The American
Prison

For their constant love and occasional wisdom,
we are fortunate to be able to dedicate this book to:

Paula Dubeck and Jordan Cullen by Francis T. Cullen

Christine Siler and Lori Vick by Cheryl Lero Jonson

Craig Hemmens and Emily Stohr-Gillmore by Mary K. Stohr

Francis T. Cullen | Cheryl Lero Jonson | Mary K. Stohr

University of Cincinnati   *Xavier University*   *Missouri State University*

The American
Prison

Imagining a Different Future

Los Angeles | London | New Delhi
Singapore | Washington DC

Los Angeles | London | New Delhi
Singapore | Washington DC

FOR INFORMATION:

SAGE Publications, Inc.
2455 Teller Road
Thousand Oaks, California 91320
E-mail: order@sagepub.com

SAGE Publications Ltd.
1 Oliver's Yard
55 City Road
London EC1Y 1SP
United Kingdom

SAGE Publications India Pvt. Ltd.
B 1/I 1 Mohan Cooperative Industrial Area
Mathura Road, New Delhi 110 044
India

SAGE Publications Asia-Pacific Pte. Ltd.
3 Church Street
#10-04 Samsung Hub
Singapore 049483

Acquisitions Editor: Jerry Westby
Editorial Assistant: MaryAnn Vail
Production Editor: Brittany Bauhaus
Copy Editor: Kristin Bergstad
Typesetter: C&M Digitals (P) Ltd.
Proofreader: Ellen Brink
Indexer: Gloria Tierney
Cover Designer: Edgar Abarca
Marketing Manager: Terra Schultz
Permissions Editor: Jennifer Barron

Copyright © 2014 by SAGE Publications, Inc.

Printed in the United States of America

Library of Congress Cataloging-in-Publication Data

The American prison : imagining a different future / editors, Francis T. Cullen, University of Cincinnati, Cheryl Lero Jonson, Xavier University, Mary K. Stohr, Missouri State University.

pages cm
Includes bibliographical references and index.

ISBN 978-1-4522-4136-4 (pbk.)

1. Prisons—United States. 2. Corrections—United States. I. Cullen, Francis T.

HV9471.A454 2013
365′.973—dc23   2012046295

This book is printed on acid-free paper.

13 14 15 16 17 10 9 8 7 6 5 4 3 2 1

Brief Contents

Contents

Preface

Beginning in the early 1970s, the United States embarked on what Todd Clear poignantly labeled a "penal harm movement." The lynchpin of this campaign was the idea that locking up more offenders for more time would not only give suffering victims the justice they were seeking but also enhance public safety. As is well known, the size of state and federal prison populations multiplied more than seven-fold from just under 200,00 to over 1.5 million. When all types of confinement were combined (e.g., jails), the inmate count came to surpass 2.4 million—meaning that about 1 in 100 adults in America was behind bars on any given day.

We, this volume's editors, have spent much of our lives in a context in which getting tough on crime was virtually hegemonic. To be sure, cracks in the penal harm movement existed—for example, calls for rehabilitating offenders were not extinguished fully—but policy makers on both sides of the political spectrum spouted law-and-order rhetoric and, in the words of Jonathan Simon, "governed through crime." Little concern seemed to exist that inmate populations rose intractably, that institutions became horribly crowded, that many facilities descended into violent warehouses, that the shameful concentration of minorities in custody evoked little national guilt, and that vast sums of the public treasury were gobbled up by a seemingly insatiable correctional system. For us—and most readers, we suspect—there seemed to be no escape from this dismal future.

Suddenly, however, things changed. In the last few years, a broad policy consensus has been reached that penal harm and mass incarceration have outlived their usefulness. A complete history of this transformation remains to be written, but we can point to three factors that have contributed to the declining popularity of incarceration. First, criminological researchers have produced a growing body of evidence showing that prisons have null or criminogenic effects on inmates' recidivism (i.e., they do not specifically deter), that too many low-risk offenders are needlessly locked up, and that crime saved through incapacitation—although meaningful—might be rivaled if resources were devoted instead to rehabilitation and prevention programs. Second, the "great American crime decline," as Franklin Zimring calls it, has largely removed law and order as a concern for the American public. Elected officials thus are reaping diminishing political capital for spouting "get tough" rhetoric. Third—and likely most important—the financial collapse of 2008 and beyond has bankrupted state treasuries. Governors, many of them

Republicans elected on pledges of lowering taxes and wiping out deficits, now face the stubborn reality that their states' prisons consume too many dollars. Unlike many other areas of state budgets where expenditures are rigidly fixed, corrections offers a tempting plasticity: If inmate populations are lowered and institutions are closed, valued cost savings can be achieved.

Regardless of the reasons, today's correctional landscape is dramatically different than it was just a short time ago. We no longer face a future that seems foreordained. In fact, we have reached what Malcolm Gladwell has termed a "tipping point." This is a phenomenon where an idea—in our case reducing prison populations— ascends and, similar to a contagious disease, spreads rapidly. When this occurs, Gladwell notes, "changes happen in a hurry." In this context, it appears that we have reached a correctional policy tipping point in which state prison populations— which have stopped rising for the first time in nearly 40 years—are starting to decline and could fall precipitously in the immediate time ahead. Indeed, it has become fashionable, rather than a case of political suicide, for elected officials to propose that the number of incarcerated offenders can and should be cut.

Most criminologists would welcome a shrinking of the nation's prison population. Scholars do not always agree on how many offenders can be safely supervised in the community; some believe that prisons house only a violent few whereas others maintain that a substantial proportion of inmates have records of chronic criminality. Still, these differences aside, there is a virtual consensus that prisons contain far too many inmates and, in particular, are likely have an iatrogenic effect on their low-risk residents.

Students of corrections, however, cannot be concerned only with the *quantity* of corrections. Although the enormous size of the prison system warrants all the attention it receives, there is a tendency among scholars and policy makers to focus almost exclusively on how many offenders can be squeezed into or let out of our secure institutions. What is lost in this discussion is the need to give equal weight to the *quality* of the correctional enterprise.

It remains to be seen how far federal, state, and local officials will go in restricting the flow of offenders into their custodial institutions. But let us assume a promising scenario in which prison and jail populations were cut by, say, 20%—a figure that would require changes in sentencing laws and practices. If this were to occur, about 1.8 million convicts would still remain behind bars on any given day. And of these, 1.2 million would still reside in a federal or state prison. Even in California, which has been forced by the U.S. Supreme Court to reduce its prison populations by upwards of 30,000 inmates due to unconstitutional medical and safety conditions, prisons will continue to house over 130,000 offenders. In short, the heartening news that the spread of the mass imprisonment epidemic has finally been halted should not divert us from understanding what has been left in its wake.

In this regard, we contend that the correctional tipping point now at hand offers ideological space to discuss not only ways of reducing inmate populations but also how corrections might serve, in Francis Allen's words, a broader social purpose. Over the past several decades, punitive rhetoric and policies have made it acceptable to envision prisons as a means of delivering pain—and little more. Prisons were thus socially constructed as a "cost" that, if high enough because sentences were long and living conditions were deplorable, would teach the wayward that crime does not pay. This stance produced a moral blindness that too often allowed correctional institutions to descend into domains that at best kept inmates on ice and at worst were criminogenic and personally damaging. As taxpayers and as a good people, Americans have the right to expect much more from corrections. In fact, opinion polls have shown repeatedly that the nation's citizenry opposes prisons that function as mere warehouses and favors prisons that save offenders from a life in crime.

Importantly, existing social realities can serve as a powerful constraint to thought and action. We come to accept a bloated, ineffective prison system as inescapable—as beyond anyone's power to control or change. The only future that is imagined is the one we have experienced—again, for much or all of our lives. But when informed by a broader historical perspective, we learn that even lengthy periods of continuity have a shelf life and that change is inevitable. But when change is possible, which direction will it take? It is here that ideas have consequences. It is here that imagining a different future is the first step to making that future—or one close to it—the new reality.

This project, *The American Prison*, thus is intended to initiate a sustained conversation about what today's prisons might entail. Written by talented corrections scholars, the volume includes 12 different ideas, divided into six parts, on how to improve the American prison. Thus, each chapter imagines a transformative correctional future—one that moves beyond the failed policies and practices of the past four decades. Taken together, the chapters offer a diverse agenda for moving forward in the change process—insights on how to make prisons truly reformative, capable of transforming the hearts and minds of offenders, more just, less harmful, fresh and inventive, and perform at a higher level. Still, despite this rich compendium of advice, we can identify at least three cross-cutting themes that inform the chapters to follow.

First, we must do a better job in our correctional system. Overcrowded, unsafe, unhealthy, damaging, and ineffective prisons are inexcusable; the banality of evil should not prevail. Those in charge must be held accountable for a higher level of performance. We have an obligation to rehabilitate offenders and to restore them to the community—and to do so in an institutional environment that is moral, healthy, and safe. We should do this in a way that not only lowers recidivism and thus protects public safety but also makes offenders more able to contribute as members of civil society. An ethos of *penal help* must replace an ethos of *penal harm* (see Chapter 13 for a more detailed discussion of the need for penal help). Second, a dose of utopianism is a good thing, especially if it moves us to consider fresh alternatives to the failed policies and practices that now prevail. Again, a future must be imagined before it can become possible. Reformers must be inspired to take action sooner rather than later. Third, we are fortunate to have a growing body of evidence on what can be done to improve correctional administration and intervention. In particular, the well-grounded insights on "what works" to build moral and effective agencies and what works to rehabilitate and improve the lives of offenders should be understood and implemented.

Thus, we stand at an important juncture in the nation's history. The opportunity for real change that leaves behind a mean season in corrections is at hand. It is time to think and act boldly. We trust that this volume will play a large role in inspiring readers to imagine and bring about such a new correctional future.

Before embarking on this collective exercise in imagining a different future for the American prison, we must acknowledge those who have helped to make this volume possible. We start with Chris Eskridge who, as General Editor of the *Journal of Contemporary Criminal Justice*, asked us to edit a special issue that came to fruition as "American Corrections in Crisis: Imagining a Different Future" (Volume 28, Issue 1, 2012). By generously presenting this opportunity, Chris allowed us to begin considering what the future of corrections might hold. We also appreciate the contributors to this special issue whose creative ideas made us realize the importance of continuing to explore how the American prison might be refashioned. These include Brandon K. Applegate, Todd R. Clear, John E. Eck, Nancy L. Hogan, W. Wesley Johnson, Ken Kerle, Eric G. Lambert, Edward J. Latessa, Lynette C. Lee, Faith E. Lutz, Joycelyn M. Pollock, Jeffrey Ian Ross, Myrinda Schweitzer, Risdon N. Slate, Paula Smith, Jeanne B. Stinchcombe, Stan Stojkovic, and Jody L. Sundt.

Two works that appeared in the journal's special issue are reprinted here: "The Therapeutic Prison" by Paula Smith and Myrinda Schweitzer, and "The Accountable Prison" by Francis T. Cullen, Cheryl Lero Jonson, and John E. Eck. Portions of the issue's Introduction also are included in this Preface. We should note as well that the current volume includes one other reprinted work, "The Virtuous Prison" by Francis T. Cullen, Jody L. Sundt, and John F. Wozniak, which appeared in Henry N. Pontell and David Shichor (Eds.), *Contemporary Issues in Crime and Criminal Justice: Essays in Honor of Gilbert Geis* (pp. 265–286). Upper Saddle River, NJ: Prentice Hall, 2001.

We must express special gratitude to Jerry Westby, who once again has supported our efforts to bring a book to press with SAGE Publications. We write for SAGE largely because of Jerry, who shows us unfailing loyalty and who respects us enough to tell us even difficult truths. Jerry also has the wisdom to surround himself with the best staff possible. In this regard, we share our special thanks with Laureen Gleason, Kristin Bergstad, and Brittany Bauhaus.

Further, we want to recognize the guidance provided by those scholars who reviewed the book's prospectus. They encouraged the book's further development and gave us much to consider in this process. Thus, our thankfulness must be extended to:

Bruce L. Bikle
California State University, Sacramento

Terry Campbell
Kaplan University

Traqina Emeka
University of Houston—Downtown

Mario L. Hesse
Saint Cloud State University

Margaret E. Leigey
The College of New Jersey

Michael Montgomery
Tennessee State University

No book is possible without the encouragement and assistance of those who touch our lives on a daily basis. We thus would like to express our appreciation to our colleagues at the University of Cincinnati, Xavier University, and Missouri State University. Our most special gratitude, however, is reserved for our families. We dedicate this book to Paula Dubeck and Jordan Cullen, Christine Siler and Lori Vick, and Craig Hemmens and Emily Stohr-Gillmore.

Part I

Reforming Offenders

1

The Therapeutic Prison

Paula Smith and
Myrinda Schweitzer

Editors' Introduction

It is instructive that American prisons are not known as "punishment facilities" or even as "justice facilities." Rather, when originally invented, they were conceptualized as "penitentiaries" and then later earned the name of "correctional institutions." Such choice of words reflects Americans' long-standing belief that prisons should not function simply as instruments to deliver retribution or as cages in which to constrain the wicked. Rather, "penitentiary" and "corrections" convey the hope that prisons will serve the broader social purpose of transforming the criminally wayward into law-abiding citizens. Notably, opinion polls from the 1960s onward repeatedly show that the public wishes rehabilitation to be a core emphasis of imprisonment. Upwards of 8 in 10 Americans favor giving inmates access to treatment services.

Despite these public preferences, the American prison has not typically lived up to its name as an institution that "corrects." To be sure, most prisons have an array of educational, vocational, substance abuse, and counseling programs. But inmates' treatment suffers from two enormous challenges. First, mass imprisonment has left many institutions far over capacity. At the height of its prison population boom, it is estimated that half of all California inmates sat idle throughout their sentence, receiving no work assignment or treatment services. Second, American prisons are not organized to be therapeutic. In nearly all cases, rehabilitation is an "add on"—an activity an inmate attends—rather than being sewn into the very fabric of institutional life. For this to occur, we would need not a prison that provides therapy but a prison that is therapeutic in its design and core practices.

In the chapter to follow, Paula Smith and Myrinda Schweitzer furnish a blueprint for constructing such a "therapeutic prison." They argue that a plan exists that is not based on speculation but on data. Thus, they propose to rely on an empirically validated instrument that assesses whether an organization is providing appropriate services. This set of guidelines for building and administering an agency capable of delivering effective rehabilitation is called the Correctional Program Assessment Inventory or the "CPAI."

An important treatment paradigm forms the core of the CPAI. This approach, invented by Canadian psychologists Donald Andrews, James Bonta, Paula Gendreau, and colleagues, is known as the "RNR model." The acronym is derived from the approach's three core principles. Thus, the risk principle (R) argues that treatment should be directed to higher-risk rather than lower-risk offenders. The need principle (N) argues that treatment should target for change those deficits or risk factors— that is, "criminogenic needs"—that are the strongest predictors of recidivism, such as antisocial values. And the responsivity principle (R) argues that treatment should be used that is "responsive to" or capable of changing criminogenic needs or risk factors (e.g., cognitive-behavioral programs).

In essence, the CPAI assesses how well a correctional agency is arranged to deliver RNR-based treatment to offenders. It covers eight domains. Assessors visiting agencies use interviews, observations, and analysis of documents to complete a 141-item instrument that measures adherence to treatment principles and practices. Smith and Schweitzer's key insight is that the CPAI can be used not only to discern what is lacking in an agency but also as a blueprint for constructing a therapeutic prison. That is, the CPAI lays out quite specifically what should be done to ensure that treatment is integral to the organization and based in the existing empirical knowledge about what works to reform offenders.

Importantly, agencies that score high on the CPAI produce lower rates of recidivism. The question thus emerges as to why any prison would not wish to use this inventory to become truly therapeutic, improve offenders' lives, and protect public safety. Defending the status quo is no longer excusable. It is time to use the CPAI as a blueprint for prison reform.

The notion that prisons should be therapeutic extends to the invention of the "penitentiary" in Jacksonian America during the 1820s and 1830s (Rothman, 1971). In fact, observers from across the Atlantic—from de Tocqueville to Dickens—were enticed to travel to the United States precisely because the penitentiary adopted a utopian vision and put it into practice. Reformers of the day, often with religious inspiration and zeal, advanced the powerful notion that prisons should not be detention centers or crude instruments of punishment, but rather social enclaves with the power to transform the criminally wayward into citizens with strong moral fiber (see Gendreau, Smith, & Goggin, 2001).

In constructing the penitentiary, its inventors contemplated how the internal design and nature of daily life could best achieve the noble goal of offender redemption. There was a firm understanding that criminals, snatched from disorderly environments where vice prevailed, should be placed into an orderly environment marked by hard work, religious influence, and separation from criminal associations. As those familiar with correctional history well know, an intense debate raged over how to ensure that inmates would be free from antisocial exposure, with those in Pennsylvania favoring solitary confinement and those in New York favoring the congregate silent system (see Cullen & Gendreau, 2000). As reformers would eventually learn, much to their dismay, crowding and the need for human contact rendered unfeasible and ineffective both methods of trying to curtail inmate interaction.

It is perhaps not surprising that in this prescientific, precriminology era, reformers would trumpet a therapeutic design that did not work as planned. But what lesson should be learned from this failure? One perspective is that prisons, by their very nature, are inherently inhumane and coercive—places where offender reform cannot take place (Rothman, 1980; Zimbardo, 2007). This perspective, however, has two disturbing features. First, it leads to a despairing view of corrections. If prisons can be only inhumane and hurtful, then why bother to try to make them humane and therapeutic? Why have any interest in offenders who are, due to the commission of their crimes, consigned to life inside these institutions of supposed intractable failure? Second, this thinking simply is empirically false. Prisons, as well as programs within prisons, differ greatly in their decency and capacity to deliver human services.

In this context, the thesis advanced here is that the inventors of the penitentiary adopted the wrong means to make prisons therapeutic, but they were prescient in suggesting that how the daily routines of prisons can have a large impact on the quality of inmates' lives and on their propensity to recidivate. The key issue, of course, is how to organize or craft the prison experience so that it is therapeutic and not, as is so often the case, coercive and counterproductive. Fortunately, a blueprint for creating a therapeutic prison exists that is theoretically and empirically well grounded: the Correctional Program Assessment Inventory (CPAI). The Correctional Program Assessment Inventory (CPAI) is a standardized tool that assesses how well intervention programs in a given correctional setting adhere to known principles of effective treatment. It identifies both strengths and areas for improvement in order to generate recommendations for enhancing the use of evidence-based practices within the organization.

In this chapter, we begin with a brief overview of the CPAI and discuss how it is currently used in the field of corrections to document the strengths and weaknesses of offender treatment programs. Furthermore, we demonstrate that the knowledge now exists to design interventions that will be successful in reducing offender recidivism, but that technology transfer remains a significant obstacle to implementation. To this end, we describe the core elements of a "therapeutic prison" that is designed with the expressed purpose of facilitating long-term behavioral change in offenders.

Correctional Program Assessment Inventory

The original version of the Correctional Program Assessment Inventory (CPAI) emanated from the extensive literature on "what works" in reducing recidivism and the principles of effective intervention with offender populations. Because space does not permit a detailed discussion, the reader is referred to Andrews and Bonta (2010) as well as to Gendreau (1996a, 1996b) for more extensive reviews of the topic. Suffice it to say, a major impetus for the development of the instrument was a criticism issued by cynics of correctional rehabilitation that it was pointless to treat offenders given that the quality of interventions in the "real world" was abysmal. Rather than abandon rehabilitative efforts as critics suggested, however, the authors of the CPAI, Paul Gendreau and Don Andrews, persuasively advocated for a more proactive approach—that is, to document the strengths and weaknesses of programs with the goal of making correctional systems more accountable and effective (Gendreau, Andrews, & Thériault, 2010).

The first and subsequent editions of the CPAI consisted of several dozen items that were based on meta-analytic reviews of the offender treatment literature, the authors' extensive managerial and clinical experience from working in a variety of correctional settings, and wisdom gleaned from colleagues who had implemented successful interventions (Gendreau et al., 2010). The CPAI was first piloted in 1990 when it was applied to 100 substance abuse programs offered by the Correctional Services of Canada (Gendreau et al., 2010). Subsequently, the CPAI has been employed in other surveys of correctional programs in Canada, Australia, and New Zealand. It has also been used in several large-scale evaluation studies in the United States involving more than 700 individual programs (Latessa, Lowenkamp, & Bechtel, 2009; Lowenkamp, 2004; Lowenkamp & Latessa, 2005).

The instrument has undergone several revisions since the original version, the latest of which is referred to as the CPAI-2000 and includes a total of 133 items across eight domains (Gendreau et al., 2010). It is perhaps useful to think about these eight domains by subdividing them into two basic areas: capacity and content. *Capacity* refers to whether or not a correctional program has the capability to deliver evidence-based interventions and services for offenders, and therefore considers a number of organizational factors and contextual issues. There are five domains associated with the capacity area: (1) organizational culture; (2) program implementation and maintenance; (3) management and staff characteristics; (4) interagency communication; and (5) evaluation and quality assurance. *Content*, on the other hand, focuses on the substantive domains of assessment and treatment, and includes three domains on the CPAI-2000: (1) client risk-need practices; (2) program characteristics; and (3) core correctional practices.

Several recent studies on both adult and juvenile programs have validated the indicators on the CPAI by correlating scores with offender recidivism. These studies yielded strong correlations with outcome between overall scores, domain areas, and individual items (Lowenkamp, 2004; Lowenkamp & Latessa, 2005; Lowenkamp, Latessa, & Smith, 2006; Nesovic, 2003). Gendreau et al. (2010, pp. 3–4) recommend that the measure can be used to: (1) evaluate proposals from prospective service providers; (2) determine whether a correctional program has a credible rationale in support of its treatment practices; (3) identify the most frequently occurring programming deficits for programs with the objective of rectifying the problems; (4) tabulate and reinforce the continued use of the best validated elements of effective correctional programs present in a particular program; (5) evaluate existing external service contracts for renewal; (6) assist in providing technology transfer to management and line staff as to what works in reducing offender recidivism; and (7) provide a concrete means of stimulating relevant research. It should also be noted that many CPAI items have been incorporated into the accreditation standards of correctional services in the United Kingdom (i.e., prisons and probation), the Correctional Service of Canada, and several jurisdictions in the United States.

Although the CPAI has been administered to an impressive number and variety of correctional treatment programs, it is disheartening to acknowledge that the majority (approximately 60%) of programs have failed to achieve a passing grade on the instrument. It should also be noted that this trend has been consistent over time and across countries (see Andrews & Bonta, 2010; Gendreau et al., 2010). This likely reflects, at least in part, the difficulties associated with technology transfer and the schism that so often exists between research and practice.

Designing a Therapeutic Prison

Taken together, the items on the CPAI-2000 delineate an "ideal" correctional program wherein a perfect score would indicate full adherence to evidence-based practices. Admittedly, the highest CPAI score in our database of more than 700 programs is 81% (and no program on record has ever received 100%). Still, the CPAI provides clear guidance on how to design a prison that moves decidedly in the direction of being therapeutic not in name only but in reality. Were the CPAI to be employed regularly by correctional agencies, the cumulative effect would be to create more prisons that scored high on the CPAI. In this sense, it would not be unreasonable to expect that in the future, a prison would reach the goal of a perfect score.

It is impossible to build a quality house without a set of blueprints that specifies the plan that must be followed and the standards that must be met. Similarly, it is impossible to build a therapeutic prison without some idea of how to do so. In fact, without plans and standards, correctional administrators at best will attempt to do what they think will work and at worst will be under no obligation to do anything to achieve offender rehabilitation. The true value of the CPAI is that it can be a source of both guidance and accountability. Its very existence raises the question of why administrators would not follow a blueprint that promises to allow for a therapeutic prison to be a reality.

Thus, the main purpose of this chapter is to describe what a therapeutic prison would look like if it embraced the principles of effective intervention and met all of the criteria on the CPAI-2000. In the two sections that follow, we discuss how the major components of the CPAI—the institutional capacity for and content of effective intervention—are integral to designing a therapeutic prison.

Capacity of the Institution

More than three decades ago, Quay (1977) made the insightful observation that the failure of a well-known prison treatment program (see Kassebaum, Ward, &

Wilner, 1971) was likely attributable to several organizational factors that diminished the capacity of the institution to deliver effective treatment programs. Specifically, he cited inadequate conceptualizations of the program, insufficient staff training protocols, and the selection of corrections professionals who did not endorse the fundamental goals of rehabilitation (Quay, 1977). In essence, this early work acknowledged that a variety of organizational and contextual level factors could negatively impact the capacity of the prison to rehabilitate offenders. Subsequent authors (e.g., Hamm & Schrink, 1989; Harris & Smith, 1996; Petersilia, 1990) have reached similar conclusions. In this section, we review a variety of organizational factors that are evaluated in the CPAI-2000 in order to provide a description of the key components of the therapeutic prison.

ORGANIZATIONAL FACTORS

Several of the organizational items included on the CPAI-2000 are derived from the general management literature (see Backer, David, & Soucy, 1995) and applied within the correctional context. All of the items discussed in this section concern the host agency (and, in this case, the therapeutic prison) where rehabilitative interventions are delivered. Careful consideration of organizational factors is critical in that it provides the context in which all rehabilitative activities occur.

To begin, the therapeutic prison should have three key documents: (1) a mandate; (2) clearly articulated goals that are shared among key administrators and frontline staff members; and (3) a documented code of ethics. The primary benefit of establishing a mandate is that it increases the likelihood that goals will be met as it provides the foundation for the mission statement and sets the framework for organizational activities. To illustrate, a prison might be charged with the mandate to reduce offender recidivism and protect the public. This mandate can then be translated into several specific goals and activities that the agency should embrace in order to achieve this end. Similarly, a documented code of ethics should be formally communicated to staff members at all levels through both initial and ongoing training. This is important for many reasons. First, a code of ethics is one factor that sets the tone of the organizational culture by establishing clear *expectations* for how staff members should interact with offenders. Second, it sets forth mechanisms for enforcement and outlines the consequences of noncompliance. Finally, and perhaps most significant, enforcement of the code of ethics affords the agency with protection from the actions of unethical employees. It is perhaps not surprising that the most effective correctional programs are ones in which the values and practices of key stakeholders are in agreement with the philosophy, mandate, and practices of the prison.

The therapeutic prison should also have a history of adopting new initiatives—and have demonstrated the capacity to make modifications within a reasonable period of time. For example, the initiation of a new program component should proceed incrementally with sufficient time for a formal pilot period in order to discuss problems and sort out logistics (Gendreau, Goggin, & Smith, 1999). In our experience, amendments to new program components are much easier to accomplish within the context of a formal pilot period versus after the modification has been implemented full scale. By contrast, two common problems should be avoided: Some agencies make changes too quickly and without sufficient planning, *whereas* other agencies cannot create the momentum necessary to implement changes.

The bureaucratic structure of the therapeutic prison should be moderately decentralized, thus allowing for a flexible response to problematic issues. This requires the establishment of formal policies and procedures to guide how problems or concerns are handled when raised within the program. As an agent of change, the program director should use reciprocity, authority (but avoid the use of threats), reinforcements, modeling, and advocacy-brokerage in order to resolve matters in a timely and nonconfrontational manner.

Finally, the therapeutic prison should be characterized by organizational harmony. This means that there should be little task or emotional-personal conflict within the organization at the interdepartmental, staff, and/or management levels. Agencies with higher levels of discord also experience higher levels of staff turnover, which compromises the stability of the program. In fact, the CPAI-2000 assesses whether or not staff turnover at all levels has been less than 25% over the previous two years.

PROGRAM IMPLEMENTATION/MAINTENANCE

Gendreau et al. (1999) contended that implementation issues have been traditionally ignored in the corrections literature. The first extensive assessment of program implementation in corrections appeared more than three decades ago when Gendreau and Andrews (1979) systematically reviewed 19 of their attempts at program implementation in correctional agencies. Since this time, other researchers in the field have contributed valuable information demonstrating that the quality of implementation is correlated with reductions in recidivism (Arbuthnot & Gordon, 1988; Byrne & Kelly, 1989; Fagan, 1990; Henggeler, Schoenwald, & Pickrel, 1995). Most notably, Lowenkamp (2004) used the CPAI to conduct 38 evaluations of offender treatment programs. Offenders who participated in these treatment programs were compared with matched comparison groups (i.e., gender, race, risk) using re-incarceration as the outcome measure. The results indicated that the program implementation domain was most strongly correlated with recidivism ($r = .54$).

Ideally, the therapeutic prison should have been initiated at a time when the agency was not confronted with far-reaching, contentious issues including significant policy changes, marked changes in the demographics or needs of clients, and staff turnover. Furthermore, the therapeutic prison should have empirically documented the need for its programs and services. This evidence should involve more than the results from community forums or aggregate-level analyses (for a more detailed review, see Posavac & Carey, 2003). To illustrate, an assessment of the prevalence of substance abuse among the offenders incarcerated in the therapeutic prison might lead to the establishment of a treatment designed to target this specific problem. In contrast, national statistics estimating the percentage of offenders with substance abuse problems (aggregate level data) or the opinions of citizens invited to a focus group (community forums) might lead to erroneous estimates of the problem and faulty decision making in this regard. Moreover, when a program has been created for a need that does not exist, it has been our experience that prison administrators can feel pressured to relax eligibility criteria and accept inappropriate referrals in order to fill beds and maintain current levels of funding.

Perhaps the most significant factor worthy of note in this domain is that the interventions offered within the therapeutic prison must be based on credible scientific evidence. In designing all components of the institution, therefore, the program director and other key staff should conduct a thorough literature review and make evidence-based decisions accordingly.

MANAGEMENT/STAFF CHARACTERISTICS

Another important consideration in the capacity area involves the qualifications and involvement of the program director (i.e., the individual responsible for overseeing the daily operations of the program). The program director of the therapeutic prison should be credentialed in terms of education and experience. Specifically, the CPAI-2000 requires that the program director be professionally trained with at least a graduate degree in one of the helping professions (e.g., education, nursing, psychology, or social work with course specialization in the correctional, forensic, or legal area) and possess full-time, direct experience with an offender treatment program for at least three years. In addition, the program director should have the support of senior agency officials and frontline staff members alike.

In the therapeutic prison, the program director should be actively engaged with staff members at all levels through training, supervision, and program delivery. These daily responsibilities of the program director are important for several reasons. First, regular contact affords the opportunity for the program director to evaluate the skills of his or her employees. Second, it provides the program director with an intimate knowledge of the demographics and needs of offenders. Third, the program director will be perceived as much more credible when initiating changes within the institution if he or she is viewed as connected to the realities of frontline service delivery. In our experience, many program directors reject this recommendation on the basis that they do not have sufficient time to be involved in direct service delivery.

The therapeutic prison should also give serious consideration to the qualifications and experience of frontline staff members. This includes clinical positions as well as security positions (i.e., correctional officers) that are typically not considered to be important agents of change within the institution. We would argue that it is indeed foolish for prison administrators to fail to recognize correctional officers as a valuable resource when one considers that inmates spend the vast majority of their time with these particular frontline staff members. As such, when considering new applicants for any position within the institution, the hiring protocol should include a criminal record check and input from personal and professional references. The CPAI-2000 also recommends that at least three quarters of employees possess an undergraduate degree in one of the helping professions and that 10% hold an advanced degree. In addition, at least 75% of frontline staff members should have previous experience working with offender populations.

Finally, the therapeutic prison should use structured mechanisms during the interview process to evaluate candidates' personal qualities (i.e., enthusiasm, warmth, respectfulness, flexibility, non-blaming, genuineness, humor, self-confidence, empathy, engagingness, reflectiveness, maturity, and intelligence) and skills related to service delivery (i.e., directive, solution-focused, structured, contingency-based, cognitive-restructuring, prosocial modeling, effective reinforcement, disapproval, and problem-solving). At the most basic level, effective programs hire staff members who are committed to human service and endorse the notion that offenders can change; it is preferable for this to occur by design rather than by accident within the organization. After they have been hired, employees should participate in bimonthly clinical supervision meetings and be assessed annually. As such, staff training is critical and should include regular instruction on the theory and practice of interventions.

INTERAGENCY COMMUNICATION

The therapeutic prison should have established formal links with other agencies to ensure services are available to meet offenders' diverse needs. Furthermore, case managers should regularly communicate with other service providers in order to effectively coordinate efforts in this regard. It is also important for corrections professionals to advocate on behalf of the offender when appropriate and necessary.

EVALUATION

The therapeutic prison should have established within-program checks such as file reviews or problem-oriented records in order to monitor offenders' treatment progress. In addition, there should be a mechanism in place that consists of regular group observations to ensure treatment fidelity and adherence to the program manual. It is interesting to note that fewer than 10% of programs in our database meet this criterion.

In order to evaluate offenders' skill acquisition, the therapeutic prison should employ periodic, objective, standardized assessments of the client on target behaviors. This can include rating scales, pre–post tests, and psychometric assessments of skills and attitudes. Similarly, the therapeutic prison should collect client rearrest, reconviction, and/or re-incarceration data during a follow-up period of at least six months. These outcome data could then be used to conduct an evaluation that compares treatment outcome with a risk-controlled comparison group. Moreover, the report forthcoming from this evaluation could be published to document the effectiveness of the therapeutic prison.

Finally, it is important for the therapeutic prison to create the capacity for ongoing assessment of topics related to service delivery. For example, the therapeutic prison might have a *specialized unit* or designated staff members for this purpose. As an alternative, the institution might utilize external consultants to advise on programming and services.

Content of Services

At the present time, there are more than 44 quantitative reviews of the assessment and treatment literature in corrections (see Smith, Gendreau, & Swartz, 2009; practitioner-friendly summaries of this literature can be found in Gendreau, 1996a, 1996b; Van Voorhis, Braswell & Lester, 2009). The results of these reviews have been replicated with remarkable consistency, and there is general consensus about which offender needs should be targeted, the best measures to use in this regard, and the most effective treatment strategies. In fact, the client risk/need practices and treatment subsections are generally considered to be the most empirically supported of all of the domains of the CPAI-2000 (see Lowenkamp, 2004; Lowenkamp et al., 2006). Below, we discuss the relevance to designing a therapeutic prison of the domains of client risk/need practices, program characteristics, and core correctional practices.

CLIENT RISK/NEED PRACTICES

Effective correctional programs establish clear admission and exclusionary criteria in order to define who is (and who is not) appropriate for the intervention. For example, a program might opt to exclude offenders with certain mental health diagnoses or violent offenders whose adaptive functioning cannot be maintained in a housing unit without more restrictive measures.

Assessment and classification is the cornerstone of effective correctional treatment. As such, the therapeutic prison should have a comprehensive intake protocol that includes the standardized assessment of offender risk and need factors in order to make placement decisions and develop case management plans. The Level of Service/Case Management Inventory (LS/CMI) is one example of a composite risk-and-need measure that has been used extensively within the United States for this purpose. Moreover, it is paramount for programs to target higher-risk offenders by varying the intensity and duration of treatment by risk level within the prison (for a detailed assessment, see Andrews & Bonta, 2010). In a prison setting, this can often be accomplished through the creation of separate housing units and/or tracks in the program for lower- versus higher-risk offenders. At a minimum, higher-risk offenders should be required to complete a greater number of hours of treatment in comparison with their lower-risk counterparts.

In addition to risk and need factors, offenders should be assessed in order to identify key factors that might impact their responsivity to treatment (e.g., gender, motivation, mental health issues, IQ). For example, an offender who has a lower IQ might not respond well to cognitive interventions that require abstract reasoning, but rather would benefit from behavioral strategies that emphasize reinforcement and incorporate additional opportunities to practice basic social skills. In this way, the assessment of these specific responsivity factors allows the corrections professional to adjust the style and mode of service delivery in order to remove and/or accommodate potential barriers to treatment.

PROGRAM CHARACTERISTICS

Previous research has consistently demonstrated that some factors are robust predictors of recidivism, whereas others are not (see Andrews & Bonta, 2010). At the most basic level, the therapeutic prison would predominantly target criminogenic needs, or the dynamic risk factors linked to criminal behavior. These include: (1) antisocial attitudes, orientations, and values favorable to law violations and procriminal role models; (2) antisocial peer associations; (3) emotional and personality factors such as anger/hostility and lack of self-control; (4) deficits in problem-solving skills; (5) lack of social skills related to interpersonal conflict resolution; (6) problems associated with alcohol/drug abuse; (7) negative attitudes and/or poor performance in areas of education and employment; (8) inadequate family affection, communication, or problem solving; and (9) poor use of leisure time. Non-criminogenic needs should be incorporated into the case management plan only if they represent relevant specific responsivity factors.

The therapeutic prison should employ a combination of treatment strategies to target the individualized criminogenic needs of offenders using evidence-based strategies. The following models are considered to be most effective in reducing recidivism: (1) *radical behavioral approaches* that are based on the principles of classical and operant conditioning; (2) *social learning approaches* that involve modeling and behavioral rehearsal techniques that engender self-efficacy; and (3) *cognitive approaches* including cognitive skills training, problem-solving therapy, self-control procedures, self-instructional training, and stress inoculation training.

In developing a contingency management system to increase appropriate target behaviors, the therapeutic prison should have a range of appropriate reinforcers that includes, at a minimum, tangible reinforcers, token reinforcers, social reinforcers, and activities (see Spiegler & Guevremont, 2010). It is advisable for correctional programs to identify reinforcers that are most meaningful to offenders by surveying inmates. Furthermore, the therapeutic prison should develop a detailed written protocol to ensure that reinforcers are administered consistently and immediately. Similarly, the therapeutic prison should develop a protocol for the administration of punishers in order to suppress antisocial behaviors using a range of consequences such as fines, loss of tokens, time out, and social disapproval (for a detailed review, see Spiegler & Guevremont, 2010). Finally, frontline staff members should assess whether or not the punishment produces any negative effects after administration, including emotional reactions (e.g., anxiety, anger), withdrawal/avoidance behaviors, and perpetuation effects (i.e., when an inmate learns to use punishment to control others' behaviors). Furthermore, punishment should not interfere with new learning, lead to response substitutions, or disrupt social relationships. Despite the fact that research has suggested that the number of reinforcers should far outweigh the number of punishers, it is our experience that most correctional programs spend more time and effort on developing protocols related to sanctions. It is also important to note that the CPAI-2000 recommends that participants engaged in a specific treatment program be separated from the rest of the population (unless the entire institution is involved in the program) given the fact that this maximizes the likelihood that offenders will generalize newly acquired behaviors beyond the treatment setting.

Meta-analyses of the treatment literature have found that institutional programs consistently produce smaller effect sizes in comparison with community-based programs (see Andrews & Bonta, 2010). This is attributable, at least in part, to the fact that community-based programs have the distinct advantage of offering interventions in vivo, that is, in more naturalistic environments where offenders can immediately practice new skills. Prisons, on the other hand, are by definition artificial environments where inmates have more limited opportunities to use skills in their own high-risk situations. In order to be successfully discharged from the institution, therefore, offenders should meet clearly defined completion criteria. In addition, offenders should be trained to observe and manage problem situations. The rehearsal of alternative, prosocial behaviors should include initial practice in a safe environment (e.g., treatment group session) using relatively simple scenarios but should eventually require the offender to practice the newly acquired skills in increasingly difficult situations (e.g., in the housing unit with peers). When clients demonstrate a new behavior, their improved competency should then be rewarded in order to encourage them to exhibit the response again. Moreover, the therapeutic prison should require offenders to prepare relapse prevention plans and train significant others to provide support during the reentry process. Participation in aftercare and booster sessions can also improve treatment outcomes in this regard.

CORE CORRECTIONAL PRACTICES

This domain of the CPAI-2000 details crucial clinical skills related to service delivery, or what is commonly referred to as *core correctional practices* (Andrews & Bonta, 2010; Gendreau et al., 2010). It is important to underscore that this does not refer to the application of any particular program or technique, but rather it refers to the skills and competencies that corrections professionals should exhibit whenever they interact with offenders (Andrews & Bonta, 2010).

First and foremost, the corrections professional should serve as an *anticriminal model* for offenders by engaging in prosocial behaviors and reinforcing clients when they do the same. This requires frontline staff members to be capable of distinguishing anticriminal from procriminal expressions (Andrews & Bonta, 2010). Furthermore, effective modeling involves the use of a coping model in which the corrections professional demonstrates the behavior in concrete and vivid ways and models a self-corrective strategy. Furthermore, the corrections professional should take care to include verbalizations of the self-instructions (or the cognitions and thoughts) that are used to support engaging in the behavior. Frontline staff members should consistently reinforce offenders for demonstrating desired behaviors, and should serve as a general source of reinforcement for these clients rather than always being punitive or negative.

Second, the most effective corrections professionals are capable of using *high-level reinforcement* to encourage prosocial behaviors as well as *effective disapproval* to discourage antisocial expressions. Effective reinforcement includes the following three main elements: (1) immediate statements of approval and support for what the offender has said or done; (2) elaboration of the reasons why this behavior is desirable; and (3) consideration of the short- and long-term benefits associated with continued use of the prosocial behavior. In contrast, *effective disapproval* should be used when the frontline staff member intends to communicate disapproval for a specific behavior and includes the following four elements: (1) immediate statements of disapproval for what the offender has said or done; (2) elaboration of the reasons why this behavior is undesirable; (3) consideration of the short- and long-term costs associated with continued use of the behavior; and (4) a clear demonstration of an alternate, prosocial behavior. Once the undesirable behavior has been corrected and appropriate prosocial behaviors are demonstrated by the offender, it is important for the staff member to immediately terminate disapproval and provide social reinforcement for the change.

Most corrections professionals are in a position of power relative to the offender, and therefore must be careful to make *effective use of authority* in order to respectfully guide the offender toward compliance. As such, staff members are encouraged to focus their messages on the behaviors exhibited (and not on the person performing it), to be direct and specific concerning their demands, and to specify the offenders' choices and attendant consequences in any given situation.

Another critical core correctional practice involves *structured learning procedures for skill building*. Goldstein (1986) identified five main components of this process: (1) define the skill to be learned by describing it in concrete steps; (2) model or demonstrate the skill for the client; (3) have the client practice the new skill by role-playing it with corrective feedback; (4) use homework assignments to extend learning opportunities; and (5) have the client practice the skill in increasingly difficult situations with feedback. It is worth noting that previous research has underscored the importance of *problem solving* as a specific social skill that should be taught to offenders because it is applicable to a wide variety of high-risk situations (Trotter, 1999, 2006).

Within the therapeutic prison, staff members should be thoroughly trained in *cognitive restructuring*. Specifically, staff members should be able to teach clients how to generate descriptions of problematic situations as well as the related thoughts and feelings. Corrections professionals should then help offenders identify risky thinking and practice more prosocial alternatives. Many correctional programs use thinking reports (see Bush, Bilodeau, & Kornick, 1995) to assist clients in identifying risky thoughts and feelings and how these affect their behavior.

Lastly, to ensure the development of a therapeutic alliance between the staff and client, there are several important relationship skills that staff working with an offender population should possess. Staff members should be open, warm, and exhibit respectful communication. Staff members should also be nonjudgmental, empathic, flexible, enthusiastic, and engaging. Furthermore, the most effective corrections professionals use humor and express optimism, and are solution-focused, structured, and directive. Moreover, these workers avoid arguments and power struggles with offenders, and work to develop internal motivation and support self-efficacy within the clients.

Conclusion

Historically, one of main purposes of the American correctional system has been to rehabilitate offenders (Cullen & Gendreau, 2000). At the present time, there is now a well-developed literature on what works in reducing offender recidivism that should be used to inform the design and implementation of offender assessment and treatment services in prison (Andrews & Bonta, 2010; Gendreau, 1996a, 1996b). In fact, meta-analyses have reported a 28% reduction in recidivism when programs adhere to the principles of effective intervention (see Andrews & Bonta, 2010). If none of the principles are followed, slight increases in recidivism have often been recorded. Moreover, corrections professionals should focus on factors beyond the content of assessment and treatment programs to include consideration of the organizational context of the prison. Using the items contained in the Correctional Program Assessment Inventory as a blueprint, institutions can develop treatments that will produce optimal results in terms of rehabilitating offenders.

References

Andrews, D. A., & Bonta, J. (2010). *The psychology of criminal conduct* (5th ed.). Cincinnati, OH: Anderson.

Arbuthnot, J., & Gordon, D. A. (1988). Disseminating effective interventions for juvenile delinquents: Cognitively-based sociomoral reasoning development programs. *Journal of Correctional Education, 39,* 48–53.

Backer, T. E., David, S. L., & Soucy, G. (1995). *Reviewing the behavioral science knowledge base on technology transfer.* Rockville, MD: U.S. Department of Health and Human Services.

Bush, J., Bilodeau, B., & Kornick, M. (1995). *Options: A cognitive change program.* Longmont, CO: National Institute of Corrections.

Byrne, J., & Kelly, L. (1989). *Restructuring probation as an intermediate sanction: An evaluation of the implementation and impact of the Massachusetts Intensive Probation Supervision Program.* Washington, DC: National Institute of Justice, Research Program on the Punishment and Control of Offenders.

Cullen, F. T., & Gendreau, P. (2000). Assessing correctional rehabilitation: Policy, practice, and prospects. In J. Horney (Ed.), *Criminal Justice 2000: Vol. 3. Policies, processes, and decisions of the criminal justice system* (pp. 109–175). Washington, DC: National Institute of Justice, U.S. Department of Justice.

Fagan, J. (1990). Treatment and reintegration of violent juvenile offenders: Experimental results. *Justice Quarterly, 7,* 233–263.

Gendreau, P. (1996a). Offender rehabilitation: What we know and what needs to be done. *Criminal Justice and Behavior, 23,* 144–161.

Gendreau, P. (1996b). The principles of effective intervention with offenders. In A. T. Harland (Ed.), *Choosing correctional options that work: Defining the demand and evaluating the supply* (pp. 117–130). Thousand Oaks, CA: Sage.

Gendreau, P., & Andrews, D. A. (1979). Psychological consultation in correctional agencies: Case studies and general issues. In J. J. Platt & R. J. Wicks (Eds.), *The psychological consultant* (pp. 177–212). New York, NY: Grune and Stratton.

Gendreau, P., Andrews, D. A., & Thériault, Y. L. (2010). *Correctional Program Assessment Inventory—2010.* Saint John, New Brunswick, Canada: University of New Brunswick.

Gendreau, P., Goggin, C., & Smith, P. (1999). The forgotten issue in effective correctional treatment: Program implementation. *International Journal of Offender Therapy and Comparative Criminology, 43,* 180–187.

Gendreau, P., Smith, P., & Goggin, C. (2001). Treatment programs in corrections. In J. Winterdyk (Ed.), *Corrections in Canada: Social reaction to crime* (pp. 238–263). Scarborough, Ontario, Canada: Prentice Hall.

Goldstein, A. P. (1986). Psychological skill training and the aggressive adolescent. In S. Apter & A. Goldstein (Eds.), *Youth violence: Program and prospects* (pp. 89–119). New York, NY: Pergamon Press.

Hamm, M. S., & Schrink, J. L. (1989). The conditions of effective implementation: A guide to accomplishing rehabilitative objectives in corrections. *Criminal Justice and Behavior, 16,* 166–182.

Harris, P., & Smith, S. (1996). Developing community corrections. In A. T. Harland (Ed.), *Choosing correctional options that work: Defining the demand and evaluating the supply* (pp. 183–222). Thousand Oaks, CA: Sage.

Henggeler, S., Schoenwald, S. K., & Pickrel, S. G. (1995). Multisystemic therapy: Bridging the gap between university and community based treatment. *Journal of Consulting and Clinical Psychology, 63,* 709–717.

Kassebaum, G., Ward, D., & Wilner, D. (1971). *Prison treatment and parole survival: An empirical assessment.* New York, NY: Wiley.

Latessa, E. J., Lowenkamp, C. T., & Bechtel, K. (2009). *Community corrections centers, parolees, and recidivism: An investigation into the characteristics of effective reentry programs in Pennsylvania, final report* (NCJ No. 230510). Washington DC: U.S. Department of Justice, Office of Justice Programs.

Lowenkamp, C. T. (2004). *A program level analysis of the relationship between correctional program integrity and treatment effectiveness.* Unpublished doctoral dissertation, University of Cincinnati, School of Criminal Justice.

Lowenkamp, C. T., & Latessa, E. J. (2005). *Evaluation of Ohio's CCA funded programs: Final report.* Cincinnati, OH: Division of Criminal Justice, Center for Criminal Justice Research, University of Cincinnati.

Lowenkamp, C. T., Latessa, E. J., & Smith, P. (2006). Does correctional program quality really matter: The impact of adhering to the principles of effective intervention. *Criminology and Public Policy, 5,* 201–220.

Nesovic, A. (2003). Psychometric evaluation of the Correctional Program Assessment Inventory. *Dissertation Abstracts International* 64 (09), 4674B. (UMI No. AAT NQ83525).

Petersilia, J. (1990). Conditions that permit intensive supervision programs to survive. *Crime and Delinquency, 36,* 126–145.

Posavac, E. J., & Carey, R. G. (2003). *Program evaluation: Methods and case studies* (6th ed.). Upper Saddle River, NJ: Prentice Hall.

Quay, H. C. (1977). The three faces of evaluation: What can be expected to work. *Criminal Justice and Behavior, 4,* 341–354.

Rothman, D. J. (1971). *The discovery of the asylum: Social order and disorder in the New Republic.* Boston, MA: Little, Brown.

Rothman, D. J. (1980). *Conscience and convenience: The asylum and its alternatives in progressive America.* Boston, MA: Little, Brown.

Smith, P., Gendreau, P., & Swartz, K. (2009). Validating the principles of effective intervention: A systematic review of the contributions of meta-analysis in the field of corrections. *Victims and Offenders, 4,* 148–169.

Spiegler, M. D., & Guevremont, D. C. (2010). *Contemporary behavior therapy* (5th ed.). Belmont, CA: Wadsworth.

Trotter, C. (1999). *Working with involuntary clients: A guide to practice.* Crows Nest, Australia: Allen and Unwin.

Trotter, C. (2006). *Working with involuntary clients: A guide to practice* (2nd ed.). Crows Nest, Australia: Allen and Unwin.

Van Voorhis, P., Braswell, M., & Lester, D. (2009). *Correctional counseling and rehabilitation* (7th ed.). New Providence, NJ: Anderson.

Zimbardo, P. G. (2007). *The Lucifer effect: Understanding how good people turn evil.* New York, NY: Random House.

2

The Restorative Prison

Lois Presser

Editors' Introduction

Prisons cause harm. Restorative justice is concerned with making amends for harm. On its face then, and as Presser notes in the following chapter, it does not appear that prisons can be restorative. Yet given the reduction or prevention of harm that might come from restorative justice programming in prisons and the fact that the use of prisons, particularly in the United States, is not going to decrease markedly any time soon, it appears prudent to explore how a prison focused on restorative justice might operate.

But what justice is, either in or outside of prison, has not always been clear. If we were to "imagine justice," we might see it as a balancing of scales between individuals or individuals and the state or as a more nuanced understanding that recognizes the parties were not equally matched at the start (see John Crank's Imagining Justice*). In Article III of the United States Constitution, our founders identified both law and equity as guiding principles for courts. What law is for students of criminal justice is understood, but the concept of equity, or the remedy the court might take to "make it right" to balance the scales of justice, is not as often attended to these days. Restorative justice is the kind of concept that might properly be considered an issue of equity. It includes a remedy that might make it right or amend the harm done.*

In her chapter, Presser argues that prisons can institute changes such that they are "minimally harmful and maximally restorative" by developing cultures of care, dialogue-based programming, and policies both inside and outside of prisons that result in decarceration. By a culture of care, she means a prison that embraces respect, rehabilitative programming, and the goal of the good life once one leaves prison. To achieve such a culture, the focus of the prison must move from an institutional culture centered on violence to one preoccupied with achieving good for oneself, for one's fellow prisoners, and for the larger community.

Dialogue-based programming in a restorative prison would open up the discussion of harms done by offenders to victims and of harms done to offenders while incarcerated. In such a way, the criminogenic needs (those needs that motivate offenders to do harm) would be exposed and hopefully dealt with (e.g., insecurity regarding safety) for the sake of preventing harms, including reoffending post-release.

Presser argues that restorative prisons must be concerned with "encounter, amends, reintegration, and inclusion." The culture must move from one of violence to one of social support and trust. Outsiders who reinforce this culture and expand the rehabilitative goals of the institution should be welcome to join it, leading to a more peaceful and regenerative environment. The end that Presser sees for prisons, restorative or not, is their end. Abolition of prisons, along an evolutionary rather than a revolutionary continuum if necessary, will, she believes, achieve the ultimate goal of restoring justice—an equitable end for the individual and the community.

> *Before I built a wall I'd ask to know*
>
> *What I was walling in or walling out,*
>
> *And to whom I was like to give offense.*
>
> *Something there is that doesn't love a wall,*
>
> *That wants it down.*

Robert Frost (1914), Excerpt from "Mending Wall"

Restorative justice is a philosophy that concerns itself with repair in the aftermath of harm. Practices based on restorative justice, such as victim-offender conferences, peer mediation, and truth-and-reconciliation commissions, aim to repair harms through both dialogue and tangible gestures such as restitution and other reparations. The core values of restorative justice—repair as well as encounter, amends, reintegration, and inclusion—are mirror opposites of standard prison practices, which involve keeping offenders away from those whom they have harmed and those whom they might harm in the future and excluding offenders from ordinary civic life (Van Ness & Heetderks Strong, 2010). In a word, restorative justice would seem to be incompatible with imprisonment.

But let us ponder the matter more specifically. Restorative justice and prisons differ from one another in at least six ways. First, given their fundamental concern with repairing harms, restorative justice practices never involve doing harm for the sake of doing harm (Zehr, 2002). In contrast, prison does harm, usually though not exclusively by design (Clear, 1994). It bears noting that the harm caused by prison is suffered by individuals, families, communities, and societies (Clear, 2007; Pattillo, Weiman, & Western, 2002; Wakefield & Uggen, 2010; Wildeman, 2009). Second, most restorative justice thinkers emphasize the collective nature of responsibility for crime. They view crime as emerging from an array of other problems, including unjust social relations (Sullivan & Tifft, 2005). In contrast, incarceration attends to the individual wrongdoer exclusively. It treats individuals as the source of crime problems. Third, restorative justice programs de-emphasize the modern state's near-total monopoly on criminal justice (Christie, 1977). Community members are vital to any restorative justice practice, even those practices sponsored by the state (Braithwaite, 1989; Dzur & Olson, 2004; Young, 1995), whereas "communities" have little to do with prisons. Fourth, restorative justice orients to crime victims as key participants, while victims have nary a thing to do with prisons. Fifth, restorative justice involves subjects doing things—specifically, taking active responsibility for harms (Braithwaite & Roche, 2001; see also Zehr, 1995, p. 42). Both practically and discursively, incarceration involves doing something *to* its subjects. Sixth, restorative justice practices for the most part involve voluntary participation; incarceration is coercive through and through. Given the logics of prison— harm-seeking, exclusionary, individualistic, state-dominant, irrelevant to victims, passivizing and coercive—restorative justice is, in fact, most compatible with its abolition.

And yet, prisons exist and get ample use—nowhere more so than in the United States (The Pew Center on the States, 2010; The Sentencing Project, 2011; West, Sabol, & Greenman, 2010). Until they are abolished, it behooves us to make prisons more restorative—for the sake of prisoners, their victims, their families, and their jailers. *Can* prisons restore? The answer in my mind is yes, somewhat, but with dramatic modifications. Van Ness and Heetderks Strong's (2010) notion of restorativeness as a continuum inspires my vision of *a restorative prison*. In their conceptualization, systems and practices may be fully, moderately, or minimally restorative. A typical expression of the latter emphasizes restitution but not the relational consequences of harm-doing and its repair. In this chapter, I assume the challenge of imagining prisons as sites of restorative justice. In particular, the stigmatization and isolation of prisoners impede full restorativeness. Barb Toews (2006, p. 75) makes this point as well:

> To be fully restorative, prison would offer more than restorative practices. It would also transform its goals, values, culture, and even architecture. A restorative transformation would radically alter the image and experience of prison. Prison would likely no longer be "prison" as we know it.

Although full restorative justice is likely beyond reach in the prison context, some elements of the restorative justice vision may nonetheless be adopted. Cheryl Swanson (2009, p. 32) maintains that the prison objectives include key restorative justice values—namely safety, respect, purposeful activity, and successful reentry.

To render prisons minimally harmful and maximally restorative, I recommend the development of cultures of care in prison, implementation of dialogue-based programming, and, more generally, limits on the use of incarceration. A restorative incarceration agenda that neglects to pursue decarceration is not restorative justice.

A Culture of Care

Braithwaite and Roche (2001) refer to communities of care in observing that "the active intervention of communities of care evokes alternative modalities of incapacitation" (p. 71). Their point is that communities of care can prevent misconduct in ways superior to coercion. The authors have in mind communities in "the free world," such as families, schools, and religious and other social groups. Geographically and discursively, prisons are located at a distance from these communities: Indeed, "incapacitation" generally signifies such distance.

Notwithstanding the dominant cultural bifurcation of prisons and communities, prisons are themselves communities. Early prison designs that segregated inmates from one another never received much use, and prisons of the 20th and 21st centuries are decidedly social environments (Rothman, 1971). Prison communities have a distinct culture. Prisoners share a language, formal and informal economies, and a hierarchical structure. They organize themselves into different social groups based on both "imported" characteristics, such as race and conviction charge, and indigenous ones, such as leadership roles. They share a knowledge base about how to cope with prison life, including a code of normative standards and sanctions for their violation.

Prison culture is violent. The popular view has inmates regularly threatening to cause and actually causing physical harm to one another. That view obscures the incidence of violence at the hands of correctional officers (Kaiser & Stannow, 2011). Consider that whereas inmates in detention centers for girls and in women's prisons do not frequently threaten or cause physical harm to one another, sexual abuse of female prisoners by officers is widespread (Buchanan, 2007; Okereke, 2006). Moreover, the emphasis on violence between prisoners obscures the fact that forcing people into physical spaces is already an infringement on bodies. The fact that medical care is generally deficient in prisons whereas medical needs are great and the risk of communicable diseases is high suggests an added dimension of bodily harm (see Wilper et al., 2009).

However, it should be noted that institutions vary in their levels of outright brutality (see, e.g., Fleisher, 1989). I would say that prisons are not necessarily characterized by violent cultures, but they are certainly characterized by cultures of violence. By cultures of violence, I mean that the reference point for prisons is violence, even where violence occurs (fortunately) irregularly. Thus, for example, prisoners may isolate themselves, physically and mentally, *or* they may form highly collegial relationships with one another in defense of violence. Where does the culture of violence come from? Prison violence follows from the element of coercion that is the paramount ethos of prisons. Prisoners use violence against one other and officers use violence against prisoners, in violation of rules or not. That the ethos of coercion begets prison violence is explicable via several criminological theories, most explicitly Colvin's (2000) perspective, but also strain (Agnew, 1992), control balance (Tittle, 1995), and defiance (Sherman, 1993): The more frustration, subordination, and degradation is experienced, the more reactive behavior we should expect. Instead of a culture of violence, the restorative prison of my imagination would house a culture of care. The work of Marshall Rosenberg on "nonviolent communication" and that of Tony Ward and Shadd Maruna on the "good life" model of rehabilitation, inform the possibilities of a prison-based culture of care.

Rosenberg (2003) conceptualizes violence as a system of communication in which the needs of speaker and audience go unspoken. When someone makes a demand without referring to a need, that gesture is "violent" (The Center for Nonviolent Communication [CNVC], 2011). In contrast, nonviolent communication, or NVC, refers to one's needs. In the NVC model, needs are basic, universal things. The most fundamental of them are autonomy, celebration, integrity, interdependence, physical nurturance, play, and spiritual communion (Rosenberg, 2003, pp. 46–47).

In addition to needs expression, NVC talk is characterized by the delivery of empathy. To summarize, NVC speakers acknowledge the needs that their interlocutors are trying to meet through their behavior and the needs that they are experiencing. They make specific requests of interlocutors in terms of their own needs: For example, "It seems that you put your books on my cot because you were cleaning your own; you value order. Would you be willing to move your belongings off of my cot to help me meet my own need for order?"

One fundamental human need that is commonly violated by and in prison is respect. I suggest that a program that teaches NVC to prisoners and prison officials critically examine the suspicion that respect is, in any given event, being violated. Often, we jump to the conclusion that others disrespect us when they are simply trying to meet their own needs, including "mundane" needs as in the example given above of order in the cell. More profoundly, the NVC framework allows its users to reinterpret what may truly be intended as displays of disrespect in terms of the perpetrator's needs, and thus diffuses interpersonal tension. An officer may *actually* be treating a prisoner with disrespect when he calls him a derogatory name. If the prisoner construes the behavior as meeting the officer's own need for respect, some of the injury may be offset.

The literature on rehabilitation is entirely pitched toward the goal of increasing public safety. It ignores the needs, desires, and interests of prisoners separate from that goal. Ward and Maruna's (2007) notion of rehabilitation for the sake of having "a good life" is innovative in that regard. These scholars view crime and other conflicts as "a direct consequence of maladaptive attempts to meet human needs" (p. 111; see also Agnew, 1992). In contrast to traditional rehabilitative approaches, Ward and Maruna explain, "correctional clients need a motivation for engaging in treatment beyond the avoidant goal of deterrence and the charitable goal of improving community safety" (p. 141). The motivation they endorse is that of living a good life. The appeal of the new culture of care in prison should be made on the basis that it will help administrators, correctional officers, *and* prisoners achieve their goals and thus make them happier.

Just as restorative justice interventions take advantage of community capacities, interventions based on a good lives model aim to take advantage of—and orient to—capacities on the part of individuals. Ward and Maruna (2007, p. 128) state:

> Intervention is therefore seen as an activity that should *add to* an individual's reper- toire of personal functioning, rather than as an activity that simply *removes* a prob- lem or is devoted to *managing* problems, as if a lifetime of grossly restricting one's activity is the only way to avoid offending. (Emphasis in the original)

In short, a good lives model of change emphasizes the positive. Doing so should, incidentally, set the tone for informal relations among prisoners that likewise orient toward the positive.

Dialogue

Dialogue—the opportunity for two or more people to share verbally and to be heard—is an essential aspect of restorative justice practice (Presser, 2004). Incarceration works *against* dialogue. The pains of imprisonment invite prisoners to disguise their true thoughts and feelings—to wear a mask. Self-disclosure is associated with vulnerability, especially in men's prisons, which prisoners are keen to avoid for the sake of thwarting victimization. Further, inmates are generally kept apart from key interlocutors, such as their victims and their supporters. They are also often kept apart from their adversaries in prison—through the use of segrega- tion. Typically, the minutia of prisoners' lives, including times and places for talk, are regulated.

The restorative prison would implement dialogue-based programming wherever possible. Dialogue would be standard procedure in the aftermath of any conflict. Dialogue would orient toward repair of conflict and harm. What to repair? The presumptive answer is the harms they have done to victims. But prisoners have also been harmed, both during the period of incarceration and prior. The harms that prisoners have caused their victims have no greater moral priority than the harms they have been subjected to. All manner of violations in prison would be dealt with through dialogue (Swanson, 2009). To do restorative justice in prison is to hold officials, and not just prisoners, accountable for such violations, because in the restorative justice view, responsibility is generally collective.

The harms of imprisonment to prisoners' families and communities are getting recent attention (Clear, 2007; Pattillo et al., 2002; Wildeman, 2009). These too can usefully be addressed in a restorative justice encounter to the extent that affected parties (or their advocates) are able to attend and represent the ways in which they have been affected.

We would get creative with restorative justice dialogue behind bars. Consider the example of victim impact panels, such as those convened by Mothers Against Drunk Driving (MADD). These get the parents of children killed by drunk driving together with persons sanctioned for that crime. Hence the "victims" and "offenders" engaged in dialogues are surrogates to one another. Ideally, victims of prisoners as well as those who have done them harm would enter into dialogue with them. Such dialogues could be convened through Skype technology. If any of the key parties are unwilling to participate, surrogates could stand in for them. For example, a counselor could receive the words that a prisoner is motivated to say to her or his victim.

Victim-offender dialogues where the offender is imprisoned can have multiple social benefits (Dhami, Mantle, & Fox, 2009). Communities and victims stand to gain better understandings about the crime and to receive symbolic and tangible reparations from the offender. They may also gain awareness of, including a critical vantage point on, the work of prisons. The offender's skills in prosocial interactions can be increased.

In this context, it is important to distinguish between restorative justice programs and cognitive-behavioral programs. The latter direct clients to understand and change their criminogenic thinking (Andrews & Bonta, 2006). Counselors instruct participants in preferred ways of thinking. Restorative justice, at least ideally, aims for more creative exchanges (see Barton, 2003). Recognizing the cultural construction of all speech, nonetheless, speakers gain by answering the call to speak what is on their hearts.

Restorative justice dialogues are not first and foremost *meant* to rehabilitate (Presser, Gaarder, & Hesselton, 2007), but they may serve that function by addressing the criminogenic needs of offenders. Unlike standard treatments, and because of their organic character, such dialogues necessarily explore patterns of offending in the context of the full range of participants' experiences. They reveal the stories that participants have been living by. Interventions into those experiences and stories are tailored to the individual, as effective rehabilitation warrants. Yet, the individual is a more active agent in the restorative justice context. As Edgar and Newell (2006, p. 28) assert, "If (prison programmes) are not based on working *with* offenders, if they are doing things for or to them, then there is a good chance that the programme is not restorative" (emphasis in the original).

Reduced Use of Incarceration

The foregoing prescriptions for a restorative prison notwithstanding, my principal recommendation is that we should use incarceration far less than we do and ideally not at all. Prisons should be used only to avert clear danger. Even then, they should be used only when other means of control have been tried.

Restorative justice practices have by no means supplanted incarceration. As John Braithwaite (2002) states, "Restorative justice has made marginal inroads into the criminal justice system" (p. 157). Yet, in this regard, it has great potential. In the restorative justice philosophy, crime is harm and justice is repair of harm, therefore justice can never be purposely harmful, and hence a tool like Braithwaite's regulatory pyramid, which formalizes such reluctance to inflict harm. Braithwaite (2002, p. 30) describes the pyramid this way:

> At the base of the pyramid is the most restorative dialogue-based approach we can craft for securing compliance with a just law. . . . As we move up the pyramid, more and more demanding and punitive interventions in people's lives are involved. The idea of the pyramid is that our presumption should always be to start at the base of the pyramid then escalate to somewhat punitive approaches only when the more modest forms of punishment fail.

More than 2.3 million people were incarcerated in the United States in 2009, an increase from an estimated 500,000 in 1980 and 1.5 million in 1990 (Bureau of Justice Statistics, 2009; Glaze, 2010). Incarceration is *not* the most often used sanction in the United States—that would be probation. Rather, incarceration *signifies* criminal justice: It is its symbol, its referent, its beating heart—the sanction one might receive, a taste of which is deprivation of liberty and agency in the forms of arrest, strip search, and pre-trial detention. To use incarceration less, then, is not simply to use it less practically speaking, but also discursively speaking. We should change the culture of criminal justice so that imprisonment loses its pride of place as a symbol. Supplant it with messier symbols—people in dialogue, emoting and venting, grief work, details of harms done shared, talk of what was and what could be—of possibilities.

A Model Restorative Prison

Efforts to do restorative justice programming in prisons are relatively sporadic and uncommon, and formal evaluations are even less typical. The United States seems to lag behind Europe in doing prison-based restorative justice (M. Brown, personal communication, Florida Atlantic University, June 7, 2012). Swanson (2009) reports that prison-based conferences with surrogate victims are under way in several countries. Alternatives to Violence workshops are held in a maximum-security correctional facility in New York. A Pennsylvania prison makes letters of apology from offenders available to their victims. Swanson (2009) also mentions victim-offender encounter programs in Minnesota, Ohio, and Texas. She focuses her full attention on the faith-based restorative justice 174-bed honor dorm in Alabama's maximum-security W. C. Holman Correctional Facility for men, which she has studied closely and where she volunteers in an instructional capacity. I will say more about the Holman honor dorm presently.

To a large extent, incarceration is an incidental feature of prison-based restorative justice programs (Dhami et al., 2009; Immarigeon, 1996; Shapland, 2008; Umbreit & Vos, 2000). That is, prison in these cases is relevant to a victim-offender encounter because that is where the offender is located. Edgar (1999) launches her review of restorative justice in prison with a consideration of victims coming into the facility to meet with incarcerated offenders. However, her attention soon turns to other innovations: "Restorative justice could imply that prisoners should mediate in response to crimes such as assaults or thefts committed by prisoners against fellow prisoners" (Edgar, 1999, p. 6). She notes that such interventions are under way in England and Wales, though greater innovation awaits.

Likewise, Dhami and colleagues (2009) emphasize a wide-ranging set of possibilities of restorative justice practice behind bars. First, they identify the following broad goals of restorative justice in prison (pp. 437–438):

- "helping prisoners take responsibility for their actions, recognize the harm they have caused, develop an awareness of victims' needs, and provide them with an opportunity to make amends to victims and give back to their communities;

- helping victims, families and communities communicate their needs to the offender, and develop an awareness of how the prison is assisting the offender in rehabilitation;

- strengthening mutually beneficial ties between the prison and community, so that the community becomes aware of the prison's work and can aid in the reintegration and resettlement of prisoners, and maintaining the prisoners' family ties; and

- by creating a prison system and culture that humanizes prisoners, gives them a decent standard of living, keeps them safe and secure, provides them with opportunities to transform themselves by using their time productively, promotes positive interactions between staff and prisoners, and resolves conflicts using alternative dispute resolution techniques."

Second, Dhami and colleagues (2009) report on existing programs such as rehabilitative workshops for prisoners run by volunteers from the community; courses aimed at helping prisoners to understand the impact of their crimes on victims and to take responsibility for same; community service projects for prisoners; and victim-offender mediation, involving both direct and indirect exchanges (e.g., letters) and surrogate victims. They report that attempts to overhaul prison culture—in line with their last goal—have been few, and these have hardly been evaluated.

My concern is with such attempts and with the goal of changing prison culture in the direction of restorative justice values. Consistent with my reading that restorative justice is first and foremost opposed to harm, and my knowledge of prisons as purveyors of harm both intended and unintended, my model restorative prison would institutionalize restorative justice principles in daily carceral life.

Shapland (2008) retains the expression "restorative justice" for victim-offender encounters, referring to the sort of thing that *I* have in mind as *restorative practices*. I would leave the instant offense that brought the individual to prison aside as an initial focus and rather use restorative practices to address life in prison. If the restorative justice philosophy is to make good on its promise to transform human relationships, I can see no better or more critical place to start than in prisons, where relationships are notoriously fraught with conflict.

Now that I have reviewed some of the conceptual considerations for a model restorative prison—one that deploys restorative justice practices to better life in prison—I would like to get more concrete. Swanson's (2009) detailed discussion of the faith-based restorative justice honor dorm at the W. C. Holman Correctional Facility in Atmore, Alabama, helps tremendously in this regard (see also, Edgar & Newell, 2006). Swanson explicates how the honor dorm, more than 10 years in operation, has managed to establish a mostly restorative subculture within the lockdown culture of a maximum-security facility.

Prisoners may live out their sentences in the restorative justice honor dorm at Holman after a two-year probationary period, during which they follow a four-semester curriculum that integrates instruction in restorative justice values and practices; victim impact education including mock letter-writing to victims and victim impact panels; and peacemaking circles for addressing institution-based conflicts. The latter are organized and facilitated by prisoners. In addition, emphasis is placed on education generally: For example, work toward the GED is required to maintain residency in the dorm. Mentoring is also a basic feature of the dorm, which Swanson (2009, p. 135) views as promoting "accountability on a level that is less rule-centered and more focused on the attachments and obligations resulting from close interpersonal relationships."

A communitarian spirit prevails, as when talk during circles emphasizes the good of the dorm, not simply that of the individuals engaged in conflict, and telling one's story over lecturing. In addition, mutual social support is the norm, as one resident shared: "The honor dorm and the inmates at Holman encouraged me daily, which was some surprise to me, where you are in a prison system where inmates tend to low rate each other" (Swanson, 2009, p. 142). Swanson observes that such an ethos has implications for reentry among those who will one day leave the facility: "The emphasis on community can be considered a rehearsal for community roles in the free world" (p. 185).

Some elements of the prison's punitive culture are found in the honor dorm. A demerit system is in place for rule violations. Neither circle participation nor community service (i.e., work in the dorm) is voluntary. Individuals can be expelled from the honor dorm for serious violations (though reapplication and readmission are available). Nor is the honor dorm wholly self-governing. Swanson (2009) explains that institutional demands and a general doubtfulness about the honor dorm exert specific pressure for order: "In a prison environment where some officers and other inmates are hostile to the dorm, there is little room for error" (p. 157). Notwithstanding its compromises, Holman's restorative justice honor dorm is commendable for prioritizing restorative justice values in daily prison life. The dorm pursues myriad opportunities for prisoners to live in a community-minded, responsible, and peaceful way. Holman has achieved mostly or moderately restorative justice under the most challenging of circumstances—a maximum-security prison in a state whose incarceration rate is among the highest in the nation.

Swanson (2009) does not weigh in as to whether the restorative justice honor dorm has shaped attitudes in the rest of the prison or attitudes about convicted people in the state. My hope is that her book gains a wide readership so that the cultural change started in the dorm might continue.

Conclusion

Of first order of importance is a reversal of the culture of violence that pervades prisons, both for the sake of limiting harm and because that culture works against candid dialogue. Beyond these changes, imprisonment should be used in select cases—only when it promises to prevent more harm than it causes (Braithwaite, 2002). A restorative *system* of criminal justice would do away with our *presumption* of incarceration. It might also suggest decarceration. Lest it seem folly to decarcerate on a wide scale, consider the folly of the status quo. It has long been documented: To wit, Quinney (1970) observed, "The modern prison is based on a paradox: it is designed to punish inmates and at the same time reform them by nonpunitive measures" (p. 177). And in a recent National Institute of Justice report, Joan Petersilia (2011) recounts the following facts:

- U.S. states spend approximately $50 billion on corrections each year. The growth in the cost of corrections over the past 20 years exceeds that of essential services, including transportation, higher education, and public assistance.

- "Even as the states were cutting back in-house prison programs most severely, in the decade from 1985 to 1995, Congress and state legislatures were passing dozens of laws closing off many job opportunities to ex-offenders and restricting their access to welfare benefits and housing subsidies" (p. 28).

- "Mass imprisonment has helped reduce crime rates, but most specialists agree that the effects have been considerably smaller than proponents claim and that we are now well past the point of diminishing returns" (p. 27).

In short, the policy of incarceration is suspect on the macro level. On the micro level—the level of inmate experience—incarceration causes serious harm. Reviewing Justice Department data from 2008, Kaiser and Stannow (2011) report that nearly 600 people, or 25 per hour, were sexually abused every day in American prisons. They caution that these numbers reflect the number of victims and not number of attacks, which is likely to be greater. They furthermore state that the numbers are likely to underestimate the extent of prison rape for various reasons including respondents' concerns about anonymity and the fact that the estimates exclude attacks in other carceral sites such as immigration detention facilities and police lockups. Still we incarcerate; still we treat prisoners' safety and well-being as an afterthought. It is folly to maintain these arrangements. Like Robert Frost in his great poem "Mending Wall," which has to do with human relationships and not prisons, we ought to question what we are walling in or walling out—in this case, healthy relationships or violence, safety and dignity or menace and disrespect.

Restorative justice is already shaping some practices in prisons, though to a limited degree (Dhami et al., 2009; Immarigeon, 1996; Shapland, 2008; Umbreit & Vos, 2000). Prison-based restorative justice programs generally have little to do with the prison itself: It is simply the place where a key participant resides. In this chapter, I have tried to construct a restorative prison—to overhaul the institution itself. Prisons can achieve some measure of restorative justice if they provide opportunities to manifest the core values of restorative justice—encounter, amends, reintegration, and inclusion (Van Ness & Heetderks Strong, 2010). In the restorative prison inmates would engage more with outsiders. Interaction within the prison would be more peaceable and candid. Talk would emphasize the panoply of basic human needs (Rosenberg, 2003).

I have emphasized reform over revolution. By rendering prisons more restorative, we accommodate to the system as it is. Compromises, the scope of which are beyond the purview of this chapter, will be necessary (see Swanson, 2009). Correctional administrators, frontline staff, and inmates may not buy into restorative justice values. We start from where we are, in terms of both goals and practices, with a restorative sort of justice as an ideal to work toward.

My argument is not incompatible with an abolitionist one. It charts abolition as an ultimate end, with intermediate steps along the way. If restorative measures are shown to improve prison life and outcomes, including misconduct, recidivism, and victim satisfaction, then abolishing prisons may eventually seem like common sense.

References

Agnew, R. (1992). Foundation for a general strain theory of crime and delinquency. *Criminology 30*(1), 47–87.

Andrews, D. A., & Bonta, J. (2006). *The psychology of criminal conduct* (4th ed.). Cincinnati, OH: Anderson.

Barton, C. K. (2003). *Restorative justice: The empowerment model*. Annandale, NSW, Australia: Hawkins Press.

Braithwaite, J. (1989). *Crime, shame and reintegration*. Cambridge, UK: Cambridge University Press.

Braithwaite, J. (2002). *Restorative justice and responsive regulation*. New York, NY: Oxford University Press.

Braithwaite, J., & Roche, D. (2001). Responsibility and restorative justice. In G. Bazemore & M. Schiff (Eds.), *Restorative community justice: Repairing harm and transforming communities* (pp. 63–84). Cincinnati, OH: Anderson.

Buchanan, K. S. (2007). Impunity: Sexual abuse in women's prisons. *Harvard Civil Rights–Civil Liberties Law Review, 42*, 45–87.

Bureau of Justice Statistics. (2009). *Prison statistics*. Washington, DC: Bureau of Justice Statistics. Retrieved May 11, 2012, from http://www.ojp.gov/bjs/prisons.htm

The Center for Nonviolent Communication. (2011). *Needs inventory*. Albuquerque, NM: CNVC. Retrieved May 11, 2012, from http://www.cnvc.org/Training/needs-inventory

Christie, N. (1977). Conflict as property. *British Journal of Criminology, 17*, 1–15.

Clear, T. R. (1994). *Harm in American penology: Offenders, victims, and their communities.* Albany: State University of New York Press.

Clear, T. R. (2007). *Imprisoning communities: How mass incarceration makes disadvantaged neighborhoods worse.* New York, NY: Oxford University Press.

Colvin, M. (2000). *Crime and coercion: An integrated theory of chronic criminality.* New York, NY: St. Martin's Press.

Dhami, M. K., Mantle, G., & Fox, D. (2009). Restorative justice in prisons. *Contemporary Justice Review, 12*(4), 433–448.

Dzur, A. W., & Olson, S. M. (2004). The value of community participation in restorative justice. *Journal of Social Philosophy, 35*(1), 91–107.

Edgar, K. (1999). Restorative justice in prison? *Prison Service Journal, 123,* 6–7.

Edgar, K., & Newell, T. (2006). *Restorative justice in prisons: A guide to making it happen.* Winchester, UK: Waterside.

Fleisher, M. S. (1989). *Warehousing violence.* Newbury, CA: Sage.

Frost, R. (1914). *Mending wall.* New York, NY: Holt.

Glaze, L. E. (2010). *Correctional populations in the United States, 2009.* Washington, DC: Bureau of Justice Statistics.

Immarigeon, R. (1996). Prison-based victim offender reconciliation programs. In B. Galaway & J. Hudson (Eds.), *Restorative justice: International perspectives* (pp. 463–476). Monsey, NY: Criminal Justice Press.

Kaiser, D., & Stannow, L. (2011, March 24). Prison rape and the government. *The New York Review of Books, 58*(5). Retrieved May 23, 2012, from http://www.nybooks.com/articles/archives/2011/mar/24/prison-rape-and-government/?pagination=false&print page=true#fnr-1

Okereke, C. (2006). Abuse of girls in US juvenile detention facilities: Why the United States should ratify the Convention on the Rights of the Child and establish a national ombudsman for children's rights. *Fordham International Law Review, 30*(6), 1709–1758.

Pattillo, M. E., Weiman, D., and Western, B. (Eds.) (2002). *Imprisoning America: The social effects of mass incarceration.* New York, NY: Russell Sage.

Petersilia, J. (2011). Beyond the prison bubble. *National Institute of Justice Journal, 268*(October), 26–31.

The Pew Center on the States. (2010). *Prison count 2010: State prison population declines for the first time in 38 years.* Washington, DC: The Pew Charitable Trusts.

Presser, L. (2004). Justice here and now: A personal reflection on the restorative and community justice paradigms. *Contemporary Justice Review, 7*(1), 101–106.

Presser, L., Gaarder, E., & Hesselton, D. (2007). Imagining restorative justice beyond recidivism. *Journal of Offender Rehabilitation, 46*(1/2), 163–176.

Quinney, R. (1970). *The social reality of crime.* Boston, MA: Little, Brown.

Rosenberg, M. (2003). *Nonviolent communication: A language of life* (2nd ed.). Encinitas, CA: Puddledancer Press.

Rothman, D. J. (1971). *The discovery of the asylum: Social order and disorder in the New Republic.* Boston, MA: Little, Brown.

The Sentencing Project. (2011). *Incarceration.* Washington, DC: The Sentencing Project.

Shapland, J. (2008). *Restorative justice and prisons: Presentation to the Commission on English Prisons Today.* Retrieved May 18, 2012, from http://www.howardleague.org/fileadmin/howard_league/user/pdf/Commission/Paper_by_Joanna_Shapland.pdf

Sherman, L. W. (1993). Defiance, deterrence, and irrelevance: A theory of the criminal sanction. *Journal of Research in Crime and Delinquency, 30*(4), 445–473.

Sullivan, D., & Tifft, L. (2005). *Restorative justice: Healing the foundations of our everyday lives* (2nd ed.). Monsey, NY: Willow Tree Press.

Swanson, C. (2009). *Restorative justice in a prison community: Or everything I didn't learn in kindergarten I learned in prison.* Lanham, MD: Lexington Books.

Tittle, C. R. (1995). *Control balance: Toward a general theory of deviance.* Boulder, CO: Westview.

Toews, B. (2006). *The little book of restorative justice for people in prison: Rebuilding the web of relationships.* Intercourse, PA: Good Books.

Umbreit, M. S., & Vos, B. (2000). Homicide survivors meet the offender prior to execution: Restorative justice through dialogue. *Homicide Studies, 4*(1), 63–87.

Van Ness, D. W., & Heetderks Strong, K. (2010). *Restoring justice: An introduction to restorative justice* (4th ed.). New Providence, NJ: LexisNexis.

Wakefield, S., & Uggen, C. (2010). Incarceration and stratification. *Annual Review of Sociology, 36,* 387–406.

Ward, T., & Maruna, S. (2007). *Rehabilitation.* London: Routledge.

West, H. C., Sabol, W. J., & Greenman, S. J. (2010). *Prisoners in 2009.* Washington, DC: U.S. Department of Justice, Bureau of Justice Statistics.

Wildeman, C. (2009). Parental imprisonment, the prison boom, and the concentration of childhood disadvantage. *Demography, 46*(2), 265–280.

Wilper, A. P., Woolhandler, S., Boyd, J. W., Lasser, K. E., McCormick, D., Bor, D. H., & Himmelstein, D. U. (2009). The health and health care of US prisoners: Results of a nationwide survey. *American Journal of Public Health, 99*(4), 666–672.

Young, M. A. (1995). *Restorative community justice: A call to action.* Washington, DC: National Organization for Victim Assistance.

Zehr, H. (1995). *Changing lenses: A new focus for crime and justice.* Scottdale, PA: Herald Press.

Zehr, H. (2002). *The little book of restorative justice.* Intercourse, PA: Good Books.

Part II

Morally Transforming Offenders

3

The Faith-Based Prison

Byron R. Johnson

Editors' Introduction

In today's context, fervent religious belief is often identified with right-wing politics. Phrases such as "The Moral Majority" and "Christian Conservatives" inspire the image of fundamentalists whose view of the sacred includes opposing women's reproductive rights, gun control, and "socialist" welfare programs. However true this view might be, it can obscure another facet of religious faith: an emphasis on a loving God who asks believers to help save the wayward and the wicked.

At his crucifixion, for example, Jesus Christ was bounded on each side by a condemned criminal. At this most crucial moment in Christian theology—the very time when Christ was to sacrifice his life for humankind's benefit—it is instructive that he offered those dying beside him the chance to be with him in heaven. As a loving God, he thus saw redemption as ever-possible and all souls as worthy of being saved. This powerful message is not lost on members of various faiths, whose beliefs urge them to value the lives even of those who have fallen by the wayside.

Indeed, religious reformers have long been involved in trying to make the prison more humane and effective. America's first prisons, invented in the 1820s, were founded by Quakers and other Christians wishing to create a pure environment in which moral fiber might be instilled. It is instructive that they called these institutions "penitentiaries"—places where offenders might do penance and be touched by God's spirit. Similarly, a half century later, another great wave of reforms was begun. In 1870, prison reformers met in Cincinnati to discuss how to create a "new penology" that might fashion an institution capable of reforming inmates. They embraced many secular practices—from classifying offenders and training guards to rewarding good behavior and providing offenders with education and industrial training.

But as people of faith, they also stressed the fundamental need to ensure that the wayward were given religious instruction. More important, they saw that religion—doing God's work—meant that the prison must be a place of reformation, not of crass and needless punishment.

In contemporary times, many reasons exist for why the American prison is seen—often correctly—as a place that diminishes inmates' physical and spiritual well-being. But it is clear that too much religion is not one of these troubling sources; quite the contrary. As Byron Johnson illuminates in this chapter, religious people and programs are an important fountain of good will in the often bleak environments of our prisons. Faith-based initiatives—for those behind bars and for those reentering society—offer not only spiritual redemption but also a range of social supports. A cognitive conversion is made possible and a community of care is provided.

The faith-based prison should not be seen as a panacea. In his book, More God, Less Crime, *Byron Johnson has made a strong case that religious belief and participation diminish criminality. But other challenges remain. For example, can religious programming overcome a range of other risk factors—criminogenic needs—that underlie an offender's antisociality? Will such interventions work well when they must be taken from the hands of volunteers and made part of the prison's organizational bureaucracy? Are faith-based programs more effective than more secular treatments? Might they be used alongside or integrated within such modalities? And what issues must be addressed to operate a religiously oriented institution in a nation committed to the separation of church and state?*

Regardless, Byron Johnson makes a compelling case for the role faith-based corrections can play in making the American prison reflect more of God's love and less of humans' harshness. In so doing, he makes us consider that faith is a critical barrier against seeing offenders as the "other" who deserve to be caged and made to suffer. Instead, faith offers a rationale for why offenders continue to matter and provides a powerful incentive for working for their worldly and heavenly salvation.

The notion that crime is a moral and spiritual problem is a common thread running throughout the history of corrections in America (Morris & Rothman, 1998). Religious believers have long maintained that the life of even the worst offender can be transformed and that faith in God is a necessary ingredient if there is to be any hope of reforming prisoners. In fact, faith-based practitioners have proclaimed this message to the incarcerated for more than two centuries. Indeed, religious instruction and training continue to play a prominent role in most correctional institutions in the United States. From a historical perspective, the primary goal of most prison ministries has been the conversion of prisoners to Christianity. Although other faith traditions have had a presence in prisons, this non-Christian activity is rare by comparison. Consequently, research to date has by necessity focused on Christian programs. This does not mean, however, that faith-based programs could not benefit from alternative faith traditions or more ecumenical approaches.

Bringing religion into prisons has been a constant throughout America's correctional history, but in recent years faith-based approaches to prison ministry have extended their reach and influence in significant ways. In the sections to follow, I will discuss how the focus of faith-motivated individuals and organizations has moved from merely preaching and teaching to inmates, to developing comprehensive faith-based programs addressing an array of offender needs (e.g., employment, substance abuse, mentoring, restorative justice, etc.), to operating faith-based dorms and units, to faith-based prisoner reentry programs, and has become a key ally in rethinking prisoner rehabilitation and prison reform.

Contemporary Prison Ministry

For many prison ministries, it is not hyperbole to suggest that a religious conversion—often referred to as a "born again" experience—has been viewed as synonymous with prisoner rehabilitation or reform. This is the very reason that many churches have a prison ministry as part of the congregation's overall outreach strategy. But even more common than church-sponsored prison ministries are congregations populated with members who are involved in their own individual jail or prison ministry. Often referred to as mom-and-pop operations, these individual-led ministries are rarely organized, and often operate in complete isolation from other outreach efforts to prisoners. Regular observers of American prisons–rural or urban, large or small, minimum or maximum security–will find that these mom-and-pop prison ministries tend to be small and insular and are primarily aimed at preaching and evangelism.

Perhaps the earliest and largest organized effort toward prison evangelism can be traced to 1969 and the Bill Glass Evangelistic Association. Now known as Champions for Life (CFL), this prison ministry was founded by former NFL football player Bill Glass and purports to be the world's largest evangelistic prison ministry. CFL's mission statement is to "assist the Church by equipping and igniting believers to share their faith in Jesus Christ with 'the least of these'" (Bill Glass Champions for Life, n.d.). Given this history, it is not surprising that prison ministries are viewed by many as nothing more than religious zealots driven by a desire to evangelize prisoners, but without any real concern for the spiritual development or maturation of inmates. Consequently, one might suspect that people driven to preach to prisoners would not really be very compassionate or have a more holistic vision for prisoner rehabilitation that prioritizes a host of non-spiritual or secular concerns related to prisoner needs like education, vocational training, life skills, and mentoring. Read the promotional material of some of these prison ministries or scan their websites (if they even have these resources), and one will find plenty of ammunition that would seem to reinforce this stereotype.

But is this stereotype of prison ministries defensible? Is evangelism really the be-all and end-all of most prison ministries? Are critics and skeptics correct to claim that all prison ministries really seek to do is proselytize inmates? In fact, the caricature of prison ministry as strictly evangelistic is far from reality. For several decades, prison ministries have done far more than simply preach to prisoners. As thousands of faith-motivated volunteers have continued to frequent prisons, there has been a steady increase in extending and rethinking traditional approaches to prison ministry. Instead of just going into correctional facilities to participate in an evangelistic service or lead a Bible study, faith-motivated volunteers as well as faith-based organizations have increasingly developed and implemented much more pervasive and comprehensive programs for prisoners, ex-prisoners, and even the families of those incarcerated.

In this chapter, I highlight some of the more visible prison ministries and how they continue to expand the boundaries of prison ministry, often in innovative and far-reaching ways that not only benefit prisoners, prisons, correctional staff, ex-prisoners, and the families of prisoners but society at large. In fact, when it comes to cost-effective and efficacious programs, prison ministries are now becoming de facto leaders in correctional reforms that address long-held and difficult correctional problems. Whether or not they are formally recognized by correctional experts, faith-based organizations and their faith-infused models are at the cutting edge of correctional strategies and reforms.

Consider the aforementioned Champions for Life, known for many years as the world's largest evangelistic prison ministry. As it turns out, CFL has several programs that target other at-risk populations, but without an evangelistic focus. For example, in 1993, CFL launched Champions for Today, which takes place in school assemblies across the country. Champions for Today relies upon former professional athletes and motivational speakers to encourage students to make positive lifestyle choices such as pursuing academic and moral excellence. They also instruct kids on the virtue of not using drugs or alcohol, as well as abstaining from sexually promiscuous behavior.[1] In 2000, CFL launched another program, Ring of Champions, a faith-based mentoring program for at-risk youth. Ring of Champions works with incarcerated youth coming through the juvenile court system. These youth are given the opportunity to voluntarily participate in a long-term mentoring relationship with an adult. Ring of Champions is led by faith-motivated volunteers who have received certified mentor training and are committed to a minimum of 12 weeks of mentoring with at-risk youth.[2]

What is the key take-away point from this example? CFL and its various ministries are dedicated to promoting virtuous and prosocial behavior to children in public schools, especially inner-city schools, as well as providing long-term mentoring relationships to adjudicated youth coming out of the juvenile court system. Thus, the organization known as the world's largest evangelistic prison ministry is actively supporting at-risk youth in non-proselytizing ways that seek to steer them away from a life of crime.

Kairos Prison Ministry International, one of the largest prison ministries in the world, seeks to address the spiritual needs of incarcerated men and women, and their families, as well as those who work in the prison environment.[3] According to the Kairos mission statement, "the people of Kairos are called by God to share the love of Christ with those impacted by incarceration." Drawing upon believers from a variety of Christian traditions, Kairos trains volunteers to work within one of three Kairos programs: Kairos Inside, Kairos Outside, *and* Kairos Torch.

Kairos Inside utilizes trained volunteer teams of men and women from communities in close proximity to an institution to present an introductory three-day weekend, deemed "a short course on Christianity." This effort is mobilized in cooperation with the prison chaplain, and an organized follow-up is part of the weekend program. The Kairos Inside program currently operates in 350 prisons in 31 states in the United States and eight additional countries.[4] More than 170,000 incarcerated men and women have been introduced to Kairos since its inception, and the current number of volunteers exceeds 20,000 per year.[5]

Kairos Outside is a special weekend retreat designed to support the female loved ones of men and women who are incarcerated. It is a safe environment for women to interact with other women in similar situations. Women are encouraged to form small groups that can support them in dealing with the many challenges facing the families of the incarcerated. The Kairos Outside program operates in 19 states and in Canada, England, Australia, and South Africa, and is active in 35 locations. Kairos Torch is a ministry that encourages young men and women who have experiences in the criminal justice system to participate in mentoring relationships. Kairos volunteers commit to a weekly mentoring process with these youthful offenders for six months following the initial weekend retreat. Currently, the Kairos Torch program is operational in 10 locations.[6]

In sum, Kairos Prison Ministry utilizes an army of trained volunteers to work with and mentor male and female prisoners. Moreover, recognizing that correctional environments are stressful, Kairos volunteers also seek to encourage the employees working within these environments. Though sharing the Christian faith is primary, Kairos volunteers provide all manners of assistance to prisoners whether through education, life skills, or ongoing mentoring. In addition, Kairos is actively mentoring youthful offenders in an effort to prevent these same youth from ending up in the adult correctional system.

The Alpha Course has been running for more than 30 years. It began in London, England, in the late 1970s as a means of presenting the basic principles of the Christian faith to new Christians. By 1990, the course was modified to appeal to non-churchgoers. Over the last two decades, the course has expanded internationally and Alpha USA has also launched Alpha for Prisons in an effort to extend this ministry to prisoners.[7] More recently, Alpha USA, through collaborative efforts with other faith-based and community organizations, is now offering prisoner reentry services to the criminal justice system.

Founded in 2000, Horizon Prison Ministry works to restore prisoners and those formerly incarcerated to healthy purposeful living through mentoring, education, skill training, and spiritual growth.[8] Horizon attempts to bring the larger community into the process of restoring offenders back to society. The 12-month Horizon program places volunteer participants into a modified housing unit. In this unit, the men work as a team to build a living and learning environment that focuses on transition preparation. Furthermore, Horizon volunteers and resident encouragers provide mentoring and guidance to participants. The preliminary evaluation research of Horizon program shows promising results (Hercik, 2005).

The Prison Entrepreneurship Program (PEP) is a Houston-based nonprofit organization that connects executives, MBA students, and leaders with convicted felons. PEP was founded on the proposition that if inmates who were committed to their own transformation were equipped to start and run legitimate companies, they could succeed in business following release from prison. PEP sponsors entrepreneurship boot camps and reentry programs for inmates.[9] It started with a "behind bars" business plan competition that drew upon the entrepreneurial acumen of inmates. The initial experiment proved so successful that the Prison Entrepreneurship Program was established in 2004.

The mission of PEP is to stimulate positive life transformation for executives and inmates, uniting them through entrepreneurial passion, education, and mentoring. Since the inception of PEP, over 700 inmates have graduated from the program. PEP graduates, on average, pay approximately $7,000 annually in taxes following release from prison. According to a recent PEP annual report, the return on investment (ROI) for PEP donors is $5 for $1 invested (Prison Entrepreneurship Program, 2012). PEP now works out of the Cleveland Correctional Center (Cleveland, Texas), a privately run correctional facility. PEP is growing quickly and now recruits prisoners from more than 60 prisons throughout the Texas Department of Criminal Justice (TDCJ). PEP is arguably one of the most innovative and promising correctional programs in the entire country. PEP is rapidly expanding within the state of Texas and is considering expansion beyond Texas in the not-too-distant future.

Founded by Charles Colson in 1976, Prison Fellowship Ministries has the most pervasive outreach of existing prison ministries.[10] At the core of Prison Fellowship's (PF) mission is the premise that crime is fundamentally a moral and spiritual problem requiring a moral and spiritual solution.[11] Prison Fellowship still believes religion is the essential ingredient in offender rehabilitation and helping former prisoners to lead a crime-free life. PF offers prisoners a variety of in-prison programs. Through one to three-day seminars and weekly Bible studies, inmates are taught to set goals that prepare them for release. Weekly Bible studies usually last an hour, and one- to three-day seminars might be offered several times a year at a particular prison. The level of prisoner exposure to such religious programs is probably no more than 50 hours of Bible study and several days of intensive seminars annually—a relatively modest correctional intervention.

There is preliminary empirical evidence that regular participation in volunteer-led Bible studies is associated with reductions in recidivism (Johnson, Larson, & Pitts, 1997). For example, I found that prisoners from four different New York prisons who attended 10 or more Bible studies during a one-year period prior to release were significantly less likely to be arrested during a one-year post-release follow-up study. In a more recent study tracking these same prisoners for an additional seven years, I found that regular participation in volunteer-led Bible studies remains significantly linked to lower rates of recidivism for two years and even three years post-release (Johnson, 2004).

It is important to understand that prison ministries are intentionally focused on *more* than the needs of prisoners serving time. Increasingly, faith-based approaches are bringing recognition to the plight of ex-prisoners, as well as the needs of the families of prisoners, and especially the children of those incarcerated. In 1972, Mary Kay Beard was in an Alabama women's prison serving a significant prison sentence for bank robbery. It was during her time in prison that she experienced a religious conversion. It was also about this time that she noticed some fellow inmates taking the toiletries given to them by local church groups and wrapping them as gifts for their own children. Beard would later explain how observing prisoners giving away these gifts was influential in her life and led her to think of how providing gifts to children of prisoners could be an important ministry. A few years after her release from prison, Beard would agree to work with Prison Fellowship to oversee this ministry in Alabama, as a Christmas project for prisoners.[12] Since its launch in 1982, Angel Tree volunteers, churches, and other partners have delivered more than 12 million gifts to children who have an incarcerated parent (Johnson & Wubbenhorst, 2012).

Before Angel Tree was launched, children of prisoners were not on the radar screen of any group or governmental agency. The government kept no records and so it was impossible even to know how many children of prisoners there were. Scholars had not studied children of prisoners or the enormous obstacles faced by this at-risk population. Practitioners as well as social service providers had simply overlooked them. It can be readily argued that Angel Tree was a forerunner of the modern movement to mentor children of prisoners. The most visible example is the Philadelphia-based Amachi program, led by Dr. W. Wilson Goode. Amachi has clearly demonstrated that partnerships between secular and faith-based groups can reach scale and produce dramatic results by identifying children of prisoners as well as mentors. In a 10-year period more than 100,000 children of prisoners have been matched with mentors.[13]

Prison Ministry Goes to the Next Level: The Emergence of Faith-Based Prison Programs

If participation in relatively small doses of religious interventions like Bible studies can have a measurable and beneficial effect on inmates, what might the effect of an extended faith-based prison program have? Believing a much more intensive intervention could lead to even better outcomes, Prison Fellowship began to strategize how to create an unapologetically faith-based community within prisons.

In the 1990s, PF tried to locate a prison partner that would allow them to launch a new initiative that would replace occasional volunteer efforts with a completely faith-based approach to prison programs. The ultimate goal would be to reform prisoners as well the prison culture. The late Charles Colson, founder of PF, unsuccessfully pitched this idea to a number of governors before finding an enthusiastic partner in then-governor George W. Bush. PF moved quickly and introduced the concept of a faith-based program to the Texas Department of Criminal Justice (TDCJ) in January of 1996. The concept described a program with a distinctly Christian orientation, "emphasizing restorative justice, in which the offender works through several phases of treatment to reshape his value system."[14] The "IFI Pre-Release Program," as it was originally named, was officially launched in April 1997.

The collaboration between TDCJ and PF represented a first for Texas, if not the country. According to PF, the InnerChange Freedom Initiative (as the IFI Pre-Release Program was later called) was different from traditional prison ministries in that it represented the first full-scale attempt to offer religious programs in a prison environment virtually around the clock. The InnerChange Freedom Initiative (IFI) promotes adult basic education, vocational training, life skills, mentoring, and aftercare, while linking each of these components in a setting permeated by faith. In this respect, IFI is a faith-saturated program whose mission is to "create and maintain a prison environment that fosters respect for God's law and rights of others, and to encourage the spiritual and moral regeneration of prisoners" (Working Group on Human Needs and Faith-Based and Community Initiatives, 2002). According to the IFI promotional material, the program is a "revolutionary, Christ-centered, Bible-based prison program supporting prison inmates through their spiritual and moral transformation beginning while incarcerated and continuing after release."[15] Not surprisingly, this description fed the mistaken notion that religious programs like IFI were at odds with a treatment model. After all, it is easy to see how some could view religion and treatment approaches to rehabilitation as opposites or adversaries—one is secular and one is faith-based. Though often overlooked by academics, IFI established an approach that viewed religion and treatment as complementary.

IFI was officially launched in April of 1997 at the Carol Vance Unit, a 378-bed prison in Richmond, Texas. The Vance Unit, one of over 100 prisons located throughout Texas, was selected because of its custody level as a pre-release facility and its proximity to the Houston area—the focus of aftercare resources and volunteer recruitment. Only offenders from Houston or surrounding counties were considered for participation in the program. Two hundred beds in the Vance Unit, or essentially half the facility, were reserved for participants in the IFI program.[16] IFI is responsible for inmate programs and TDCJ is responsible for security and custody. Together, PF and the TDCJ formed a unique private-public partnership that would test the proposition that a sacred-secular collaboration could achieve the civic purpose of reducing recidivism and thereby increase public safety.

Anchored in Biblical teaching, life-skills education, and group accountability, IFI established a three-phase program involving prisoners in 16 to 24 months of in-prison Biblical programs and 6 to 12 months of aftercare while on parole. Phase I provides a spiritual and moral foundation on which the rest of the program is based. Phase II tests the inmate's value system in real-life settings in hopes of preparing him for life after prison. Commonly referred to as aftercare, Phase III is the reentry component of IFI and is designed to help assimilate the inmate back into the community through productive and supportive relationships with family, local churches, and the workplace.

Phase I of IFI lasts approximately 12 months and focuses on rebuilding the inmate's spiritual and moral foundation as well as providing educational and survival skills. A heavy emphasis is placed on:

- Biblical education, a general equivalency diploma (GED), tutoring, substance abuse prevention, and life skills

- work (jobs are similar to those of other prisoners in the general population)

- support groups designed to increase an inmate's personal faith

- support groups for enriching relations with family members and crime victims

- mentoring

- peer groups (Community Bible Study)

Phase I is designed to transform the criminal thinking process and establish a new foundation for growth. Six months into Phase I, IFI participants are supposed to be matched with a mentor. Mentors are Christian men from the Houston community who meet with IFI prisoners one-on-one for a minimum of two hours per week.

Phase II of the IFI program lasts 6 to 12 months and seeks to continue the educational, work, and support group aspect of the program. The main difference in Phase II is that IFI participants are allowed to perform community service work during the day at off-site locations, such as Habitat for Humanity. IFI members in Phase II continue with Christian-based education, Bible study courses, mentoring, and support groups, but with a special emphasis on leadership issues. Since IFI operates under the assumption that the program encourages spiritual growth, it is expected that in Phase II participants will begin to take on leadership roles within the program. Evening programs are also offered to IFI participants throughout the week with support groups focusing on a different topic each night: Personal Faith, Mentoring, Substance Abuse, Family/Crime Victims, Community Bible Study. In addition, intensive spiritual weekend retreats are offered periodically through Kairos, a nationally recognized prison ministry.

Phase III of IFI is the aftercare component of the faith-based program and lasts for an additional 6 to 12 months. The mission of the aftercare program is to assist participants in their reentry into society by helping with housing and employment referrals, facilitating the mentoring relationship, and making connections between the offender and local church communities that will provide a nurturing environment to continue the former prisoner's spiritual growth. Aftercare workers recruit new churches and volunteers to assist in the mentoring of IFI participants, and to help with other critical reentry needs such as housing, transportation, and employment. IFI made the decision early on that the target of aftercare services would be directed toward those offenders completing at least 16 months of the IFI prison program at the Carol Vance Unit. Therefore, those offenders who did not complete the program because of an opportunity for early parole, or who were asked to leave the program early (typically for disciplinary reasons), for example, were not guaranteed reentry assistance from IFI's aftercare workers. The justification for this controversial decision was that PF wanted to encourage and reward successful behavior (completing the program) with additional assistance beyond the prison walls. Arguably, those offenders most in need of aftercare may well be those who did not receive aftercare because they did not complete the program. IFI leadership ultimately decided it was more prudent to "invest" already limited aftercare resources in only those program participants who had exhibited the most progress by completing the program rather than investing in individuals who had not shown progress in the program.

Evaluating the InnerChange Freedom Initiative

The 75th Texas Legislature directed the Texas Department of Criminal Justice to develop a tier of rehabilitation programs, and required these programs (including IFI) to be monitored and evaluated by the Criminal Justice Policy Council (CJPC; 2003).[17] However, in addition to documenting outcomes like recidivism, PF felt it vital to commission an independent evaluation that would focus more on IFI participants and the program itself. The findings were generated from the recidivism and outcome data generated by the CJPC, as well as data I collected on the IFI program, participants, staff, volunteers, and correctional staff.

The evaluation combined a quantitative study and a qualitative study. Like the CJPC evaluation, the quantitative aspect of the independent evaluation essentially focused on recidivism outcomes, namely arrest and incarceration of former IFI participants (Johnson & Larson, 2003). The qualitative component, however, relied largely upon observational work and field interviews. This approach helped to document the workings of the faith-based prison program, the spiritual changes in the participants as well as the prison environment, and the experiences of IFI participants following release from prison (Johnson, 2011). Findings presented in Table 3.1 compare the measures of recidivism between the total sample of IFI participants and each of the three comparison groups. As can be seen, 36.2% of IFI participants were arrested during the two-year period following release. Similarly, 35% of the matched group, 34.9% of the screened group, and 29.3% of the volunteered group were arrested during the two-year follow-up period. Likewise, there is little difference between IFI members (24.3%) and the matched group (20.3%), the screened group (22.3%), and the volunteered group (19.1%) in terms of the percentage of former prisoners who were once again incarcerated in the two-year post-release period.

Since IFI's launch in early 1997, PF has maintained that in order for the program to be effective in reducing recidivism, participants would need to complete all three phases of the program because each phase of the program builds upon the previous phase. As it turned out, 75 of the 177 IFI participants (42%) completed all program phases and graduated from the program, while 102 members (58%) did not complete all three phases of the program. Hispanics are most likely to "graduate" from the program (61%) and African Americans are least likely to complete all the components of IFI (37%). Prisoners over the age of 35 are more likely than those under 35 to have graduated or completed all three phases of the IFI program (52% vs. 35%). Inmates with low Salient Factor Risk Scores were more likely than those with high Salient Factor Scores to graduate from the program (57% vs. 42%).

Among the 102 who did not graduate from the IFI program, 51 (50%) were released via parole or mandatory release before they could finish all phases of IFI.

Table 3.1 Results of IFI Texas Two-Year Recidivism Analysis

Recidivism Type	Full Sample (N = 1931) (1a) IFI vs. (2a) Match Group		IFI Sample (n = 177) (1b) IFI Graduates vs. (3b) Non-Completers		IFI Graduates (n = 75) (1c) < 16 months vs. (3c) > 16 months		IFI Non-completers (n = 102) (1d) < 16 months vs. (3d) > 16 months	
	(1a)	(2a)	(1b)	(3b)	(1c)	(3c)	(1c)	(3c)
Arrest								
Percent Arrested	36.2%	35.0%	17.3%	50.0%	15.0%	20.0%	46.5%	68.8%
No. Arrested	64	614	13	51	6	7	40	11
Sample Size	177	1,754	75	102	40	35	86	16
Chi-Square	0.09, p = .76		19.98, p < .0001		0.33, p < .5652		2.67, p < .1023	
Incarceration								
Percent Incarcerated	24.3%	20.3%	8.0%	36.3%	5.0%	11.4%	34.9%	43.8%
No. Incarcerated	43	356	6	37	2	4	30	7
Sample Size	177	1,754	75	102	40	35	86	16
Chi-Square	1.57, p = .21		18.79, p < .0001		1.05, p < .3059		0.46, p < .4982	

SOURCE: Johnson, B. R. (2011). *More God, less crime: Why faith matters and how it could matter more* (p. 109). West Conshohocken, PA: Templeton Press.

NOTE: All tests used the Pearson X^2 statistic with one degree of freedom for a 2×2 table.

Early release on parole was a significant problem for several of the first few cohorts or groups entering IFI, as the Texas Parole Board came under pressure in 1998 and 1999 to stabilize the size of the prison population. Not surprisingly, among the first to be paroled early were minimum-custody prisoners, including those from IFI. The problem of early release on parole was subsequently minimized after the first several cohorts were admitted into the program. Another 48 inmates were removed before they could complete the IFI program for the following reasons: 19 for disciplinary reasons, four at the request of IFI staff, one for medical problems, and 24 at the voluntary request of the applicant.

IFI program graduates have significantly lower rates of rearrest than the matched group (17.3% vs. 35%), or either of the two comparison groups—the screened group (34.9%) and the volunteered group (29.3%). Similarly, those completing the IFI program have significantly lower rates of re-incarceration than the matched group (8% vs. 20.3%), as well as the screened group (22.3%) and the volunteered group (19.1%). The fact that IFI graduates are significantly less likely to be either rearrested or re-incarcerated during the two-year period following release from prison offers initial evidence that program completion of this faith-based initiative is associated with lower rates of recidivism for former prisoners. The recidivism reductions found in the two-year post-release study of IFI are over 17% for arrest and 12% for incarceration. Though the number of offenders in the current study group is quite small ($n = 177$), the results are nonetheless promising.

After release from prison, IFI participants continue on parole in Phase III for another 6 to 12 months. During this aftercare phase of the program, it is expected that IFI participants, like others released from prison, will meet regularly with parole officers. What is different, however, is that IFI mentors are also encouraged to attend these meetings, especially during the weeks and months following release from prison. When comparing those cases where the mentor was known to the parole officer versus those cases where the mentor was not known to the parole officer, the IFI participant was less likely to be rearrested (20% vs. 30%) or re-incarcerated (8% vs. 17%). Further, if the parole officer had documented regular contact versus little or no contact between the mentor and the IFI participant, then the IFI member was also less likely to be rearrested (17% vs. 28%) or re-incarcerated (9% vs. 15%).

To summarize, the quantitative analysis yields the following recidivism findings:

1. No statistical difference between the total sample of IFI prisoners and the matched group on either measure of recidivism during the two-year tracking period

2. A high percentage of IFI participants (58%) were not able to complete the program (half were paroled early and another 25% voluntarily withdrew); these "non-completers" were much more likely than the comparison group to be rearrested or re-incarcerated

3. IFI program graduates were significantly less likely than the matched group to be rearrested (17.3% vs. 35%) during the two-year post-release period

4. IFI program graduates were significantly less likely than the matched group to be re-incarcerated (8% vs. 20.3%) during the two-year follow-up period

5. Mentor contact is associated with lower rates of recidivism

Replicating InnerChange: An Outcome Evaluation in Minnesota

Using the Prison Fellowship's InnerChange Freedom Initiative in Texas as a model, the Minnesota Department of Correction (DOC) established in 2002 the InnerChange Freedom Initiative (InnerChange), a faith-based prisoner reentry program located at the Minnesota Correctional Facility (MCF)-Lino Lakes, on the edge of the Twin Cities. MCF-Lino Lakes is a medium-security facility. The program gives preference to offenders nearing release but is also available for offenders with longer sentences. Reentry programs are tailored to meet individual release plans for members, including transfer to a minimum security institution or to a halfway house or parole. InnerChange is privately funded, and the program depends heavily on volunteers from local churches and religious organizations for the delivery of many of the services provided.[18] Developed and operated by Prison Fellowship Ministries, InnerChange is a 30-month-long program that attempts to help participants successfully transition from prison to the community through the delivery of educational, faith-based programs. Although InnerChange programs are based on two values reflected in the life and teaching of Jesus Christ, inmates do not have to be Christian to apply or participate in the program. InnerChange programs cover areas related to substance abuse education, victim impact awareness, life skills development, cognitive skill development, educational attainment, community reentry, religious instruction, and moral development. InnerChange also strives to build community support for participants by not only involving local faith communities in religious events and activities but also by matching each participant with a mentor.

The Minnesota DOC recently completed an outcome evaluation of the InnerChange program (Duwe & King, 2012). The evaluation assessed the impact of InnerChange on recidivism among 732 male offenders at MCF-Lino Lakes released from Minnesota prisons between 2003 and 2009. The average follow-up period for the 732 offenders was a little more than three years. There were 366 offenders who participated in InnerChange, had their recidivism risk assessed, and had been released from prison during the 2003–2009 period. Offenders whose recidivism risk had been assessed and who had been released during the 2003–2009 period, but did not participate in InnerChange ($n = 366$), were matched to those in the InnerChange group on commonly known risk factors. Multivariate statistical analyses were performed to further control for factors other than InnerChange participation that may have had an impact on recidivism. To minimize selection bias, propensity scores were used to individually match the nonparticipants with those who entered InnerChange (Duwe & King, 2012, p. 4). These measures were used to ensure that any observed differences in recidivism between the 366 InnerChange participants and the 366 offenders in the comparison group were due strictly to participation in InnerChange.

As can be seen in Figure 3.1, InnerChange participants had lower recidivism rates than the offenders in the comparison group. For example, 42% of the InnerChange participants had been rearrested for a new offense by the end of December 2011 compared with 51% of the comparison group offenders. The results also show that 25% of the InnerChange participants were reconvicted for a new offense compared to 34% in the comparison group. In addition, 9% of the InnerChange participants were re-incarcerated for a new criminal offense compared to 13% of the comparison group offenders. The results from the multivariate statistical analyses, which controlled for time at risk and other rival causal factors, revealed that participating in InnerChange significantly lowered the risk of recidivism by 26% for rearrest, 35% for reconviction, and 40% for new offenses leading to re-incarceration.

In an effort to better understand the factors linking participation in InnerChange with significantly reduced reoffending, mentoring data were examined. Analyses of

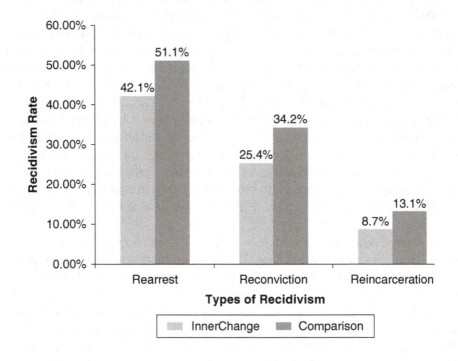

Figure 3.1   Recidivism Rates for InnerChange Minnesota and Comparison Group Offenders

SOURCE: Duwe, G., & King, M. (2012). Can faith-based correctional programs work? An outcome evaluation of the InnerChange Freedom Initiative in Minnesota. *International Journal of Offender Therapy and Comparative Criminology, 20*, 17. Reprinted with permission from SAGE Publications.

these data revealed that 173 (or 47%) of the 366 InnerChange participants met with a mentor, whereas the remaining 193 (53%) did not. Among the 173 who met with a mentor, 131 (76%) had a mentoring continuum insofar as they met with their mentors both in prison and in the community. In addition to providing spiritual advice, mentors can assist offenders by holding them accountable, being a friend, and providing a host of services from transportation to life skills. The findings confirm that a mentoring continuum significantly reduced measures of recidivism.

According to Duwe and King (2012), there are likely several reasons why InnerChange reduces recidivism. Through traditional Christian beliefs and a doctrine that promotes living a prosocial and crime-free life, InnerChange also attempted to lessen the recidivism risk of those who participated by focusing on issues such as education, criminal thinking, and chemical dependency. Not unlike other contemporary programs (e.g., therapeutic communities addressing the criminogenic needs of participants) that have been found to be effective in reducing recidivism, InnerChange participants live in a separate housing unit. Further, InnerChange participants receive a continuum of care that connects the delivery of programs in the institution to those found in the community. Finally, and perhaps most importantly, InnerChange expands offender social support networks by connecting participants to mentors and linking them with faith-based communities after their release from prison. The findings suggest that faith-based correctional programs can work, but only if they incorporate elements of other correctional programs that are known to be effective. Although the evaluation did not include a cost-benefit analysis, Duwe and King indicate InnerChange is a cost-effective program for the State of Minnesota. Since InnerChange relies heavily on volunteers and program costs are privately funded, the state of Minnesota does not have to bear any additional costs for the program. Moreover, InnerChange provides a tangible benefit in the form of reduced recidivism, which includes fewer incarceration and victimization costs.

Joan Petersilia (2003) has identified several major prisoner reintegration practices in need of correctional reform. First, Petersilia argues it is necessary to alter the in-prison experience and essentially change the prison environment from one fostering antisocial behavior to one promoting prosocial behavior. This shift in philosophy would call for fundamentally changing the prison culture so as to teach skills and values that more closely resemble those found in society at large. Second, it is critical that relevant criminal justice authorities revise post-release services and supervision while targeting inmates with high-need and high-risk profiles. In other words, provide closer supervision and assistance to those most likely to recidivate. Third, there is a need to seek out and foster collaborations with community organizations and thereby enhance mechanisms of informal social control. Stated differently, there is a need to establish partnerships that will provide a network of critically needed social support to newly released offenders facing a series of reintegration obstacles.

InnerChange incorporates all three of these correctional reforms. This unique faith-based prison program not only attempts to transform prisoners, but, as Petersilia suggests, attempts to change the prison culture from one that tends to promote antisocial behavior to one that is both conducive to and promotes prosocial behavior. Additionally, InnerChange provides critically needed aftercare services to prisoners following release from prison. Employment and housing are two of the main areas where InnerChange aftercare workers provide invaluable assistance. Petersilia has also noted it is important to prioritize risk and provide extra close supervision and assistance to those most likely to get in trouble. This is exactly the role InnerChange aftercare workers assumed as most prudent for them to play. Indeed, InnerChange aftercare staff focus a great deal of their energies on parolees following release from prison. Central to this process of aftercare is the role of InnerChange mentors—an asset missing from the vast majority of prisoner reentry initiatives.

Finally, InnerChange has made a concerted effort to partner with both parole officials and congregations in the surrounding communities. Collaborating with parole officials has been important because it has allowed both parole officers and InnerChange aftercare workers to pool their resources in supervising parolees. Partnerships with churches have made it possible to recruit scores of volunteers who teach a wide variety of classes in the InnerChange program. Similarly, these congregations have been the places InnerChange has targeted for recruiting mentors, and indeed entire congregations, to agree to work with both prisoners and former prisoners. Without the partnership with these faith-based organizations, InnerChange would not be possible. Petersilia argues that community-based organizations, local businesses, and faith-based organizations are showing themselves to be critical partners in assisting offenders with the transition back into society. The key word in this observation, however, is the reference to *promising* rather than *proven* programs. These two InnerChange studies contribute preliminary evidence that a faith-based prison program combining education, work, life skills, mentoring, and aftercare can be effective in reducing recidivism.

Moving Beyond Faith-Based Prison Programs: Introducing the Prison Seminary

Helping prisoners to rewrite their life narratives can be a powerful and redemptive experience, giving ex-prisoners the hope and purpose needed to start a new and positive life, while at the same time helping them to come to grips with the antisocial life they have left behind (Johnson, 2011). Preliminary evidence indicates that faith-based pre-release/reentry prison programs can be effective in reducing recidivism (Duwe & King, 2012; Johnson, 2011; Johnson & Larson, 2003). However, most faith-based programs do not last very long and one can readily argue that to have the biggest possible salutary effect, prisoners need a more substantial or sustained faith-based intervention. Moreover, the most serious offenders tend to have longer prison sentences and are typically ineligible for consideration when it comes to participation in programs. This is unfortunate since most faith-based programs operate under the assumption that any life can be transformed regardless of the severity of the crime. However, two experimental programs are now ready to test the proposition that a four-year prison seminary can be effective with even the hardest of those criminals serving very long sentences—even life sentences—within our nation's maximum-security prisons.

The Darrington Unit (Rosharon, TX) resembles most other maximum-security prisons around the country, except for the fact that it now offers a four-year seminary within the prison. On August 29, 2011, 39 prisoners were formally installed as the first class of seminarians studying to become ministers under a new program that operates within this maximum-security prison. Referred to as the Darrington Seminary, it is an extension of the Fort Worth–based Southwestern Baptist Theological Seminary. The nondenominational program is carefully modeled after a similar initiative at the Louisiana State Penitentiary, often referred to as Angola. Initiated by Warden Burl Cain, the Angola Bible College, which is an extension of the New Orleans Baptist Theological Seminar, has received considerable attention from sacred media outlets since its inception in 1995. Though the Angola seminary has received recognition in some religious circles, it has not been the subject of serious consideration by national policy makers or viewed by criminologists as a worthy avenue to pursue much less to replicate. The unique aspect of these two seminaries is that they focus on enrolling "lifers" and those with extremely long prison sentences, so that the men, once graduated, will have many years to spend in sharing their faith and their moral convictions with others inside the prison.

Although Angola has a notorious and well-documented history as one of the most violent prisons in America, in recent years an increasing number of observers have reported a far less violent institution. Many have suggested that Angola has undergone a total change in the prison culture during the last 17 years (Rideau, 2010). Moreover, they credit this change to the fact that the Angola seminary graduates have remained inside the prison. Using this particular "lifer-student" approach, correctional leaders at Angola and Darrington are convinced they have the potential not only to rehabilitate prisoners but to transform the prison environment itself. Transforming the culture of prisons through the power of faith may hold the potential for: (1) enhancing the prospect of rehabilitating prisoners, (2) reducing prison violence (e.g., inmate-on-inmate, inmate-on-staff), (3) lowering the level of gang activity, (4) decreasing the prevalence of suicide, (5) improving morale (among prisoners as well as staff), (6) reducing staff turnover, and (7) lowering recidivism following release from prison. Since faith-based programs tend to be privately funded and largely staffed by volunteers, they come at no cost to taxpayers. In a time of shrinking budgets and program cutbacks, correctional administrators may be open to the idea of volunteer-led faith-based programs and especially seminaries, a prospect that will be enhanced if the evidence indicates that they can be effective.

Again, the difference in Angola and Darrington, where faith-based programs are concerned, is that these two seminaries will accept only those inmates with extremely long sentences, so the inmates can be returned to service inside the prison system and therefore exert for many years an influence for moral change and spiritual renewal among the rest of the inmates. The most critical aspect of these two seminaries is their commitment to send their graduates out as "Field Ministers" to other prisons in their respective states. Angola has been sending out their graduates as "missionaries" for a number of years, and the Darrington Seminary now has approval from the highest levels of the TDCJ to follow this same approach. This will mean the influence of the seminary graduates will gradually permeate all the prisons in Texas—just as it has done in all the prisons in Louisiana.

Although the idea of placing seminaries within prisons may sound bizarre, PF is currently planning to launch more than 20 seminaries within California's prison system in 2012 alone, and serious discussions are taking place between PF and officials from a host of other states regarding the possibility of allowing prison seminaries to become part of their existing prison systems. If these discussions take root, we could be witnessing a major shift in the American prison system within the next few years.

Baylor University's Program on Prosocial Behavior and the Institute for Studies of Religion (of which the author is a member) recently received a major five-year grant (2012–2017) to conduct an assessment of the effectiveness of both the Angola and Darrington seminaries. The Angola and Darrington studies will incorporate a number of different research perspectives from qualitative to quantitative methodologies. For example, during the five-year study period, the research team will conduct ongoing interviews with inmates, correctional staff, seminary instructors, and other faith-based volunteers. These interviews at different time points will allow the study team to assess and monitor the degree to which a prisoner's faith journey grows or changes over time. We will observe classes, worship services, vocational training and work, and even recreational activities, in order to gain an accurate picture of life within the prison. Further, we will compare and contrast the seminary with the general population of the wider prison populations at both Angola and Darrington. Specifically, we want gauge the influence of the seminary on the broader prison culture outside of the seminary. We will analyze all official and relevant data made available to us from the prisons as well as the Department of Corrections in Louisiana and the Texas Department of Criminal Justice. In addition to studying standard recidivism measures (e.g., prison infractions, post-release arrest, conviction, or incarceration), we will conduct Return on Investment (ROI) analyses.

The prison seminaries at Angola and Darrington are producing seminary graduates who plan to become Field Ministers or missionaries to other prisons in Louisiana and Texas. We will collect data in order to determine the long-term effects of a prisoner having graduated with a seminary degree. For example, among other outcomes, we plan to determine the extent to which seminary graduates:

1.   are viewed as positive role models in the general prison population by staff and inmates;

2.   engage in ministry and the sharing of their faith;

3.   are able to counter those antisocial aspects of prison culture; and

4.   are less likely to break institutional rules.

In the case of Angola, we will collect data as far back as possible on seminary participants. This will allow us to identify for tracking purposes those prisoners who completed the seminary program and to examine the behavior of prisoners who were transferred to other prisons.

The Role of Faith-Based Organizations in Prisoner Reentry

In less than three decades, the U.S. prison population has grown from roughly 300,000 to more than 1.6 million, and the number of former prisoners on parole has increased from around 220,000 to 825,000 (Glaze & Bonczar, 2009). This unprecedented growth means that some 2,000 prisoners are being released from prisons around the country each day. The transition back to society is not a new problem—former prisoners as well as the communities receiving them have always struggled with the issue—but the sheer magnitude of the number of prisoners returning to society has turned the problem into a national crisis (Travis, 2005). Despite various correctional experiments designed to assist former prisoners with this difficult transition period, the likelihood of a former prisoner successfully reintegrating back into the community has not improved. Roughly two thirds of all offenders released from prison will be rearrested within three years of their release (Langan & Levin, 2002). It is not unreasonable, therefore, for politicians and decision makers to fear that the increasing number of ex-prisoners returning to society poses a threat to public safety (Committee on Community Supervision and Desistance from Crime, 2007).

Most correctional experts agree that any comprehensive prisoner reentry strategy must include the following components: close community supervision, access to substance abuse treatment, mental health services, educational programs, vocational training, and job placement. The reality, however, is that our criminal justice system does not have a good track record for providing these much needed components. In fact, correctional budgets are being cut in many states and it is likely we will continue to see more cuts rather than expansion of programs—especially those designed to address prisoner reentry. Consequently, recommendations for a comprehensive and well-resourced prisoner reentry plan to be delivered and shouldered exclusively by the government are shortsighted, cost prohibitive, and untenable. Finding sustainable and replicable solutions to prisoner reentry requires a much more holistic approach than academics, corrections experts, stakeholders, and decision makers have been willing to consider.

THE FEDERAL GOVERNMENT TAKES AN INITIAL STEP IN ADDRESSING PRISONER REENTRY

Two major prisoner reentry initiatives have now given us some preliminary evidence that sacred-secular partnerships hold promise for addressing the prisoner reentry crisis. In 2003, the U.S. Department of Labor launched Ready4Work, a three-year pilot program to address the needs of ex-prisoners through faith-based and community organizations (FBCOs). Ready4Work placed an emphasis on job training, job placement, case management, mentoring, and other aftercare services. FBCOs were selected to provide services to adult ex-offenders in 11 cities. Ready4Work purposely targeted participants with a high probability of recidivism. Once individuals entered the program, they were eligible for services lasting up to one year. Participants were also matched with mentors in one-to-one and/or group mentoring relationships. Job placement specialists helped participants find jobs and case managers continued to provide assistance after participants were employed. Results from Ready4Work provide preliminary evidence of what is possible when an intermediary brings together public and private partnerships to address prisoner reentry in a holistic and coordinated strategy.

The Prisoner Reentry Initiative (PRI) was announced in 2004 and grew out of the Department of Labor's Ready4Work project. PRI was designed to further test the proposition that prisoner reentry could be effectively accomplished with a comprehensive strategy designed to draw heavily from partnerships with FBCOs. The PRI helped to connect former prisoners with faith-motivated groups as well as secular community-based organizations willing to help ex-prisoners locate employment and to stay out of trouble by following prosocial paths. A total of 30 PRI grantees across the country were selected to provide mentoring, employment, and other transitional services to thousands of ex-inmates. PRI sites began serving program participants in the spring of 2006 and, like Ready4Work, preliminary results were promising. These alliances confirm the premise that sacred and secular partnerships can indeed be critical partners in establishing a network of social supports necessary for comprehensive and coordinated prisoner reentry.

EXTENDING FAITH-BASED EFFORTS TO THE COMMUNITY

Any prisoner reentry plan that is comprehensive and able to reach scale (i.e., be replicated in other jurisdictions) will require a massive influx of new people and programs that do not currently exist in most jurisdictions. Since the government alone cannot provide these programs, faith-based groups represent a critical piece of the reentry puzzle that has yet to be courted as an ally. Indeed, many faith-based groups feel they are marginalized and even mistrusted by government entities. Historically speaking, the reasons for this lack of cooperation, unfortunately, have dealt with stereotypes, prejudice, and even discrimination. Most secular groups as well as the government do not have solid track records for being "faith friendly." Likewise, many faith-based organizations are often reluctant to partner with government and secular institutions. There is, consequently, a degree of distrust among faith-motivated individuals toward perceived outsiders, and the opposite is also true.

Out4Life, Prison Fellowship's newest initiative, seeks to develop a national reentry network to assist the 700,000 plus prisoners released each year in the United

States to make a successful transition back to their families and communities. For example, Out4Life argues faith-motivated individuals can assist prisoner reentry efforts by agreeing to undergo necessary training to specifically assist parole and other community-based correctional personnel. Ultimately, a truly comprehensive prisoner reentry plan will require very large numbers of committed and trained volunteers (e.g., probation and parole) who will agree to bring to bear their varied networks of social and spiritual support to correctional, governmental, and secular entities committed to prisoner reentry and aftercare. Without a comprehensive approach that coordinates public and private and secular and sacred partnerships, prisoner reentry support will remain fragmented and poorly resourced, and continue to be a national crisis. There is great promise if government and faith-based groups collaborate in meaningful partnerships to successfully address prisoner reentry problems.

It is readily acknowledged that lack of housing, employment, transportation, counseling, and mentoring are substantial obstacles making the transition from prison to society so difficult for ex-prisoners. Tackling these problems is going to require a great deal of new human and financial resources as well as the participation of key community leaders. Out4Life also recognizes and proposes that any comprehensive strategy for confronting the problems of prisoner reentry will require an infusion of an unprecedented number of new volunteers—drawn heavily from communities of faith—that have or can develop strategic alliances focused on each of the problems ex-prisoners encounter.

Out4Life, therefore, seeks to create a paradigm shift for how many have thought about ministry to ex-offenders. Instead of leading a Bible study in prison, many new religious volunteers may be asked to consider developing strategies to improve the housing and employment conditions for ex-offenders already living in the community as well as prisoners who will eventually be returning home. The importance of mentoring relationships that are established in prison and carry over to the community cannot be overemphasized. We know that mentoring matters for youth and children, but it also matters for adults. The real problem is the severe shortage of mentors for prisoners, and an even more dramatic shortage of mentors for ex-prisoners. This is precisely why communities of faith, by far America's most volunteer-rich organizations, are uniquely positioned to assist in alleviating the mentoring deficit (Cornwell & Harrison, 2004; Musick & Wilson, 2007). Tragically, almost all the 700,000 leaving prison this year will do so without the benefit of a mentor. Communities have not been approached in any systematic or meaningful way about how they can provide these mentors. However, there is no other source more volunteer-rich than America's houses of worship (Musick & Wilson, 2007). There are approximately 375,000 congregations in the United States, and Out4Life intends to make widely known what would seem obvious to any objective observer; namely, that the "faith factor" should be front and center when developing strategies for prisoner reentry. Indeed, Out4Life believes the coordination and mobilization of faith-motivated volunteers and organizations should be considered a non-negotiable ingredient for any successful prisoner reentry plan.

Out4Life was launched in Louisiana in 2008, in Arkansas in 2009, and in 2010, it was launched . . . in the following states: Arizona, Georgia, Michigan, Minnesota, Ohio, Oregon, Tennessee, Texas, and Virginia. Out4Life seeks to build a national reentry and aftercare movement by supporting three distinct stages of action: (1) sponsoring reentry conferences, (2) establishing coalitions, and (3) building a national network. Out4Life engages stakeholders in a national reentry network to help make this happen. Out4Life works to: (1) generate awareness of the needs and obstacles facing newly released prisoners and the urgency to address those needs; (2) pull together government agencies, businesses, churches and faith-based organizations, and civic groups in a collaborative effort to help ex-prisoners successfully reintegrate into society; (3) identify and offer best practices that prove effective in restoring formerly incarcerated men and women to their families and to society; (4) build regional and state coalitions and support existing coalitions to help offer a comprehensive array of services and support to returning prisoners; and (5) network all of these coalitions to change lives and reduce recidivism throughout the nation.

Reentry conferences build awareness by bringing together representatives from the government, community, and church to discuss both the needs and the potential of returning prisoners. Through plenary talks and workshops these conferences provide a platform for addressing barriers to reintegration as well as the opportunity to identify strategies for overcoming these barriers, and to begin the process of cultivating collaborative relationships. Out4Life Coalitions include agencies, faith-based organizations, businesses, community organizations, and other social service providers who reach out to formerly incarcerated men and women with much needed resources and ongoing support. These regional and state-level collaborative teams offer diverse services that may include mentoring, support groups, housing, assistance, job placement, educational opportunities, counseling, and other supportive services. The Out4Life National Network seeks to link all of these regional and statewide coalitions together to maximize the exchange of information and the shared use of best practices for successful reentry. Prisoner reentry and aftercare are formidable problems for every community in the country. Consequently, it is essential to build a national network that pays attention not only to urban centers where so many offenders will be returning but to small and rural communities that have their own unique set of challenges.

Ready4Work, the Prisoner Reentry Initiative, and Out4Life represent preliminary but positive developments in the effort to confront the obstacles associated with prisoner reentry. Out4Life holds considerable potential because it corrects an oversight common in prison ministry for many decades, namely, the disproportionate emphasis on faith-motivated volunteerism in prisons rather than communities. Out4Life seeks to bring a whole new generation of volunteers—and the vast network of services these volunteers can systematically tap—to address the needs of reentry and aftercare. In addition, Out4Life acknowledges that government programs as well as faith-based and community efforts tend to operate in isolation from each other and are thus unable to adequately address prisoner reentry and aftercare. Stated differently, the solution to reentry and aftercare cannot be achieved by the faith community or government alone. Thus, Out4Life is all about coalition building and networking in an effort to build and sustain the necessary capacity to achieve what otherwise will be an unattainable civic good. By intentionally focusing on reentry and aftercare best practices, and supporting public-private as well as sacred-secular collaborations, Out4Life has the potential to inspire a serious paradigm shift in the field of corrections.

What has been missing until recently is a prisoner reentry model or template that links all the non-negotiable elements of reentry together in a way that can be replicated and sustained in cost-effective ways in local communities, in regions, or statewide. We are in need of a plan where coordination and collaboration are central, where the goals of the reentry model are realistically achievable, where the specific elements of the plan are replicable in any community, and finally, where the plan is affordable and does not add new costs to already overburdened correctional budgets. Out4Life recognizes prisoner reentry requires the active engagement of multiple sectors, private and public, secular and sacred, in order to make a difference. Faith- and community-based networks dedicated to prisoner reentry that do not presently exist must be created. Partnerships, for example, must be forged between faith-based organizations and governmental agencies—entities that have not always had a track record of working together—uniting for the civic good. In order to be effective, these efforts must be bolstered by intermediary organizations that will provide oversight, technical assistance, capacity building, and accountability. Out4Life is providing leadership in this area by organizing local, regional, and national forums for facilitating these vital discussions and challenging individuals, groups, and agencies to think intentionally about meeting one of the most vexing problems facing our society.

Conclusion

The title of this chapter—The Faith-Based Prison—is somewhat misleading. Technically, I do not believe there will ever be (or should be) a completely faith-based prison in America. On the other hand, faith-based programs are continuing to extend their presence and influence in positive ways in prisons as well as the communities to which prisoners will return. Because of this increasing momentum some may be assuming or wondering if totally faith-based prisons will actually become a viable option within the American correctional system. Even if future research demonstrates extraordinary cost savings and significant recidivism reductions associated with faith-based prison programs, it is unlikely that completely faith-based prisons will ever exist in America.

For example, the InnerChange Freedom Initiative (described in this chapter) is a faith-based program that initially co-existed alongside the general prison population of the Carol Vance Unit in Richmond, Texas. Over time the success of the IFI program led to an agreement between TDCJ and Prison Fellowship to dedicate all of the beds in the prison to this faith-based program. One might readily argue, therefore, that the Carol Vance Unit has been a completely faith-based prison for more than a decade.

Indeed, a tour of the Carol Vance Unit might seem to confirm that notion. Yet a closer look reveals that the prison, like any other correctional institution, has a warden, associate wardens, custodial staff, and a host of other correctional employees not affiliated with the IFI program. IFI simply provides privately funded faith-based programs, largely driven by faith-motivated volunteers. This 15-year experiment is a public-private partnership designed to reduce recidivism; it is not a fully faith-based prison. Over time IFI and TDCJ have established a very positive rapport and respectful working relationship and have become a model for what is possible when one considers reaching scale with a faith-based program. I would argue it is not desirable or possible to have a completely faith-based prison. Such a concept would require turning over every function and role of the prison to the faith-based community, which would raise insurmountable legal and ethical concerns. Indeed, I have never heard one proponent of faith-based approaches suggest a completely faith-based prison to be an outcome either remotely desirable or worth considering.

Though I think it is unlikely we will ever see a fully faith-based prison, this should not be interpreted as diminishing the role of faith-based prison programs. In fact, I believe that faith-based approaches are at the leading edge of correctional reform and innovation. From reaching out to children of prisoners through one-on-one mentoring, to establishing faith-based dorms, faith-based pre-release or reentry prison programs, prison seminaries, and faith-based prisoner reentry and aftercare, faith-based organizations and individuals are touching every difficult-to-address problem area within corrections. These faith-motivated individuals and groups are volunteering their faith-based services in large numbers and research is beginning to demonstrate their worth. Moreover, there exists a new receptivity from correctional administrators for these faith-based prison interventions since they can offset shrinking correctional budgets, which have necessitated cutting already scarce offender programs.

Endnotes

1. Since its inception in 1993, *Champions for Today* has presented nearly 4,400 programs across the United States and world to over 1.5 million students, with many of these presentations made in inner-city schools (http://www.billglass.org/cft.htm).

2. http://www.ringofchampions.org/

3. Kairos sprang from the Cursillo movement and is supported by Christian volunteers, including those from Cursillo and those other movements that consider Cursillo as their root.

4. United Kingdom, Australia, South Africa, Costa Rica, Honduras, Nicaragua, Peru, and Canada.

5. http://www.kairosprisonministry.org/

6. http://www.kairosprisonministry.org/

7. There are more than 60,000 Alpha courses running in 169 countries and an estimated 18 million people have participated. The Alpha course is supported by all major denominations (http://www.alphausa.org/).

8. http://www.horizonprisonministry.org/

9. http://www.pep.org/

10. Prison Fellowship is the largest organized prison ministry in the United States. According to Prison Fellowship's most recent Annual Report, the ministry is supported by the efforts of over 300,000 volunteers. Approximately 200,000 prisoners per month participate in either Bible studies or seminars led by PF-trained volunteers in over 1,300 of the country's 1,850 state and federal correctional facilities (www.prisonfellowship.org).

11. Prison Fellowship identifies itself as a not-for-profit, volunteer-reliant ministry whose mission is to "exhort, equip, and assist the Church in its ministry to prisoners, ex-prisoners, victims, and their families, and to promote biblical standards of justice in the criminal justice system."

12. http://www.angeltree.org/angeltreehome

13. http://www.amachimentoring.org/

14. From the TDCJ Feasibility Study for monitoring and tracking participants in "IFI."

15. See http://www.prisonfellowship.org/programs/reentry/ifi/

16. The Texas Department of Criminal Justice and Prison Fellowship later agreed to increase the IFI population at the Vance Unit. As of April 2003, the IFI program held over 200 prisoners, and currently houses more than 300 prisoners.

17. The CJPC was an official Texas agency independent of TDCJ or other criminal justice agencies and existed from 1983 to 2003.

18. For example, Prison Fellowship's costs to operate IFI in fiscal year 2000–2001 alone were $1.45 million.

References

Bill Glass Champions for Life. (n.d.). Retrieved June 1, 2012, from http://www.billglass.org/statementoffaith.htm

Committee on Community Supervision and Desistance from Crime. (2007). *Parole, desistance from crime, and community integration.* Washington, DC: The National Academies Press.

Cornwell, B., & Harrison, J. A. (2004). Labor unions and voluntary association membership. *American Sociological Review, 69,* 751–767.

Criminal Justice Policy Council. (2003). *Initial process and outcome evaluation of the InnerChange Freedom Initiative: The faith-based prison program in TDCJ.* Austin, TX: Criminal Justice Policy Council.

Duwe, G. & King, M. (2012). Can faith-based correctional programs work? An outcome evaluation of the InnerChange Freedom Initiative in Minnesota. *International Journal of Offender Therapy and Comparative Criminology, 20,* 1–29.

Glaze, L. E., & Bonczar, T. P. (2009). *Probation and parole in the United States, 2008.* Washington, DC: U.S. Department of Justice, Bureau of Justice Statistics.

Hercik, J. M. (2005). *Rediscovering compassion: An evaluation of Kairos Horizon communities in prison.* West Pointe, PA: Caliber Associates.

Johnson, B. R. (2004). Religious programs and recidivism among former inmates in prison fellowship programs: A long-term follow-up study. *Justice Quarterly, 21,* 329–354.

Johnson, B. R. (2011). *More God, less crime: Why religion matters and how it could matter more.* West Conshohocken, PA: Templeton Press.

Johnson, B. R., & Larson, D. B. (2003). *The InnerChange Freedom Initiative: A preliminary evaluation of a faith-based prison program.* Waco, TX: Baylor University, Institute for Studies of Religion.

Johnson, B. R., Larson, D. B., & Pitts, T. G. (1997). Religious programs, institutional adjustment, and recidivism among former inmates in prison fellowship programs. *Justice Quarterly, 14,* 145–166.

Johnson, B. R., & Wubbenhorst, W. (2012). *Building relationships between prisoners, their families, and churches: A case study of Angel Tree.* Waco, TX: Baylor University, Institute for Studies of Religion, Program for Prosocial Behavior.

Langan, P. A., & Levin, D. J. (2002). *Recidivism of prisoners released in 1994.* Washington, DC: U.S. Department of Justice, Bureau of Justice Statistics.

Morris, N., & Rothman, D. J. (1998). *The Oxford history of the prison: The practice of punishment in Western society.* New York, NY: Oxford University Press.

Musick, M., & Wilson, J. (2007). *Volunteers: A social profile.* Bloomington: Indiana University Press.

Petersilia, J. (2003). *When prisoners come home: Parole and prisoner reentry.* New York, NY: Oxford University Press.

Prison Entrepreneurship Program. (2012). *Prison entrepreneurship program: 2011 annual report.* Houston: Author.

Rideau, W. (2010). *In the place of justice: A story of punishment and deliverance.* New York, NY: Knopf.

Travis, J. (2005). *But they all come back: Facing the challenges of prisoner reentry.* Washington, DC: Urban Institute Press.

Working Group on Human Needs and Faith-Based and Community Initiatives. (2002). *Finding common ground: 29 recommendations of the Working Group on Human Needs and Faith-Based and Community Initiatives.* Washington, DC: Search for Common Ground.

4

The Virtuous Prison

Toward a Restorative Rehabilitation

Francis T. Cullen, Jody L. Sundt, and John F. Wozniak

Editors' Introduction

Jonathan Simon is a scholar known for his judicious, not hyperbolic, commentary on correctional issues. It is thus disquieting that he has described contemporary American corrections as a "waste-management system." Similar to other toxins, observes Simon, offenders are seen as dangerous and unredeemable. The task for managers is to determine how toxic offenders are and then to place the highest-risk inmates in the most secure container available (i.e., a super-max or high-security prison). Overall, the job is to move the large flow of "toxic materials"—offenders— through the system as efficiently and inexpensively as possible.

All metaphors, of course, have their limits. The American prison is not devoid of people of good will or of practices aimed at saving the wayward. But Simon's use of the concept of "waste management" captures a fundamental reality of our recent correctional history. As mass imprisonment overwhelmed resources and punitive rhetoric flourished, inmates were often reduced from fellow community members to be reformed into inputs to be turned eventually into outputs. Many correctional officials thus focused on the dual tasks of finding enough beds for, and managing the diverse risks posed by, the constant overflow of inmates into institutions crowded far beyond their built capacity.

Francis Cullen, Jody Sundt, and John Wozniak decry this amoral penology. They remind us that the inventors of the penitentiary, as well as of the modern rehabilitative ideal in the years leading up to the Progressive Era, were anything but amoral. For them, corrections was driven by a higher purpose—often a religiously inspired purpose—that called reformers to inculcate morality into the hearts and minds of offenders. In retrospect, not all of these reformers' methods would strike us as sensible today (e.g., solitary confinement for inmates). But with the advantage of modern criminology and research on what works to change offenders, we now have the means to accomplish the optimistic goals they articulated.

Importantly, Cullen, Sundt, and Wozniak argue that the key to restoring the moral purpose of American corrections is to transform custodial institutions into virtuous prisons. At its core, this vision rejects any inclination to devalue inmates and to treat them as mere toxic wastes to be managed. Rather, corrections is unabashedly conceptualized as a moral enterprise in which the pursuit of virtue should define all activities inside the prison walls. At the moment, this goal might appear overly bold and unattainable. But the embrace of virtue is a necessary first step in transforming prisons from containers for toxic waste into social domains in which moral improvement is privileged in policy and practice decisions.

To accomplish this ambitious goal, Cullen and his colleagues propose a practical strategy—that prison life should be governed by what they call "restorative rehabilitation." As might be recalled, the concepts of restorative justice and rehabilitation were discussed previously in Chapters 1 and 2. To Cullen and his coauthors, the appeal of restorative justice resides in its emphasis on offenders recognizing and taking responsibility for the harm they have caused and then in taking steps to help restore their victims. This process will lead to their restoration to the community. However, to become prosocial citizens, offenders must also address their deep-seated criminogenic needs that led to their incarceration. Here, the authors argue that empirically validated principles of effective treatment should be used to guide these rehabilitation efforts.

In the end, Cullen, Sundt, and Wozniak do not shy away from asserting that corrections is not simply a technical task of managing inmate populations but a moral enterprise. In the absence of clear values, corrections risks forfeiting its sense of higher social purpose and of becoming mired in the daily challenges of so-called waste management. In this context, the call for a virtuous prison reminds us that values matter, and comprise is a key component in any attempt to fashion a more promising future for the American prison.

In American corrections, mass incarceration is the elephant in the room that nobody can ignore. Although the seemingly unstoppable rise in prison populations finally appears to have stopped, the nation is left with a disquietingly large number of its citizens behind bars (Pew Center on the States, 2010). The enormity of what has occurred is revealed by a brief look to the past. In 1970, the count of inmates in state and federal prisons on any given day did not reach 200,000; four decades later, this figure had increased more than seven-fold, with the population coming to surpass 1.5 million (Glaze, 2011; Langan, Fundis, Greenfeld, & Schneider, 1988). When offenders in jail are added in, America's incarcerated population now tops 2.2 million (Glaze, 2011). Not surprisingly, most criminologists decry this enormous jump in imprisonment. They often note that the United States has the highest incarceration rate worldwide—several times higher than most advanced industrial nations (Cullen & Jonson, 2012). Merely making this observation, it seems, is enough to confirm that something is amiss in our correctional policy.

The most common assertion is that the United States should not place so many of its residents behind bars. Although we largely agree with this contention, we will leave the specific merits of this claim for others to debate (compare, e.g., Bennett, DiIulio, & Walters, 1996, and Reynolds, 1997, with Clear, 1994, Currie, 1998, Irwin & Austin, 1994, and Pratt, 2009). What concerns us here, however, is the corresponding tendency for criminologists to remain silent on precisely *what prisons should be like*. Because criminologists' main concern is that imprisonment should be used sparingly (i.e., only for the incorrigibly violent or for those committing truly heinous crimes), they couple their criticism of the "imprisonment binge" with a call for policy makers to create more viable "alternatives to incarceration." Although the logic here makes sense—if too many people are locked up, alternatives to prison are essential—this kind of thinking obscures or neglects a related question: Short of releasing them, what should be done with the offenders who remain incarcerated? If criminologists respond at all, it is with the admonition that prisons should be "more humane." Exactly what this means is only infrequently spelled out (for exceptions, see Johnson, 1996; Toch, 1997; see also the chapters in this volume).

Why do criminologists generally fail to draft a blueprint for the prison environment? To an extent, their scholarly interests lie outside the substantive area of institutional corrections; instead, their critique of "imprisonment" is part of a broader salvo against the conservatives' "get tough" movement on crime. We suspect, however, that something else is also involved. Since the stunning critique of institutionalization elucidated in Goffman's (1961) *Asylums* and illustrated by the Stanford prison experiment (Haney, Banks, & Zimbardo, 1973; Zimbardo, 2007), many criminologists have embraced the view that total institutions, and correctional facilities in particular, are *inherently* inhumane. Efforts to improve prisons are thus seen as doomed and, even worse, as serving to legitimate the very idea that prisons are *potentially* humane. In this view, a "humane prison" is an oxymoron and a dangerous one at that. The stubborn reality is that even when prison administrators have the best of intentions, institutions will remain coercive and dehumanizing (see, e.g., Rothman, 1980).

This conceptualization of prisons is part of a more general view of so-called state social control that has been nearly hegemonic in criminology over the past generation. By the early 1970s, criminologists—by all accounts a progressive group politically—had embraced the view that "nothing works" in corrections and, more generally, that virtually all attempts by the state to control crime were coercive. Scarcely a decade before, they were optimistic—sometimes cautiously, sometimes wildly—that government was an integral part of the solution to crime (President's Commission on Law and Enforcement and Administration of Justice,

1968). The continuing turmoil of the 1960s and revelations of abuse of power by state officials, however, diminished this hope and resulted in a jaundiced view of the willingness and capacity of the government's "agents of social control" to improve offenders' lives (Cullen & Gilbert, 1982; Garland, 1990). Criminologists, especially those of a "critical" perspective, were prone to see virtually any intervention to control crime as a strategy of power concealed beneath a phony rhetoric voiced by naïve reformers or disingenuous state officials. In subsequent years, this view became, ironically, often uncritically accepted and part of the professional ideology of criminologists (Cullen & Gendreau, 2001; Matthews, 2009; Sherman, 1993).

Binder and Geis (1984) capture this phenomenon in their revealing analysis of how criminologists portray juvenile diversion programs. They note that diversion might legitimately be described as an effort to spare juveniles criminal sanctions in exchange for their participation in programs that provide these youths—many at risk for future illegal conduct—with much-needed social services. These programs are run by youth and nonprofit agencies and provide "family counseling, restitutive arrangements, help with securing work, employment counseling, and intervention with schools" (p. 635). Instead, criminologists commonly portray diversion as "stigmatizing" and as "dramatizing the evil" of "kids." This labeling is carried out by "agents of social control." Positive program results are dismissed as methodologically unsound (see also Gottfredson, 1979). Most salient, diversion is said to invidiously "widen the net of social control." Such rhetoric, argues Binder and Geis (1984, p. 630), should be deconstructed to illuminate its ideological purpose:

> The phrase "widening the net" is, of course, employed pejoratively, with the intent to evoke an emotional response. It conjures up visions of a mesh net that is thrown over thrashing victims, incapacitating them, as they flail about, desperately seeking to avoid captivity. The net is maneuvered by "agents of social control," another image-provoking term, this one carrying a Nazi-like connotation. Both terms are employed for purposes of propaganda rather than to enlighten.

Where does this kind of thinking lead us? Binder and Geis (1984, p. 636) contend that the favored policy recommendation is a preference for "no action"—for nonintervention by the criminal justice system (see also Travis & Cullen, 1984). When taking "no action" is patently absurd (i.e., when a serious crime had been committed), then the preference is for exercising the least control possible. In this view, the goal should not be to "do good" but to "do the least harm possible" (Fogel, 1988; Gaylin, Glasser, Marcus, & Rothman, 1978). As rising prison populations over the past 40 years reveal, this minimalist approach to crime control has not proven persuasive. It also has led, as we have argued, to an absence among criminologists of systematic thinking about what prisons should be like.

We do not believe that it is responsible for criminologists to refrain from entering the ongoing conversation about what prisons are for and how they should be organized. As noted, the failure to participate in this policy discourse has not stemmed the use of imprisonment in the United States. In this context, the risk of somehow "legitimizing" prisons seems the least of our worries. Worse still, by not articulating a compelling vision for imprisonment—by merely being naysayers for 40 years—criminologists have provided the get tough crowd with an unprecedented opportunity to redefine the purpose and nature of imprisonment. As Clear (1994) observes, the result has been a "penal harm movement" that has made the infliction of misery on inmates not something to hide but to celebrate. Further, the generic critique of prisons as inherently inhumane, while correct in the sense that all institutions are depriving, ignores the reality that not all prisons are equally depriving (DiIulio, 1987; Wright, 1994). Some facilities expose inmates to violence and inspire fear, some do not; some provide decent amenities, some do not; some provide opportunities to be productive and to change, some do not. To ignore this reality is to forfeit the opportunity to improve the quality of life for America's inmate population.

Given these considerations, we propose that it is time for criminologists—especially progressive criminologists—to speak up and articulate what prisons should be for and like (as our fellow scholars are doing in this volume). In the end, we anticipate that a cacophony of voices will be needed to clarify what a progressive approach to institutional corrections should entail. Our purpose here thus must be seen as modest and as advancing but one possible option. This caveat stated, we offer as a model for corrections *the virtuous prison*.

At its core, this approach suggests that the fundamental goal of the prison experience should be to foster in inmates "virtue," which is usually defined as "moral goodness" or "moral excellence" (*Webster's New Universal Unabridged Dictionary*, 1979, p. 2042). Prisons should be considered moral institutions and corrections as a moral enterprise. Inmates should be seen as having the obligation to become virtuous people and to manifest moral goodness. This statement announces that there are standards of right and wrong and that offenders must conform to them inside and outside prisons. The notion of a virtuous prison, however, also suggests that the correctional regime should be organized to fulfill the reciprocal obligation of providing offenders with the means to become virtuous. Much like the founders of the penitentiary did when they designed detailed daily routines for inmates to follow (Rothman, 1971), careful attention should be paid to how each prison would be arranged to enhance the goal of moral regeneration. Such efforts should include using existing criminological knowledge on "what works" to change offenders.

The virtuous prison is being advanced as a *progressive* reform—as a way of humanizing imprisonment and of contributing to the commonweal of communities. We recognize the dangers inherent in preaching morality, but we also suggest that there are dangers—already realized—in rejecting morality. A progressive approach is, by its very nature, value-laden, not value-free. We should not be afraid of *rediscovering the morality* that informed earlier Progressive-oriented prison reforms. We also assert that the idea of a virtuous prison has decided advantages over two other models for imprisonment: "the legal prison" and "the painful prison." These issues are explored in the pages ahead.

Rediscovering Morality

Progressive criminologists are not without the capacity for moral outrage. They (and we) are indignant about the social and economic injustices that contribute to the uneven distribution of crime in the United States. They show little sympathy for white-collar offenders and castigate corporations that wantonly exploit the environment and commit violence against workers and consumers. And so on. Even so, it is politically incorrect or, in the least, unfashionable to speak of traditional "street" offenders and their misdeeds as "immoral." Take, for example, James Q. Wilson's (1975, p. 235) now-famous claim that "wicked people exist. Nothing avails except to set them apart from innocent people." Why should this assertion—arguably correct to a degree—bother progressive criminologists (and us) so much? Why does such moral judgmentalism evoke a visceral feeling of discomfort and make us flush with anger?

In part, we suspect, the rejection of moralism as applied to individual offenders is not so much what it says but what it may unwittingly—or not so unwittingly—obfuscate. By focusing on an individual offender's moral failing, it is easy to ignore the role of the social structure and material inequity—the so-called root causes—in the individual's wayward life course. It also is easy to claim that we must "set apart" this individual law-breaker without pricking our consciences about how we, as a society, may have played a role in the offender becoming "wicked."

Another consideration, however, is the evolving belief among progressives that the trumpeting of morality is not done in good faith but is merely another strategy of power. Moral claims thus are not true but are merely exercises in rhetoric that mask darker political and class-based interests. "Moral crusades" and the speeches of "moral entrepreneurs" are not to be taken at face value but are to be viewed skeptically and deconstructed. What are they really after? What's the hidden agenda?

This view of morality has had salient effects within corrections, most notably with the attack on rehabilitation in the 1970s and beyond. Because advocates often borrowed the language and logic of the medical model, offender treatment has at times been portrayed strictly as a scientific, technical task: finding and using the most scientifically appropriate treatments to change law-breakers into law-abiders. But rehabilitation is, at its core, a moral enterprise. It depends on the existence of social consensus about shared values—about what is right and what is wrong (see Allen, 1981). It is morally judgmental; it accepts a standard for moral and legal behavior and defines those not meeting this standard as in need of adjustment (see Garland, 1995).

Beginning in the late 1960s and early 1970s, progressive criminologists became uneasy about rehabilitation for these very reasons; the treatment ideal's moral claims were seen as illegitimate. Thus, once upon a time, the founders of the penitentiary and of the juvenile court were viewed as humanitarian reformers. Now, they were unmasked as seeking to "discipline" poor offenders so that they could be productive workers for the capitalists and as becoming "child savers" to reaffirm existing class arrangements and to provide themselves with gender-appropriate occupational opportunities (e.g., social work)

(Foucault, 1977; Platt, 1969). Moral crusades thus were redefined as immoral crusades. Similarly, social workers, counselors, and all others tied to the correctional "establishment" were transformed from members of the "helping professions" into "agents of social control" who abused their power so as to control, not improve, offenders (Rothman, 1980). Benevolence thus was supposedly unmasked for what it "really" was: coercion. And offenders, as Binder and Geis (1984, p. 644) note, became the "underdog, who tends to be seen as a romantic force engaged in a liberating struggle with retrogressive establishment institutions." In their more extreme forms, "crime" and "criminals" were reduced to social constructions—words always to be bracketed by quotes to show that there is no objective standard of morality or legality. In its milder form, criminologists simply denied that offenders were different and in need of any change—a position that subsequent research has shown to be foolish (Andrews & Bonta, 2010; Raine, 1993; Wright, Tibbetts, & Daigle, 2008). Moral condemnation of offenders and their harmful behavior was not in vogue. Regardless, if there was nothing really wrong with offenders, then rehabilitation had no legitimate function: There was nothing in them to fix.

Let us hasten to say that these criticisms of rehabilitation had important kernels of truth in them, although not nearly the amount of truth that their advocates confidently imagined (Cullen & Gilbert, 1982; see also Garland, 1990). This way of thinking, however, also had the distinct disadvantage of constraining how a whole generation of criminologists understood corrections (see Cullen & Gendreau, 2001). In particular, it became "taken for granted" that prisons were inhumane and immoral places; that "nothing worked" in prisons for the betterment of offenders; and that correctional workers' claims of helping offenders were a camouflage for their desire to continue to exercise unfettered discretion over powerless inmates. In this context, there was a tendency to see inmates as twice victimized—once by the social injustices that prompted them to break the law, and a second time by the correctional system that subjected them to inhumane conditions certain to drive them further into crime. The idea that offenders might have engaged in morally reprehensible conduct and that prisons should serve to morally reform them was—and, to a large extent, still is—out of sync with this line of reasoning (Newman, 1983). Discussions of a virtuous prison would have been dismissed out of hand and those proposing such a foolish venture would have been characterized as criminologically illiterate. This may remain the case.

The difficulty for many criminologists, however, is that they were, and are, largely bereft of any positive agenda for the prison—short, again, of abolishing it or minimizing its use. As they turned away from rehabilitation, most criminologists followed the crowd and embraced the "justice model." They liked this approach because it argued that offenders, including the incarcerated, should be accorded an array of legal rights that would protect them against the power of the state to sanction them unfairly or too harshly. After all, who could be against justice? But this approach was strangely disconnected from the very criminology they practiced. The justice model is based on the legal fiction of the atomized individual offender who freely chooses to break the law and earn the right to be punished. Most criminologists, however, spent their professional lives documenting that, at most, the choice of crime is socially bounded and, in too many cases, that the odds of law-breaking among people exposed to at-risk environments—the victims of social injustice—are astronomical. We return to the limits of a legal model shortly.

In the end, then, we propose that criminologists, especially progressive scholars, recognize the importance of talking about virtue or morality *in formulating correctional policy in prisons*. This call is not, we believe, a departure from progressive principles but a rediscovery of them. The great reforms in American corrections—for example, the penitentiary and the rehabilitative ideal that led to offender classification and treatment programs—drew their power in large part from the willingness of their advocates to speak about right and wrong and about what prisons should be about. As Zebulon Brockway (1871, p. 42) eloquently observed more than a century ago in Cincinnati at the National Congress on Penitentiary and Reformatory Discipline:

> It will be noticed that there is a wide difference in these two views of crime; a difference so wide that every prison system must be founded upon one or the other of them, and not by any possibility upon both; for a system, so founded, would be divided against itself, and could not stand. Just here, thorough discussion is needed, for irrevocable choice must be made. If punishment, suffering, degradation are deemed deterrent, if they are the best means to reform the criminal and prevent crime, then let prison reform go backward to the pillory, the whipping-post, the gallows, the stake; to corporal violence and extermination! But if the dawn of Christianity has reached us, if we have learned the lesson that *evil is to be overcome with good*, then let prisons and prison systems be lighted by this law of love. Let us leave, for the present, the thought of inflicting punishment upon prisoners to satisfy so-called justice, and turn toward the two grand divisions of our subject, the real objects of the system, viz.: *the protection of society by the prevention of crime and reformation of criminals.* (Emphasis in the original)

We recognize that our views risk being discounted as naïve—as ignoring that many progressive reforms have had untoward consequences and that these reforms rarely were constructed to ruffle the feathers of the rich and powerful by calling for the redistribution of valued resources. We cannot fully debate this issue here, but we will make three brief responses. First, critics of past progressive reforms somehow assume that "things would have been better" in the absence of these reforms. Our experiences over the past several decades, however, provide a sobering rebuttal to the view that the opposite of the traditional progressive model of individualized treatment is the dawn of a new era of humanity in corrections. Second, with appropriate reflection and caution, the mistakes of the past are not inevitably repeated. The alternative view—that all correctional reforms are doomed to corruption and failure—is a recipe for continued inaction. Third, conservatives have rushed into the correctional arena equipped with their moral interpretation of offenders and of what should be done *to*—not *for*—them. Without a competing moral vision, the odds of achieving a more humane corrections are diminished.

Finally, we should take notice that our urgings to rediscover morality and to create virtuous prisons are not completely pie-in-the-sky ideas. Later, for example, we will discuss a closely allied development: the emergence of faith-based prison units. But we can also draw attention to the growing restorative justice movement (Levrant, Cullen, Fulton, & Wozniak, 1999; Sullivan & Tifft, 2008; Van Ness & Strong, 2010). This approach, which many progressives are now embracing because it is community based and not prison based, is at its core a moral enterprise. It is unabashed in defining the misdeeds of offenders as blameworthy and inexcusable; but it is equally unabashed in holding out the possibility that through the offenders' hard work to compensate victims and to change for the better, the gift of forgiveness from victims, and the support of the community, the restoration of offenders—as well as victims and the community—is possible. Whatever its faults and potential problems (Cullen & Jonson, 2012; Daly, 2008), restorative justice shows that correctional responses are not limited to the infliction of pain but can attempt to achieve nobler goals and real-life outcomes. This is a lesson, we trust, that might be fruitfully generalized to our understanding of prisons—a possibility we will revisit later.

The Legal Prison

The attack on rehabilitation in the 1970s fractured the consensus that corrections should be about correcting people. As the hegemony of the treatment ideal shattered, conservatives rushed in to propose an alternative approach: using prisons to inflict pain on offenders for lengthy periods of time. As noted, those on the Left, including progressive-oriented criminologists, trumpeted the alternative "justice model of corrections" (see, e.g., Fogel, 1979; Fogel & Hudson, 1981; Morris, 1974).

Within prisons, the prime target of the leftists was the discretion exercised by correctional staff and by parole boards. They bristled at the idea that offenders should be "coerced" into treatment under the threat that their early release from prison depended on program participation and their being "cured." In an inhumane prison environment, staff could not be trusted to exercise their discretion fairly and with expertise. Parole boards were depicted as either political hacks or as well-meaning folks who unwittingly placed inmates in the position of having to "con" board members so as to earn their release from prison. Justice model advocates thus argued that all indeterminacy in sentencing, parole boards, and enforced therapy should be eliminated. But this approach wanted something more: the allocation to inmates of an array of legal rights that would ensure their protection against the abuses visited upon them by correctional staff and by life in an inhumane environment.

In short, whereas advocates of rehabilitation hoped to fashion therapeutic communities, those favoring the justice model wished to construct a "legal prison"—an institutional community built on the principles of restraining state power and of according inmates virtually every legal right available to them in the free society. At times, this approach was characterized as a "citizenship model of corrections." In Conrad's (1981, pp. 17–19) words, the prison "should become a school for citizenship" in which inmates were granted the rights to personal safety, to care, to personal dignity, to work, to self-improvement, to vote, and to a future. Although based on pure speculation, Conrad and other reformers believed that once inmates were offered the opportunity to enjoy and exercise the rights of citizens, the prison would become orderly and more humane. Once citizenship was learned inside prisons, its effects might generalize and make offenders more responsible as they returned to the free society. As Conrad (1981, p. 19) observed:

> Justice depends on reciprocity between the state and its citizens and among citizens themselves. A man whose rights are not protected by the state has no rights. A man who has no rights cannot be expected to observe the rights of others. If justice is really therapy, as I believe, it can only be administered to a citizen, not to a civilly dead convict.

Although naïve sounding, the justice model is hardly foolish, and it might even have proven a boon to prison life in a different political context. In the 1970s, those on the political Left had reason to believe that the law was an instrument of change and of good. Until this time period, inmates had been virtual "slaves of the state" as courts practiced a "hands off" doctrine inside prisons. Prison litigation did much to improve basic standards of living within correctional facilities and to accord offenders religious and legal rights (DiIulio, 1990; Jacobs, 1983). What the justice model advocates did not anticipate, however, was that the expansion of constitutional protections to prisons would, when confronted by more conservative courts, stop far short of ensuring that inmates had a right to citizenship or a humane environment. Instead, the courts have taken a minimalist approach, protecting offenders from "cruel and unusual" prison conditions but not from much more than this (Palmer & Palmer, 1999).

One fundamental problem with the justice model, then, is that it is out of step with the times (Cullen & Jonson, 2012; Rothman, 2002). In the early 1970s—in the midst of the Civil Rights Movement and in the shocking aftermath of the Attica riot and slaughter—it seemed reasonable to suggest that inmates were victims in need of rights. Today, however, policy makers and the public are likely to concur that inmates "have too many rights." Talk of "democratizing corrections" and turning "inmates into citizens" would prompt skepticism if not the acerbic query of "who's running the joint now"? The justice model may have done some good, but it has now exhausted itself. It is incapable of fueling a new age of correctional reform in the 21st century.

The justice model and its legal prison also failed to provide a compelling answer to the "utilitarian" question of what role prisons would play in reducing crime. Advocates wished to suggest that through "voluntary rehabilitation" and the learning of "citizenship" offenders *might* lower their subsequent criminal participation. But having criticized rehabilitation as coercive and ineffective—the "noble lie" as Morris (1974, pp. 20–22) put it—they were reluctant to say that offenders *should* change and that corrections should ultimately be about facilitating this outcome. As a result, they were wishy-washy on crime, failing to articulate how prisons could be employed to protect innocent citizens—whether through rehabilitation or through tougher means, such as long-term incapacitation. Caught up with rectifying the injustices done to inmates, they largely forfeited the opportunity to show how their progressive-oriented reforms would make society safer. This mistake was not only intellectual but also political, for conservative commentators rushed into this void to tell policy makers and the public how to put an end to the lawlessness in the nation's streets.

The Painful Prison

Clear (1994) characterizes American corrections over the past decades as being in the throes of a "penal harm movement"—of a concerted effort to inflict an increasing amount of pain on offenders. The most visible sign of this campaign is the successful policy agenda to cram more and more law-breakers behind bars for longer and longer periods of time. Although given less consideration, a collateral sign of the penal harm movement is the attempt to make inmates' stays in prison not only lengthier but also increasing physically uncomfortable—what Sparks (1996) calls the policy of "penal austerity."

Given their progressive bent and their attraction to preaching that even the worst among us deserve humane treatment, criminologists have generally been disconcerted by these developments. Even so, while not brutish in their views, some criminologists have warmed up to the idea that prisons should be painful rather than, say, therapeutic or contexts in which to practice citizenship.

Take, for example, Newman's (1983) "punishment manifesto" conveyed in his controversial *Just and Painful*. Embracing a retributivist position, Newman argues that imprisonment as a form of punishment should be used sparingly; instead, he favors corporal punishment, delivered most often through electric shocks and calibrated to the seriousness of the crime committed. When prison sentences are given, however, he contends that they should be reserved for those who have engaged in serious and/or repeated crimes. In these cases, the minimum penalty should be 15 years of incarceration. Most noteworthy for our purposes, he envisions "prisons as purgatory" (p. 61); they should be harsh places so that inmates will suffer. Such punishments are justified, says Newman, because they are deserved and because they offer offenders the opportunity to truly atone for their evil acts and, in a sense, to save their souls.

Newman's proposals are provocative and tempting: Would we be willing to take the current massive overuse of imprisonment and exchange it for the application of electric shocks to a great many offenders and lengthy sentences of extreme suffering to a few offenders? But this deal will remain hypothetical because of Americans' cultural ambivalence about punishing the body of offenders and their embrace of imprisonment as a preferred sanction. The risk of Newman's proposal, then, is that it will be used in a piecemeal fashion. While it will not reduce the use of imprisonment, it potentially could add legitimacy to claims that prisons should be places in which *all* offenders, not a select few, suffer.

A milder version of the painful prison is set forth by Logan and Gaes (1993). These authors do not favor making prisons a purgatory or exposing inmates to gratuitous pain. They believe that prisons should meet constitutional standards of safety, decency, and amenities and should be governed firmly and fairly, not harshly and arbitrarily. Their "confinement model," however, embraces retribution or just deserts as its guiding principle and sees prison as a means of punishing. Unlike the more liberal advocates of just deserts, who looked to the justice model as a way of protecting inmates from the inherent coerciveness of imprisonment—and more like Newman (1983)—Logan and Gaes favor "punitive confinement" as a way of dramatizing the immorality of the offender's crime and of affirming the offender's "autonomy, responsibility, and dignity" (p. 255).

Logan and Gaes state clearly that they wish offenders to be sent to prison *as* punishment and not *for* punishment. Unless we misread between the lines of their essay, however, this caveat is meant to go only so far. They may not want prisons to be warehouses, but they seemingly do want them to be punitive and to involve no-frills living—to send, as they would say, a "cultural message" to the citizenry that crime is evil and will be judged harshly. Their view of rehabilitation is revealing. Treatment programs, they speculate, are paternalistic and convey the wrong message about crime and criminals to society; they deny offender responsibility and presumably increase the sales of Dershowitz's (1994) *The Abuse Excuse.* Rehabilitation is not to be fully excluded by their confinement model, but it is to be permitted only when it is "voluntary, is separated from punishment, and is not a privilege unavailable to those who are not in prison" (p. 257). Thus, participation in treatment is not to be tied to privileges of any sort; programs are to be delivered after imprisonment or inside prison by outside community social service agencies—and then only to foster institutional order, not to change offenders; and services given to offenders are to be governed by the principle of less eligibility.

Logan and Gaes's model of punitive confinement is principled, but it is not based on principles we wish to embrace. First, as with other retributivists, they must accept the legal fiction that crime is a free and autonomous choice. Even the economists—from a discipline based on the assumption of rationality—understand that choice is bounded and is influenced by socially induced "tastes" or "preferences" (see also Boudon, 1998; Kahneman, 2011). Although we concur with their desire to hold offenders morally responsible, we believe that this is only half the moral equation: Society, too, should be held accountable for its role in the criminal choices offenders make, and the correctional process should reflect this reality. Second, we are equally troubled by their rejection of the utility—the crime savings—that can be achieved through effective correctional intervention, especially with high-risk offenders (Andrews & Bonta, 2010). The easy sacrifice of this goal is tantamount to saying that prisons should play no role in *protecting future victims* from crime. Such a state interest is not only constitutionally permissible but, we believe, moral to pursue. Third, while this may be a case of "what's in the eye of the beholder," we reject their view that prison treatment programs send the cultural message that "crime's not the offender's fault." Rehabilitation can send other messages: that offenders have an obligation to change; that offenders are not a form of refuse but have the human dignity to be renewed; that offenders are worth investing in because they can change and contribute to society; and that we, as a society, are not only about "hating the sin" but, at least under some circumstances, about "loving the sinner."

Perhaps more important, we are troubled that like Newman, Logan and Gaes are seemingly untroubled by the prospect that their call for "punitive confinement" will not go as planned. We worry, however, that once the punitive genie is out of the bottle, it will not prove to be principled but more akin to Jafar—the evil Disney character in the *Aladdin* films who attempted to use his new-found, genie-like powers for self-interest and to harm others. We wonder, in particular, where the restraint will come from if we accept that prisons are an instrument for punishment— pure and simple. What will occur when even responsible scholars such as Logan and Gaes do not challenge the principle of less eligibility? What cultural message will politicians hear and what can they be trusted to do?

The events from the penal harm movement give us considerable reason for concern. As Lacayo (1995, p. 31) observed when this movement was in full swing, the "hottest development in criminal justice is a fast-spreading impulse to eliminate anything that might make it easier to endure a sentence behind bars." The impulse to create a "no frills" prison (Finn, 1996) might have slowed in recent years, but its effects have proven enduring. Indeed, the roster of these austerity policies remains familiar: sending inmates out on chain gangs; barring inmates from Pell grants and opportunities to participate in college programs; banning computers and televisions in cells; forbidding weightlifting; housing inmates in tents; eliminating steak from inmate diets; and so on (Applegate, 2001; Lenz, 2002; Tewksbury & Mustaine, 2005). These policies are hardly part of a principled confinement model. Rather they are intended to ensure that inmates are in prison *for punishment* and are undertaken with the utilitarian and criminologically ill-conceived notion that exposing offenders to rotten living conditions will deter their future wrongdoing. There is no evidence to support the view that painful prison—or, for that matter, a custodial as opposed to a noncustodial sentence—reduces reoffending (Cullen & Jonson, 2012; Listwan, Sullivan, Agnew, Cullen, & Colvin, 2013). Worse still, these policies are trumpeted by politicians whose new-found campaign to immiserate inmates' lives seems rooted less in morality and more in a calculated desire to capture headlines and electoral capital. Such a vision for corrections should not go unchallenged—a task to which we now turn.

The Virtuous Prison

Because nearly all correctional reforms historically have been misshapen when put into place and have failed to realize their ideals (Cullen & Gilbert, 1982; Rothman, 1980), we approach the task of outlining an alternative vision for the prison with much trepidation. It also is daunting to realize that a crafty critic could soon home in on our proposal's vulnerabilities (e.g., the potential arrogance in claiming to be virtuous, its embrace of utility as a central correctional goal). Still, as argued previously, we are persuaded that progressives inadvertently have allowed agendas like the "painful prison" to gain influence by paying insufficient attention to correctional policy as it pertains to life inside institutions. Even if the recent financial crisis has tarnished the appeal of mass imprisonment, there is still a "culture war" over what the internal regimen and ultimate purpose of the nation's prisons should be (see, e.g., see Kruttschnitt & Gartner, 2005; Page, 2011). Without fresh ideas—others' if not ours—progressives will remain on the defensive and do little to shape prison policies in the time ahead.

RESTORATIVE REHABILITATION

The mission of the virtuous prison is to use offenders' time of incarceration to cultivate moral awareness and the capacity to act virtuously. Although recognizing the deprivations inherent in total institutional life, the approach rejects the progressive view, held by many criminologists, that nothing productive can be accomplished in prison. This approach also rejects the notion of the painful or austere prison as having no utility—other than inflicting suffering—and as inhibiting the inculcation of virtue in offenders. The virtuous-prison approach rejects incapacitation because it is a utilitarian theory that, by not endorsing the goal of offender change, needlessly limits the crime savings—and thus the utility—that prisons can achieve. And this approach rejects retributivist ideas for their disinterest in crime control and for their belief, as Newman (1983, p. 142) writes, that "the most basic of all freedoms in a society" is "the freedom to break the law" and to be punished for it. The virtuous prison has a different vision—the idea that people, including inmates, have an *obligation* to obey the law, not to harm others, and that societal institutions, including the prison, should be organized to facilitate this goal.

Two principles form the foundation of the virtuous prison: *restorative justice* and the *rehabilitative ideal* (see Wilkinson, 1998). As alluded to earlier, restorative justice hinges on the premise that the harm from crime is morally wrong and that its effects need to be remedied. Offenders thus are called on to announce and publicly accept the blame for their wrongdoing. They are then expected to act virtuously by restoring victims they have harmed. Such restoration for victims might be emotional, such as when offenders apologize for their misdeeds, or might be material, such as when offenders provide restitution. Offenders also must recognize that breaches of the law damage the commonweal; therefore, restoring the community through service activities is often mandated. The precise nature of this restorative justice remedy is reached at a conference where the offender, victim, family members, and concerned others meet to express their disappointment and hurt and to work out a way in which the offender can restore the harm he or she has caused. Ideally, and over time, the victim forgives and reconciles with the offender. The community is expected to do its part, too, by reintegrating, not rejecting, the repentant offender. In this whole process, the state is present but involved mainly as an arbiter helping the parties to reach agreement.

Restorative justice is morally clear and it is unambiguous about requiring offenders to make amends. But this approach is sympathetic as well to the view that people, including law-breakers, are capable of change. It also proposes that criminal sanctions should be used to rectify harm and to do good—not to heap more suffering on offenders in an aimless way or for purposes of mere retribution. It is backward looking, shaming the conduct that has occurred; it is present looking, applying a criminal sanction that does good; and it is future looking, trying to create victims who are restored and offenders capable of moral conduct (see, e.g., Braithwaite, 1998; Hahn, 1998; Van Ness & Strong, 2010).

Can restorative justice be imported into the prison? To date, it has largely been conceptualized as a *community-based* approach; indeed, progressives have rushed to embrace it precisely because it is presented as an alternative to prison (for exceptions, see Dhami, Mantle, & Fox, 2009; Hahn, 1998; Van Ness & Strong, 2010; see also Lund, 1997; Wilkinson, 1998). In an otherwise thoughtful analysis of restorative justice, for example, Braithwaite (1998, p. 336) will "concede" only that "for a tiny fraction of people in our prisons, it may actually be necessary to protect the community from them by incarceration." This view not only is empirically problematic in its optimistic view of inmates (Logan & DiIulio, 1992) but also errs, we believe, in not seeing the role of restorative justice *within* prisons—a place, again, in which over 2.2 million people now reside in the United States. Regardless, prisons present two challenges to restorative justice: the removal of offenders from the community and a population of more serious, hardened offenders.

Although various scenarios could be devised to reconcile victims with prison-bound or prison-based offenders, the removal of the offender from the local community will make victim-offender conferences less likely to occur. Yet, even if specific agreements with specific victims are not reached, a virtuous prison could be organized around the principle that inmates should be engaged in activities that are restorative (e.g., contributing to a victim compensation fund, community service). In this way, what inmates do would be imbued with a clear moral and practical purpose: to repair, or make amends for, the harm to society that they and their fellow offenders have caused. In this approach, prisons thus would be an instrument for doing good for society. Although limited, it is noteworthy that prison programs based on restorative justice are beginning to emerge (see, e.g., Dhami et al., 2009; Lund, 1997; Swanson, 2009; Wilkinson, 1998; see also Chapter 2 in this volume by Lois Presser).

Perhaps the more daunting challenge, however, is the depth of the criminality of the offenders who enter prison. A weakness of restorative justice is that the approach's understanding of offender behavioral change is speculative and based, at most, on only a slice of the criminological research about offenders (see Levrant et al., 1999). The idea that the kind of high-risk offenders who frequently populate prisons will, with any regularity, be morally regenerated by a two-hour victim-offender reconciliation meeting or merely by furnishing restitution strains credulity. Such an understanding denies the pathology within many offenders that has been developing over a lifetime. It will take tough work and appropriate therapeutic techniques to change offenders—to prepare them to act morally outside the prison walls (see Wilkinson, 1998).

It is at this juncture, therefore, that the rehabilitative ideal should be merged with restorative justice—for two reasons. First, even more strongly than restorative justice, rehabilitation identifies the reform of the offender as a legitimate and important correctional goal—a goal whose attainment simultaneously benefits inmates and, by preventing crime, society. Second, there is now a growing body of empirically based knowledge specifying the correctional interventions that "work" to reduce recidivism, including among high-risk serious offenders (see, e.g., Andrews & Bonta, 2010; Henggeler, 1997; Lipsey & Wilson, 1998; MacKenzie, 2006; see also Chapter 1 in this volume by Paula Smith and Myrinda Schweitzer). This research suggests that certain "principles of effective intervention" should be followed in seeking to rehabilitate offenders (e.g., those outlined in the risk-need-responsivity or "RNR" model) (Andrews & Bonta, 2010). To a large extent, these principles are consistent with restorative justice because primary targets for change in this correctional approach are offenders' antisocial values and thinking (Andrews & Bonta, 2010; Gendreau, 1996). In any case, a restorative corrections will likely fail to impact recidivism if it is not informed by the extant research on rehabilitation. If one prefers, the principles of effective intervention can be seen as supplying the needed technology for offender restoration.

PRISON PARTICULARS

The goal of prison organization would be to create a "virtuous milieu." The task would be how to surround inmates with positive moral influences. Although our thoughts are still preliminary, we would propose seven general considerations:

First, inmate idleness would be eliminated. "Idle hands" may or may not be "the devil's workshop," but they are no friend to virtuous living. Wright (1994) contends that a "productive environment" reduces prisoner violence and disruption and also fosters hope—a sense of purpose—among inmates.

Second, the activities in which inmates engage would have a restorative purpose. Prison employment, for example, should not merely be to pass the time or to equip offenders with occupational skills but rather should have a larger purpose beyond the inmate's self-interest. Thus, inmate wages might be used to compensate victims, with offenders writing and sending the checks to victims. Or inmates might be engaged in jobs that produce products for the needy—toys for poor children or prefabricated houses for Habitat for Humanity. Similarly, community service would be encouraged—first inside the prison (e.g., writing to elderly shut-ins, training dogs for the seeing impaired, holding bake sales for "good causes"), and then during the day outside the prison (e.g., fixing up a playground, making a house livable for a family) (Lund, 1997). When possible, moreover, inmates would be prompted to help restore one another, such as by tutoring someone who is less educated or leading self-help sessions. Which activities ultimately are implemented is less important than the fact that inmates are engaged in activities that have a *moral purpose*—that provide opportunities to be virtuous (see Van Ness & Strong, 2010, pp. 94–95).

Third, contact with virtuous people would be encouraged. Although not unmindful of security risks, the virtuous prison would encourage as many upstanding community people as possible, including those religiously inspired, to lead and/or participate in prison programs, to mentor inmates, and to visit and socialize with inmates. These volunteers should be seen not as a potential disruption but as sources of valuable human capital who will share their knowledge and values with inmates. Further, by coming into the prison—by devoting their time and effort to a worthy cause—such volunteers are modeling the very kind of prosocial, virtuous behavior that we wish inmates to learn.

Fourth, inmates would participate in rehabilitation programs that are based on criminological research and the principles of effective correctional intervention (again, see Andrews & Bonta, 2010; Gendreau, 1996). An important principle of the virtuous prison would be that offenders have the *obligation* to seek restoration so as not to misbehave inside the institution or to recidivate in the community. The reciprocal obligation of the state is to provide quality treatment programs that have the greatest chance of facilitating this restoration. In this spirit, criminological knowledge would be welcomed and not dismissed. Programs shown not to work—such as boot camps—would be relegated to the therapeutic dustbin. Alternatively, programs shown to work—cognitive-behavioral interventions—would be implemented and evaluated. In the end, programs would be intended to give offenders the values, understanding of the world, and skills to live a productive life. This approach is much different, we should note, than punitive strategies that threaten offenders with punishment but provide no positive instruction on how to lead a life outside crime.

Fifth, the standard of inmate living would be as high as possible. A low standard of living—inflicting pain on offenders—serves no defensible moral or utilitarian purpose. It also is inconsistent with the very purpose of a virtuous prison, which takes seriously the maxim that "virtue begets virtue." Politically, the restorative orientation of the virtuous prison might make it less vulnerable to attempts to immiserate its population. Often, inmates are seen as part of the undeserving poor who no longer should receive social welfare "entitlements." In the virtuous prison, however, inmates will be engaged in activities in which they "give back to victims and the community"; in short, they may become more "deserving" in the eyes of policy makers and thus less attractive as targets for meanness.

Sixth, prison guards would be encouraged to function as "correctional" officers. In the virtuous prison, guards would be seen as professionals who deliver various types of human services (Johnson, 1996). Their tasks obviously would involve maintaining order, ensuring custody, and enforcing rules. But they also would be integral to the central institutional mission of fostering virtue in inmates. One cannot bifurcate staff into two neat divisions—"custodial" and "treatment"—because correctional officers are potentially too involved in inmates' daily lives and routines not to affect programmatic outcomes and the quality of the institution. Thus, while guards have their distinctive duties, they should, through participatory management, be brought into the planning of how best to achieve the virtuous prison's central mission. In particular, they should be relied on to advance, not stymie, the restoration or correction of the offenders in their charge. Research suggests that many correctional officers might well welcome this enrichment of their occupational role (Johnson, 1996; Toch & Klofas, 1982). Although supportive of custodial objectives, a number of guards also see rehabilitation as an important goal of imprisonment (see, e.g., Cullen, Lutze, Link, & Wolfe, 1989; Kifer, Hemmens, & Stohr, 2003).

Seventh, the virtuous prison would not be for all inmates. We would like to see the model of the virtuous prison spread far and wide, and we are confident that with enough experimentation and organizational development, this model could eventually be effective with a large proportion of the inmate population. Still, we are realistic enough to know that not every inmate could function effectively in this environment (e.g., the intractably recalcitrant, violent, or mentally disturbed inmate). At the very least, however, the virtuous prison would be appropriate for at least *some* inmates, with precisely how many remaining an empirical question to be discovered. If so, then there is reason to undertake an experiment with the prison we have proposed. The salient point is that success with even one model virtuous prison would be valuable because it would show that prisons can serve lofty goals and can be administered, within the limits of good sense, humanely. Some support for these views can be drawn from the current experimentation with "faith-based" prisons.

FAITH-BASED PRISONS

Is a virtuous prison possible? One hint that it might be can be found in the faith-based correctional movement (see Chapter 3 in this volume by Byron Johnson). In April of 1997, Prison Fellowship Ministries—the religiously based prison reform group begun by Charles Colson (of Watergate fame)—established the InnerChange Freedom Initiative in the Carol Vance Unit of a minimum-security prison (Jester II) located outside Houston and under the auspices of the Texas Department of Correction. Based on a model used to reform and administer prisons in Brazil (Leal, 1998), this initiative sought to develop a faith-based prison community. The inmate participants had diverse criminal histories and were required to be within 21 to 24 months of parole or release from prison. To ensure separation of church and state, Prison Fellowship Ministries funded the program's staff and operation (but not the correctional officers or inmate living costs) and accepted only inmates who volunteered. The program is still in existence and has spread to other states, such as Minnesota (for a full account of this initiative, see Johnson's detailed discussion in Chapter 3; see also Eisenberg & Trusty, 2002; Prison Fellowship Ministries, 1999).

This prison initiative is based on the belief that behavior is a reflection of values and worldview. For inmates, it is proposed that rehabilitation depends on a fundamental "inner change" that reconciles the person with Christ. This sacred relationship then allows the offender to reconcile human relationships and to embark on genuine, long-term behavioral change. The special focus on a religious transformation is a distinctive feature of the InnerChange Freedom Initiative. It also is what limits its widespread use, since the separation of church and state sets burdensome legal restrictions on the programmatic services a department of corrections can fund.

From our perspective, however, the InnerChange Freedom Initiative is instructive because the features incorporated into its prison community *besides religion* make it quite similar to the virtuous prison we have proposed. Thus, the Texas initiative largely embraces the dual principles of moral restoration and rehabilitation. It is extensively programmed and relies heavily on church-based volunteers to serve as chaplains, lead small groups, mentor inmates, provide educational and artistic tutoring, facilitate family support groups, and coordinate the community service project. It also has inmates participate in productive work so as to teach them to be "stewards of their time." The initiative is unabashed in expressing its desire not to inflict pain on inmates but to create a community of strong social bonds and love. Further, it is committed to using an aftercare program to reintegrate offenders, upon their release, into a supportive religious community.

To be sure, the appeal of the InnerChange Freedom Initiative stems in an important way from its faith-based orientation and because it was proposed by an influential religious ministry, Prison Fellowship. Still, the kind of prison community being created—a focus on moral restoration, concerted efforts to rehabilitate offenders, substantial support given to offenders during and after incarceration, a lack of mean-spirited rhetoric—did not render this project politically unfeasible. Indeed, by requiring inmates to strive in concrete ways toward change—to show that they were deserving of support—this program was the kind of "compassionate conservatism" that then-Texas Governor George W. Bush could embrace and use to bump up his ratings in the polls. This ongoing initiative thus shows that space exists to experiment with different models of imprisonment. It is relevant as well that, while the American public is punitive toward crime, repeated surveys reveal that there also is substantial support among citizens for the principles of restorative justice and of prison-based rehabilitation (see, e.g., Cullen, Fisher, & Applegate, 2000; Cullen, Pealer, Fisher, Applegate, & Santana, 2002; see also Cullen, Pealer, Santana, Fisher, Applegate, & Blevins, 2007). In this context, the prospect of creating a virtuous prison does not seem far-fetched.

Conclusion: Doing Good

As Binder and Geis (1984) show, criminologists have a tendency to feel happy when they can show that nothing the government does has any effect on crime (see also

Cullen & Gendreau, 2001; Matthews, 2009; Sherman, 1993). At times, there seems to be a special glee—a gotcha!—when scholars can reveal how people who hope to "do good" and express benevolent intentions put reforms into place that end up having untoward, unanticipated consequences. There is, of course, a need to puncture false claims and to save offenders from foolish, if not repressive, efforts to supposedly save them. Pushed too far, however, this professionally supported desire to delegitimate "state control" is smug and counterproductive. Nothing constructive— nothing that can work—is ever proposed.

Prisons, we believe, have suffered from criminologists' unwillingness to entertain the possibility that correctional institutions could be administered more humanely and more effectively. The risk of taking action is failure and, at times, messing things up. But the past four decades of penal harm should have taught us two lessons about corrections: First, doing good sometimes means that good is actually achieved. And second, doing good is almost always preferable to the alternative—neglect or, even worse, the conscious attempt to inflict pain. The challenge now is to devise those strategies that can, in fact, realize our benevolent sentiments in the difficult area of corrections. The virtuous prison is but one suggestion on how to "do good" in prison. Hopefully, it will soon be followed by many others.

References

Allen, F. A. (1981). *The decline of the rehabilitative ideal: Penal policy and social purpose.* New Haven, CT: Yale University Press.

Andrews, D. A., & Bonta, J. (2010). *The psychology of criminal conduct* (5th ed.). New Providence, NJ: Anderson/LexisNexis.

Applegate, B. K. (2001). Penal austerity: Perceived utility, desert, and public attitudes toward prison amenities. *American Journal of Criminal Justice, 25,* 253–267.

Bennett, W. J., DiIulio, J. J., Jr., & Walters, J. P. (1996). *Body count: Moral poverty and how to win America's war against crime and drugs.* New York, NY: Simon & Shuster.

Binder, A., & Geis, G. (1984). *Ad populum* argumentation in criminology: Juvenile diversion as rhetoric. *Crime and Delinquency, 30,* 624–647.

Boudon, R. (1998). Limitations of rational choice theory. *American Journal of Sociology, 3,* 817–828.

Braithwaite, J. (1998). Restorative justice. In M. Tonry (Ed.), *A handbook of crime and punishment* (pp. 323–344). New York, NY: Oxford University Press.

Brockway, Z. R. (1871). The ideal of a true prison system for a state." In E. C. Wines (Ed.), *Transactions of the National Congress on Penitentiary and Reformatory Discipline* (pp. 38–65). Albany, NY: Weed, Parsons.

Clear, T. R. (1994). *Harm in American penology: Offenders, victims, and their communities.* Albany: State University of New York Press.

Conrad, J. P. (1981). Where there's hope there's life. In D. Fogel & J. Hudson (Eds.), *Justice as fairness: Perspectives on the justice model.* Cincinnati, OH: Anderson.

Cullen, F. T., Fisher, B. S., & Applegate, B. K. (2000). Public opinion about punishment and corrections. In M. Tonry (Ed.), *Crime and justice: A review of research* (Vol. 14, pp. 1–79). Chicago, IL: University of Chicago Press.

Cullen, F. T., & Gendreau, P. (2001). From nothing works to what works: Changing professional ideology in the 21st century. *The Prison Journal, 81,* 313–338.

Cullen, F. T., & Gilbert, K. E. (1982). *Reaffirming rehabilitation.* Cincinnati, OH: Anderson.

Cullen, F. T., & Jonson, C. L. (2012). *Correctional theory: Context and consequences.* Thousand Oaks, CA: Sage.

Cullen, F. T., Lutze, F. E., Link B. G., & Wolfe, N. T. (1989). The correctional orientation of prison guards: Do officers support rehabilitation? *Federal Probation, 53*(1), 33–42.

Cullen, F. T., Pealer, J. A., Fisher, B. S., Applegate, B. K., & Santana, S. A. (2002). Public support for correctional rehabilitation in America: Change or consistency? In J. V. Roberts & M. Hough (Eds.), *Changing attitudes to punishment: Public opinion, crime and justice* (pp. 128–147). Cullompton, Devon, UK: Willan.

Cullen, F. T., Pealer, J. A., Santana, S. A., Fisher, B. S., Applegate, B. K., & Blevins, K. R. (2007). Public support for faith-based correctional programs: Should sacred places serve civic purposes? *Journal of Offender Rehabilitation, 43*(3–4), 29–46.

Currie, E. (1998). *Crime and punishment in America.* New York, NY: Metropolitan Books.

Daly, K. (2008). The limits of restorative justice. In D. Sullivan & L. Tifft (Eds.), *Handbook of restorative justice: A global perspective* (pp. 134–145). New York, NY: Routledge.

Dhami, M. K., Mantle, G., & Fox, D. (2009). Restorative justice in prisons. *Contemporary Justice Review, 12,* 433–448.

Dershowitz, A. M. (1994). *The abuse excuse—And other cop-outs, sob stories, and evasions of responsibility.* Boston, MA: Little, Brown.

DiIulio, J. J., Jr. (1987). *Governing prisons: A comparative study of correctional treatment.* New York, NY: Free Press.

DiIulio, J. J., Jr., (Ed.). (1990). *Courts, corrections, and the constitution: The impact of judicial intervention on prisons and jails.* New York, NY: Oxford University Press.

Eisenberg, M., & Trusty, B. (2002). *Overview of the InnerChange Freedom Initiative: The faith-based prison program within the Texas Department of Criminal Justice.* Austin, TX: Criminal Justice Policy Council.

Finn, P. (1996). No frills prisons and jails: A movement in flux. *Federal Probation, 60*(3), 35–44.

Fogel, D. (1979). *"We are the living proof": The justice model for corrections* (2nd ed.). Cincinnati, OH: Anderson.

Fogel, D. (1988). *On doing less harm: Western European alternatives to incarceration.* Chicago: University of Illinois at Chicago, Office of the International Criminal Justice.

Fogel, D., & Hudson, J. (Eds.). (1981). *Justice as fairness: Perspectives on the justice model.* Cincinnati, OH: Anderson.

Foucault, M. (1977). *Discipline and punish: The birth of the prison.* New York, NY: Pantheon.

Garland, D. (1990). *Punishment and modern society: A study in social theory.* Chicago, IL: University of Chicago Press.

Garland, D. (1995). Penal modernism and postmodernism. In T. G. Blomberg & S. Cohen (Eds.), *Punishment and social control* (pp. 181–209). New York, NY: Aldine de Gruyter.

Gaylin, W., Glasser, I., Marcus, S., & Rothman, D. (Eds.). (1978). *Doing good: The limits of benevolence.* New York, NY: Pantheon.

Gendreau, P. (1996). The principles of effective intervention with offenders. In A. T. Harland (Ed.), *Choosing correctional options that work: Defining the demand and evaluating the supply* (pp. 117–130). Thousand Oaks, CA: Sage.

Glaze, L. E. (2011). *Correctional populations in the United States, 2010*. Washington, DC: U.S. Department of Justice, Bureau of Justice Statistics.

Goffman, E. (1961). *Asylums: Essays on the social situation of mental patients and other inmates*. Garden City, NY: Anchor.

Gottfredson, M. R. (1979). Treatment destruction techniques. *Journal of Research in Crime and Delinquency, 16*, 39–54.

Hahn, P. H. (1998). *Emerging criminal justice: Three pillars of a proactive justice system*. Thousand Oaks, CA: Sage.

Haney, C. W., Banks, C., & Zimbardo, P. G. (1973). Interpersonal dynamics in a simulated prison. *International Journal of Criminology and Penology, 1*, 69–97.

Henggeler, S. W. (1997). *Treating serious anti-social behavior in youth: The MST approach*. Washington, DC: U.S. Department of Justice, Office of Juvenile Justice and Delinquency Prevention.

Irwin, J., & Austin, J. (1994). *It's about time: America's imprisonment binge*. Belmont, CA: Wadsworth.

Jacobs, J. B. (Ed.). (1983). *New perspectives on prisons and imprisonment*. Ithaca, NY: Cornell University Press.

Johnson, R. (1996). *Hard time: Understanding and reforming the prison* (2nd ed.). Belmont, CA: Wadsworth.

Kahneman, D. (2011). *Thinking, fast and slow*. New York, NY: Farrar, Straus and Giroux.

Kifer, M., Hemmens, C., & Stohr, M. K. (2003). The goals of corrections: Perspectives from the line. *Criminal Justice Review, 28*, 47–69.

Kruttschnitt, C., & Gartner, R. (2005). *Marking time in the Golden State: Women's imprisonment in California*. New York, NY: Cambridge University Press.

Lacayo, R. (1995, September 4). The real hard cell: Lawmakers are stripping inmates of their perks. *Time*, pp. 31–32.

Langan, P. A., Fundis, J. V., Greenfeld, L. A., & Schneider, V. W. (1988). *Historical statistics on prisoners in state and federal institutions, yearend 1925–86*. Washington, DC: U.S. Department of Justice, Bureau of Justice Statistics.

Leal, C. B. (1998). *The Association for the Protection and Assistance to the Convict: A Brazilian Experience*. Paper presented at the annual meeting of the American Society of Criminology, November, Washington, DC.

Lenz, N. (2002). "Luxuries" in prison: The relationship between amenity funding and public support. *Crime and Delinquency, 48*, 499–525.

Levrant, S., Cullen, F. T., Fulton, B., & Wozniak, J. F. (1999). Reconsidering restorative justice: The corruption of benevolence revisited? *Crime and Delinquency, 45*, 3–27.

Lipsey, M. W., & Wilson, D. B. (1998). Effective intervention for serious juvenile offenders: A synthesis of research. In R. Loeber & D. P. Farrington (Eds.), *Serious and violent juvenile offenders: Risk factors and successful interventions* (pp. 313–336). Thousand Oaks, CA: Sage.

Listwan, S. J., Sullivan, C. J., Agnew, R., Cullen, F. T., & Colvin, M. (2013). The pains of imprisonment revisited: The impact of strain on inmate recidivism. *Justice Quarterly, 30*, 144–168.

Logan, C. H., & DiIulio, J. J., Jr. (1992). Ten deadly myths about crime and punishment in the U.S. *Wisconsin Interest, 1*(1), 21–35.

Logan, C. H., & Gaes, G. (1993). Meta-analysis and the rehabilitation of punishment. *Justice Quarterly, 10,* 245–263.

Lund, L. (1997). Restorative justice from prison. *ICCA Journal on Community Corrections, 8* (August), 50–51, 55.

MacKenzie, D. L. (2006). *What works in corrections: Reducing the criminal activities of offenders and delinquents.* New York, NY: Cambridge University Press.

Matthews, R. (2009). Beyond "so what" criminology: Rediscovering realism. *Theoretical Criminology, 13,* 341–362.

Morris, N. (1974). *The future of imprisonment.* Chicago, IL: University of Chicago Press.

Newman, G. (1983). *Just and painful: A case for corporal punishment of criminals.* New York, NY: Harrow and Heston/Macmillan.

Page, J. (2011). *The toughest beat: Politics, punishment, and the prison officers union in California.* New York, NY: Oxford University Press.

Palmer, J. W., & Palmer, S. E. (1999). *Constitutional rights of prisoners* (6th ed.). Cincinnati, OH: Anderson.

Pew Center on the States. (2010). *Prison count 2010: State population declines for the first time in 38 years.* Washington, DC: Pew Charitable Trusts.

Platt, A. M. (1969). *The child savers: The invention of delinquency.* Chicago, IL: University of Chicago Press.

Pratt, T. C. (2009). *Addicted to incarceration: Corrections policy and the politics of misinformation in the United States.* Thousand Oaks, CA: Sage.

President's Commission on Law Enforcement and Administration of Justice. (1968). *The challenge of crime in a free society.* New York, NY: Avon.

Prison Fellowship Ministries. (1999). *The InnerChange Freedom Initiative: Background, fact sheet, history, FAQs, and legal basis.* Washington, DC: Prison Fellowship Ministries.

Raine, A. (1993). *The psychopathology of crime: Criminal behavior as a clinical disorder.* San Diego, CA: Academic Press.

Reynolds, M. O. (1997). *Crime and punishment in America: 1997 update.* Dallas, TX: National Center for Policy Analysis.

Rothman, D. J. (1971). *The discovery of the asylum: Social order and disorder in the New Republic.* Boston, MA: Little, Brown.

Rothman, D. J. (1980). *Conscience and convenience: The asylum and its alternatives in Progressive America.* Boston, MA: Little, Brown.

Rothman, D. J. (2002). *Conscience and convenience: The asylum and its alternatives in Progressive America* (Rev. Ed.). New York, NY: Aldine de Gruyter.

Sherman, L. W. (1993). Why crime control is not reactionary. In D. Weisburd & C. Uchida (Eds.), *Police innovation and control of the police* (pp. 171–189). New York, NY: Springer-Verlag.

Sparks, R. (1996). Penal "austerity": The doctrine of less eligibility reborn? In R. Matthews & P. Francis (Eds.), *Prisons 2000: An international perspective on the current state and future of imprisonment* (pp. 74–93). Hampshire, UK: MacMillan.

Sullivan, D., & Tifft, L. (Eds.). (2008). *Handbook of restorative justice: A global perspective.* New York, NY: Routledge.

Swanson, C. (2009). *Restorative justice in a prison community: Or everything I didn't learn in kindergarten I learned in prison.* Lanham, MD: Lexington Books.

Tewksbury, R., & Mustaine, E. E. (2005). Insiders' views of prison amenities: Beliefs and perceptions of correctional staff members. *Criminal Justice Review, 30,* 174–188.

Toch, H. (1997). *Corrections: A humanistic approach.* Guilderland, NY: Harrow and Heston.

Toch, H., & Klofas, J. (1982). Alienation and desire for job enrichment among correction officers. *Federal Probation, 46*(1), 35–44.

Travis, L. F., III, & Cullen, F. T. (1984). Radical non-intervention: The myth of doing no harm. *Federal Probation, 48*(1), 29–32.

Van Ness, D. W., & Strong, K. H. (2010). *Restoring justice* (4th ed.). New Providence, NJ: Anderson/LexisNexis.

Webster's new unabridged dictionary. (1979). Second edition. New York, NY: Simon & Schuster.

Wilkinson, R. A. (1998). *The impact of community service work on adult state prisoners using a restorative justice framework.* Unpublished doctoral dissertation, Department of Educational Foundations, University of Cincinnati.

Wilson, J. Q. (1975). *Thinking about crime.* New York, NY: Vintage.

Wright, J. P., Tibbetts, S. G., & Daigle, L. E. (2008). *Criminals in the making: Criminality across the life course.* Thousand Oaks, CA: Sage.

Wright, K. N. (1994). *Effective prison leadership.* Binghamton, NY: William Neil.

Zimbardo, P. G. (2007). *The Lucifer effect: Understanding how good people turn evil.* New York, NY: Random House.

Part III

Doing Justice

5

The Feminist Prison

Kristi Holsinger

Editors' Introduction

Women's experience in prisons has always been defined by their otherness. They were and are the "other" when compared to the much more numerous male offenders. In patriarchal societies that valued women as lesser than their male counterparts, this "otherness" only exacerbated their less powerful and less noticeable status. In the first prisons built in this country, women were relegated to small sections and assigned kitchen, laundry, or sewing duties. They were subject to sexual assault by male staff and inmates in such facilities.

Once moved to their own facilities, which did not happen in most states until later in the 1800s or early 1900s, their female staff were often paid less than males in comparable positions in male prisons. Work programming for the women tended to focus on traditional gender roles rather than prepare them to support themselves and their children once they left prison. Other programming that they received was geared toward male inmates whose life circumstances and predispositions might be similar to, but not the same as females'. Women inmates, before the feminist movement of the early 1970s, were little studied and often misunderstood by scholars and practitioners in the field.

In the following chapter, Holsinger documents how this otherness has played out for women in prisons and the news is not heartening. "Women in prison make up one of the most oppressed, vulnerable, and invisible groups in society," she writes. They are often born poor and experience all of the life deficits that status entails, such as inferior schooling, little or no health care, a higher incidence of abuse and neglect as children, greater exposure to and subsequent engagement in abusive relationships, substance abuse, and criminal involvement (usually of the more minor kind). Prison for such women is just another stop along a pathway of despair, coming from nothing and going right back there once released.

It is the combination of the structural nature of women's crime, the poverty and all the baggage that comes with it, along with little social support for women both in and outside of prison that reinforces the belief that such crime and abuse ridden pathways are the only option. The 40 years worth of a drug war—with its focus on low-level offenders, a disproportionate number of whom are minority and female— has served to vastly increase the incarceration of women and has pushed them farther along this pathway of cumulative disadvantage. Similar effects are produced by the supposed equalizing of sentencing for men and women, despite the fact that women tend to initiate crime less and commit the least violent offenses.

Feminist scholars have traced the effect of this war and the "get tough on crime" initiatives on women and girls involved in the criminal justice system. They have also documented all of the needs and deficits for female offenders that put them on that path of despair and how to differentiate between what programming works and what programming does not to lessen their criminality and improve their lives. Their scholarship has illuminated another, alternative path that might be constructed for many women offenders.

Holsinger's Model Feminist Prison, as presented in this chapter, encompasses this research by feminist scholars. Holsinger envisions a prison reserved for a smaller number of incarcerated women where staff, programming, and a predominant purpose of the facility is to show women how to get off of the seemingly predetermined and destructive pathway they are on and instead support them as they traverse another way. This alternative path would bring women offenders reentering communities into the mainstream of American life where they are no longer the other, but are productive and possibly happy with their own lives.

W omen involved in the criminal justice system have always made up and continue to make up a small proportion compared to males. However, beginning in the early 1980s, and particularly over the next two decades, there were dramatic increases in incarceration rates for women, drawing new attention to this small subgroup within corrections. Due to the skyrocketing numbers that have come to define our new incarceration practices of the past three decades, and to increasing numbers of feminist scholars in the criminal justice and criminology fields, new attempts are being made to offer a more accurate and in-depth picture of who these women are, why they are increasingly being incarcerated, and how they should be treated by the court systems and correctional institutions.

These are significant and important changes in light of a legacy of ignoring females, primarily due to their low representation in the criminal justice system, or assigning sexist and inaccurate interpretations of their behavior that unfortunately resulted in programs that did little to address their real and pressing needs. Research on criminal women in the past was more likely to focus on their sexuality, or their failure to conform to appropriate gender roles as causal factors, as well as an interest in how they responded to incarceration, rather than an examination of their life circumstances that might explain their route into the criminal justice system. Not surprisingly, given the increases in women's incarceration rates, many modern scholars have attempted to understand and explain that growth. Their answers provide complex explanations that reject the simple but incorrect conclusion that women are becoming more violent or more criminal, or more like men. Rather, cultural and political shifts reflecting an increased punitiveness related to women's involvement in criminal behavior are seen as largely responsible; shifts that have also affected men.

The punishment model that took hold for incarcerated men was similarly adopted for women under the rationale of gender equality (Chesney-Lind, 1998); however, equitable treatment does not and should not imply identical treatment (Rafter, 1990). Gender differences exist between incarcerated men and women that are often ignored under the guise of providing gender parity. Yet these gender differences will require different responses to provide truly equal treatment that meets the needs of both women and men. Most of these differences are social factors—the result of gendered socialization and existing inequalities.

Women in prison make up one of the most oppressed, vulnerable, and invisible groups in society (Belknap, 2006; Sokoloff, 2005). One only need look at who is incarcerated in a given society to grasp who the most disadvantaged groups are, and that disadvantage only deepens as a result of their incarceration. Social inequality produced by mass incarceration is often difficult to see since it is hidden; hidden from view for most of society and hidden when the incarcerated are not included in measures of poverty and unemployment (Western & Pettit, 2010). It has been argued that criminal justice practices are creating a permanent underclass as effectively as slavery practices of the past, with much less critique (Alexander, 2010). The cost of ignoring these women or providing them treatment that is mismatched to their needs, however, is high in terms of the negative effects on society. For women (who typically have custody of their minor children), the social inequality they experience becomes cumulative when the effects on their children are examined. Women's caretaking frequently extends to the elderly and the sick in their families and communities, making their absence keenly felt by many.

These realities have culminated in an interesting and important time in correctional practices for women. Jurisdictions across the country are beginning to grapple with what it might mean to provide programs for system-involved women that are "gender-responsive" rather than rely on policies, programs, and practices that were developed for men in correctional institutions. Questions are being raised about what it might look like if programs had been designed for women at the outset, and how "best practices" in correctional rehabilitation and treatment might be merged with these new approaches based on the unique set of needs these women have.

The contemporary landscape even allows for imagining what a "feminist prison" might look like, even though at first glance this term may appear to be an oxymoron. Feminism historically has implied attaining gender equality in the social, political, legal, and economic facets of society. A broader, more complete understanding of feminist thought recognizes that gender is culturally created and maintained in ways that afford men greater power and influence and that to create equality, women, their experiences and knowledge, will need to be at the "center of intellectual inquiry" (Daly & Chesney-Lind, 1988, p. 504). The expected outcome will be the empowerment of women and social change. In criminology, feminist scholars have brought attention to exclusion of women from theories of crime, sexism within existing theories, sexism within juvenile and adult justice systems, and violence against women (Daly & Chesney-Lind, 1988). The next steps required by a feminist perspective include an even more critical examination of prisons and their conditions that goes beyond seeking equality to questioning if prisons ultimately do women more harm than good by depriving them of respect, rights, and dignity and ignoring the sociopolitical and cultural contexts they live in.

Women in Prison

THE NUMBERS AND TRENDS

Approximately 88% of women in prison are in the state systems, with the remaining 12% doing time in federal prisons. Sentenced women under the jurisdiction of state and federal correctional authorities make up slightly less than 7% of adults under correctional supervision in this country. In real numbers and according to the most recent statistics available, that means 104,629 women were incarcerated at yearend 2010 in various correctional facilities (Guerino, Harrison, & Sabol, 2011).

The United States is well known for having some of the highest incarceration rates in the world; this status has become particularly striking given the increases of the last 30 years. The rate at which women were incarcerated remained stable and below 10 per 100,000 women in the population from 1925 through the early 1980s; however, at that point in time, a dramatic shift occurred and rates of incarcerated women climbed sharply, driving us to the current incarceration rate of 67 per 100,000 women (Guerino et al., 2011). The greatest growth occurred between 1980 and 2000, accounting for a seven-fold increase in women serving time in prison with the rates of growth most dramatic for non-White women (Sokoloff, 2005). Prior to this historic rise, female sentencing was more likely to be from a non-incarcerative, rehabilitative model with shorter sentences and a greater use of probation (Faris & Miller, 2010).

Generally speaking, women's crime is less serious, less frequent, and more often concentrated in low-level property and public order offenses such as prostitution when compared with men's crime. Women's involvement in violent crime has been declining, with the largest increases instead seen in drug-related crimes (and drug-related parole violations) and property offenses (Chesney-Lind, 1998; Sokoloff, 2005). Even within the category of violence, women's rates of committing murder do not make up the bulk of arrests; rather, it is the broad category of assaults that has gone up.

In state prisons, based on 2009 data, 36% of females serving sentences are incarcerated for violent offenses, 30% for property offenses, and 26% for drug offenses, with public order and other/unspecified offenses contributing the remaining 8% of offenses (Guerino et al., 2011). Compare this to men's sentences, which are 54% for violent offenses, 18% for property offenses, and 17% for drug offenses, and significant gender differences emerge. Further, many differences exist within these broad offense classifications. Women serving time for a violent offense are twice as likely as men to have victimized someone they know (Snell, 1994). While prevalence of offending rates decline with age for both sexes, they do so more dramatically for women (Block, Bokland, van der Werff, van Os, & Nieuwbeerta, 2010).

Policy changes related to the War on Drugs deserve special attention, and have been particularly damaging for women. Primarily through mandatory sentencing laws dictating prison sentences for minor drug charges and longer sentences, women are increasingly being incarcerated for minor drug offenses; for example, being a courier, a high-visibility position in the drug distribution network. Further, women's low status in low-level positions in the drug world means that they do not have access to intelligence that could assist them in prosecutorial bargaining. As a result, women are unable to reduce the charge severity and are often given harsher sentences for crimes relatively minor in nature (Sokoloff, 2005). Unfortunately the women-harming effects do not end there as drug offenses affect policies limiting welfare, public housing, federal educational grants, employment, and parental custodial rights (Bloom, Owen, & Covington, 2004).

Similarly, pro-arrest policy changes related to domestic violence have increased the likelihood that women will be arrested and charged for participation in any physical altercation (Chesney-Lind, 2002). Policy changes like these take away judicial discretion, when in the past considerations could be made about the family members relying on a sentenced woman for support. Attempts to remove bias from the correctional system on gender, or other demographic variables, also have the ultimate effect of reducing discretion when it may be warranted.

Research on gender differences in processing generally produce mixed findings. However, research focusing on the interaction of gender and race find more consistent results showing the disadvantage minority women experience in processing (Crawford, 2000; Crow & Kunselman, 2009; Griffin & Wooldredge, 2006). Harsher processing also has been found to exist for poorer and younger women (Gilbert, 2001). One explanation being put forth to elucidate these differences is that criminal justice decision makers assess a person's blameworthiness or dangerousness based on race and other social factors (Crow & Kunselman, 2009).

THEIR CHARACTERISTICS

Women in prison are typically from the lower socioeconomic classes. Not surprisingly, then, they often manifest conditions related to living in poverty—inadequate health care, poor nutrition, more physical health problems, and substandard education than their counterparts in the general population. Their problems range from chronic conditions that have not been adequately addressed to dental problems resulting from a lack of preventative care. Women have higher rates of HIV/AIDS compared to men in prison, a fact likely related to intravenous drug use, trading sex for money, and sexual abuse (DeGroot, 2001). Related to their economic situation, they often experience a lack of safe, stable housing and have had inadequate and limited educational and vocational histories.

Most women of color in the prison system come from communities of poverty, putting them in "triple jeopardy" for incarceration based on their gender, race, and socioeconomic status (Bloom, Owen, & Covington, 2003). Racial and ethnic minorities are overrepresented in prison when compared to their lower representation in the population. African American non-Hispanic women's imprisonment rates were nearly three times that of White non-Hispanic women (133 vs. 47 per 100,000 in the population) while Hispanic women were incarcerated at a rate of 77 per 100,000 (Guerino et al., 2011). One potential explanation, although there are many, can be seen by looking at how policy changes related to drugs have disproportionately affected women's incarceration rates. Between 1986 and 1991, there was a 241% increase for White women, a 328% increase for Latina women, and a shocking 828% increase for African American women (Mauer & Huling, 1995).

Typically, women in prison are young, yet they are often the heads of households and mothers of young children. Separation from their children is one of, if not the main cause of, anxiety and stress for incarcerated women (Bloom et al., 2003; Hardyman & Van Voorhis, 2004). Incarcerated women are likely to be parents; about two thirds are mothers of minor children (Mumola, 2000). In interviews with 74 mothers, Celinska and Siegel (2010) found incarcerated mothers use multiple coping strategies to deal with separation from their children. All of the mothers reported that being a good mother was central to their identity and they were planning and preparing for the future in regard to their children. The vast majority (95%) used available strategies that allowed them to mother their children from prison, such as maintaining contact and/or visits with their children. Another large percentage (88%) indicated using prison as a time of self-transformation. All of these responses indicate the importance of motherhood to their identity and how this role can be a strong source of motivation for making positive changes in their lives.

Women who are incarcerated in prison also have more extensive histories of abuse, victimization, domestic violence (victim), and battery compared to incarcerated men. Rates of trauma are also consistently found to be much higher in incarcerated female samples compared to females in the general population. A recent and comprehensive study of the abuse histories of incarcerated women found that 70% of the women reported one violation of rape or a serious sexual assault and half reported being abused as a child (McDaniels & Belknap, 2008). Another study of a large Southern prison found lifetime sexual victimization rates to be 68%, with homosexual and bisexual women being more likely to report sexual victimization (Blackburn, Mullings, & Marquart, 2008). Younger women were also more likely to report this experience, which may indicate that sexual violence leads females onto a criminal path at an early age. Researchers interviewing women in a jail setting found the women faced increased victimization when they were on drugs, engaging in criminal activity, involved in a relationship, residing with a significant other, and lacking stable living conditions (Armstrong & Griffin, 2007). This study highlights an important gender difference: the increased risks women face in their private, domestic lives.

Several critical issues for women appear to be highly correlated with their high rates of victimization. It has been estimated that 60% of women in prison have a history of drug dependence (Mumola & Karberg, 2006) and that use is often described in terms of self-medication to cope with extremely difficult life circumstances. Studies indicate that as many as 80% of women in prison suffer from at least one psychiatric disorder, the most common being post-traumatic stress disorder and depression (Jordan, Schlenger, Fairbank, & Caddell, 1996; Teplin, Abram, & McClellan, 1996). Another study found symptoms of a mental disorder to be 73% in a prison sample of women versus 55% of male prisoners; both high rates when compared with the estimate of 12% for the general population of women (James & Glaze, 2006).

It is thought that about half of incarcerated women have engaged in self-harming behaviors (Borrill et al., 2003). One of the few studies exploring this phenomenon found that being White, younger, and having a higher than average sentence was associated with self-harming behavior. This group also had more abuse, risk-taking behavior, eating disorders, and domestic violence in their childhoods, and were more likely to have incarcerated and substance-using family members and a history of prostitution (Roe-Sepowitz, 2007). This study provides a reminder of how women's experiences are shaped based on basic demographic variables.

PROGRAMS AND POLICIES

Gender differences have existed in prisons throughout history, and were particularly notable once separate institutions were established beginning in the 1870s (Belknap, 2006). Although fewer treatment programs have always been available to women compared to men, one early difference was in the type of treatment programs available. Early theories suggested that "deviant" women needed to learn the proper gender role to "cure" them, thus cottage style prisons emerged, run largely by women. The programs often prepared inmates for traditional female roles that would develop their skills in domestic work or skills that would lead to employment in low-paying jobs. Many of the programs that would logically be recommended following an examination of the characteristics of incarcerated women are not widely available in prison, as programs providing vocational skill development, further education, and substance abuse treatment are the exception rather than the norm (The Sentencing Project, 2007).

One impetus for the establishment of separate prisons for women was their vulnerability to victimization, particularly at the hands of male staff. Unbelievably, this type of victimization has not been eradicated and is likely related to the power dynamics that exist in prisons. One recent study found that 17% of women in a southern prison reported experiencing sexual victimization while in prison (Blackburn et al., 2008). In fact, abuse, exploitative relationships, and verbal and emotional abuse by staff and by other inmates (while staff turn a blind eye) have come to be part of most prison settings (George, 2010). Unfortunately many individuals working in the field do not have training in female development or knowledge of the structural oppression that affects women, racial and ethnic minorities, and the poor, much less a critique of their own beliefs. As such, it is not uncommon to hear staff negatively describe females as emotional, manipulative, and more difficult to work with than males (Pollock, 1986), contributing to an environment where abuse is more likely.

Trauma, a common factor in many women's histories and one duly noted by feminist scholars, typically goes unaddressed in the prison environment. Psychological needs, such as issues related to safety, trust, esteem, and intimacy, and a host of other post-traumatic stress disorder symptoms that are the result of trauma are often only made worse in the typical prison setting (Fournier, Hughes, Hurford, & Sainio, 2011). Medication, often psychotropic drugs, is the most common response to women's mental health needs (Proctor, 2009; Severson, Berry, & Postmus, 2007). Similarly, treatment for substance use problems, which are often related to trauma, is deemed to be largely inadequate, ineffective, or unavailable in prison, and the prison setting itself is not judged to be the ideal environment for treatment (Hagan & Coleman, 2001; Radosh, 2002).

Lack of adequate health care for incarcerated women is well documented, largely as a result of law suits, investigative journalism, research, legislative studies, and government reports (Proctor, 2009). In particular, gynecological and obstetrical services are most lacking along with an inability to deal with the chronic and ongoing health conditions that come with aging and living in poverty. Current practices related to prenatal care, birthing accommodations, postnatal care, and hygiene needs are not effectively addressing the needs of women. One study found that the majority of women in a prison that had contracted with a private health care corporation felt that the quality of their health care declined while they were in prison and that they were not believed by staff when they reported health problems. They also reported a lack of prompt care and found services to be available at inconvenient times of the day and cost prohibitive with the inmates having two dollars deducted from their funds each time they received medical services, discouraging utilization (Proctor, 2009).

While some promising programs exist, prisons have not made maintaining mother-child contact a priority. Both mothers and children are adversely affected by forced separation resulting from incarceration. Mothers suffer guilt, remorse, and anxiety about the care of their children and the effects of their incarceration on them. The negative effects on children are also well documented and include emotional problems such as post-traumatic stress disorder, and behavioral problems such as school misconduct and criminal justice involvement (Snyder, 2009).

Research findings suggest that the percentage of children who never visit their mother while she is incarcerated is somewhere between 40% and 71% (Celinska &

Siegel, 2010). Many institutional policies exist today that work against mothers maintaining contact with their children, such as inconvenient visiting hours, limits on the number and length of phone calls, geographical distance, and lack of programs supporting positive interactions (Celinska & Siegel, 2010; Snyder, 2009). Due to the lower numbers of incarcerated women and fewer facilities, women are estimated to be 160 miles farther from their families than incarcerated men, with fewer opportunities to transfer (Bastick & Townhead, 2008; Coughenour, 1995). Further, policies are in place that allow for the termination of parental rights if a child was in the foster care system for 15 of the last 22 months (Adoptions and Safe Families Act of 1997). Bad parenting is not the reason most women are incarcerated, so the role of state intervention in breaking families apart should be critically examined, especially in light of the harm done to the child (Snyder, 2009).

Rehabilitation in Prison Programs

Countless challenges continue to plague institutional correctional treatment programs that go against "best practices" established in the field. The organizational structure and primary goals of prisons are not treatment, and as such the conflicting goals of custody and punishment often take precedence (Calhoun, Messina, Cartier, & Torrs, 2010). Prisons are noisy, unpredictable places where environmental disruptions and the existing culture can easily undo any progress in treatment. Staff turnover and frequent roommate reassignments can also contribute to unstable conditions. Further, prisons are artificial environments where treatment is more likely to be coercive in nature and does not allow for the involvement of family or the opportunity to practice new skills in real life settings. One typical problem in correctional treatment programs in prison is putting everyone in an available program whether that program is one that they need or not, largely due to a lack of variety in existing programs.

Best practices in corrections dictate that agencies adhere to the risk, need, and responsivity principles for the greatest reductions in recidivism—yet they often do not. These principles, in sum, suggest that high-risk offenders be targeted with the most intensive resources, that targets of intervention be criminogenic needs that when addressed will reduce criminal behavior, and that treatment modalities are matched to individual personalities and competencies (Andrews & Bonta, 2010). Cognitive-behavioral programs, as well as several other theoretical approaches, are deemed to be the most effective (Gendreau, Little, & Goggin, 1996). These principles ideally are used to guide offender assessment, case planning, and treatment.

In addition to the general lack of adherence to these best practices, feminist theorists have several concerns for how these principles play out in relation to incarcerated women. In the case of criminalized women, the focus should be on women's needs since generally women are relatively low risk for reoffending and are less of a threat to public safety, particularly compared to incarcerated men (Holtfreter & Morash, 2003). Incorporating these needs into risk assessments is problematic in that this practice has had the effect of penalizing women with more restrictive placements, reduced access to educational and vocational opportunities, and less family contact (Bastick & Townhead, 2008; Hannah-Moffat, 1999). The smaller numbers of institutions for women also mean that women will be more likely to be overclassified by being placed in a facility that is more restrictive than warranted by their risk level (Bastick & Townhead, 2008).

Further, this practice in essence blames women for tragic life circumstances like their abuse as children, for example, and ignores the fact that they lacked protection from the abuse (Severson et al., 2007). Shoshana Pollack (2007) notes that the concept of risk is ultimately used to scrutinize and control populations that are already the most socially excluded due to poverty, addictions, and mental health issues. Rather than paying attention to the structural conditions that are contributing factors, these approaches are in danger of pathologizing women and may "decontextualize gendered, racialized, and classed experiences and focus instead on changing thinking patterns" (p. 163).

Women inmates deemed the counseling they receive in prison as largely ineffective due to long waiting lists, groups that were too big, and/or groups that were not addressing their needs. Further, the crucial missing component was a lack of a meaningful relationship with a therapist since they were seen sporadically, or, even worse, given a limited number of sessions or were seen by multiple counselors (Fournier et al., 2011). Given that advocates of best correctional practices are recognizing the importance of the relationship between the counselor and client, we cannot expect that the counseling practices typically provided to female inmates will be beneficial.

As noted, another mistake made in correctional practices is to use programs, policies, and procedures developed for men, giving women fewer opportunities to receive appropriate treatment (Holtfreter & Morash, 2003). One example is the use of classification or assessment instruments that have never been statistically validated on a sample of women, which was found to be the case in 36 states (Van Voorhis, Pealer, Spiropoulis, & Sutherland, 2001). The potential for misuse of these instruments and how they can negatively affect women is varied and significant (see Holsinger & Van Voorhis, 2005) and can serve to legitimize damaging correctional practices rather than question the role of the state in further harming women.

Feminist Approaches

RESEARCH DIRECTIONS

One direction taken by feminist theorists is to develop theories on female offending that do not rely on sexist and stereotypical ideas about women. This task is best accomplished by listening to the voices of women and girls to understand how they came to be involved in the criminal justice system. Feminist scholars also seek to document and raise awareness about criminal justice processing and current conditions and practices in correctional institutions for women and, when necessary, advocate for change. Another approach taken is to build on new theoretical development and the critique of current practices by making policy and programmatic recommendations for institutions that would be truly "gender specific" or "gender responsive" to the challenges faced by women inmates. Each of these initiatives suggests that gender matters and is a critical concept to examine when it comes to criminal behavior, processing, and treatment. Despite some reforms in this realm, system changes are lagging considerably behind the contributions of feminist scholars (Pollack, 2007).

A growing body of literature has developed alongside the work of feminist criminologists that is consistent and supportive of research findings on criminalized women. Largely coming from the voices of currently and previously incarcerated women, they document how women come to be criminalized, their experiences of incarceration, and life after prison (see George, 2010; Levi & Waldman, 2011). Similarly, investigative journalists and authors outside of criminal justice and criminology scholarship rely heavily on the words of incarcerated women to document their lives and experiences of incarceration (see Lamb, 2003, 2007; Rathbone, 2006; Salvi, 2007). These works increase the visibility of incarcerated women and add to the urgency of pursuing more humane and effective strategies related to punishment.

THEORETICAL PERSPECTIVES ON WOMEN'S OFFENDING

Theories developed from a feminist perspective purport that female offending cannot be understood without an examination of the gendered life circumstances of women and men. Childbirth and parenting, being a caretaker, the experience of trauma, abuse and victimization, the lack of support networks, and the likelihood of living in poverty with blocked opportunities are all gendered conditions of life for women. The greatest strength, then, of this perspective is an analysis of the assemblage of causes of offending that is developed by hearing from system-involved women (Block et al., 2010). In fact, when incarcerated women were interviewed about what girls involved in the system need, their comments were remarkably consistent with what the existing literature base says girls need (Garcia & Lane, 2010).

A feminist perspective would also advocate for investigating the intersecting oppressions and intersecting marginalized identities that impact this population, such as race, class, gender, sexuality, nationality, age, and other defining social characteristics (Burgess-Proctor, 2006). Theoretical work by feminist scholars seeks to identify subgroups, looking at the policy implications of each pathway, rather than the alternative of lumping all women together, creating a unified "female offender" (Holtfreter & Morash, 2003).

Feminist theorists often use the word *pathways* to describe the complex routes that different women take into involvement with the correctional system. Daly

(1992) developed five unique pathways for women: street women, harmed and harming women, battered women, drug-connected women, and economically motivated women. Similarly, Gilfus (1992) outlines six pathways that link attempts to cope with victimization to the likelihood of being criminalized. For girls, and subsequently women, one common pathway is the runaway who, to escape a dysfunctional or abusive home, uses the resources at her disposal (i.e., her body, stealing, drug selling) to survive. The fact that she is a runaway has historically been a punishable status offense, although this practice is now viewed as a less acceptable response than in the past. Drug use, one coping strategy at her disposal, is also a response that is criminalized. One small study supporting these ideas found that addicted women inmates often began using and eventually abusing substances due to traumatic events in their lives (McDonald, 2008).

Research linking abuse and victimization to pathways to crime has some problematic implications that need to be guarded against. When focusing on the psychological impact of trauma on individuals, there is the danger of ignoring existing structural conditions that cause such high rates of violence against women and girls. This focus also takes attention off of the policies in institutions that exacerbate these traumas. Another problematic development is viewing victimizations as risk factors that can then be used to justify decisions about confinement and privileges (Pollack, 2007). Pollack found evidence this phenomenon happens in the context of women's relationships. The risk factor of being abused by a man required higher levels of supervision and reporting with respect to new intimate relationships, a perfect illustration of focusing on her personal failing in choosing intimate partners rather than on the realities of violence against women. This outcome would be unlikely for a man, highlighting another way in which gender affects processing and treatment.

Other theorists have focused on the economic marginalization and the feminization of poverty (rates of poverty are highest and fastest growing for women and their children) to explain women's criminal involvement. Gender matters, and it shapes women's responses to poverty; involvement in criminality is often related to economic need. Barriers to the labor market, including early motherhood and limited skills, lead women to using the resources they have to survive. Poverty can easily be linked with women's imprisonment when examining current bail and restitution practices. Interesting differences emerge when comparing men's and women's motivation to commit crime. Women's offenses are more likely to be economically driven and motivated by poverty (Bloom et al., 2004). Similarly, women with children report engaging in crime as a realistic alternative to homelessness and hunger (Ferraro & Moe, 2003). The stigma criminalized women carry and the guilt they experience is greater than that of men; women experience a greater disjuncture between being an "offender" and the idealized gender roles that exist in society.

Patriarchy, particularly as it is related to high rates of violence against women and high rates of poverty of women and children, shapes their criminal behaviors and how they interact in the world (Garcia & Lane, 2010). There is concern among feminist scholars that these factors and their effects are ignored in favor of locating the cause of crime within a woman's psyche (Pollack, 2007). While programming can and should address individual psychological issues that are the result of women's experiences, it cannot ignore the larger sociological context.

CONDITIONS AND PRACTICES IN WOMEN'S PRISONS

The extent to which current practices and policies, and in some cases even programs, exacerbate women's problems while they are in prison, and actually increase the likelihood of reoffense, is concerning. This section considers the effect these practices have on women. The section also highlights recent research that illuminates how women's identities, pre-prison experiences, and the structure of the institution shape how they do their time (Kruttschnitt & Gartner, 2003; Owen, 1998).

The California Coalition of Women Prisoners, a feminist advocacy group, found that women were more likely to blame themselves for their problems rather than understand their situations in light of oppressive social problems (Whitehead, 2007). Women misplace their anger toward the criminal justice system on themselves or other inmates (Zaitzow, 2003). Again, this finding exemplifies a problem seen in many treatment programs where structural conditions, from the War on Drugs to the effects of living in poverty, are ignored in favor of an individualization of the problem. Prison fosters dependency in women and raises the question of how is it possible to raise consciousness and empower women in the context of a prison given the existing power inequalities that exist within that environment (Whitehead, 2007).

Strip searches, sexual harassment, and abuse continue in prison with guards who have power over them, just as an abuser did outside of prison. Women report being controlled, manipulated, and threatened while incarcerated (Richie, 2001). These exploitative exchanges, unfortunately, only reinforce a woman's lack of power. One woman rather insightfully noted that the self-esteem program she received helped her deal with the prison strip search she experienced (Pollack, 2007). Pollack notes, "The same system that is humiliating her is offering her ways of feeling better about being violated" (p. 169).

In the words of one formerly incarcerated woman, Tina Reynolds,

> As I relived my experiences within the criminal justice system, I began to realize that I had been severely traumatized by the practices and policies exercised upon me and enforced over me while in the jails and the prisons I had been confined at. I realized that the way I had been treated was both dehumanizing and oppressive. I took and accepted this treatment as the status quo because I had done wrong, I had committed crimes, and I considered this part of my punishment. (2010, p. 454)

Research on incarcerated women finds that stressors of life in prison often include staff inconsistencies in the enforcement of rules and a lack of respect from prison staff (Fox, 1988; McDonald, 2008). Owen's (1998) research on women in prison suggests that women's lives prior to incarceration, the abuse they may have experienced, their marginality in society, and their subsequent criminality, greatly influence their experience while in prison. Also troubling was the finding that women who failed to use the language of the treatment program to explain their correctional therapeutic experiences were judged by staff to be at a higher risk for violent offending (Hannah-Moffat, 2004).

There are important gender differences in institutional misconduct that highlight differences in how women and men adjust to and cope with life behind bars. Women are less likely to commit serious infractions while incarcerated, and more likely than men to engage in individual opposition to prison staff, as opposed to collective action (Kruttschnitt & Gartner, 2003). Women with prior incarcerations had lower infractions than men. Age (being younger), race (being non-White), education (having less), sentence length (having a shorter one), and perceptions of staff treatment (more caring) were predictive factors for infractions for women but not for men (Gover, Perez, & Jennings, 2008).

A MODEL FEMINIST PRISON

Given these documented realities and challenges, the task at hand requires imagining a future that is different from our current prison system for women, one that rather than existing peripherally and secondarily to what has been created for the male offender, puts the experiences and needs of incarcerated women at the center. As outlined, the women in today's prison system suffer the worst of the gendered ramifications of our society, such as a lack of power, blocked opportunities, the primary responsibility for caring for children, and the like. So while addressing women's individual problems related to addiction, educational opportunities, and vocational and life skills is important, feminist prisons would also need to empower these women by supporting them in addressing the sociopolitical and cultural contexts they find themselves in.

At this point in time and thanks largely to feminist research, women's needs are well known, along with many ideas about how to respond to those needs. What remains missing is widespread implementation of these more feminist and gender-responsive practices, an integration of these approaches with the "best practices" correctional literature, and a systematic evaluation of the effectiveness of these approaches. The prison system for women has considerable room for improvement! Prisons must start by recognizing the constellation of needs that exist for incarcerated women.

Richie (2001) notes that "the demands and needs form a complex web of concerns and stressors that often compete and exacerbate one another" (p. 380). Therefore, services addressing these issues must be comprehensive, integrated, and culturally relevant (Bloom et al., 2004). They include case management that assesses needs on an ongoing basis and links them to multifaceted services in the broad areas of education, skill development, housing, medical/mental health care, and parenting (Holtfreter & Morash, 2003). Model feminist programs also share a variety of key components.

THE PRISON ENVIRONMENT

In addition to the needs women bring with them to prison, they unfortunately have likely developed new ones as a result of the experience of incarceration. Compelling arguments have been made highlighting the psychological degradation women experience in prison (George, 2010; Irwin & Owen, 2005). Being incarcerated should not result in worsening women's physical and mental health, but it usually does. Sound nutrition, opportunities to exercise, and ample access to appropriate health care, particularly for long-term and gender-related health conditions, are needed.

Emotions that women may need special assistance learning to cope with include guilt and shame, social stigma, and distrust. The prison environment only fosters dependency as women get used to following repetitive and restrictive schedules and rules they have no input on. They have little control over any decision that affects their daily life, fostering existing anger, resentment, and a sense of injustice. As a result, model programs must fundamentally alter the prison environment in ways that allow greater input in the operations of the facility; decisions that will increase women's sense of ownership of the environment will likely include increases in privacy, support, and services.

Prisons for women have to do a better job protecting women living there, particularly in light of their extensive histories of trauma. Until abuse is eradicated in prisons, great care must be taken in determining the capacities in which male staff may work in women's prisons, with female prisoner safety given priority over gender equality in the workplace (Bastick & Townhead, 2008). Reporting systems are often inadequate; Muscat (2008) recommends that the location and receipt of information reported be separate from correctional institutional personnel and in a variety of locations. The recipient of these reports should handle multiple issues, not just violence and safety concerns, to provide greater anonymity and confidentiality to those who report. This person must be trained in crisis intervention and trauma, be objective and impartial, and maintain boundaries that promote trust. A trained team then should review these reports and handle them appropriately with the victim's care at the forefront of concern.

THE NATURE OF THE INTERVENTION: RELATIONAL AND REHABILITATIVE

Scholars in the field of correctional rehabilitation and treatment are beginning to acknowledge the importance of the therapeutic relationship. Perhaps one of the biggest changes needed in many prisons is a dramatic culture change among staff (meaning everyone who has direct contact with clients) in order to create environments that are safe and treat women respectfully and with dignity (Bloom et al., 2004). This shift needs to start with the initial hiring decision by assessing interpersonal skills such as empathy, relational styles, personality, and support for the treatment offered. In other correctional settings, warm and motivating staff interactions were critical in offender success (Robinson, Lowenkamp, Holsinger, VanBenschoten, Alexander, & Oleson, 2012).

Dehumanizing offenders has long been a part of the history of the American prison system, but staff need to be hired and trained to see the humanness of the women they work with—to see the person as authentic, complex, and autonomous in order to develop life-changing bonds with them (Vogelvang, 2012).

Similar and supportive of the staff qualifications necessary to create a better prison environment, it is often recommended that gender-specific programs for women be relational in nature due to the socialization women receive to value and nurture relationships. Gender-responsive curricula for addiction and recovery that are modeled on relational theory have found this approach to be a good fit for incarcerated women (Calhoun et al., 2010). Relationships matter and by paying attention to the quality of the relationship and promoting mentoring relationships, more effective outcomes with incarcerated women are more likely.

From an evidence-based perspective, much is known about creating an ideal program. An ideal program for women, beyond addressing the critical components mentioned above, would be thoughtfully developed and based on a sound theoretical model that is applied consistently throughout the program by qualified and well-trained staff. Ideal programs use assessment as a tool to individualize treatment and assess qualities of the individual that should affect the type of intervention the person receives. In the best case, assessments as well as direct input from the woman about her needs would guide treatment decisions. Women should have the opportunity to provide input into existing programs as well. The best programs pay attention to the length and intensity of the treatment, the size of the groups, and teaching and then practicing the skills being taught. Quality assurance measures and systematic program evaluation are critical components as well (Gendreau & Andrews, 1994).

Antithetical to the literature on best practices, some feminist scholars argue that prisons *should* target women's non-criminogenic needs even though the expectation is not necessarily to reduce recidivism but to achieve other positive outcomes that might ultimately impact criminal involvement in the future (Holtfreter & Morash, 2003). Women typically come to America's prison system with a host of needs that go far beyond criminogenic needs. Much of the program deconstruction resulting from the implementation of best practices has occurred under the belief that correctional programs were straying far from effective intervention via the targeting of "non-criminogenic" needs. This might be the best prescription for programs that are designed to serve men only, as men come to the prison system with many more advantages (or at least fewer deficiencies) than women. Women, on the other hand, enter the prison system disadvantaged in ways that are expressed via their criminogenic needs, as well as needs in many other areas—important areas that are vital to prosocial functionality. To insist that programs for women target only criminogenic needs will by definition miss the mark in fixing the whole person in a gendered society.

ADDRESSING TRAUMA, SUBSTANCE USE, AND MENTAL HEALTH

Prisons must start by recognizing the constellation of needs that exist for incarcerated women. For example, trauma, substance use, and mental health issues (particularly post-traumatic stress disorder) are seen as profoundly inter-related issues that are common in this population (Arditti & Few, 2006; Bloom & Covington, 2009). Services that are trauma based are relatively well developed with a strong theoretical base containing clear content and structure; however, their use is far from widespread. These approaches are careful to avoid re-traumatizing or revictimizing women and provide individualized, therapeutic approaches in a women-only context with empowerment being the ultimate goal. Unfortunately, few methodologically strong studies have been done to assess the outcomes of such programs, but this avenue of treatment appears logical given the existing needs in this area.

CONTACT WITH CHILDREN

Maintaining contact between incarcerated women and their children is best. Doing so ultimately increases the chances for a successful reunification with their children and a positive readjustment to parenting. Even educational parent-ing programs that have not included structured visits with children report improvements in women's parenting attitudes, self-esteem, and legal knowledge regarding parental rights and responsibilities (Kennon, Mackintosh, & Myers, 2009). Through qualitative analysis, it was assessed that women learned more about their children's needs (including their need to know that what happened to their mother was not their fault) as well as the importance of maintaining regular communication with their children and their children's caretakers. Education in negotiating the mother-caregiver relationship is crucial as this can affect the regularity of contact (Enos, 2001).

In the case of parenting programs it is easy to see that the benefits, including reduced recidivism by mothers, decreased emotional and behavioral problems and delinquency for children, and reductions in state-supported foster care, outweigh the costs (Poehlmann, 2005; Sandifer, 2008; Snyder, 2009). Existing research indicates that it is in the best interest of mothers and children both to be directly involved in parenting programs, a practice uncommon in most U.S. prisons, but more common in other countries (Hoffman, Byrd, & Kightlinger, 2010). Any avenues for increasing parent-child contact are worth pursuing, including keeping women closer to their homes, allowing for leaves and visits as much as possible, and evaluating the best interest of the children, even regarding the decision to imprison (Bastick & Townhead, 2008).

SKILL DEVELOPMENT AND EMPOWERMENT

Women need the opportunity to develop skills so they can support themselves and their children upon release. Providing opportunities for women to acquire further education or to learn new skills to improve their economic status is a likely way to address some of these long-standing needs. If women do not emerge from prison with these skills they will be pulled back into illegal ways of making money as a result of their need (Richie, 2001). One unique vocational program in prison taught women plumbing skills. Analysis of this program uncovered that having support from the prison administration, the necessary physical space, an awareness and responsiveness to low literacy levels, and peer mentoring for areas of difficulty were key factors for success (Young & Mattucci, 2006).

When incarcerated women rank what they perceive to be the most helpful types of programs, they identify long-term, tangible supports such as child care, housing, welfare, food banks, and educational services and also note that these are the supports they are *least* likely to receive (Severson et al., 2007). Meanwhile, services they are more likely to receive, like support groups, counseling, education, and legal services, were evaluated as least helpful. While these services are no doubt important, it is informative that they are ranked lower than the basic survival needs the women have.

Richie (2001) advocates for empowerment and consciousness-raising in programs that help women understand how structural influences have affected their personal choices, not an easy task in a prison environment that takes away autonomy and decision-making opportunities. Additionally, these types of programs would require highly trained professionals who themselves have an understanding of patriarchy, sexism, and poverty, to name a few, in order to provide effective education. Women need to work on decision making in the context of their limited choices and in ways that help them develop a sense of hope.

COMMUNITY REENTRY FOR WOMEN

Women are largely released back into the community with the needs they had when they went in—economic independence, safe and affordable housing, and adequate health care. If the goal is to avoid a speedy return to prison, it would seem logical that efforts would be made while women are incarcerated to address these underlying problems. At the very least, correctional institutions should be developing reentry plans that prepare for these needs through case management, and "wraparound services" would follow women returning to their communities.

Further, women return to their communities with post-prison penalties that add to existing problems as they will likely experience the denial of necessary supports such as public housing, welfare benefits, financial assistance for further education, and employment (Samuels & Mukamal, 2004). One study comparing women who succeeded on parole with those who had failed identified important variables for success (Cobbina, 2010). Having access to services post-release, such as housing, employment, access to child care, parenting classes, and other needs like clothing were associated with successful return to the community, as were family support and supportive parole officers. Again, officers who listened, encouraged, were supportive, and who offered concrete assistance were identified as important for success, again emphasizing the importance of this relational role in reducing recidivism. Clearly, reentry programs must be comprehensive and gender sensitive.

FEMINIST ALTERNATIVES AND ACTIVISM

A multitude of reasons suggest that many incarcerated women could be better served in community-based programs, and that prisons should be used only as a last resort. Promoting healthy relationships with children and others could best be achieved in a community setting, allowing for community mentoring (Bloom et al., 2004; Richie, 2001). The community is also a less expensive alternative to incarceration and is becoming increasingly appealing as state budgets for education are being surpassed by correctional expenses.

Prisons with the focus on security are simply not set up to interface with community social service agencies or respond to the complex array of needs that women have. It is clear we are inappropriately incarcerating many women in this country; women who are not a threat to public safety, women who have been criminalized for their attempts to survive difficult circumstances, and women with addiction issues requiring treatment, not punishment. Women with histories of abuse and victimization are further harmed by correctional practices that reinforce their disempowerment and deepen existing psychological wounds. International human rights standards (The United Nations Standard Minimum Rules for the Treatment of Prisoners, for example, but also other prison-specific guidelines and human rights instruments) can be used to improve the lives of imprisoned women as there is overwhelming evidence that these standards are routinely violated by U.S. practices (Bastick & Townhead, 2008).

Policy changes, many at the state level, will have to be made. There are still policies in place that prevent those with a felony conviction (sometimes specifically tied to a felony drug conviction) from receiving social service assistance, public housing, Pell grants, employment, and regaining custody of their children (Bloom et al., 2004). For example, more policies that encourage employers to hire previously incarcerated individuals are needed (Young & Mattucci, 2006). States that have made significant strides in reducing their female prison populations can be emulated. By diverting more drug addicted offenders from prison to treatment, New York experienced a historic drop in its prison population. Similarly, California responded to U.S. Supreme Court orders to reduce its prison population by releasing mothers with nonserious offenses to serve the remainder of their sentences in the community.

Other policy changes to consider that would drastically impact women's incarceration rates would be the release of nonviolent offenders to supervision in the community and the complete decriminalization of drug use (Davis, 2003). A reinterpretation of substance use as a medical issue requiring treatment, rather than a criminal justice issue requiring punishment for a moral failing, would lead to huge reductions in the prison population since this large proportion of women currently incarcerated could be transferred to community-based programs.

Our overreliance on incarceration to address existing entrenched social problems is foolish, particularly when incarceration allows for the root causes of crime that are embedded in the political, economic, and social contexts to be ignored. Our current policies criminalize poor women, particularly poor women of color. A better strategy for reducing crime could be reinvesting in low-income communities, particularly through the provision of housing, employment, education, and health care (Bhavnani & Davis, 2000; Richie, 2001). It is advocating for change in current destructive society and community conditions that will ultimately improve the lives of women who are too frequently ensnared in the criminal justice system.

For the women who remain in the U.S. prison system, drastic changes must be made to provide a "feminist prison." Many of these changes will have to be fought for through activism on the part of feminists outside of the prison structure. First, we must acknowledge the gendered society we live in and the ramifications of that reality for the lives of women, particularly the most marginalized women in society. The prison setting must provide a safe and positive environment in which a relational, rehabilitative, holistic, and individualized approach can be achieved that recognizes and responds to the unique needs of women. Treating women with respect, listening to them to understand the complexities of their lives, and then responding with compassion and real support would provide a profoundly different future for incarcerated women than is provided by current practices. Many lives, both of the women themselves and of their families, are at stake.

References

Adoptions and Safe Families Act of 1997. (PL 105-89, Nov. 19, 1997).

Alexander, M. (2010). *The new Jim Crow: Mass incarceration in the age of colorblindness.* New York: The New Press.

Andrews, D. A., & Bonta, J. (2010). *The psychology of criminal conduct* (5th ed.). New Providence, NJ: Anderson.

Arditti, J. A., & Few, A. L. (2006). Mothers' reentry into family life following incarceration. *Criminal Justice Policy Review, 17,* 103–123.

Armstrong, G. S., & Griffin, M. L. (2007). The effect of local life circumstances on victimization of drug-involved women. *Justice Quarterly, 24,* 80–105.

Bastick, M., & Townhead, L. (2008, June). *Women in prison: A commentary on the UN Standard Minimum Rules for the Treatment of Prisoners.* New York: Quaker United Nations Office.

Belknap, J. (2006). *The invisible woman: Gender, crime, and justice* (3rd ed.). Cincinnati, OH: Wadsworth.

Bhavnani, K. K., & Davis, A. Y. (2000). Women in prison: Researching race in three national contexts. In F. W. Twine & J. Warren (Eds.), *Racing research, researching race: Methodological dilemmas in critical race studies* (pp. 227–246). New York: New York University Press.

Blackburn, A. G., Mullings, J. L., & Marquart, J. W. (2008). Sexual assault in prison and beyond: Toward an understanding of lifetime sexual assault among incarcerated women. *The Prison Journal, 88,* 351–377.

Block, C. R., Bokland, A. A. J., van der Werff, C., van Os, R., & Nieuwbeerta, P. (2010). Long-term patterns of offending in women. *Feminist Criminology, 5,* 73–107.

Bloom, B., & Covington, S. (2009). Addressing the mental health needs of women offenders. In R. L. Gido & L. P. Dalley (Eds.), *Women's mental health issues across the criminal justice system* (pp. 160–176). Upper Saddle River, NJ: Prentice Hall.

Bloom, B., Owen, B., & Covington, S. (2003). *Gender responsive strategies: Research, practice, and guiding principles for women offenders.* Washington, DC: National Institute of Justice.

Bloom, B., Owen, B., & Covington, S. (2004). Women offenders and the gendered effects of public policy. *Review of Policy Research, 21*(1), 31–48.

Borrill, J., Burnett, R., Atkins, R., Miller, S., Briggs, D., Weaver, T., & Maden, A. (2003). Patterns of self-mutilation and attempted suicide among White and Black/mixed race female prisoners. *Criminal Behavior and Mental Health, 13*, 229–240.

Burgess-Proctor, A. (2006). Intersections of race, class, gender, and crime: Future directions for feminist criminology. *Feminist Criminology, 1*, 27–47.

Calhoun, S., Messina, N., Cartier, J., & Torrs, S. (2010). Implementing gender-responsive treatment for women in prison: Client and staff perspectives. *Federal Probation, 74*(3), 27–33.

Celinska, K., & Siegel, J. A. (2010). Mothers in trouble: Coping with actual or pending separation from children due to incarceration. *The Prison Journal, 90*, 447–474.

Chesney-Lind, M. (1998). The forgotten offender: Women in prison: From partial justice to vengeful equity. *Corrections Today, 60*(7), 66–73.

Chesney-Lind, M. (2002). Criminalizing victimization: The unintended consequences of pro-arrest policies for girls and women. *Criminology and Public Policy, 2*, 81–90.

Cobbina, J. E. (2010). Reintegration success and failures: Factors impacting reintegration among incarcerated and formerly incarcerated women. *Journal of Offender Rehabilitation, 49*, 210–232.

Coughenour, J. C. (1995). Separate and unequal: Women in the federal criminal justice system. *Federal Sentencing Reporter, 8*, 142–144.

Crawford, C. (2000). Gender, race, and habitual offender sentencing in Florida. *Criminology, 38*, 263–280.

Crow, M. S., & Kunselman, J. C. (2009). Sentencing female drug offenders: Reexamining racial and ethnic disparities. *Women and Criminal Justice, 19*, 191–216.

DeGroot, A. S. (2001). HIV among incarcerated women: An epidemic behind the walls. *Corrections Today, 63*(1), 77–81.

Daly, K. (1992). Women's pathways to felony court: Feminist theories of lawbreaking and problems of representation. *Southern California Review of Law and Women's Studies, 2*(1), 11–52.

Daly, K., & Chesney-Lind, M. (1988). Feminism and criminology. *Justice Quarterly, 5*, 497–538.

Davis, A. Y. (2003). *Are prisons obsolete?* New York, NY: Seven Stories Press.

Enos, S. (2001). *Mothering from the inside: Parenting in a women's prison.* Albany: State University of New York Press.

Faris, J., & Miller, J. (2010). Family matters: Perceptions of fairness among incarcerated women. *The Prison Journal, 90*, 139–160.

Ferraro, K. J., & Moe, A. M. (2003). Mothering, crime, and incarceration. *Journal of Contemporary Ethnography, 32*, 9–40.

Fournier, A. K., Hughes, M. E., Hurford, D. P., & Sainio, C. (2011). Investigating trauma history and related psychosocial deficits of women in prison: Implications for treatment and rehabilitation. *Women and Criminal Justice, 21*, 83–99.

Fox, J. G. (1988). Women in prison: A case study in the social reality of stress. In R. Johnson & H. Toch (Eds.), *The pains of imprisonment* (pp. 205–220). Prospect Heights, IL: Waveland Press.

Garcia, C. A., & Lane, J. (2010). Looking in the rearview mirror: What incarcerated women think girls need from the system. *Feminist Criminology, 5*, 227–243.

George, E. (2010). *A woman doing life: Notes from a prison for women.* New York: Oxford University Press.

Gendreau, P., & Andrews, D. A. (1994). *Correctional Program Assessment Inventory.* St. John, New Brunswick, Canada: University of New Brunswick.

Gendreau, P., Little, T., & Goggin, C. (1996). A meta-analysis of the predictors of adult offender recidivism: What works! *Criminology, 34*, 575–608.

Gilbert, E. (2001). Women, race, and criminal justice processing. In C. Renzetti & L. Goodstein (Eds.), *Women, crime, and criminal justice: Original feminist readings* (pp. 222–231). Los Angeles: Roxbury.

Gilfus, M. E. (1992). From victims to survivors to offenders: Women's routes of entry and immersion into street crime. *Women and Criminal Justice, 4*, 63–90.

Gover, A., Perez, D. M., & Jennings, W. G. (2008). Gender differences in factors contributing to institutional misconduct. *The Prison Journal, 88*, 378–403.

Griffin, T., & Wooldredge, J. (2006). Sex-based differences in felony dispositions before versus after sentencing reform in Ohio. *Criminology, 44*, 893–923.

Guerino, P., Harrison, P. M., & Sabol, W. J. (2011). *Prisoners in 2010.* Washington, DC: U.S. Department of Justice, Bureau of Justice Statistics.

Hagan J., & Coleman, J. P. (2001). Returning captives of the American War on Drugs: Issues of community and family reentry. *Crime and Delinquency, 47*, 352–367.

Hannah-Moffat, K. (1999). Moral agent or actuarial subject: Risk and Canadian women's imprisonment. *Theoretical Criminology, 3*, 363–385.

Hannah-Moffat, K. (2004). Losing ground: Gendered knowledge, parole risk, and responsibility. *Social Politics, 11*, 363–385.

Hardyman, P. L., & Van Voorhis, P. (2004). *Developing gender-specific classification systems for women offenders.* Washington, DC: National Institute of Corrections.

Hoffman, H. C., Byrd, A. L., & Knightlinger, A. M. (2010). Prison programs and services for incarcerated parents and their underage children: Results from a national survey of correctional facilities. *The Prison Journal, 90*, 397–416.

Holsinger, K., & Van Voorhis, P. (2005). Examining gender inequities in classification systems: Missouri's development of a gender-responsive assessment instrument. *Women, Girls and Criminal Justice, 6*(3), 33–34, 44–47.

Holtfreter, K., & Morash, M. (2003). The needs of women offenders: Implications for correctional programming. *Women and Criminal Justice, 14*, 137–160.

Irwin, J., and Owen, B. (2005). Harm and the contemporary prison. In A. Liebling & S. Maruna (Eds.), *The effects of imprisonment* (pp. 94–118). Cullompton, Devon, UK: Willan.

James, D., & Glaze, L. (2006). *Mental health problems of prison and jail inmates.* Washington, DC: U.S. Department of Justice, Bureau of Justice Statistics.

Jordan, B., Schlenger, W., Fairbank, J., & Caddell, J. (1996). Prevalence of psychiatric disorders among incarcerated women. *Archives of General Psychiatry, 53*, 1048–1060.

Kennon, S. S., Mackintosh, V. H., & Myers, B. J. (2009). Parenting education for incarcerated mothers. *The Journal of Correctional Education, 60*, 10–30.

Kruttschnitt, C., & Gartner, R. (2003). Women's imprisonment. *Crime and Justice, 30*, 1–81.

Lamb, W. (2003). *Couldn't keep it to myself: Testimonies from our imprisoned sisters.* New York: HarperCollins.

Lamb, W. (2007). *I'll fly away: Further testimonials from the women of York prison.* New York: HarperCollins.

Levi, R., & Waldman, A. (2011). *Inside this place, not of it: Narratives from women's prisons.* New York: McSweeneys.

Mauer, M., & Huling, T. (1995). *Young Black Americans and the criminal justice system: Five years later.* Washington, DC: The Sentencing Project.

McDaniels, C., & Belknap, J. (2008). The extensive sexual violation and sexual abuse histories of incarcerated women. *Violence Against Women, 14*, 1090–1127.

McDonald, D. (2008). Gender-responsive treatment and the need to examine female inmates' lives in prison and prior to prison. *Corrections Compendium, 33*(6), 7–12, 29–30.

Mumola, C. J. (2000). *Incarcerated parents and their children.* Washington, DC: U.S. Department of Justice, Bureau of Justice Statistics.

Mumola, C. J. & Karberg, J. C. (2006). *Drug use and dependence, state and federal prisoners, 2004.* Washington, DC: U.S. Department of Justice, Bureau of Justice Statistics.

Muscat, B. T. (2008, November). *Violence and safety programs in women's prisons and jails: Addressing prevention, intervention and treatment* (NIJ Award # 2006-RP-BX-0016). Retrieved from Gendered Violence and Safety: A Contextual Approach to Improving Security in Women's Facilities. Retrieved May 11, 2012, https://www.ncjrs.gov/pdffiles1/nij/grants/225342.pdf

Owen, B. (1998). *"In the mix": Struggle and survival in a women's prison.* Albany: State University of New York Press.

Poehlmann, J. (2005). Representations of attachment relationships in children of incarcerated mothers. *Child Development, 76*, 579–696.

Pollack, S. (2007). "I'm just not good in relationships": Victimization discourses and the gendered regulation of criminalized women. *Feminist Criminology, 2*, 158–174.

Pollock, J. M. (1986). *Sex and supervision: Guarding male and female inmates.* New York: Greenwood.

Proctor, J. (2009). The impact imprisonment has on women's health and health care from the perspective of female inmates in Kansas. *Women and Criminal Justice, 19*, 1–36.

Radosh, P. F. (2002). Reflections on women's crime and mothers in prison: A peacemaking approach. *Crime and Delinquency, 48*, 300–315.

Rafter, N. (1990). *Partial justice: Women, prisons, and social control.* New Brunswick, NJ: Transaction Books.

Rathbone, C. (2006). *A world apart: Women, prison, and life behind bars.* New York: Random House.

Reynolds, T. (2010). A formerly incarcerated woman takes on policy. *Dialectic Anthropology, 34*, 453–457.

Richie, B. E. (2001). Challenges incarcerated women face as they return to their communities: Findings from life history interviews. *Crime and Delinquency 47*, 368–389.

Robinson, C. R., Lowenkamp, C. T., Holsinger, A. M., VanBenschoten, S., Alexander, M., & Oleson, J. C. (2012). A random study of Staff Training Aimed at Reducing Re-arrest (STARR): Using core correctional practices in probation interactions. *Journal of Crime and Justice, 35*, 167–188.

Roe-Sepowitz, D. (2007). Characteristics and predictors of self-mutilation: A study of incarcerated women. *Criminal Behaviour and Mental Health, 17*, 312–321.

Salvi, S. (2007). *Women behind bars: The crisis of women in the U.S. prison system.* Emeryville, CA: Seal Press.

Samuels, P., & Mukamal, D. (2004). *After prison: Roadblocks to reentry.* New York: Legal Action Center.

Sandifer, J. L. (2008). Evaluating the efficacy of a parenting program for incarcerated mothers. *The Prison Journal, 88*, 423–445.

The Sentencing Project. (2007, May). *Women in the criminal justice system: Briefing sheets.* Washington, DC: Author.

Severson, M., Berry, M., & Postmus, J. (2007). Risks and needs: Factors that predict women's incarceration and inform service planning. In R. Sheehan, G. McIvor, & C. Trotter (Eds.), *What works with women offenders* (pp. 61–90). Cullompton, Devon, UK: Willan.

Snell, T. L. (1994). *Survey of prison inmates, 1991: Women in prison.* Washington, DC: Government Printing Office.

Snyder, Z. K. (2009). Keeping families together: The importance of maintaining mother-child contact for incarcerated women. *Women and Criminal Justice, 19*, 37–59.

Sokoloff, N. J. (2005). Women prisoners at the dawn of the 21st century. *Women and Criminal Justice, 16*, 127–137.

Teplin, L., Abram, K., & McClellan, G. (1996). Prevalence of psychiatric disorders among incarcerated women: 1. Pretrial detainees. *Archives of General Psychiatry, 53*, 505–512.

Van Voorhis, P., Pealer, J., Spiropoulis, G., & Sutherland, J. (2001). *Classification of women offenders: A national assessment of current practices and the experience of 3 states.* Cincinnati, OH: University of Cincinnati, The Center for Criminal Justice Research.

Vogelvang, B. (2012). *A communication model for offender supervision: Eight steps to make sense of science in a street-level dialogue.* Den Bosch, The Netherlands: Avans University of Applied Science.

Western, B., & Pettit, B. (2010). Incarceration and social inequality. *Daedalus, 139*(3), 8–19.

Whitehead, J. C. (2007). Feminist prison activism: An assessment of empowerment. *Feminist Theory, 8*, 299–314.

Young, D. S., & Mattucci, R. F. (2006). Enhancing the vocational skills of incarcerated women through a plumbing maintenance program. *The Journal of Correctional Education, 57*, 126–140.

Zaitzow, B. H. (2003). "Doing gender" in women's prison. In B. H. Zaitzow & J. Thomas (Eds.) *Women in prison: Gender and social control* (pp. 21–38). Boulder, CO: Lynne Rienner.

6

The Racially Just Prison

Craig Hemmens and
Mary K. Stohr

Editors' Introduction

American prisons and jails were shaped by racial and class prejudices from their inception. In colonial days, if offenders could pay for their incarceration, and few people of color could at the start of this country, then their circumstances were materially different while incarcerated and they were less likely even to be incarcerated. Before the Civil War in the 1860s, skin color mattered and would determine whether and how someone was incarcerated. Thus, if you were an African American man or woman, and residing in a southern or border state, it might mean that you were kept enslaved, or were re-enslaved, in the "free community" so that your labor would not be lost by your owners; if in a free state, you might be incarcerated, but in inferior conditions. For a person of color before the Civil Rights Movement of the 1960s in any part of this country, but particularly in the South, it might mean that your housing, work, and general treatment would be inferior to that of your White counterparts. It might also mean that on your way to incarceration, you suffered mistreatment and discrimination at the hands of racist police or court personnel.

Even today in some states, as Craig Hemmens and Mary Stohr describe in the following chapter, there is racial (including ethnic) segregation based on gang affiliation. Sometimes this segregation is by choice and sometimes it is imposed by staff to avoid altercations between warring gangs. Latinos separate into different gangs than African Americans and Whites; even within these groupings there are rival gangs aligned to fight for power and position in large and violent prisons of some states. In other states, usually smaller and less racially and ethnically diverse, the prisons are not so taxed with a formal segregation, though informal racial and ethnic division may simmer just beneath the surface. The difference in racial and ethnic makeup between the staff and inmates serves only to exacerbate such tensions in all prisons.

By the time this book is published, it will have been 50 years since Martin Luther King, Jr. delivered his "I Have a Dream" speech in 1963 on the steps of the Lincoln Memorial in Washington, DC (available at http://www.huffingtonpost.com/ 2012/01/16/i-have-a-dream-speech-text-martin-luther-king-jr_n_1207734.html). In that historic speech, Dr. King spoke of a society where there was racial justice and all were treated equally, a society free of racial segregation: "Now is the time to rise from the dark and desolate valley of segregation to the sunlit path of racial justice." The segregation he spoke of was in housing, schools, and other public and private facilities in the free community, but we might fruitfully apply it to prisons. As long as there is segregation, even when based on the justification of "security," there will be differential treatment accorded the racial and ethnic groups, and, just as importantly, there will be little chance to bridge the chasm in understanding that separates these groups in prisons. As the authors of this chapter note, it almost goes without saying that we cannot have racially just prisons until we have a racially just society, or what Dr. King dreamed of. And there is much progress that can still be made in that direction in prisons. The authors of this chapter offer some suggestions to move us closer to that dream of racial justice that Reverend King articulated 50 years ago.

While the first American prison did not open until 1790, racism in America has existed for much longer. Indeed, American history is dominated by race relations. Slavery was a major issue during the debates over the ratification of the Constitution and eventually resulted in the Civil War. The end of slavery did not mean the elimination of racism, however. The failure of Reconstruction and the passage of Black Codes and Jim Crow laws in the South kept the race question alive. Southern leaders developed the doctrine of "separate but equal" as a means of controlling Blacks (Ayres, 1984; Williamson, 1984), a policy endorsed by the U.S. Supreme Court in the infamous *Plessey v. Ferguson* (1896) decision.

Prisons have long mirrored other social institutions. Segregation was the norm in most prisons, including many in the nominally desegregated North, and racism was as prevalent inside the walls as outside. For much of the 20th century, prison demographics also mirrored those of the free world, with the inmate population being largely White. Beginning in the 1960s, prisons began to see an influx of Black and Hispanic inmates. Today, the prison is one of the few social institutions in which African Americans (and other minorities) are in the majority and, in some ways, exert dominance. This disquieting reality has led scholars such as Loïc Wacquant (2001) to argue that the prison is an extension of the urban ghetto—two places in which Blacks are concentrated and controlled. Even if this claim is hyperbolic, it illuminates the disproportionate confinement of people of color. In this chapter, we document the extent of racial inequality in imprisonment in the United

States, the history of racial segregation in prison, and some of the consequences of this inequality on inmates and staff. We then explore ways both to lessen the imprisonment of minorities and to develop a prison environment that is racially sensitive and takes racial justice seriously.

Racial Inequality in American Prisons

HISTORICAL BACKGROUND

American prisons have been shaped from the beginning by race as they were created in the context of a racist society. From the very founding of the United States, slavery, the ultimate imprisonment, was reserved for people from Africa or of African descent. Enslaved people had no liberty and no rights, and their movements were completely controlled—all of which pretty much describes the lot of prisoners. As an indication of how closely the circumstances of slaves and prisoners resembled each other in the eyes of policy makers, the Thirteenth Amendment to the Constitution (ratified in 1865) outlawed slavery and involuntary servitude, except in the case of prisoners convicted of a crime. This meant that prisoners were considered slaves at this time. This status was reinforced by Virginia's Court of Appeals in *Ruffin v. Commonwealth* (1871), when the court noted that inmates were "slaves of the state." As a consequence, inmates had no right to seek legal redress in courts. This led to the development of the so-called hands-off doctrine, wherein courts left the operation and oversight of prisons to the executive branch (e.g., governors in states and the president for the national government).

The difference between slaves and prisoners, however, was that slaves had done nothing legally wrong to merit their status as slaves, whereas inmates in prisons of the time had been convicted of a crime. Moreover, in the case of slavery, private individuals directly, as opposed to the government in the case of prison inmates, deprived slaves of their rights and liberties. Admittedly, this latter difference was sometimes difficult to discern in the case of both slaves and inmates as the government legally sanctioned slavery, and private individuals were involved in "leasing" or contracting for the labor of prison inmates, from government operated prisons, to work on their farms or to make their products.

The history of America also includes the imprisonment of other racial and ethnic groups solely due to their racial or ethnic status rather than any criminal offending. American Indians, or Native Americans, were forcibly removed to reservations (which in effect were much like correctional institutions) in the 1800s so that their land might be confiscated by European immigrants. Reservations were operated by the federal government, and though their inhabitants were mostly free to roam within the reservation boundaries, movement outside of those boundaries was controlled and often prohibited (Mann, 2006). Japanese American citizens, in 1942 and during World War II, were another racial and ethnic group that was forced into prison-like facilities—so-called internment camps, which were much like reservations and prisons—solely for their race and ancestral nationality. Their land and property were also confiscated, and their movement and freedom in, and from, the camps was limited (Mercier, 2010).

The first American prison (some scholars would argue it was the first fully developed prison anywhere) was the Walnut Street Jail (partially modified to become a prison), whose prison section was opened in 1790, in Philadelphia, Pennsylvania. Prisons in other states were built shortly thereafter. Notably, in the late 1700s when a section of the Walnut Street Jail was refashioned into a prison, slavery was legal in the United States, though some states and localities in the North outlawed it within their boundaries even before the ratification of the Thirteenth Amendment.

As slave owners would be deprived of the labor of their property should Black men and women be incarcerated, early American prisons, especially in states where slavery was legal, were mostly populated by Whites (including the foreign born), free Blacks, or other non-Whites. In her research on historical prison use for women in the border state of Maryland from 1812 to 1869, Young (2001) found that foreign-born Whites (Irish and German) and free Blacks were more likely to be incarcerated than native White women, even before the Civil War. In the 1825 prisoners' list for Newgate Prison in Connecticut, the number of Blacks and Whites (based solely on complexion) was 78 (67%) and 39 (33%), respectively (Phelps, 1996, p. 108). Connecticut gradually began to eliminate slavery as early as 1784, whereas Maryland did not until the Civil War (Menschel, 2001). As a more northern state than Maryland, and in a state where slavery was illegal (though some were still enslaved there), it is likely that many of the Blacks mentioned in Newgate prison were free rather than enslaved prior to their incarceration. In fact, the Maryland legislature in 1858 passed a law that provided that free Blacks convicted of some crimes be subject to public sale rather than imprisonment, a factor that may have reduced their numbers in prisons (Young, 2001).

According to a first-hand account by three White men sentenced to the Missouri State Prison in 1841 for trying to help slaves escape to free states, the conditions for all in the prison were abhorrent, but were particularly hard for the Black men who were subjected to even more abuse and degradation than the Whites (Thompson, 1847). Similarly, in his research on the Parchman Prison in Mississippi, Oshinsky (1996) found that after the Civil War, Blacks were arrested and imprisoned for even minor offenses and forced to work in segregated prisons on prison plantations or on plantations of Southern farmers; sometimes these were the same plantations they had been imprisoned on as slaves before the war. The conditions for both Blacks and Whites in the Parchman Prison were horrific, but materially worse for the Black men incarcerated there.

THE CIVIL RIGHTS MOVEMENT IN PRISONS

Because of the disparity in treatment between Whites and minorities in prisons, it is hardly surprising that prisons were a crucible for change as regards prisoners' rights. As indicated by *Ruffin v. Commonwealth* (1871), courts were reluctant to engage in an area of administration that they thought belonged to the executive branch of government. As Belbot and Hemmens (2010, p. 4) note in their book *The Legal Rights of the Convicted,* "Federal judges who reviewed lawsuits filed by state prison inmates were particularly wary of intruding on the business of state governments." By the time of the Civil Rights Movement in the 1960s and early 1970s, the federal courts had been incorporating (or applying) many of the civil liberties delineated in the federal Constitution's Bill of Rights to state citizens appearing before state courts (via the Fourteenth Amendment's due process clause).

Civil liberties have to do with telling the government to stay out of the individual citizen's life; they caution the government with "shall nots" (e.g., limiting searches or prohibiting cruel and unusual punishment). Civil rights have to do with asking the government to respect and protect certain rights (e.g., voting rights or equal protection in hiring). Yet inmates, as slaves of the state, had no rights and were not considered citizens. This changed in the 20th century as inmates increasingly were given access to the courts, even the federal courts, and a shift really took hold when the United States Supreme Court issued the decision *Cooper v. Pate* (1964).

Dealing with the fundamental First Amendment right to practice religion free of government interference, and certainly affected by the increased incidence of the incarceration of Blacks, just as the Civil Rights Movement was heating up outside the prison walls, the *Cooper* decision changed everything. Cooper, an African American inmate of Illinois's Stateville prison, claimed his placement in administrative segregation was retribution because he wanted to practice his Muslim religion. He claimed he was denied access to the Koran and clergy. The Supreme Court determined that he had a right to access to the courts on this issue and to file an injunction to end his placement in administrative segregation. As a result of this case, the hands-off doctrine was weakened and a number of other issues for inmates were now matters for court consideration (e.g., searches, use of force, due process, conditions of confinement) (Belbot & Hemmens, 2010).

One should not take away from this discussion the belief that as a result of the Supreme Court decisions on these matters, inmates now possess the rights of regular citizens; nothing could be further from the truth (Rideau, 2010). In fact, the courts have determined that inmates still possess very few rights or liberties. All that happened with the prisoners' rights movement was a recognition that inmates are not slaves of the state and have a right to access to courts (though this has been restricted by recent Supreme Court decisions and federal legislation), and that they have some very basic rights to due process in some instances, and to decent accommodations, nutritional food, and freedom from excessive punishment or blatantly cruel treatment.

CURRENT RACIAL AND ETHNIC DIFFERENCES IN PRISON USE

Despite this progress in the protection of inmate rights and liberties, or at least the acknowledgment that prisoners might have some rights, the incarceration of African Americans, Latinos/Latinas, and other racial and ethnic minorities has increased exponentially over the last few decades. According to the latest available data (for year-end 2010) from the Bureau of Justice Statistics, Black, non-Hispanic males and females had imprisonment rates that were almost seven times and three times, respectively, higher than White non-Hispanic males and females (Guerino, Harrison, & Sabol, 2012, p. 7). Hispanic males and females were almost three times and two times, respectively, more likely to be incarcerated than Whites. And Black males and females were more than two and almost two times, respectively, more likely to be incarcerated than Hispanic males and females (Guerino et al., 2012, p. 27).

As of 2010, the federal prison population had continued to increase. At this time, however, the overall count of those incarcerated in the United States—including offenders imprisoned in half of the states—decreased for the first time since 1972 (Guerino et al., 2012, p. 1). Notably, 18% of state inmates and fully 51% of federal inmates were serving sentences for drug offenses in 2009 (Guerino et al., 2012, p. 1). These numbers, however, somewhat mask the changes in imprisonment by race and ethnicity between 2000 and 2010. During this decade, the total number of White and Hispanic inmates continued to increase, while the total number of Black inmates actually decreased slightly. Despite this slight decline in the number of Black inmates, Blacks and Hispanics remain disproportionately represented in inmate populations in state and federal correctional institutions.

Most commentators on this phenomenal increase in the imprisonment of minority group members over the past several decades blame the drug war and other harsh sentencing practices (Alexander, 2010; Lurigio & Loose, 2008). The practical effect of this war, as waged and funded by all presidents since Richard Nixon (with the exception of Jimmy Carter and up to and including President Obama), virtually all governors, most congressmen and -women and state legisla- tors, and the tough-on-crime legislation, has been to incarcerate an unprecedented number of minority men and women, particularly African Americans and Latinos/ Latinas. There are indications that the war might be waning in the states as eco- nomic concerns take precedence, evidence that incarceration has a negligible effect on crime (if not a criminogenic one) becomes common knowledge, and the public becomes more amenable to legalization and decriminalization of marijuana (Cullen, Jonson, & Nagin, 2011; Hogan, Garland, Wodahl, Hass, Stohr, & Lambert, 2012; Nagin, Cullen, & Jonson, 2009; Stohr & Walsh, 2012). But the drug war at the federal level is still being waged and incarceration at the federal level continues apace, though there have been decreases in some states.

While these data on late 20th century and early 21st century incarceration rates present a troubling picture of a racially unbalanced and unjust prison system, this is nothing new. American correctional history is replete with evidence of racist policies and practices, as the next section makes clear.

Racial Segregation in American Prisons: A Short History

In *Plessey v. Ferguson* (1896), the Supreme Court endorsed the Jim Crow policy of separation of the races—the doctrine of supposedly "separate but equal." This was used in virtually all public facilities, including prisons. White prisoners were kept in the penitentiary, while Black prisoners were utilized in the convict lease system outside the prison walls (Oshinsky, 1996; Taylor, 1993; Walker, 1988).

In 1954, in *Brown v. Board of Education*, the Supreme Court determined the doctrine of "separate but equal" in public schools was unconstitutional because it deprived Black children of equal educational opportunities and branded them with a badge of inferiority. The Supreme Court over the next decade consistently struck down segregation on the basis of race in a number of other public facilities.

As for prisons, beginning in the 1960s, federal courts began to discard the traditional hands-off doctrine and to examine critically the conditions of prison life. Finally, in the 1968 decision of *Lee v. Washington*, the Supreme Court declared that mandatory racial segregation in correctional facilities was unconstitutional. However, a concurring opinion suggested that, in limited circumstances, racial segregation might be permitted if necessary to maintain institutional security. Thus, although the high court voided official policies mandating racial segregation in correctional facilities, it left the door open for the use of racial segregation in circumstances where correctional administrators could show that institutional security necessitated it. The Court also neglected to address whether prison officials had an affirmative duty to integrate, rather than simply being prohibited from enforcing racial segregation. While *Lee* was supposed to mark the end of racial segregation in prisons, it left an opening for administrators to use race as a proxy for other issues, such as violence and, in the latter part of the 20th century, gang membership.

Racial tensions became a major security issue in the 1980s as inmate gangs formed along racial and ethnic lines (Rideau, 2010). A number of prison systems experienced significant increases in inmate-on-staff and inmate-on-inmate assaults, many of which were apparently racially motivated (Fong, 1990; Ralph, 1997). Prison administrators responded by separating warring gang factions (Fleisher & Decker, 2001). Given that gang membership is largely based on race, the practical result of these administrative actions was separation of the races, supposedly based not on the "natural" social inferiority of minority group members, but on gang membership.

Using race as a proxy for gang membership and as a justification for racial segregation was struck down by the Supreme Court in *Johnson v. California* (2005). In *Johnson*, the Court held that prisons must operate by the same rules as the wider society when it comes to the use of race—that prison administrators cannot use race to segregate inmates except under extraordinary circumstances to ensure the safety and security of inmates, staff, and institutions. According to the Court, "by insisting that inmates be housed only with other inmates of the same race, it is possible that prison officials will breed further hostility among prisoners and reinforce racial and ethnic divisions" (*Johnson v. California*, 2005).

Although the *Johnson* case dealt with California's practice of automatic, or mandatory, racial segregation, evidence suggests that California was not alone in the practice of racially segregating inmates. The reality is that the racial segregation of inmates continues in American prison systems to varying degrees. The best evidence on the extent of racial segregation in American prisons comes from a national survey of prison wardens in 2000. This study revealed that 4% of prison wardens reported that inmates are not racially integrated within cells. Another 45% of wardens reported that their department of corrections does not have an official policy of racially integrating inmates within cells (Henderson, Cullen, Carroll, & Feinberg, 2000). Almost 3% of wardens reported that inmates are not housed on racially integrated cellblocks. Moreover, nearly 60% of prison wardens revealed that inmates within their institutions could request an exemption from being integrated with an inmate of a different race, subject to the warden's discretion. Henderson and colleagues (2000) summarized the state of racial desegregation in American prisons by noting that "the racial integration of prison cells is largely left to the discretion of the prison warden"—and that among inmates sharing a cell in U.S. prisons, only 30% of these cells are integrated by race (Henderson et al., 2000, pp. 305–307).

While prison administrators in California and elsewhere have argued that inmates prefer segregated housing units, the support for this assertion is mixed. In a survey of 775 inmates just released from the Texas prison system, Hemmens and Marquart (1999) posed two questions specific to race relations and prison desegregation. First, the researchers asked the recently released inmates the extent to which they agreed with the statement that "race is a big problem in TDC" (the Texas Department of Corrections). Whites and Hispanics tended to agree or strongly agree with that statement, whereas Blacks tended to disagree that race was a big problem in the TDC. Second, the researchers sampled members to respond to the question of whether "allowing inmates of different races to live in separate living areas is a good idea." Overall, the recently released inmates tended to disagree that inmates of different races should be separated in living areas. Blacks were more likely to support an integrated housing policy than Whites or Hispanics, although the latter racial groups still leaned toward integrated housing.

While mandatory racial segregation is permissible in only the most extreme circumstances, there is evidence that it is still occurring as the result of habit or official acquiescence to inmate demands. This sort of "voluntary" racial segregation creates a dilemma for corrections officials. It is one thing to require desegregation; it is another thing altogether to mandate integration. This has proven difficult in the free world, and is even more difficult in the prison setting, given the intellectual, emotional, and social limitations of the inmate population.

Cases involving voluntary racial segregation are much more difficult to resolve than those involving official segregation policies. Many of the mandatory racial segregation polices are based on antiquated notions of racial inferiority or on the mere speculation that desegregation will inevitably lead to violence. But when there is clear evidence that inmates may prefer the company of those of like skin color, what are administrators to do? They are duty bound to respect the constitutional rights of inmates. This means that racial segregation is prohibited except in narrowly defined circumstances. Courts have upheld segregation after a prison riot, but little else.

Administrators may also have an affirmative duty to integrate, especially when there is a history of racial segregation within a particular institution. Supreme Court precedent in other areas, such as schools, holds that a history of discrimination mandates not just abrogation of official policies requiring segregation, but additionally imposes an affirmative duty to integrate, as a remedy for past injustices.

Coupled with the duty not to discriminate on the basis of race is the constitutional duty not to ignore dangers to inmates. The "deliberate indifference" standard requires prison administrators not choose to ignore potential dangers to inmates under their care and supervision. This requirement may come into play if an administrator requires integration when there is clear evidence that the result will be inmate violence.

Racism and American prisons have been linked since the early days of the United States. And while the form racism has taken has changed over time, it remains a concern today. But what are the effects of racist policies and practices on inmates and prison staff? And do these effects carry over to the outside world? In the next section we examine some of the consequences of racist prisons and policies.

Consequences of Disproportionate Minority Confinement: Inside and Outside Prison

That a disproportionate number of African Americans and Hispanics are incarcerated is clear. While the debate rages about the reasons for this, there is ample evidence that racism in its many forms is to blame for this phenomenon; in any case the fact remains that prisons are overpopulated by people of color. What impact does this disproportionate incarceration rate have on society? Here are just a few of the most serious consequences.

First, the high number of African American men in prison means there are high numbers of African American mothers raising their children without a father present. Inner-city African American communities already have a higher percentage of single-parent families, and the disproportionate incarceration of African American men contributes to this statistic. This has the effect of weakening African American communities (Clear, 2007; Woldoff & Washington, 2008).

Second, the enforcement of laws that have a disparate impact on minorities negatively affects individual defendants. For instance, the crack/powder cocaine disparity in sentencing has resulted in much harsher/longer prison sentences being given to African American drug possessors, as crack cocaine weighs significantly more than powder cocaine. Until recently, someone convicted of possessing 2 grams of crack cocaine received the same sentence as someone convicted at the federal level of possessing 150 grams of powder cocaine, a disparity of 75 to 1. While this disparity was reduced in 2012 to 18 to 1 (similar to the modified federal sentencing guidelines), an enormous difference remains. This is a prime example of modern racism, where racial disparities are created or maintained through "colorblind" policies and practices—what some have referred to as the "new Jim Crow" (Alexander, 2010).

Third, the imposition of mandatory sentences and sentence enhancements based on behaviors that are strongly correlated with race result in African

Americans being treated differently by the court system than Whites (Case, 2008). Research indicates that Blacks are more likely to receive sentence enhancements and Whites more likely to receive downward departures (Schlesinger, 2011; Wang & Mears, 2010; Warren, Chiricos, & Bales, 2012). An example is the imposition of life without parole for offenses committed by juveniles. One out of every eight African American juveniles convicted of murder is sentenced to life without parole, while only one out of every 13 White juveniles convicted of murder is sentenced to life without parole (Racial Inequality in Youth Sentencing, 2012).

Fourth, the effects of incarceration do not end upon release. In virtually every state, a felony conviction results in some degree of disenfranchisement and loss of other civil rights (Uggen, Shannon, & Manza, 2012); in addition there are the so-called collateral consequences of a felony conviction, which include difficulty in finding gainful employment with a criminal record (Pager, Western, & Sugie, 2009) and greater health inequalities (Sykes & Piquero, 2009). Furthermore, families are put at risk, not only during incarceration, when parents are limited in their opportunities to see their children, but afterward; there is research that indicates incarcerated and released felons are less engaged with their children (Woldoff & Washington, 2008).

Beyond the high levels of imprisonment and the effect on society, what does this mean for those in prison? A number of issues are associated with racially unjust prisons. Three merit consideration. First, segregation in prison (Trulson, Marquart, Hemmens, & Carroll, 2008), whether mandatory or voluntary, sends a message that the races are in some way different and that this difference requires separation. There is no empirical evidence to support this assertion, and to either enforce or simply allow segregation is to give in to the ghosts of the past. Second, victimization in prison varies by race (Steiner & Wooldredge, 2009; Wooldredge & Steiner, 2012), and this differential may be related to racist beliefs that are acted upon by inmates with negative feelings about members of other races and ethnicities. Inmate victimization is a serious issue in prisons, and prison administrators are responsible for making prisons reasonably safe. If racist beliefs increase the likelihood of victimization, then steps must be taken to change the policies and practices that either give rise to or enable these beliefs. Third, inmates are not the only ones who suffer from racially unjust prisons; so too do correctional staff. As noted above, correctional work forces were, historically, overwhelmingly White (and male). Racist beliefs limited the opportunities for minorities to work in prisons or, once employed, to advance through the ranks (Ayres, 1984; Oshinsky, 1996). While the number of minority employees has increased in the past quarter century, in many prison systems there is still a long way to go.

A Racially Just Prison

What would a racially just prison look like? Different from prisons of today, to be sure. Possible to create? If we did not think so, we would not have written this chapter. That does not mean it will be easy. Here are some proposals for creating a racially just prison:

RACIAL INTEGRATION

Segregation, either by law or custom, is unacceptable. It sends the message that the races are different and cannot live together. Such outmoded ways of thinking must not be allowed to affect how prisons are operated or structured. Yes, race relations in prison are a troublesome issue. This is no surprise, given the poor history of race relations in society, generally, and the limited educational and social development of the inmate population. Requiring prison administrators to do what society has been largely unable to do, in the closed and often violent world of the prison, no doubt places increased pressure on the prison. Nevertheless, we must strive to create the society we envision in dreams. Eliminating mandatory segregation policies and practices is not enough—institutions must take affirmative steps to integrate every aspect of the prison, from cells to workplaces and recreation areas to the cafeteria and programming areas.

While racial segregation can be rationalized as a matter of safety, it is really only a short-term solution to crisis situations. As Robert Johnson (1996) points out, the effectiveness of racial segregation as a tool for managing prisoner behavior has been questioned and has the negative effect of reinforcing racial stereotypes. The vast majority of prisoners are released back into society, and the manner in which inmates are treated in prison influences their post-prison experience. Corrections officials must take the lead in breaking the vicious cycle of hatred and intolerance.

Voluntary racial segregation policies lend credibility to an unacceptable belief. Acquiescing to unreasonable inmate demands weakens both the moral and actual authority of corrections administrators. If rehabilitation is a meaningful component of the prison experience, then teaching tolerance and racial equality is an important activity. Failing to look beyond race in making prison management decisions is not only poor management and reflective of a simplistic view of the world as black and white (pun intended), but it is also unconstitutional, and, most significantly, immoral.

Those inmates who threaten or practice violence in an effort to prevent integration must be dealt with, rather than letting fear of their response to integration prevent integration. The response to violent reactions to integration should be to punish the violent, not give in to their demands. If the American public and political leaders had done that during the Civil Rights Movement, we would have given in to the likes of infamous racists "Bull" Connor (Birmingham, Alabama, Public Safety Commissioner) and Arkansas governor Orval Faubus. This is unacceptable in modern society. As a means of ensuring maximum integration of prisons, corrections officials should be required to document their efforts to integrate their facilities at all levels.

PROGRAMMING/TREATMENT

If prisons are to be places of correction and treatment and not just warehouses, educational and treatment programming must be readily and widely available. Historically, this has not been the case. After the Civil War, Southern prisons were largely reserved for Whites, and Blacks were sent out to work in convict work camps run by private parties looking for cheap labor (Oshinsky, 1996; Taylor, 1993). During the Progressive Era, many prisons sought to implement educational and rehabilitation programming in prisons. These programs were limited to only some inmates in the prisons, and in many instances Blacks and other minorities were excluded (Walker, 1988). In the latter part of the 20th century, as prison populations exploded, correctional programming was actually reduced. Claims that such programming either did not work or was cost prohibitive (Lipton, Martinson, & Wilks, 1975; Martinson, 1974) led to a dramatic reduction in opportunities for inmate rehabilitation. As prison systems moved to increased use of close custody and so-called super-max prisons, programming was in some institutions virtually eliminated.

Interestingly, the decrease in inmate programming opportunities took place at the same time that prisons were experiencing a dramatic increase in the number of minority inmates. Consequently, minority inmates suffered most dramatically from the reduction in programming opportunities. A racially just prison requires that all inmates have the opportunity to engage in programming that will both improve their chances for social and economic success upon release and reduce the likelihood that they will recidivate. A prison without equal opportunity to improve one's lot in life is a racially unjust prison.

VISITATION

As prison systems expanded in the 1980s and 1990s, the politics of prison siting (Martin, 2000) led to a tremendous increase in the number of prisons located in rural areas. While some prisons have historically been located in rural communities, during the latter part of the 20th century this became the norm. Rural communities sought prisons as means of improving the economy, and rural land was often cheaper, providing prison system administrators and state legislators with dual motivation to site new prisons in rural areas.

As the increase in prison population was based in large part upon an increase in the number of African American men from urban areas being sentenced to prison, the result was a tremendous increase in the number of minorities who were incarcerated in prisons often quite far removed from their homes. This meant that, in many instances, families of inmates could not afford to travel to visit. Research has shown that the negative effect of incarceration is worse for African Americans than it is for Whites, and that incarceration weakens the parent-child relationship and family bonds in general (Mumola, 2000; Woldoff & Washington, 2008). Prison siting and its disparate impact on minorities is another example of color-blind racism. A racially just prison is one that eliminates the disparate impact on incarceration. This requires that inmates be housed in prisons near their homes so that family members have relatively easy access for visits. Additionally, because personal interaction is crucial to developing and maintaining familial and parental bonds, visitation polices must be reconfigured to provide for maximal visitation opportunities, opportunities that include all of the familial activities. Inmates must be able to spend time with and have personal contact with family members. This obviously has significant implications for prison security, but the fact that it is difficult to do is not justification for denying a child meaningful access to his or her parent.

STAFFING

While the focus of this chapter has been on the impact of prison on inmates, that is only a part of the equation. Staff members "live" in prison as well. A racially just prison is one in which staff members are treated the same regardless of race. Historically, prison staffs have been dominated by White men. Only recently has this begun to change. Today, minorities make up approximately 25% of prison staff. Clearly, progress has been made. Equally as clear, there remains work to be done.

One of the unintended consequences of siting so many prisons in rural areas is the limitation on opportunities for minorities, who are disproportionately located in urban areas, to seek employment in prisons near where they live. Sending minorities from urban areas to prisons in rural areas that are staffed largely by Whites is a prescription for the continuation of racial stereotypes. A racially just prison requires equal hiring and promotion opportunities for minorities.

SENTENCING POLICIES

While this chapter is focused on the changes needed to create a racially just prison, correctional institutions do not operate in a vacuum. For America to create racially just prisons, we must deal with the criminal justice system policies, practices, and laws that create the inmate population. So long as a disparate number of African Americans and Hispanics are being incarcerated, prisons are, by definition, places of racial inequality. We must, first and foremost, eliminate the racist policies and practices that send minorities to prison in disproportionate numbers. Even if these policies and practices may be color-blind by design, they remain unacceptable so long as they have differential racial impacts.

Prisons should be more than warehouses. They should be places of corrections, of treatment and rehabilitation, and of education. For much of our history, we have been content to incarcerate those who have violated the law but had little regard for the morality of either the law or the sentence associated with it. And once offenders are incarcerated, we have given little consideration to their well-being in prison, or the impact of incarceration on them after release. As Blacks and, increasingly, Hispanics are incarcerated at rates much higher than that for Whites, this represents racial injustice. While state-endorsed segregation and racism are things of the past, our prisons serve to create significant racially disparate outcomes. And these racial disparities carry with them the unintended and generally hidden cost of worsening existing racial divisions (Unnever, Cullen, & Jonson, 2008). How can we expect minorities to view the criminal justice system as legitimate when they see every day in their own communities the differential impact? Racism in any form is unacceptable; state policies and institutions that contribute to the racial divide must not be allowed to continue. We must and can do better.

References

Alexander, M. (2010). *The new Jim Crow: Mass incarceration in the age of colorblindness.* New York, NY: New Press.

Ayres, E. L. (1984). *Vengeance and justice: Crime and punishment in the nineteenth century American south.* New York, NY: Oxford University Press.

Belbot, B., & Hemmens, C. (2010). *The legal rights of the convicted.* El Paso, TX: LFB Scholarly Publishing.

Brown v. Board of Education, 347 U.S. 483 (1954).

Case, P. (2008). The relationship of race and criminal behavior: Challenging cultural explanations for a structural problem. *Critical Sociology, 34,* 213–238.

Clear, T. R. (2007). *Imprisoned communities: How mass incarceration makes disadvantaged neighborhoods worse.* New York, NY: Oxford University Press.

Cooper v. Pate, 378 U.S. 546 (1964).

Cullen, F. T., Jonson, C. L., & Nagin, D. S. (2011). Prisons do not reduce recidivism: The high cost of ignoring science. *The Prison Journal, 91,* 48S–65S.

Fleisher, M., & Decker, S. (2001). An overview of the challenge of prison gangs. *Corrections Management Quarterly, 5,* 1–9.

Fong, R. S. (1990). The organizational structure of prison gangs: A Texas case study. *Federal Probation, 54,* 36–43.

Guerino, P., Harrison, P. M., & Sabol, W. J. (2012). *Prisoners in 2010.* Washington, DC: U.S. Department of Justice, Bureau of Justice Statistics.

Hemmens, C., & Marquart, J. (1999). The impact of inmate characteristics on perceptions of race relations in prison. *International Journal of Offender Therapy and Comparative Criminology, 43,* 230–247.

Henderson, M. L., Cullen, F. T., Carroll, L., & Feinberg, W. (2000). Race, rights, and order in prison: A national survey of wardens on the racial integration of prison cells. *The Prison Journal, 80,* 295–308.

Hogan, N., Garland, B., Wodahl, E., Hass, A., Stohr, M. K., & Lambert, E. (2012, March). Closing the iron bar inn: The issue of decarceration and its possible effects on inmates, staff and communities. Paper presented at the annual Academy of Criminal Justice Sciences Meeting, New York, New York.

Johnson, R. (1996). *Hard time: Understanding and reforming the prison.* Belmont, CA: Wadsworth.

Johnson v. California, 545 U.S. 162 (2005).

Lee v. Washington, 390 U.S. 333 (1968).

Lipton, D., Martinson, R., & Wilks, J. (1975). *The effectiveness of correctional treatment.* New York, NY: Praeger.

Lurigio, A., & Loose, P. (2008). The disproportionate incarceration of African Americans for drug offenses: The national and Illinois perspective. *Journal of Ethnicity in Criminal Justice, 6,* 223–247.

Mann, C. C. (2006). *1491: New revelations of the Americas before Columbus.* New York, NY: Vintage Books.

Martin, R. (2000). Community perceptions about prison construction: Why not in my backyard? *The Prison Journal, 80,* 265–294.

Martinson, R. (1974). What works? Questions and answers about prison reform. *The Public Interest, 33,* 22–54.

Menschel, D. (2001). Abolition without deliverance: The law of Connecticut slavery 1784–1848. *The Yale Law Journal, 111,* 183–222.

Mercier, M. (2010). *Japanese Americans in the Columbia River basin.* Retrieved August 1, 2012, from http://archive.vancouver.wsu.edu/crbeha/jrojteam

Mumola, C. (2000). *Incarcerated parents and their children.* Washington, DC: U.S. Department of Justice, Bureau of Justice Statistics.

Nagin, D. S., Cullen, F. T., & Johnson, C. L. (2009). Imprisonment and reoffending. In M. Tonry (Ed.), *Crime and justice: An annual review of research* (Vol. 38, pp. 115–200). Chicago, IL: University of Chicago Press.

Oshinsky, D. M. (1996). *Worse than slavery: Parchman Farm and the ordeal of Jim Crow justice.* New York, NY: Free Press.

Pager, D., Western, B., & Sugie, N. (2009). Sequencing disadvantage: Barriers to employment facing young Black and White men with criminal records. *The Annals of the American Academy of Political and Social Science, 623,* 195–213.

Phelps, R. (1996). *Newgate of Connecticut: Its origin and early history.* Camden, ME: Picton Press.

Plessey v. Ferguson, 163 U.S. 537 (1896).

Racial Inequality in Youth Sentencing. (2012). *The Campaign for the Fair Sentencing of Youth.* Retrieved August 1, 2012, from http://www.endjlwop.org/the-issue/advocacy-resource-bank/racial--inequality-in-youth-sentencing/

Ralph, P. H. (1997). From self-preservation to organized crime: The evolution of inmate gangs. In J. W. Marquart & J. R. Sorenson (Eds.), *Correctional contexts* (pp. 182–186). Los Angeles: Roxbury.

Rideau, W. (2010). *In the place of justice: A story of punishment and deliverance.* New York, NY: Knopf.

Ruffin v. Commonwealth, 62 Va. 790 (1871).

Schlesinger, T. (2011). The failure of race neutral policies: How mandatory terms and sentencing enhancements contribute to mass racialized incarceration. *Crime and Delinquency, 57,* 58–81.

Steiner, B., & Wooldredge, J. (2009). The relevance of inmate race/ethnicity versus population composition for understanding prison rules violations. *Punishment and Society, 11,* 459–489.

Stohr, M. K., & Walsh, A. (2012). *Corrections: The essentials.* Los Angeles: Sage.

Sykes, B. L., & Piquero, A. R. (2009). Structuring and re-creating inequality: Health testing policies, race, and the criminal justice system. *The Annals of the American Academy of Political and Social Science, 623,* 214–227.

Taylor, W. B. (1993). *Brokered justice: Race, politics, and Mississippi prisons 1798–1992.* Columbus: Ohio State University Press.

Thompson, G. (1847). *Prison life and reflections.* Oberlin, OH: Oberlin Press.

Trulson, C. R., Marquart, J., Hemmens, C., & Carroll, L. (2008). Racial desegregation in prisons. *The Prison Journal, 88,* 270–299.

Uggen, C., Shannon, S., & Manza, J. (2012). *Street-level estimates of felon disenfranchisement in the United States, 2010.* Retrieved August 1, 2012, from http://sentencingproject.org/doc/publications/fd_State_Level_Estimates_of_Felon_Disen_2010.pdf

Unnever, J. D., Cullen, F. T., & Jonson, C. L. (2008). Race, racism, and support for capital punishment. In M. Tonry (Ed.), *Crime and justice: A review of research* (Vol. 37, pp. 45–96). Chicago, IL: University of Chicago Press.

Wacquant, L. (2001). Deadly symbiosis: When ghetto and prison meet and mesh. *Punishment and Society, 3,* 95–133.

Walker, D. R. (1988). *Penology for profit: A history of the Texas prison system 1867–1912.* College Station: Texas A&M University Press.

Wang, X., & Mears, D. P. (2010). Examining the direct and interactive effects of changes in racial and ethnic threat on sentencing decisions. *Journal of Research in Crime and Delinquency, 47,* 522–557.

Warren, P., Chiricos, T., & Bales, W. (2012). The imprisonment penalty for young Black and Hispanic males: A crime-specific analysis. *Journal of Research in Crime and Delinquency, 49,* 56–80.

Williamson, J. (1984). *The crucible of race.* New York, NY: Oxford University Press.

Woldoff, R. A., & Washington, H. M. (2008). Arrested conduct: The criminal justice system, race, and father engagement. *The Prison Journal, 88,* 179–206.

Wooldredge, J., & Steiner, B. (2012). Race group differences in prison victimization experiences. *Crime and Delinquency, 40,* 358–369.

Young, V. D. (2001). All the women in the Maryland State Penitentiary: 1812–1869. *The Prison Journal, 81,* 113–132.

Part IV

Doing No Harm

7

The Safe Prison

Benjamin Steiner and
Benjamin Meade

Editors' Introduction

For a while, "scared straight" programs captured the nation's fancy. It was heartening to see older and now wiser inmates, many serving life terms for crime committed in their misguided youthful days, attempting to divert juvenile delinquents from a life in crime. Using aggressive, if not threatening language, they tried to illuminate the brutal realities of the unsafe prison that the youngsters surely would enter unless they changed their ways. They made it clear that were these kids to end up in the society of captives, they would be extorted, beaten, and perhaps sexually assaulted.

As it turned out, scared straight programs proved to be ineffective, if not slightly criminogenic. But what was often lost in the debate over whether this intervention worked was the unquestioned acceptance of the fact that prisons were places where offenders risked victimization. To an extent, a subtext to the scared straight approach was that wayward youth should understand that prisons were populated by dangerous offenders. The fact that prisons were unsafe was thus an unavoidable reality. Play with fire, and you will get burned. In another way, there was even some glee over the fact that prisons were hot spots for criminal victimization. Prisons might pack a more deterrent punch because inmates not only would lose their freedom but also suffer fear and injury. It was an added source of deterrence that cost the state nothing!

This acceptance of the unsafe prison is troubling on three grounds. First and most important, it is morally appalling in a democratic society to allow a state-run social institution to descend into such a condition. When we place offenders behind bars, we assume a responsibility to ensure that, while being deprived of their freedom, they are kept free from harm. Second, research shows that heightening the pains of imprisonment has no deterrent effect on released offenders and, if anything, increases their recidivism. Third, as John DiIulio has shown in Governing Prisons, *the management of correctional institutions matters. Some facilities are orderly and safe, whereas others are disorderly and unsafe. The difference is not a random outcome but rather due to the quality of how the prisons are administered by those in charge. Phrased more generally, whether prisons are safe or unsafe is a choice—a matter of governance and not a foreordained, uncontrollable event.*

In the chapter to follow, Benjamin Steiner and Benjamin Meade first provide an invaluable analysis of the sources of inmate crime and victimization and then set forth a blueprint for making prisons safer. They suggest that reducing prison crowding would facilitate the capacity of administrators to address this issue. But they also share two more important insights. First, to improve safety, it is not sufficient to monitor the risk level of offenders. It also is essential to know more about the inmates under our control and care. We must have an understanding of their treatment needs—which can be achieved through assessment instruments—and provide these offenders with quality, evidence-based rehabilitation programs. Such programming might involve an up-front expense, but the cost of ignoring inmates' criminogenic needs can be far worse—disruptive conduct in prison and recidivism upon reentry.

Second, Steiner and Meade offer the innovative insight that safety also is tied to whether inmates perceive their treatment as legitimate. Creating such legitimacy involves administering a prison that shows inmates that they are respected and valued as human beings. Part of this task requires that the inmates not live in crowded facilities that provide few opportunities for meaningful activity and improvement. But another part of this task requires giving inmates a voice about institutional decisions, and training correctional officers to understand the importance of their dealing with inmates fairly. In making this recommendation, Steiner and Meade are not advocating allowing the inmates "to run the place." Rather, they are cautioning that similar to the rest of us, inmates will act less defiantly and with more civility when they are valued, respected, and treated justly than when they are devalued, degraded, and treated coercively.

Prisons are institutions where individuals who have been convicted of crimes are physically removed from society and confined. An underlying rationale of imprisonment is the protection of the public from individuals who, by virtue of their behavior, are considered a danger to public safety (Clear, Cole, & Reisig, 2013). Placing so many offenders in close proximity to one another would seemingly increase the odds that prisons would be unsafe places for both inmates and staff by maximizing the convergence in time and space of suitable targets and persons who are likely to offend if given the opportunity.

Most people perceive that prisons are unsafe places (Fleisher & Kreinert, 2009). Nearly all media reports related to prisons revolve around incidents such as stabbings, riots, and escapes. Movies such as *American Me* and *The Shawshank Redemption*, along with popular television shows such as *Lock-up* and *Oz,* depict prisons as places where violent and sexual victimization are a part of the everyday fabric of prison life. Even though prisons are not really as unsafe as the media and Hollywood portrayals might suggest, the existing data do suggest that rates of victimization in prisons are higher than in the general population (Catalano, 2005; Wolff, Shi, & Siegel, 2009; Wooldredge, 1998). However, researchers have also uncovered that there is variation in rates of inmate crime and victimization between prisons (e.g., Camp, Gaes, Langan, & Saylor, 2003; Steiner, 2009; Steiner & Wooldredge, 2008a; Wolff et al., 2009; Wooldredge, 1998), which suggests that some prisons are safer than others. But, what makes some prisons safer or more orderly than others? We address that question in this chapter.

We begin with a discussion of the importance of maintaining order and safety in prisons, followed by a description of the extent of inmate crime and victimization within prisons. We then review the evidence concerning causes/correlates of inmate crime and victimization. Next, we discuss some of the current efforts states are using to make prisons safer, and underscore which of these strategies are more promising than others. Finally, we conclude with recommendations for creating "the safe prison."

Safety and Order in Prisons

A discussion of safety and order in prisons is potentially paradoxical because prisons are institutions that forcibly confine individuals who have violated the laws that regulate society. Once inside prisons, individuals become inmates who are subjected to rules and regulations largely defined by correctional staff. Given such conditions, compliance on the part of the inmates would seem unlikely. Yet, despite the fact that inmates have violated the laws of society, inmates also share a basic need to feel safe and secure (Irwin, 1980; Irwin & Cressey, 1962; Toch, 1977). The inmates' need for safety and security forms the basis for agreement regarding which actions can threaten their well-being. In order to feel safe and secure, inmates recognize that some minimum rules prohibiting these acts are required (Bottoms & Tankebe, 2012; Sparks, Bottoms, & Hay, 1996). Thus, the consensus among the confined about the necessity of many of the facility rules and the officials with the power to enforce those rules reflects agreement regarding the value of living in a safe and orderly environment.

Maintaining orderly and safe institutions is also a high priority of correctional administrators (DiIulio, 1987; Gendreau, Goggin, & Law, 1997; Toch, Adams, & Grant, 1989). In his book, *Governing Prisons*, John J. DiIulio (1987) observed that order, amenity, and service are the three factors that are relevant to the quality of prison life, but he also noted that without order, prisons cannot provide amenity or service. Most correctional administrators would agree with DiIulio's assertion because indicators of "disorder" such as rule violations, assaults, disturbances, and so forth, threaten the smooth operation of a prison as they often disrupt the daily schedule or routine. Correctional administrators are also legally responsible for protecting the individuals who have been confined (Park, 2000), and both line staff and facility administrators are often evaluated, in part, by levels of indicators of disorder (Camp et al., 2003; DiIulio, 1987; Lombardo, 1989). Further, much like inmates, correctional staff share a need to feel safe and secure (Lombardo, 1989). The agreement regarding the importance of living and working in a safe and orderly environment constitutes a goal shared by inmates and the staff, albeit one potentially motivated by different reasons (Irwin & Cressey, 1962; Ramirez, 1984; Wheeler, 1961).

THE EXTENT OF INMATE CRIME AND VICTIMIZATION IN PRISONS

Despite the common need among inmates and correctional staff to feel safe and secure, prisons are still less safe than the larger society. The Bureau of Justice provides several sources of data collected from inmates and correctional administrators that permit an assessment of the safety of prisons in the United States. According to the 2005 Uniform Crime Report (UCR), the rate of assaults per 1,000 persons in the general population was 0.44 (Federal Bureau of Investigation, 2005, table 30). Based on data collected as a part of the 2005 Census of Adult State and Federal Correctional Facilities, the average within-facility rate of assaults on inmates was 16.25 assaults per 1,000 inmates. Similar to neighborhoods in the general population, however, assaults were not randomly distributed across facilities. For the 2005 Census mentioned above, most facilities reported one or fewer assaults per 1,000 inmates, only 30% of facilities reported an assault against a staff member, and less than 6% of facilities reported a major disturbance, defined as an incident that resulted in serious injury or property damage and a loss of control of a portion of the facility, requiring an extraordinary measure to regain control.

Data from the 2004 Survey of Inmates in State Correctional Facilities showed that 13% of inmates reported committing a physical assault on another inmate during their current period of incarceration, while 3% of inmates reported committing a physical assault on a staff member. The survey also revealed that roughly 15% of inmates reported being intentionally injured by someone else since their incarceration. Studies of inmate victimization conducted by other researchers have revealed varied estimates, including 20% of inmates victimized by physical violence and/or threats of violence during a six-month period (Wolff, Blitz, Shi, & Bachman, 2007, p. 593), 10% victimized by physical assaults and robberies during a six-month period (Wooldredge, 1998, p. 488–489), 7% victimized by physical assaults during a six-month period (Wooldredge & Steiner, in press), and 14% of inmates victimized by personal crimes during a three-month period (Wooldredge, 1994, p. 373). Although these data reflect the prevalence of events that occurred over different periods of time, including inmates' entire period of incarceration, it is, perhaps, still illustrative to compare these estimates to those generated from the National Crime Victimization Survey (NCVS). Data from the NCVS showed that the rate of victimization per 1,000 persons experiencing an assault in the past year has ranged from 16 to 18 persons between 2004 and 2009, or less than 2% of the population (Catalano, 2005, p. 2; Catalano, 2006, p. 2; Rand, 2009, p. 1).

Following the passage of the Prison Rape Elimination Act in 2003, the Bureau of Justice began collecting national-level data on the extent of sexual victimization in prisons. The 2008 National Former Prisoner Survey (NFPS) showed that approximately 7.5% of former state inmates reported experiencing one or more incidents of sexual victimization during their most recent period of imprisonment (Beck & Johnson, 2012, p. 8). Over 5% (5.4%) reported an incident that involved another inmate, while 5.3% of prisoners reported an incident involving facility staff (Beck & Johnson, 2012, p. 8). The 2008–2009 National Inmate Survey (NIS) revealed that approximately 4.4% of inmates reported experiencing one or more sexual victimizations in the past year, 2.1% reported being sexually victimized by another inmate, while 2.8% of inmates reported sexual victimization by staff members (Beck & Harrison, 2010, p. 6). In comparison, data from the NCVS showed that less than 1% of persons reported being sexually assaulted in 2008 (Rand, 2009, p. 1), and data from the UCR revealed even fewer individuals reported being forcibly raped (Federal Bureau of Investigation, 2009). Thus, the odds of experiencing violent or sexual victimization are higher in prison than the general population, but researchers have also found that, similar to neighborhoods or communities, the odds of experiencing victimization varies considerably across prisons (e.g., Beck & Harrison, 2010; Wolff et al., 2007; Wooldredge, 1998; Wooldredge & Steiner, in press).

Although the evidence reviewed above suggests that prisons are less safe than the general population, an exception to these findings does exist. The odds of being a victim of a homicide in prison are lower than the odds of being murdered in the general population. According to data collected for the UCR, the homicide rate in the United States was 5.6 homicides per 100,000 persons in 2002 (Federal Bureau of Investigation, 2003, p. 15), while the homicide rate in state prisons was 4 homicides per 100,000 inmates (Mumola, 2005, p. 1). The majority of prisons did not experience a homicide in 2002 (Mumola, 2005).

Researchers have also uncovered considerable variability between inmates and prisons in the prevalence and incidence of inmate violence and victimization (e.g., Beck & Harrison, 2010; Camp et al., 2003; Steiner, 2009; Steiner & Wooldredge, 2008a, 2008b; Wolff et al., 2007; Wolff et al., 2009; Wooldredge, 1998; Wooldredge & Steiner, in press). In fact, Wolff and Shi (2009) found that a majority of inmates in the prisons they examined actually felt safe. These findings suggest that inmate violence and victimization is a nonrandom process.

CAUSES AND CORRELATES OF INMATE CRIME AND VICTIMIZATION

"Crimes" are defined as behaviors that violate the criminal law (Sutherland & Cressey, 1978), while inmate "crimes" or "misconduct" are behaviors that violate the rules of the facilities in which the inmates are confined (Eichenthal & Jacobs, 1991; Irwin, 1980; Wooldredge, 1994, 1998). The importance of maintaining safe and orderly prisons has generated a number of studies of the causes and correlates of inmate crime and deviance, but reviews of this literature have revealed few consistencies across studies (e.g., Bottoms, 1999; Meade, 2012; Steiner, 2008). Potential reasons for these inconsistencies are beyond the scope of this chapter; interested readers should consult the aforementioned reviews.

At the inmate level, the evidence suggests that the most consistent predictors of misconduct are age and a history of antisocial behaviors (e.g., number of prior incarcerations, a history of drug use). Younger inmates and inmates with a longer history of antisocial behavior have higher odds of perpetrating misconduct (Cunningham & Sorensen, 2006; Griffin & Hepburn, 2006; Morris, Longmire, Buffington-Vollum, & Vollum, 2010; Steiner & Wooldredge, 2008b; Wooldredge, Griffin, & Pratt, 2001). A few studies have also found that involvement with antisocial peers or gangs before or during imprisonment is associated with higher odds of misconduct (Andia et al., 2005; Berk, Kriegler, & Back, 2006; Drury & DeLisi, 2008; Gaes, Wallace, Gilman, Klein-Saffran, & Suppa, 2002; Griffin & Hepburn, 2006; Meade, 2012).

Other inmate-level measures that are frequently examined by researchers include inmates' sex, race/ethnicity, committing offense type, sentence length, time served, and level of involvement in conventional behaviors before (e.g., marriage, education, employment) and during (work assignments, treatment programs) their incarceration. However, the evidence concerning the relevance of these measures has been mixed across studies (see, e.g., Berk et al., 2006; Camp et al., 2003; Drury & DeLisi, 2008; Griffin & Hepburn, 2006; Harer & Steffensmeier, 1996; Huebner, 2003; Jiang & Winfree, 2006; Morris et al., 2010; Steiner & Wooldredge, 2008b, 2009a, 2009b; Wooldredge et al., 2001; Wooldredge & Steiner, 2009).

There have been significantly fewer studies of inmate victimization compared to studies of inmate misconduct and crime. However, it is important to distinguish the correlates and causes of inmate offending from those of victimization because the policy implications of each focus differ somewhat (Wooldredge & Steiner, in press). An understanding of the influences of offending is more useful for proactive approaches to preventing increases in the precursors to crime, while an understanding of victimization is more useful for crime prevention strategies designed to reduce opportunities for offenders (Clarke, 1995).

Most researchers have uncovered that victimization is more likely among younger inmates (Kerbs & Jolley, 2007; Wolff et al., 2009; Wooldredge, 1994, 1998; Wooldredge & Steiner, in press; but see Ireland, 1999). Involvement in conventional activities such as prison jobs, recreation, education classes, and so forth has been linked to lower odds of personal victimization, yet higher odds of theft victimization (Wooldredge, 1998; Wooldredge & Steiner, 2012, in press). The evidence concerning the effects of inmates' sex, race/ethnicity, education, marital status, and criminal history has been mixed across studies (Beck & Harrison, 2010; Beck & Johnson, 2012; Perez, Gover, Tennyson, & Santos, 2010; Wolff et al., 2009; Wolff, Shi, & Blitz, 2008; Wooldredge, 1994, 1998; Wooldredge & Steiner, 2012, in press).

Most studies of inmate victimization have been limited to samples of inmates confined in one to perhaps a few prisons, while some studies of inmate crime have involved analyses of samples from multiple facilities, permitting the examination of facility-level effects on rates of inmate crime. Findings pertaining to facility-level effects should be consistent across studies of offending and victimization, however, because prisons with higher offense rates would necessarily have higher victimization rates. To date, the only facility-level finding that has been relatively consistent across studies is the effect of facility security level or custody level of the inmate population. Higher security facilities and facilities with a greater density of inmates classified as higher custody levels also have higher rates of misconduct (Camp et al., 2003; Griffin & Hepburn, 2006; McCorkle, Miethe, & Drass, 1995; Steiner & Wooldredge, 2009b).

Other facility-level measures that have been examined in related studies include the demographic composition of inmate and staff populations, the ratio of inmates to officers, institutional crowding, involvement in institutional programming or work assignments, and the use of disciplinary housing (e.g., Beck & Johnson, 2012; Camp et al., 2003; Huebner, 2003; McCorkle et al., 1995; Meade, 2012; Steiner, 2009; Steiner & Wooldredge, 2008b, 2009a, 2009b; Wooldredge et al., 2001; Wooldredge & Steiner, 2009, in press). Findings regarding the effects of these measures are mixed across studies, possibly due to the limited number of studies, differences in operationalizations of these measures, sample sizes, and so forth.

Taken together, the extant research concerning the causes and correlates of inmate crime and victimization has offered few insights regarding how to make prisons safer, albeit with a few notable exceptions. Younger inmates are at risk for victimization, but they also have higher odds of perpetrating misconduct. Inmates who have a longer history of antisocial behavior or associate with antisocial peers are also more likely to offend in prison. Structuring inmates' routines by involving them in facility programming or work assignments might reduce opportunities for some forms of victimization. Facilities that are higher security or contain higher risk populations have higher rates of inmate crime and victimization. Future studies should continue to seek to uncover the sources of inmate crime and victimization. Of particular importance could be an understanding of the effects of dynamic influences on misconduct and victimization at both the inmate and facility levels because dynamic factors are subject to intervention.

Current Efforts to Make Prisons Safe

Correctional staff bear the primary responsibility of making prisons safe (Park, 2000), yet there has been very little research directed at evaluating different strategies for making prisons safer. Most studies focus on predicting inmate crime and misconduct or on evaluating in-prison programs in terms of whether they reduce offenders' odds of recidivism. Below we describe some of the more common strategies that have been applied in prisons. These strategies include inmate classification, inmate programming, and different managerial styles.

INMATE CLASSIFICATION

Assessment tools are typically administered to inmates soon after their incarceration. The purpose of most assessment tools is to classify inmates into risk categories based on their probability of exhibiting behaviors that threaten the security of an institution (e.g., misconduct) (Van Voorhis, 2009). Although the information derived from assessment tools can be used to inform custody and treatment decisions, most states currently use them primarily for custody decisions.

The approach to managing inmates and prisons used by most correctional administrators has changed considerably over the past several decades. Prisons have become subject to legal intervention and oversight (see, e.g., Jacobs, 1980). Prisons have also become more open institutions, permeated by rapidly changing populations, visitors, and various interest groups (e.g., faith-based organizations). And, owing to mass incarceration, nearly all prisons have become overcrowded (Steiner & Wooldredge, 2008b; Vaughn, 1993). These structural changes have contributed to a shift in thinking away from focusing on individual considerations and rehabilitating inmates, toward the goal of simply "managing" large offender populations through the use of assessment tools and custodial classification (see, e.g., Feeley & Simon, 1992; Irwin, 2005; Kruttschnitt & Gartner, 2005; Silver & Miller, 2001).

In many respects, this shift away from more humanitarian goals toward managing aggregate populations could be viewed as recognition on the part of correctional administrators that inmate deviance is inevitable in the era of mass incarceration. By using custody classification, administrators can segregate high-risk inmates into a few facilities and protect lower risk inmates. Findings from an experiment conducted by Berk, Ladd, Graziano, and Baek (2003) are illustrative. Berk and his colleagues compared the odds of misconduct among California prisoners randomly assigned for placement under either the existing classification system or a "new" security classification system. Aggregate misconduct levels were nearly identical for both groups during a two-year follow-up. However, the new classification system did a better job of predicting who engaged in misconduct and, as such, placed more inmates who committed misconduct into more secure settings. In other words, the new classification system shifted more misconduct into higher security units, but overall system-wide levels of misconduct remained the same. The new system was considered successful in light of the California Department of Corrections' goal of placing inmates in the least restrictive security level consistent with internal and public safety (Berk et al., 2003). These findings suggest that using custodial classification can keep inmates in some prisons more safe, but custodial classification also decreases safety in other prisons. System-wide safety remains the same (see Irwin, 2005, for a similar observation).

The point of the above discussion is not to bemoan the use of assessment tools, as there is considerable evidence to suggest that they do what they were designed to do: predict behavior (Van Voorhis, 2009). Our point is simply that it might make prisons safer if the information derived from these tools were used to inform decisions that reduced inmate crime and victimization, as opposed to simply displacing it. We elaborate on this point later on in the chapter.

INMATE PROGRAMMING

A prison program is any formal structured activity that takes inmates out of their cells and involves them in instrumental activities (Clear et al., 2013). There have been relatively few studies of the effects of different types of inmate programming on institutional behavior. Most evaluations of in-prison programs have examined the effects of these programs on recidivism (for a review, see Gaes, Flanagan, Motiuk, & Stewart, 1999). Although a meta-analysis of the effects of in-prison treatment programs on inmate misconduct did turn up 68 evaluations of such programs, a close inspection of the studies included in the authors' sample revealed that many of the studies were evaluations of programs for juveniles, and the vast majority of the studies were published prior to 1990, with over half of the studies being published before 1980 (French & Gendreau, 2006). With these caveats in mind, the evidence regarding the effectiveness of in-prison programs is encouraging; participation in most programs is associated with lower odds of institutional misbehavior.

The most common programs found within prisons are education and work programs (Gaes et al., 1999; Gerber & Fritsch, 1994). Education programs include those that provide basic and college education, as well as those programs that provide vocational training. The available evidence suggests that participation in each type of education program is associated with modest reductions in the odds of inmate misconduct. Prison work programs also vary considerably across prisons and state systems. Most all prisons rely on inmate labor to assist with basic institutional operations (e.g., food service). Some states also contract inmate labor for jobs outside of the institutions (e.g., highway clean-up) or offer inmates opportunities for paid labor positions. Studies have not assessed the efficacy of each type of work program, but the available evidence does suggest that participation in a prison work program is linked to reductions in institutional misbehavior (Gaes et al., 1999; Gerber & Fritsch, 1994).

Finally, French and Gendreau's (2006) meta-analysis of in-prison treatment programs revealed an effect size of .14, which means that inmates who participated in an in-prison treatment program were 14% less likely to commit misconduct than inmates who did not participate. French and Gendreau also found that some programs were more effective than others; specifically, those programs that contained a behavioral component were associated with greater reductions in misconducts.

Overall then, the evidence concerning the effects of prison programs on institutional safety, while limited, is encouraging. More research on the effects of in-prison programs on in-prison behavior is sorely needed. Particularly important could be studies that shed light on which programs are more effective than others (e.g., behavioral).

MANAGERIAL STYLES

In an important contribution to penology, DiIulio (1987) observed that prisons vary in their quality of life, and the quality of life in prisons is primarily influenced by how prisons are managed. Based on findings from his ethnographic case study of the Texas, California, and Michigan penal systems, DiIulio argued that a "control model" of facility management achieved the most orderly prisons. Under a control model, all facilities are run as a maximum-security facility. Communications between staff and between staff and inmates are formal, and inmates are not allowed to participate in decision making related to facility affairs. Inmates are generally kept busy and permitted to participate in work and treatment programs. Rules and regulations are followed carefully and strictly enforced. Discipline for inmates who violate facility rules is swift and certain, but so are rewards for inmates who comply.

DiIulio's (1987) "administrative control theory" has resonated well with prison administrators for several reasons. First, an unrelated study of prison riots that occurred between 1971 and 1986 conducted by Useem and Kimball (1989) reached similar conclusions. Second, DiIulio's theory was introduced at the same time the rapid increase in prison populations served to change the social order of prisons and led to a greater reliance on formal controls by prison management in order to maintain institutional safety (Simon, 2000). Finally, the control model also fit nicely with the "get tough" approach to offender treatment that gained favor during the 1970s and 1980s.

Yet despite its popularity, the available empirical evidence regarding the effectiveness of an administrative control model is mixed. Researchers have found that coercive controls such as higher levels of supervision, greater use of segregation, and so forth can reduce levels of misconduct, but overall the evidence regarding these strategies is mixed (Bottoms, 1999; Reisig, 1998; Steiner, 2009; Useem & Reisig, 1999; Wooldredge & Steiner, in press). Colvin (1992) underscored the relevance of remunerative controls (e.g., program participation and paid jobs) for reducing inmate deviance. According to Colvin, remunerative controls offer incentives for inmates to comply with facility rules without damaging their dignity and without feeding their cynicism toward authority. A greater involvement in services such as work assignments or facility programming has been correlated with lower levels of inmate misconduct in some studies (e.g., Huebner, 2003; Jiang & Winfree, 2006; Steiner, 2009; Steiner & Wooldredge, 2009b).

All told, there is simply too little evidence to support one style of management over another. It is also unclear how relevant management really is, considering most wardens or superintendents have limited contact with the inmates on a day-to-day basis. It could be that the actions of line-level correctional officers are more important for making prisons safer and more orderly (Bottoms, 1999; Liebling, 2004; Steiner, 2008). After all, correctional officers translate managerial policy into action (Garland, 1990; Liebling, Price, & Shefer, 2011; Lipsky, 1980; Lombardo, 1989). We return to this idea shortly.

Mass Incarceration, Prison Crowding, and Prison Safety

With some exceptions, the above discussion paints a relatively bleak picture of prisons in terms of strategies to make prisons safer. However, the observations above must be tempered by the fact that, for nearly 30 years, prison administrators have been operating in the era of mass incarceration. Mass incarceration has contributed to overcrowding in most state prison systems (Steiner & Wooldredge, 2008b; Vaughn, 1993), and even though the evidence regarding a direct link between facility crowding and inmate crime is mixed (see, e.g., Gaes, 1994; Steiner & Wooldredge, 2009c), crowding could contribute to higher rates of inmate crime and victimization indirectly by impacting prison administrators' capacity to effectively manage their facilities.

Official estimates of "crowding" are often based on the rated capacity of prisons, rather than their design capacity, and the former is easily manipulated by correctional administrators (Zimring & Hawkins, 1991). Although using rated capacities to determine whether prisons are crowded is legally permissible, it also presents problems for effective inmate classification, programming, supervision, and discipline. For instance, we discussed above how assessment and classification is primarily used to inform custody decisions in prisons. Assessment tools were designed in part to facilitate treatment decisions and fit inmates to environments that best addressed their emotional and rehabilitative needs (Toch, 1977; Van Voorhis, 2009). However, administrative flexibility, in decisions regarding inmate classification and movement within a facility, begins to be reduced when the inmate population reaches 80% of the facility's *design capacity* (Klofas, Stojkovic, & Kalinich, 1992). Since most facilities are operating above 80% of their *rated capacities*, prison administrators may not be able to use the information derived from assessment tools to fit inmates into the best environment to meet their needs.

Crowding can also impact the effectiveness of facility programming (Steiner & Wooldredge, 2009c). Most facilities are designed with areas for inmate programming. However, in the era of mass incarceration, these spaces have been converted to dormitory housing in many prisons. Even if facility administrators are able to retain programming space, the opportunity for inmates to access these programs is limited in facilities that are filled to their rated capacities, rather than design capacities. This is because the available programming space in most facilities was constructed based on the number of inmates those facilities were designed to house, rather than the number of inmates the facilities could legally house. As discussed above, programming is one way to reduce inmates' odds of crime or violent victimization. By reducing inmates' opportunity to access programming, more inmates do not receive the services they need and more inmates have idle time, each of which could make prisons less safe.

Finally, crowding could hinder supervision. Crowding impacts staff-to-inmate ratios, which could directly impact inmate safety by increasing the opportunity for the convergence of potential victims and offenders in the absence of supervision (Steiner & Wooldredge, 2009c). Crowding could also weaken the effectiveness of inmate discipline. The sizes of segregation units within prisons are based on each facility's design capacity. If prisons are filled up to or beyond their rated capacities, the proportion of the total beds that were designed for segregation is necessarily reduced. Such reductions limit the tools facility administrators have at their disposal to punish inmate behaviors that threaten the safety of an institution. Even if facility administrators are willing to double bunk segregation cells, the effectiveness of the punishment is reduced. For all of these reasons, any serious effort to make prisons safer should begin by reducing prison populations.

Legitimacy and Prison Safety

Although we have offered a less than optimistic view regarding strategies for making prisons safer, recent research conducted primarily in prisons in the United Kingdom (UK) has offered some evidence that the safety of prisons can be improved (e.g., Liebling, 2004; Sparks et al., 1996). Researchers have found that prisons can be made more safe or orderly by improving the legitimacy of those prisons (e.g., Liebling, 2004; Sparks et al., 1996). *Legitimacy* refers to "the belief that authorities, institutions, and social arrangements are appropriate, proper and just" (Tyler, 2006, p. 376; see also Bottoms, 1999; Tyler, 1990). It is "a quality possessed by an authority, a law, or an institution that often leads individuals to feel obligated to obey its decisions and directives" (Tyler, 2003, p. 308). But, how might correctional administrators make prisons more legitimate?

Regarding the institutions, inmates who serve their time in prisons that are falling apart; structurally unsafe; overcrowded; provide substandard food; and limit access to recreation, self-improvement classes, and so forth might hold weaker beliefs regarding the legitimacy of those institutions (Sparks et al., 1996). Inmates confined in facilities with policies that degrade and dehumanize inmates, or completely deprive them of their autonomy might also be less likely to view those prisons as legitimate. In contrast, legitimate prisons are those in which the conditions are such that inmates feel they are respected and retain some of their dignity (Liebling, 2004; Tyler, 2010). Legitimate prisons permit inmates to have a voice in decisions that impact their daily lives (Franke, Bierie, & MacKenzie, 2010; Sparks et al., 1996; Tyler, 2010). This does not mean correctional administrators should grant every inmate request, but simply that inmates should have an opportunity to be heard regarding the policy decisions that impact their treatment and be provided with an explanation of the justification underlying the outcomes of the decision-making process. When individuals are offered a voice in the decision-making process, they are more likely to feel involved and perceive that they are being treated with dignity and respect (Tyler, 2010).

Legitimate prisons provide inmates with due process regarding decisions that impact their liberty (Tyler, 2010). Most prisons do afford inmates due process in disciplinary proceedings, and most prisons also have policies related to procedures for inmates to air their grievances (Clear et al., 2013). Yet there is also considerable variation between prisons in these policies, and the potential for arbitrary decision making exists (Bottoms, 1999). Inmates who are confined in prisons where policies have been put in place to permit them access to the process they are due and to guard against arbitrary decision making might hold stronger beliefs regarding the legitimacy of the institution. Similarly, inmates who are housed in prisons where the policies pertaining to inmate grievances are fair, impartial, and designed to make the process accessible to all inmates will probably hold stronger beliefs regarding the legitimacy of those facilities.

Finally, inmates who feel that the policies of the prison in which they are confined, and the institution itself, are designed to do what is right are more likely to view their prison as legitimate (Tyler, 2010). Individuals are often motivated by their perceptions regarding the motivations of the authorities that they come into contact with; individuals wish to believe that, regardless of the situation, the authorities are interested in their well-being (Tyler, 1990). Inmates who feel that the prison they are housed in is designed to help them in some way will be more likely to view that prison more positively and as more legitimate than inmates who feel that their institution is designed simply to warehouse them or make them worse (Franke et al., 2010; Liebling, 2004).

The above considerations related to making prisons legitimate could be influenced by correctional administrators within prisons; however, they are also primarily a function of state policy, available resources, and so forth. Prison administrators often have little control over such matters. Equally, if not more important for institutional safety, could be whether inmates perceive prison management as legitimate. Recall from the discussion above that levels of disorder vary across facilities, and management practices help to shape these differences (Bottoms, 1999; Camp et al., 2003; DiIulio, 1987). Yet it is unclear whether managerial philosophies or styles are the primary influence of this variation. It could be that it is the normal everyday encounters between line-level correctional officers and inmates that have the most influence on facility order. In other words, fundamental to the potential link between management practices and order maintenance could be the manner in which inmates are supervised as well as how they are treated during their encounters with staff (Bottoms, 1999; DiIulio, 1987; Henderson, Wells, Maguire, & Gray, 2010; Liebling, 2004; Reisig & Mesko, 2009; Sparks et al., 1996; Vuolo & Kruttschnitt, 2008).

Practitioners and academics have suggested that the correctional officers' treatment of inmates can affect those inmates' odds of misconduct and the overall stability of the facility environment (Bottoms, 1999; Clemmer, 1940; DiIulio, 1987; Hepburn, 1985; Irwin, 1980; Lombardo, 1989; O'Donnell & Edgar, 1998; Sparks et al., 1996; Sykes, 1958). How inmates are treated by correctional officers may influence inmates' perceptions regarding the legitimacy of the correctional staff's authority and, in turn, the ability of staff to gain inmate compliance (Bottoms, 1999; DiIulio, 1987; Hepburn, 1985; Irwin, 1980; Lombardo, 1989). When individuals believe that authorities are legitimate, they are more likely to accept and comply with the decisions of those authorities, regardless of their self-interests. This is because when individuals believe authorities are legitimate they are more likely to "buy into" the decisions made by those authorities (Franke et al., 2010; Tyler, 1990, 2003).

Inmates' perceptions of correctional officer legitimacy will no doubt be influenced by instrumental concerns such as the outcomes of their encounters with staff and their level of satisfaction with those outcomes. However, normative considerations such as individuals' perceptions of the distributive and procedural justice, or the perceived fairness of the outcomes and the treatment they received during those encounters have been shown to be stronger influences of perceptions of legitimacy (e.g., Bottoms & Tankebe, 2012; Casper, Tyler, & Fisher, 1988; Liebling, 2004; Tyler, 1990, 2003). Regarding procedural justice, individuals typically desire to have a voice and participate in the decision-making process. They expect authorities to remain neutral and treat them with dignity and respect. Individuals also want to believe that authorities are acting out of a desire to do what is right and that the authorities can morally justify their decisions that affect them (Bottoms, 1999; Sparks et al., 1996; Tyler, 1990, 2010). On the other hand, inconsistent treatment by authorities can influence perceptions of authority as illegitimate, and in turn, provoke defiance of the rules (Colvin, 2007; Sherman, 1993).

Evidence derived from studies of citizens' perceptions of the police and courts supports the relationship between legitimacy and compliance (e.g., Paternoster, Brame, Bachman, & Sherman, 1997; Tyler, 1990). Ethnographic studies of prison environments have also underscored the link between correctional officer legitimacy and prison order (e.g., Clemmer, 1940; Irwin, 1980; Liebling, 2004; Liebling & Price, 1999; Sparks et al., 1996). Additionally, Reisig and Mesko (2009) observed that inmates' perceptions of procedural justice were linked to their odds of misconduct, and Steiner (2008) found that inmates with stronger beliefs regarding the legitimacy of correctional staff had lower odds of perpetrating inmate crimes and rule violations. Thus, with regard to institutional safety, inmates' perceptions of the legitimacy of correctional staff could matter as much or more than the legitimacy of the institution in which the inmates are confined.

Conclusion: Creating the Safe Prison

Prisons are less safe than the general population. However, some prisons are safer than others, and some types of inmates are more at risk for perpetrating inmate crimes or being victims of other inmates. We have shown that very little is known about how to make prisons safer. Much more research on this topic is needed. Still, the available research does permit us to make five tentative recommendations for creating the safe prison.

RECOMMENDATION 1: REDUCE PRISON POPULATIONS

Although the evidence reviewed above does not show a direct link between crowding and prison misconduct, we have illustrated how crowding can impact safety indirectly by limiting correctional administrators' abilities to manage their facilities effectively (e.g., reducing supervision, limiting programming space). A safe prison would have an inmate population that is below its design capacity.

RECOMMENDATION 2: CLASSIFY INMATES BASED ON THEIR NEEDS RATHER THAN RISK

We have discussed above how prison classification is primarily used for making custody decisions as opposed to treatment decisions. We have also shown how this strategy has not improved the safety of prison systems, suggesting that classification solely for the purpose of informing custody decisions is not an effective strategy for making prisons safer. In contrast, prison programming can be an effective way of making prisons safer. Yet, providing effective programming begins with an understanding of inmates' needs. This information can be gained through assessment tools that are designed to assess not only the risk inmates pose to institutional safety, but also their unique treatment needs. If our first recommendation can be followed, then inmates should be matched to prison environments with programming that will match their unique needs. Assuming, however, that opportunities for rehabilitative services will remain limited, the evidence suggests that available services should be directed to high-risk/need inmates (Van Voorhis, 2009).

RECOMMENDATION 3: PROVIDE INMATES WITH OPPORTUNITIES FOR EVIDENCE-BASED PROGRAMMING

We have discussed the efficacy of prison programming for making prisons safer, and another chapter in this volume offers a vision of a rehabilitative prison (see Chapter 1). It is worth noting that there is some evidence to suggest certain types of programming applied to certain types of offenders could be an even more effective way of making prisons safer than simply providing programming. For instance, programs with a cognitive and/or behavioral component have been shown to be more effective than most other types of programs (French & Gendreau, 2006; Smith, Gendreau, & Goggin, 2009). Most reviews of the correctional treatment literature have focused on the effects of cognitive and/or behavioral programs on offenders' odds of recidivism; however, it is reasonable to infer that if participation in cognitive and/or behavioral programs is associated with the largest reductions in recidivism, then participation in those programs is also likely to be associated with larger reductions in other indicators of criminality, such as institutional misbehavior. Prison administrators would be wise to implement programs for high-risk/need inmates that have a cognitive or behavioral component. This is not to say that other effective programs such as education and work programs should be disbanded. After all, education and employment are needs that hold great importance upon inmates' release back into society. Similarly, participation in these types of programs has been linked to lower odds of inmate crime and personal victimization within prisons. Our point is simply that correctional managers need to implement programs that, based on the available evidence, achieve some sort of measureable goal, whether it be reductions in institutional misbehavior, recidivism, or the improvement of other indicators of inmate well-being.

RECOMMENDATION 4: MAKE PRISONS MORE LEGITIMATE

Reducing a prison's population (Recommendation 1) would go a long way toward making that prison more legitimate. Improving other physical and structural conditions within a prison might also contribute to the perception among inmates that they are respected and valued as human beings; such perceptions might promote stronger beliefs regarding the legitimacy of the institution. Implementing policies that permit inmates to have a voice in the decisions that impact their treatment could also contribute to institutional legitimacy. An opportunity for inmates to voice their opinions would not necessarily need to be provided in a formal setting, but perhaps more informally within the housing units or even through the use of an anonymous suggestion box. A legitimate prison would also provide inmates with due process during disciplinary proceedings. Grievance procedures would be made accessible to individuals with little or no legal training, and often with limited education. Policies would also be in place to ensure fair and impartial decision making during the disciplinary or grievance process. Finally, ensuring that all policies are designed to do what is right for the inmate population might strengthen inmates' beliefs regarding the legitimacy of a prison.

RECOMMENDATION 5: IMPROVE THE LEGITIMACY OF CORRECTIONAL STAFF

Correctional officers are aware of the importance of their work, but less well understood among officers is just how important their everyday encounters with inmates are (Liebling et al., 2011; Sparks et al., 1996). This is because within the close confines of a prison environment, the outcomes of most incidents are more widely known compared to a community context (Bottoms & Tankebe, 2012; Sparks et al., 1996). Inmates' perceptions regarding the legitimacy of correctional officers could be central to their odds of complying with the rules, and consequently prison safety (Bottoms, 1999; Tyler, 2010). This is because when individuals believe that legal authorities are legitimate, they are more likely to accept and comply with the decisions of those authorities (or the rules they enforce), regardless of their self-interests (Tyler, 1990, 2003). Perceptions of correctional staff as "legitimate" require that the actions of officers and administrators are just or fair (i.e., their actions must be morally justifiable to inmates under their supervision) (Bottoms, 1999; Sparks et al., 1996). Thus, fundamental to creating a safe prison is ensuring that correctional staff understand that they have been granted legal authority, but that the legitimacy of that authority is conditional upon the strength of inmates' beliefs regarding the legitimacy of those officers (Bottoms & Tankebe, 2012). In a safe prison, correctional staff would understand the importance of cultivating the perception that they are legitimate.

In closing, based on the extant evidence concerning what works and what is promising regarding prison safety, we can reasonably argue that following the five recommendations outlined above could create a safe prison. Although it will take resources to reduce a prison's population, implement effective classification and programs, and make aspects of a prison more legitimate, these costs must be weighed alongside the costs to public safety of ignoring the confined population. Experiencing violent victimization in prison has implications for the risk of subsequent criminality after release (Boxer, Middlemass, & Delorenzo, 2009; Listwan, Sullivan, Agnew, Cullen, & Colvin, 2013), and violent experiences may feed inmates' disrespect and cynicism toward legal authority since the state has failed to protect them from harm (Wooldredge & Steiner, in press). Nearly all prisoners will rejoin society, and so it is a great risk to public safety to be complacent about bettering these individuals' chances of desisting from offending upon their release. In the meantime, a prison could be made more legitimate with relatively little expense by training staff on the importance of cultivating inmates' perceptions regarding correctional officer legitimacy. As Sparks and Bottoms (1995, p. 60) observed:

> Every instance of brutality in prisons, every casual racist joke and demeaning remark, every ignored petition, every unwarranted bureaucratic delay, every inedible meal, every arbitrary decision to segregate or transfer without giving clear and well founded reasons, every petty miscarriage of justice, every futile and inactive period of time is delegitimating.

Ensuring that correctional staff understand the importance of their day-to-day encounters with inmates could go a long way toward making a prison more legitimate, and ultimately more safe.

References

Andia, J. F., Deren, S., Robles, R. R., Kang, S.-Y., Colon, H. M., Oliver-Velez, D., & Finlinson, A. (2005). Factors associated with injection and noninjection drug use during incarceration among Puerto Rican drug injectors in New York and Puerto Rico. *The Prison Journal*, 8, 329–342.

Beck, A. J., & Harrison, P. M. (2010). *Sexual victimization in prisons and jails reported by inmates, 2008–2009*. Washington, DC: Bureau of Justice Statistics, Office of Justice Programs.

Beck, A. J., & Johnson, C. (2012). *Sexual victimization reported by former state prisoners, 2008*. Washington, DC: Bureau of Justice Statistics, Office of Justice Programs.

Berk, R. A., Kriegler, B., & Back, J.-H. (2006). Forecasting dangerous inmate misconduct: An application of ensemble statistical procedures. *Journal of Quantitative Criminology*, 22, 131–145.

Berk, R. A., Ladd, H., Graziano, H., & Baek, J.-H. (2003). A randomized experiment testing inmate classification systems. *Criminology and Public Policy, 2*, 215–242.

Bottoms, A., & Tankebe, J. (2012). Beyond procedural justice: A dialogic approach to legitimacy in criminal justice. *Journal of Criminal Law and Criminology, 102*, 119–170.

Bottoms, A. E. (1999). Interpersonal violence and social order in prison. In M. Tonry & J. Petersilia (Eds.), *Crime and justice: A review of research* (Vol. 26, pp. 205–282). Chicago, IL: University of Chicago Press.

Boxer, P., Middlemass, K., & Delorenzo, T. (2009). Exposure to violent crime during incarceration: Effects on psychological adjustment following release. *Criminal Justice and Behavior, 36*, 793–807.

Camp, S. D., Gaes, G. G., Langan, N. P., & Saylor, W. G. (2003). The influence of prisons on inmate misconduct: A multilevel investigation. *Justice Quarterly, 20*, 501–533.

Casper, J. D., Tyler, T. R., & Fisher, B. (1988). Procedural justice in felony cases. *Law and Society Review, 22*, 483–508.

Catalano, S. M. (2005). *Criminal victimization, 2004.* Washington, DC: U.S. Department of Justice, Bureau of Justice Statistics, Office of Justice Programs.

Catalano, S. M. (2006). *Criminal victimization, 2005.* Washington, DC: U.S. Department of Justice, Bureau of Justice Statistics, Office of Justice Programs.

Clarke, R. V. (1995). Situational crime prevention. In M. Tonry & D. P. Farrington (Eds.), *Crime and justice: A review of research* (Vol. 19, pp. 91–150). Chicago, IL: University of Chicago Press.

Clear, T. C., Cole, G. F., & Reisig, M. D. (2013). *American corrections* (10th ed.). Belmont, CA: Wadsworth, Cengage Learning.

Clemmer, D. (1940). *The prison community.* New York, NY: Rinehart and Company.

Colvin, M. (1992). *The penitentiary in crisis: From accommodation to riot in New Mexico.* Albany: State University of New York Press.

Colvin, M. (2007). Applying differential coercion and social support theory to prison organizations: The case of the penitentiary of New Mexico. *The Prison Journal, 87*, 367–387.

Cunningham, M. D., & Sorensen, J. R. (2006). Nothing to lose? A comparative examination of prison misconduct rates among life-without-parole and other long-term high-security inmates. *Criminal Justice and Behavior, 33*, 683–705.

DiIulio, J. J., Jr. (1987). *Governing prisons: A comparative study of correctional management.* New York, NY: Free Press.

Drury, A. J., & DeLisi, M. (2008). Gangkill: An exploratory empirical assessment of gang membership, homicide offending, and prison misconduct. *Crime and Delinquency, 57*, 130–146.

Eichenthal, D. R., & Jacobs, J. B. (1991). Enforcing the criminal law in state prisons. *Justice Quarterly, 8*, 283–303.

Federal Bureau of Investigation. (2003). *Crime in the United States: 2002.* Washington, DC: Author.

Federal Bureau of Investigation. (2005). *Crime in the United States: 2004.* Washington, DC: Author.

Federal Bureau of Investigation. (2009). *Crime in the United States: 2008.* Washington, DC: Author.

Feeley, M., M. & Simon, J. N. (1992). The new penology: Notes on the emerging strategy of corrections and its implications. *Criminology, 30*, 449–474.

Fleisher, M. S., & Kreinert, J. L. (2009). *The myth of prison rape: Sexual culture in American prisons.* Lanham, MD: Rowman and Littlefield.

Franke, D., Bierie, D., & MacKenzie, D. L. (2010). Legitimacy in corrections: A randomized experiment comparing a boot camp with a prison. *Criminology and Public Policy, 9*(1), 89–118.

French, S. A., & Gendreau, P. (2006). Reducing prison misconducts: What works! *Criminal Justice and Behavior, 33*, 185–218.

Gaes, G. G. (1994). Prison crowding research reexamined. *The Prison Journal, 74*, 329–364.

Gaes, G. G., Flanagan, T. J., Motiuk, L. L., & Stewart, L. (1999). Adult correctional treatment. In M. Tonry & J. Petersilia (Eds.), *Crime and justice: A review of research* (Vol. 26, pp. 361–426). Chicago, IL: University of Chicago Press.

Gaes, G. G., Wallace, S., Gilman, E., Klein-Saffran, J., & Suppa, S. (2002). The influence of prison gang affiliation on violence and other prison misconduct. *The Prison Journal, 82*, 359–385.

Garland, D. (1990). *Punishment in modern society: A study in social theory.* Chicago, IL: University of Chicago Press.

Gendreau, P., Goggin, C. E., & Law, M. A. (1997). Predicting prison misconducts. *Criminal Justice and Behavior, 24*, 414–431.

Gerber, J., & Fritsch, E. J. (1994). The effects of academic and vocational program participation on inmate misconduct and reincarceration. In Sam Houston State University (Ed.), *Prison Education Research Project: Final report.* Huntsville, TX: Sam Houston State University.

Griffin, M L.., & Hepburn, J. R. (2006). The effect of gang affiliation on violent misconduct among inmates during the early years of confinement. *Criminal Justice and Behavior, 33*, 419–448.

Harer, M. D., & Steffensmeier, D. J. (1996). Race and prison violence. *Criminology, 34*, 323–355.

Henderson, H., Wells, W., Maguire, E. R., & Gray, J. (2010). Evaluating the measurement properties of procedural justice in a correctional setting. *Criminal Justice and Behavior, 37*, 384–399.

Hepburn, J. R. (1985). The exercise of power in coercive organizations: A study of prison guards. *Criminology, 23*, 145–164.

Huebner, B. M. (2003). Administrative determinants of inmate violence: A multilevel analysis. *Journal of Criminal Justice, 31*, 107–117.

Ireland, J. L. (1999). Bullying behaviors among male and female prisoners: A study of adult and young offenders. *Aggressive Behavior, 25*, 161–178.

Irwin, J. (1980). *Prisons in turmoil.* Boston, MA: Little, Brown.

Irwin, J. (2005). *The warehouse prison: Disposal of the new dangerous class.* Los Angeles, CA: Roxbury Press.

Irwin, J., & Cressey, D. R. (1962). Thieves, convicts, and the inmate culture. *Social Problems, 10*, 142–155.

Jacobs, J. B. (1980). The prisoners' rights movement and its impact, 1960–1980. In N. Morris & M. Tonry (Eds.), *Crime and justice: A review of the research* (Vol. 2, pp. 429–470). Chicago, IL: University of Chicago Press.

Jiang, S., & Winfree, L. T. (2006). Social support, gender, and inmate adjustment to prison life: Insights from a national sample. *The Prison Journal, 86*, 32–55.

Kerbs, J. J., & Jolley, J. M. (2007). Inmate-on-inmate victimization among older male prisoners. *Crime and Delinquency, 53*, 187–218.

Klofas, J. M., Stojkovic, S., & Kalinich, D. A. (1992). The meaning of correctional crowding: Steps toward an index of severity. *Crime and Delinquency, 38*, 171–188.

Kruttschnitt, C., & Gartner, R. (2005). *Marking time in the Golden State: Women's imprisonment in California.* Cambridge, UK: Cambridge University Press.

Liebling, A. (2004). *Prisons and their moral performance: A study of values, quality, and prison life.* New York, NY: Oxford University Press.

Liebling, A., & Price, D. (1999). *An exploration of the staff-prisoner relationships at HMP Whitemoor.* London, UK: Prison Services.

Liebling, A., Price, D., & Shefer, G. (2011). *The prison officer* (2nd ed.). New York, NY: Willan.

Lipsky, M. (1980). *Street-level bureaucracy.* New York, NY: Russell Sage.

Listwan, S. J., Sullivan, C. J., Agnew, R., Cullen, F. T., & Colvin, M. (2013). The pains of imprisonment revisited: The impact of strain on inmate recidivism. *Justice Quarterly, 30*, 144–168.

Lombardo, L. X. (1989). *Guards imprisoned: Correctional officers at work* (2nd ed.). Cincinnati, OH: Anderson.

McCorkle, R. C., Miethe, T. D., & Drass, K. A. (1995). The roots of prison violence: A test of the deprivation, management, and "not-so-total" institution models. *Crime and Delinquency, 41*, 317–331.

Meade, B. (2012). *Examining the effects of religiosity and religious environments on inmate misconduct.* Unpublished doctoral dissertation, University of South Carolina, Columbia.

Morris, R. G., Longmire, D. R., Buffington-Vollum, J., & Vollum, S. (2010). Institutional misconduct and differential parole eligibility among capital inmates. *Criminal Justice and Behavior, 37*, 417–438.

Mumola, C. J. (2005). *Suicide and homicide in state prisons and local jails.* Washington, DC: Bureau of Justice Statistics, Office of Justice Programs.

O'Donnell, I., & Edgar, K. (1998). Routine victimisation in prisons. *The Howard Journal, 37*, 266–279.

Park, J. J. (2000). Redefining Eighth Amendment punishments: A new standard for determining the liability of prison officials for failing to protect inmates from serious harm. *Quinnipiac Law Review, 20*, 407–466.

Paternoster, R., Brame, R., Bachman, R., & Sherman, L. W. (1997). Do fair procedures matter? The effect of procedural justice on spouse assault. *Law and Society Review, 31*, 163–204.

Perez, D. M, Gover, A. R., Tennyson, K. M., & Santos, S. D. (2010). Individual and institutional characteristics related to inmate victimization. *International Journal of Offender Therapy and Comparative Criminology, 54*, 378–394.

Ramirez, J. (1984). Prisonization, staff, and inmates: Is it really about us versus them? *Criminal Justice and Behavior, 11*, 423–460.

Rand, M. R. (2009). *Criminal victimizations, 2008.* Washington, DC: U.S. Department of Justice, Bureau of Justice Statistics.

Reisig, M. D. (1998). Rates of disorder in higher-custody state prisons: A comparative analysis of managerial practices. *Crime and Delinquency, 44*, 229–244.

Reisig, M. D., & Mesko, G. (2009). Procedural justice, legitimacy, and prisoner misconduct. *Psychology, Crime and Law, 15,* 41–59.

Sherman, L. W. (1993). Defiance, deterrence, and irrelevance: A theory of the criminal sanction. *Journal of Research in Crime and Delinquency, 30,* 445–473.

Simon, J. (2000). From the big house to the warehouse: Rethinking prisons and state government in the 20th century. *Punishment and Society, 2,* 213–234.

Silver, E., & Miller, L. L. (2001). A cautionary note on the use of actuarial risk assessment tools for social control. *Crime and Delinquency, 48,* 138–161.

Smith, P., Gendreau, P., & Goggin, C. (2009). Correctional treatment: Accomplishments and realities. In P. Van Voorhis, M. Braswell, & D. Lester (Eds.), *Correctional counseling and rehabilitation* (5th ed., pp. 285–294). Cincinnati, OH: Anderson.

Sparks, J. R., & Bottoms, A. E. (1995). Legitimacy and order in prisons. *The British Journal of Sociology, 46,* 45–62.

Sparks, J. R., Bottoms, A. E., & Hay, W. (1996). *Prisons and the problem of order.* Oxford, UK: Oxford University Press.

Steiner, B. (2008). *Maintaining prison order: Understanding causes of inmate misconduct within and across Ohio prisons.* Unpublished doctoral dissertation, University of Cincinnati, Cincinnati, OH.

Steiner, B. (2009). Assessing static and dynamic influences on inmate violence levels. *Crime and Delinquency, 55,* 134–161.

Steiner, B., & Wooldredge, J. (2008a). Comparing state- versus facility-level effects on crowding in U.S. correctional facilities. *Crime and Delinquency, 54,* 259–290.

Steiner, B., & Wooldredge, J. (2008b). Inmate versus environmental effects on prison rule violations. *Criminal Justice and Behavior, 35,* 438–456.

Steiner, B., & Wooldredge, J. (2009a). Individual and environmental effects on assaults and nonviolent rule-breaking by women in prison. *Journal of Research in Crime and Delinquency, 46,* 437–467.

Steiner, B., & Wooldredge, J. (2009b). The relevance of inmate race/ethnicity versus population composition for understanding prison rule violations. *Punishment and Society, 11,* 459–489.

Steiner, B., & Wooldredge, J. (2009c). Rethinking the link between institutional crowding and inmate misconduct. *The Prison Journal, 89,* 205–233.

Sutherland, E. H., & Cressey, D. R. (1978). *Criminology* (10th ed.). Philadelphia, PA: J. B. Lippincott.

Sykes, G. M. (1958). *The society of captives.* Princeton, NJ: Princeton University Press.

Toch, H. (1977). *Living in prison.* New York, NY: Free Press.

Toch, H., Adams, K., & Grant, J. D. (1989). *Coping: Maladaptation in prisons.* New Brunswick, NJ: Transaction Publishers.

Tyler, T. R. (1990). *Why people obey the law.* New Haven, CT: Yale University Press.

Tyler, T. R. (2003). Procedural justice, legitimacy, and the effective rule of law. In M. Tonry (Ed.), *Crime and justice: A review of research* (Vol. 30, pp. 283–358). Chicago, IL: University of Chicago Press.

Tyler, T. R. (2006). Psychological perspectives on legitimacy and legitimation. *Annual Review of Psychology, 57,* 375–400.

Tyler, T. R. (2010). "Legitimacy in corrections": Policy implications. *Criminology and Public Policy, 9,* 127–134.

Useem, B., & Kimball, P. (1989). *States of siege: U.S. prison riots, 1971–1986*. New York, NY: Oxford University Press.

Useem, B., & Reisig, M. D. (1999). Collective action in prisons: Protests, disturbances, and riots. *Criminology, 37*, 735–759.

Van Voorhis, P. (2009). An overview of classification systems. In P. Van Voorhis, M. Braswell, & D. Lester (Eds.), *Correctional counseling and rehabilitation* (5th ed., pp. 133–160). Cincinnati, OH: Anderson.

Vaughn, M. S. (1993). Listening to the experts: A national study of correctional administrators' responses to prison overcrowding. *Criminal Justice Review, 18*, 12–25.

Vuolo, M., & Kruttschnitt, C. (2008). Prisoners' adjustment, correctional officers, and context: The foreground and background of punishment in late modernity. *Law and Society Review, 42*, 307–336.

Wheeler, S. (1961). Role conflict in correctional communities. In D. R. Cressey (Ed.), *The prison: Studies in institutional organization and change*. (pp. 229–259). New York, NY: Holt, Rinehart & Winston.

Wolff, N., Blitz, C. L., Shi, J., & Bachman, R. (2007). Physical violence inside prison: Rates of victimization. *Criminal Justice and Behavior, 34*, 588–599.

Wolff, N., & Shi, J. (2009). Type, sources, and patterns of physical victimization. *The Prison Journal, 89*, 172–191.

Wolff, N., Shi, J., & Blitz, C. L. (2008). Racial and ethnic disparities in types and sources of victimization inside prison. *The Prison Journal, 88*, 451–472.

Wolff, N., Shi, J., & Siegel, J. (2009). Understanding physical victimization inside prisons: Factors that predict risk. *Justice Quarterly, 26*, 445–475.

Wooldredge, J. (1994). Inmate crime and victimization in a southwestern correctional facility. *Journal of Criminal Justice, 22*, 367–381.

Wooldredge, J. (1998). Inmate lifestyles and opportunities for victimization. *Journal of Research in Crime and Delinquency, 35*, 480–502.

Wooldredge, J., Griffin, T., & Pratt, T. (2001). Considering hierarchical models for research on inmate behavior: Predicting misconduct with multilevel data. *Justice Quarterly 18*, 203–231.

Wooldredge, J., & Steiner, B. (2009). Comparing methods for examining relationships between prison crowding and inmate violence. *Justice Quarterly, 26*, 795–826.

Wooldredge, J., & Steiner, B. (2012). Race group differences in prison victimization experiences. *Journal of Criminal Justice, 40*, 358–369.

Wooldredge, J., & Steiner, B. (in press). Violent victimization in state prisons. *Violence and Victims*.

Zimring, F. E., & Hawkins, G. (1991). *The scale of imprisonment*. Chicago, IL: University of Chicago Press.

8

The Healthy Prison

Roberto Hugh Potter and
Jeffrey W. Rosky

Editors' Introduction

With the passage of the Affordable Care Act—so-called Obamacare—the United States moved toward what citizens in all other advanced industrial nations take for granted: universal access to health care. Implicit in this reform is the view that health care should not be based on sheer wealth or having employment with medical benefits. Rather, the Act suggests that health care—and having the opportunity to live a pain-free or disease-free life—is a basic human right that any good society should provide.

The right not just to some form of health care, but to quality health care, is complicated still further when we turn to those the state has chosen to deprive of their freedom: prison inmates. An inevitable tension arises when deciding how much social welfare services—whether education, job training, or medical attention—to give to those who have violated the rights of others, at times badly harming their victims. The impulse can arise to let inmates live impoverished, unhappy lives—to provide them with few services and, if they have the misfortunate of becoming ill, to let them suffer. But doing bad things to bad people is unacceptable—for two reasons.

First, as has been said many times, how we treat the least among us is a reflection of the moral health of our society. We have the legal obligation to not impose punishments that are cruel and unusual. But we have the deeper obligation to be ethical. We provide inmates with a decent life because it is the decent thing to do. Second, there is the matter of utility. When we choose to warehouse offenders in crowded prisons devoid of meaningful services, we risk returning to society a steady flow of inmates who burden their kids, families, and communities. They will be uneducated, unemployable, unhealthy, and unreformed. Thus, we provide inmates with a decent life because it is our interest to do so.

In the chapter to follow, Roberto Hugh Potter and Jeffrey Rosky build on these arguments to show why creating a healthy prison is sound correctional policy. Many inmates, who often lived risky and unhealthy lives, walk through the prison gates with substance abuse problems, mental health disorders, infectious diseases, and an array of other health concerns. They then live in a society of captives in close proximity with other inmates, conditions ripe for exacerbating and, for some problems, spreading their illnesses. If we choose to ignore these stubborn realities, then the mental and physical health of inmates can decline decidedly. The result is the reentry of offenders who will import their problems into the larger society. The other result is that a health crisis can arise within the prison society—one that will lead to judicial intervention (as has recently occurred in California) and to the need to expend resources on serious illness that might have been prevented.

Potter and Rosky thus make a compelling case for a more proactive, sensible approach to inmate health. The opportunity exists to make inmates mentally healthier and to curtail the development of infectious diseases and progressive medical conditions. But the authors also point out that a truly healthy prison would seek to teach inmates to eat correctly, to engage in appropriate exercise, and generally have a healthy lifestyle. If this were to occur in a serious and systematic way, then, ironically, what goes on inside the society of captives might provide a model for how to improve the lives of those in the society of free citizens.

O n June 9, 2011, James Verone walked into the RBC Bank in Gastonia, North Carolina, and attempted to rob it. He asked for only one dollar and committed his robbery without a weapon. After his attempt, he sat down on the couch and waited for the police. Suffering from a number of health problems, his goal was not to rob the bank but to be sentenced to prison so that he could obtain the necessary health care that he could not afford until he qualified for Medicaid (Turbyfill, 2011). Mr. Verone felt that prison was the only place he could find affordable health care. Only three weeks earlier, the United States Supreme Court had found that the overcrowding in the California Department of Corrections and Rehabilitation was deliberately indifferent to the health care needs of prisoners and constituted an Eighth Amendment constitutional violation, resulting in multiple unnecessary deaths from deficiencies in how health care was delivered in the California prison system (*Brown v. Plata*, 2011).

While this chapter is to imagine what a healthy prison would look like, these two events help frame where we are currently with prison health care delivery: On one extreme, we have a man so desperate for affordable health care that he committed crime to get it, while on the other, we have the U.S. Supreme Court saying that the largest prison system in the country is killing its inmates because of how poorly it delivers its constitutionally mandated health care. But this false dichotomy between a hospital of hope and a sanatorium of death hides the scope within prisons of health care and medical needs that include but are not limited to the following:

- Prenatal and neonatal care for infants born to female inmates;

- Preventive care including diet, exercise, immunizations, and other health promotions;

- Acute care for injury, infectious disease, and other urgent conditions;

- Psychiatric care for mental illness and addictive disorders;

- Chronic care for infectious diseases, cancers, cardiovascular diseases, and metabolic disorders;

- Geriatric care for aging inmates, including for dementia; and

- Hospice care and compassionate release for terminally ill inmates.

Part and parcel with health care treatment is the need for the cost containment that requires prisons to institute managed care plans that create drug formularies, elicit co-payments from inmates, create contracts with outside medical providers, and craft responsible and adequate standards to discern between deliberate indifference and malpractice. In addition, staffing issues, which beleaguer regular health care providers, are at the forefront of delivering health care in prisons, with difficulties in recruiting and retaining physicians, physician assistants and nurse practitioners, RN and LPN nurses, and mental health providers.

As we can see, the scope of the problem is wide and difficult and does not easily fall into either Mr. Verone's hospital of hope or the Supreme Court's sanatorium of death. So how can we imagine the healthy prison? How can we get to that future where Mr. Verone's vision is unnecessary but a future that is constitutional? Let us examine the past to see how we can chart that path.

The Healthy Prison's Ancestry

The constitutional guarantees of prisoner access to health care were not always clear cut. The first real case dealing with access to health care was *Spicer v. Williamson* (1926). It involved a situation in Duplin County, North Carolina, where an armed robbery offender shot while fleeing a local deputy was taken to a local doctor for emergency treatment by the sheriff. The county commissioners refused to pay the doctor for the treatment so the doctor sued the sheriff, winning the case and establishing a legal precedent that custodians of prisoners had an obligation to provide and pay for emergency care. It took another 50 years and *Estelle v. Gamble* (1976) for the standard to move beyond urgent care to also include emergent and chronic care. This case involved an inmate who sued the

Texas correctional system after hurting his back while working on the prison farm, claiming that he was denied adequate treatment for his injury. Ironically, in *Estelle*, the U.S. Supreme Court rejected the inmate's claims, but they set forth a new legal standard for prison health care, albeit more of a "floor" standard than a "ceiling" standard. That is, so long as prisons provide "adequate, reactive" health care, avoiding "deliberate indifference" in the provision of care, they have met the standard established by the U.S. Supreme Court. In the healthy prison, we will need to exceed this minimum standard to restore health and promote healthy lifestyles. The question at hand is how to best address standards of care for correctional health services.

Beyond these legal standards, prisons and correctional systems were already trying to establish proper prison health care. Indeed, Anno (2001, pp. 23–24) provides an overview of the evolution of correctional health standards. She notes that as early as 1966 the American Correctional Association (ACA) began to directly address health and medical care standards. The National Advisory Commission on Criminal Justice Standards and Goals and the National Sheriffs' Association (NSA) also began to develop health care–related standards in the early 1970s. The American Public Health Association (APHA) published national health care standards specifically for prisons and jails in 1976, which were later revised in 1986 and 2003. In 1977, the American Medical Association (AMA) published health care standards for jails, followed by a set of standards for prisons in 1979. Moreover, the ACA was utilizing the AMA standards as the basis of its revised health care standards by 1977, according to Anno (2001).

Evidence shows that most industry standards in the United States are voluntary consensus standards developed within industry sectors (Office of Management and Budget, 1998). Correctional health standards, while falling into this category, are generally proprietary standards, linked to accreditation by private organizations such as the ACA and the National Commission on Correctional Health Care (NCCHC). For those prison facilities that operate infirmaries or hospitals, the Joint Commission (2012) standards also apply. But while participation in voluntary standards of its face would seem to produce better outcomes, it remains an open question whether participation in such standards actually produces better outcomes. The only mandated prison health care standards to carry federal regulatory authority are those associated with the Prison Rape Elimination Act (PREA) of 2003 (42 U.S.C. 15601 et seq.). While the medical and mental health standards in the PREA standards are specific to sexual assault cases, they require all of the voluntary accrediting agencies, as well as prison systems that do not participate in any of those accrediting programs, to adopt this set of standards or risk losing federal funding.

The final ancestral piece for the healthy prison is the aforementioned *Brown v. Plata* (2011) decision. In *Brown*, the U.S. Supreme Court ordered California to release approximately 37,000 inmates due to constitutional deficiencies in health care delivery resulting from severe overcrowding. Quite simply, California had too many prisoners, which affected its ability to provide constitutionally mandated health services. The long-term ramifications for the California system and other state correctional systems from the *Brown* decision is unknown, and California's reaction to *Brown* was to shift the overpopulation burden to the state's jail system (California Department of Corrections and Rehabilitation, 2011); whether this solves California's problem remains to be seen. But while *Brown* does not directly state what types of care *should* be available, it does cover the range of problems that *can* disrupt access to adequate health care, including overcrowding, understaffing, and poorly maintained facilities that confront most American correctional systems at the federal, state, and local levels. Given the impact of *Estelle* on correctional health care, *Brown* will likely have a similar and significant impact as prisons and jails continue to struggle to meet their statutory and constitutional requirements in the current economic climate.

From this brief history, we can see that courts have created a health care standard for correctional systems and that these systems are liable if they do not deliver adequate and reactive health care in a constitutional manner. Professional organizations and accrediting bodies also have created some health care standards and practices. But the question remains, beyond these constitutional and professional standards, what should the healthy prison look like?

The Healthy Prison's Mandate

Scholars have already set forth visions and mandates for prison health care. Indeed, Cullen, Sundt, and Wozniak (2001, p. 268) argued that it was time to develop a vision of prisons for the 21st century, what they termed the "virtuous prison":

> Prisons should be considered moral institutions and corrections a moral enterprise. Inmates should be seen as having the obligation to become virtuous people and to manifest moral goodness. This statement announces that there are standards of right and wrong and that offenders must conform to them inside and outside of prisons. *The notion of a virtuous prison, however, also suggests that the correctional regime should be organized to fulfill the reciprocal obligation of providing offenders with the means to become virtuous. . . . The virtuous prison is being advanced as a progressive reform, as a way of humanizing imprisonment and of contributing to the commonwealth of communities.* (Emphasis added)

In their text on decision making and rationality in the criminal justice system, Gottfredson and Gottfredson (1988, pp. 271–272) noted that decisions required "alternative courses of action" be available to decision makers. These alternative decisions—which we invent—are parts of the evolution of the criminal justice system. This chapter is intended as part of that imagination/invention process with regard to health and corrections as part of a "virtuous prison."

The idea of a healthy prison also cannot be divorced from the concept of rehabilitation. While most attention to prisoner health has focused on the relatively rare transmission of non-respiratory infectious diseases (a point we will address later), less has been paid to what walks through the sally port. This seems odd, as "importation" (Clemmer, 1949) remains a key concept in discussing other aspects of prisoners' lives we hope to affect during their incarceration.

Marquart, Merianos, Hebert, and Carroll (1997), in an article aimed at examining how external sociopolitical factors might affect correctional health care, address two of the key issues before us:

> An important contribution of research on the criminal justice system is the identification of background characteristics of persons brought into the system and an examination of how the system affects their lives. To accomplish this goal as it relates to prisoners, researchers must come to understand health condition and ultimately morbidity/mortality within correctional populations as an outcome linked to personal attributes, acquired risks, biological risks, efforts at self-care—the pre-institutional dimension. In short, scholars must examine the health condition of prisoners prior to confinement and explore how prisoner health condition during confinement is affect by confinement. (p. 186)

All that is missing from their statement is asking how correctional health care, or the lack thereof, affects the community once prisoners are released into the free world, and how health care delivered during incarceration can continue into the free world. Their basic thesis, conceptual framework, and the research agenda proposed stress the relationships among criminal justice enforcement and sentencing policies and a wide range of correctional health issues. The arguments presented address not only infectious and chronic diseases often associated with substance abuse, but also the impact of increasing numbers of violent inmates being sentenced and the aging inmate population.

Marquart et al. (1997) weave the life-course perspective (now a staple of developmental criminology) with existing research on the general decline of health status in the United States (and minority groups in particular) and the profile of inmates entering prison systems (in particular). They point out the impact of social conditions on the health chances (and life chances) of segments of society most likely to enter prisons. These preexisting, or imported, health conditions are then affected by the prison experience. They cite the work of Wallace, Klein-Saffran, Gaes, and Moritsugu (1991), focusing on federal prisoners, to argue that, at that point in time, the health status of the vast majority (90%) of prisoners did not change from entry to exit from prison, while 6% worsened and 4% improved. Their basic point is that the health status of a prisoner is a result of complex interactions between the prisoner's pre-incarceration status and the incarceration experience. Theirs is also one of the first articles in the literature to link physical and psychological health concerns entering correctional facilities. In a theme echoed in several later studies, they state that the best predictor of health status while incarcerated is health status before incarceration.

Hence, in imagining the healthy prison and its mandate, these preexisting conditions feed the majority of medical needs of inmates and require the healthy prison to comport to clinical and constitutional standards. Moreover, the Hippocratic Oath's requirement to "keep them from harm and injustice"—that is, the long-standing ethical standard to "first, do no harm"—is paramount in the mandate. But this requires knowledge of inmate health status both pre-incarceration and while incarcerated. So what is the health status of inmates when they enter the gates of the healthy prison? In the next section, we will examine this in greater detail.

The Healthy Prison's Patients

Anno (1997) provides an overview of research on the health status of inmates entering correctional facilities through the mid-1990s. Her presentation summarizes prior research on specific health risk behaviors. She found that prisoners tend to utilize tobacco, alcohol, and other substances at higher rates than in the general public, and that the initiation of these behaviors is at younger ages than among the non-incarcerated population. With regard to sexual behaviors, Anno notes that our knowledge of pre-incarceration sexual behavior is primarily based on inferences "from their lower socioeconomic status, their criminal histories of sex offenses including prostitution, their heavy substance abuse, and their medical conditions" (p. 293). Drawing especially on the results of mostly single jail-based seroprevalence studies, Anno notes the high rates of sexually transmitted diseases (STDs) entering correctional facilities, but adds little information about actual sexual behaviors pre-incarceration.

Anno concludes that we know very little about problematic pre-incarceration health behaviors such as nutrition and exercise, self-mutilation and suicidal behaviors, or violent victimization and/or perpetration. Nutrition and exercise experience, along with substance use, will have a longer term impact on chronic health conditions as prisoners age (a theme in later research). Self-harm and harm to others will also play a role on in-prison health and health care utilization, as well as possible exportation back into the community upon release.

Hart's (1971) "inverse care law" suggests that quality medical care is least available in those communities where it is needed most. This is especially true in market economies such as the United States. Since we draw our prison populations disproportionately from lower socioeconomic status and minority communities, it follows that these people, mostly males, are also likely to have received little health care prior to arrival in prison (or perhaps in jail). This is particularly true of preventative and chronic health care.

These differences in burden of disease and access to and utilization of health care are demonstrated in mortality outcomes across race/ethnic groups in the United States (see Table 8.1). In every cause-of-death category, African Americans die at higher rates than other ethnic groups. Hispanics and Native Americans demonstrate higher death rates than Whites in diabetes. The final two columns of Table 8.1 compare the mortality rates from these diseases for the nation in 2004 and among state prisoners from 2001 to 2004. Although the rates are quite different, with the exception of mortality from diabetes, the ranking of the causes is very similar. Thus, the diseases that disproportionately affect minority and poor people in the "free world" quite likely affect the burden of disease and mortality observed inside prison walls.

Moreover, little information about the health of prisoners at entry, during their incarceration, or at the time they leave the prison is available to criminal justice researchers. What little we do have comes from occasional self-reports of inmate health problems, reviews of administrative records, or single facility studies.

Table 8.1   Death Rates (per 100,000 population) for Selected Chronic Diseases[a] and National Total (2004) Compared to Prisoners (per 100,000 population[b])

Disease	Whites	African American	Asian/ Pacific Islanders	American Indian/ Alaska Native	Hispanic	U.S. Total 2004[c]	Prisoners (2001– 2004)
Heart Disease	267.8	346.4	158.6	185.1	176.1	222.2	68
Stroke	60.6	84.8	54.0	42.9	40.0	51.1	8
All Cancers	204.3	262.5	129.3	136.8	122.1	188.6	58
Diabetes	22.0	51.6	19.0	54.2	33.6	24.9	—

a. Anderson, R. N., & Smith, B. L. (2005). Deaths: Leading causes for 2002. *National Vital Statistics Reports, 53*, 17.

b. Mumola, C. J. (2007). *Medical causes of death in state prisons, 2001–2004*. Washington, DC: Bureau of Justice Statistics.

c. National Center for Health Statistics, Centers for Disease Control and Prevention. (2004). *Deaths, percent of total deaths, and death rate for the 15 leading causes of death in 5-year age groups, by race and sex: United States, 2004*. Retrieved June 1, 2012, from http://www.cdc.gov/nchs/data/dvs/LCWK1_2004.pdf.

Maruschak and Beck (2001) reported data from federal and state inmates (respectively) in 1997 summarizing administrative records of medical conditions. Among those incarcerated, 1.1% and 1.3% had heart problems, 0.2% and 0.3% had cancer, 0.9% and 1.5% had diabetes, 0.9% and 0.5% had liver/kidney problems, 0.9% and 1.4% had respiratory problems, and 0.7% and 0.4% had neurological problems. Data taken from official medical records in the Federal Bureau of Prisons for 2000 on a variety of diseases are also reported here. Among the federal prisoners, 4.4% had asthma, 3.6% had diabetes, 2.5% had heart disease, and 7.8% were hypertensive. Their report also examined medical problems such as injuries, which increase with age and length of time spent in incarceration.

Using data on health care utilization by state inmates in Kentucky imprisoned during the 1993–1998 time frame, Garrity, Hiller, Staton, Webster, and Leukefeld (2002) examined health conditions among state prisoners, some of whom had participated in drug treatment programs and others who had not done so. Their research questions focused on the impact of pre-incarceration variables on in-prison health status, and utilization of both physical and mental health services. Their basic conclusion with regard to health status while incarcerated is that "ill health prior to incarceration continues during incarceration. . . . It is possible that underlying emotional distress consistently experienced from before to after incarceration provokes the perception of and/or the reality of consistent physical illness" (p. 306). They also found that self-rated health status in the six months prior to the interview was one of the strongest predictors of in-prison illness (p. 306). Basically, the healthier prisoners perceived themselves to be, the fewer illness episodes were reported in official records.

Colsher, Wallace, Loeffelholz, and Sales (1992) presented data on the health status of prisoners aged 50 and older ("older inmates") incarcerated in Iowa's state prison system during 1989. While 65% of the 119 respondents characterized their current health as "excellent or good," more than half noted their health had deteriorated since their confinement. Unfortunately, there were no controls entered for how long individuals had been incarcerated. Thus, we are unable to determine whether it is the age at confinement, or growing older inside the walls that contributed to the perceived deterioration. The problematic conditions identified by the respondents included chronic illnesses such as arthritis, hypertension, ulcers, prostate problems, and myocardial infarction. The seriousness and number of problems increased with age, those above the age of 60 having significantly more problem conditions than those between 50 and 60.

Hepatitis C (HCV) has emerged as one of the most widespread and potentially serious health threats among incarcerated individuals. Ruiz, Molitor, and Plagenhoef (2002) conducted a comparison of HCV and HIV seroprevalence rates among entrants to a California state correctional facility in 1999 and 1994. Of all entrants in 1994, 41.2% (39.4% of males and 54.5% of females) were HCV positive and 3.2% (2.4% of males and 3.2% of females) were HIV positive. In 1999, the percentage of men testing positive for HCV had dropped to 34.2% and for women to 25.3% (drops of 13% and 54%, respectively). HIV positivity for men dropped to 1.4% and for women to 1.7% (declines of 42% and 47%, respectively). The authors attribute declines in prevalence to possible reduction in intravenous drug use (IDU) or an increase in safer injecting practices, though there was a general decline in reported drug arrests in the state. Offsetting the generally progressive declines was a 16% rise in the number of African American men testing positive for HCV antibodies over the five-year period, and that African Americans in general had the highest rates of infection among racially defined groups among the new prisoners in 1999.

Baillargeon et al. (2004) examined infectious disease codes (ICD-10) for medical problems diagnosed at intake physicals on all incoming prisoners in the Texas state correctional system from January 1999 through December 2001 ($N = 336,688$). The diseases, in ranked order (rate per 100,000 prisoners), were latent TB (tuberculosis) (16,511), HCV (8,377), HIV/AIDS (1,458), syphilis (655), methicillin-resistant staphylococcus aureus (MRSA; 328), herpes zostor (206), hepatitis B (HVB; 84), active TB (39), pneumonia (27), gonorrhea (15), and encephalitis (4). The latent TB rate was highest among African Americans, Latinos, and males. HCV rates were highest among Whites and females. HIV/AIDS and syphilis rates were highest among African Americans and women. MRSA and HVB rates were highest among Whites and women. Herpes and encephalitis rates were highest among Whites and males. Active TB rates were highest among Latinos and males. Pneumonia and gonorrhea rates were highest among African Americans and males. Regardless of the disease, rates tended to be higher as the age of the inmate increased. Unfortunately, there were no controls for prior incarceration history included in the analysis to examine whether first-time entrants were in better or worse health status in terms of these infections. Prevalence rates, while not directly comparable, were higher than the general community for HIV/AIDS, HCV, and marginally higher for active TB, but the same or lower for the remaining diseases.

In an attempt to provide comparisons to national disease rates, Hammett, Harmon, and Rhodes (2002; see also National Commission on Correctional Health Care, 2002) compared diagnoses among prisoners to those in a variety of national studies conducted by researchers at the Centers for Disease Control and Prevention (CDC). The authors note that their estimates are based on disease prevalence in state and federal prison systems, though the sources of those data are quite variable in scope and completeness. Thus, the authors warn that these should be considered "rough rates" (Hammett et al., 2002, p. 1792) for comparison purposes. Overall, their results suggest that, particularly among infectious diseases, the burden of these diseases was anywhere from 12 to 35 times higher among prisoners than observed in the general public. We have reproduced their data in Table 8.2.

The latest available national-level self-reports of state and federal prisoner health issues (Maruschak, 2008) continue to show how the diseases brought into prisons compare with national-level disease rates (see Table 8.3). Information on prisoners held in state prison systems is collected in the Survey of Inmates in State Correctional Facilities (SISCF), collected "periodically," with the most recent collection in 2004. Finally, conducted jointly by the Bureau of Justice Statistics (BJS) and the Federal Bureau of Prisons (FBOP), the Survey of Inmates in Federal Correctional Facilities (SIFCF) is conducted at the same time as the SISCF, and the most recent data are from the 2004 survey. The primary results from these surveys are summarized in Table 8.2, along with comparisons from the 2009–2010 national data from the CDC.

Because the prisoner reports are not confirmed medical diagnoses, and the CDC data are test results, we urge readers not to draw firm conclusions. Rather, we offer these to show how widely estimates of a variety of disease burdens range when self-reports and clinical data are compared. In looking at the two sources of data, we note that in some areas self-reported conditions are higher in prisoners than the clinical data among the national sample. This is especially true of HIV, arguably the disease receiving the most attention from health researchers. When other chronic and lifestyle diseases are examined, however, prisoners are either below or comparable to the national estimates. This is, in all probability, the younger age profile of prisoners than in the national sample. As the prisoner population ages, we may see a narrowing of these gaps. In some cases, we may even see prisoners surpass the general public due to diseases associated with behaviors such as substance abuse and trauma associated with violence, especially traumatic brain injuries.

It has been necessary to understand the dynamics and scope of the health issues that come into the prison systems around the nation in order to begin to frame the development of the healthy prison. There is first the issue of restoration to health for those who enter the gates ill. For some, the disease state is transitory and restoration can be achieved for the future (e.g., bacterial STDs, hepatitis A). Others bring chronic disease burdens whose maintenance, or continuity of care, will require continuous monitoring for the remainder of the lifespan (e.g., diabetes, HIV).

Table 8.2 National Estimates of Selected Infectious Diseases Among Inmates and Releasees and Prevalence in U.S.

Disease	Estimated Prevalence Among Inmates, %		Prevalence in U.S. Population, 1996, %	Estimated Number of Inmates w/Condition 1997	Estimated Number of Releasees w/Condition 1996	Number in U.S. Population w/Condition, 1996	Releasees With Condition as % of Total in U.S. Population w/ Condition, 1996
	Prisons	Jails					
AIDS	0.5[a]	0.5[a]	0.09	8,900	39,000	229,000[b]	17.0
HIV infection (non-AIDS)	2.3–2.98[c]	1.2–1.8[d]	0.3	35,000–47,000	98,000–145,000	750,000[e]	13.1–19.3
Syphilis Infection	2.6–4.3	2.6–4.3	N/A	46,000–76,000	202,000–332,000	N/A	—
Chlamydia	2.4	2.4	N/A	43,000	186,000	N/A	—
Gonorrhea	1.0	1.0	N/A	18,000	77,000	N/A	—
Hepatitis B Infection	2.0[f]	2.0	N/A	36,000	155,000	1,000,000–1,250,000[g]	12.4–15.5
Hepatitis C Infection	17.0–18.6[f,h]	17.0–18.6[h]	1.8	303,000–332,000	1,300,000–1,400,000	4,500,000[i]	28.9–32.0
TB Disease	0.04[j]	0.17[k]	0.01	1,400	12,000	34,000[l]	35.0
TB Infection	7.4	7.3	N/A	131,000	566,000	N/A	—

SOURCE: (unless otherwise noted in the footnotes): Hammett, T. M., Harmon, M. P., & Rhodes, W. (2002). The burden of infectious disease among inmates of and releasees from U.S. correctional facilities, 1997. *American Journal of Public Health, 92,* 1789–1794.

a. More than five times the prevalence in the U.S. population (0.09%).

b. U.S. Centers for Disease Control and Prevention. (1997). *HIV/AIDS Surveillance Report, 9(2),* 1–43.

c. Eight to ten times the prevalence in the U.S. population (0.3%).

d. Four to six times the prevalence in the U.S. population (0.3%).

e. CDC estimate, based on midpoint of 1993 estimate in Rosenberg, P. S. (1995). Scope of the AIDS epidemic in the United States. *Science, 270,* 1372–1375.

f. Current or chronic.

g. U.S. Centers for Disease Control. (1991). Hepatitis B virus: A comprehensive strategy for eliminating transmission in the United States through universal childhood vaccination: Recommendations of the Immunization Practices Advisory Committee (ACIP). *Morbidity and Mortality Weekly Report, 40*(RR-13), 1–19.

h. Nine to 10 times the prevalence in the U.S. population (1.8%).

i. Based on prevalence estimate in McQuillan G. M., Alter, M. J., Moyer, L. A., Lambert, S. B., & Margolis, H.S. (1997). A population-based serologic survey of hepatitis C virus infection in the U.S. In M. Rizzetto, R. H. Purcell, G. L. Gerin, and G. Verme (Eds.), *Viral hepatitis and liver disease* (pp. 267–270). Turin, Italy: Edizioni Minerva Medica.

j. Four times the prevalence in the U.S. population (0.01%).

k. Seventeen times the prevalence in the U.S. population (0.01%).

l. Estimated from CDC, TB Registry Reports, 1992–1994.

Table 8.3   Medical Problems Reported by State and Federal Prisoners in 2004 with Comparison to 2009–2010 National Data from the Centers for Disease Control and Prevention

		Prisoners, 2004	
Medical Problem	National	State	Federal
Chronic Diseases			
Arthritis	22.7%	15.3%	12.4%
Hypertension	31.9	13.8	13.2
Asthma	8.2	9.1	7.2
Heart Problems	11.8	6.1	6.0
Renal (Kidney) Problems	1.7	3.2	3.1
Diabetes	10.7	4.0	5.1
Hepatitis (unspecified)	26.7 – A 4.6 – B 1.3 – C	5.3	4.2
Liver Problems	0.9	1.1	1.1
Infectious Diseases			
TB (Lifetime)	3.6/100,000	9.4	7.1
HIV	0.54	1.6	1.0
Other Sexually Transmitted Diseases (STDs)	0.54	0.8	0.4

SOURCES: National Center for Health Statistics, Centers for Disease Control and Prevention. (2009–2010). *Fast stats, A–Z*. Retrieved June 1, 2012, from http://www.cdc.gov/nchs/fastats/Default.htm; Maruschak, L. (2008). *Medical problems of prisoners*. Washington, DC: U.S. Department of Justice.

Finally, for those who have not yet developed chronic diseases, there is the issue of prevention and education, sometimes known as disease prevention and health promotion.

The ultimate measure of health is death, or mortality. National-level information on causes of death among state prisoners in the United States has become available since the passage of the Deaths in Custody Reporting Act of 2000 (Public Law 106-297). Examining data from 2001 to 2004, Mumola (2007, p. 1) listed heart attacks (27%), cancers (23%; 1 in 3 from lung cancer), diseases of the liver (10%), HIV/AIDS (7%), and suicide (6%) as the causes of 80% of all deaths; homicide contributed just under 2% of deaths. Men died at higher rates than did women in prison. Mortality rates were higher as prisoner age increased (two thirds among prisoners over age 45), except for suicide, which was flat across age categories reported. Among those older prisoners who died, 85% were over the age of 45 when they were admitted to prison. Having been in prison for more than 10 years raised the probability of dying in prison by three times over those who had served five years. Sixty-eight percent of the fatal conditions had been diagnosed upon admission to the prison system (i.e., imported). Ninety-four percent of those who died had received medical evaluations for their condition, 89% had received some form of diagnostic test, and 93% had received medication for the condition that eventually caused their deaths.

The overall mortality rate among prisoners from 2001 to 2004 was 19% lower than in the resident population of the United States. Whether this is because of a "healthy prisoner" effect (Fazel & Benning, 2006), or some protective factor of imprisonment, as suggested by Spaulding et al. (2011), is another empirical question. Ironically, it appears that imprisonment is an overall protective factor for African American men, as Mumola (2007) reported a 57% reduction in death rates compared to their age-adjusted peers in the community. This was consistent with Spaulding et al.'s (2011) data from the Georgia Department of Corrections (GDOC) 15-year cohort, where Black men demonstrated a lower probability of dying in prison than their community peers, while non-Black men were likely to die at higher rates than their community peers. There were too few deaths among women prisoners in the GDOC cohort to draw conclusions. Rosen, Wohl, and Schoenbach (2011) observed similar results for prisoners held in North Carolina prisons. Black male prisoner death rates in prison were lower than their community peers' in all categories. White male prisoner death rates were lower for accidental deaths, but higher for most other key disease conditions than their community counterparts.

In sum, the data available on health conditions among state and federal prisoners in the United States do not suggest that they are a generally "diseased" population. There are higher rates of certain diseases in prisons than those observed in the community, to be sure. However, all of the available data suggest the majority of those diseases are brought into the facility, or "imported," from the community. That disease transmission does occur is a certainty. How much it occurs is the question to be answered.

Whether or not the health care delivered in prisons is adequate to meet the burden of disease entering the prison and developing during imprisonment is yet another question. In terms of certain states (e.g., California), we see the courts have determined that it is not adequate in all cases. The Texas, California, Florida, New York, and Pennsylvania prison systems accounted for 41% of the deaths reported in the 2001–2004 reporting period. Louisiana, Tennessee, Pennsylvania, West Virginia, and Kentucky reported the highest mortality rates during that time period. Thus, we see variation in the number, rates, and composition of deaths reported across the states (Mumola, 2007), making blanket statements about prison health somewhat perilous. In the end, the healthy prison system must be equipped to handle the treatment of a variety of diseases among its population. We examine whether or not blanket standards will improve this situation later in this chapter.

In spite of the sorts of data reported above, one of the enduring metaphors for prison health is that prisons are "reservoirs of disease" (e.g., Fazel & Baillargeon, 2011). Yet, those statements are generally followed by the admission that we know relatively little about the health of prisoners, as noted above. Assuming that acute, bacterial sorts of infectious diseases are addressed by prison health care, the primary "threat" prisoners pose to the public health upon their return to the community is from either chronic, infectious viral diseases or the cost burden associated with chronic noninfectious diseases.

One of the few areas where published information about prisoner health post-release can be found is in the areas of tuberculosis and HIV. Overall, the evidence that most people who obtain treatment in correctional settings for diseases as diverse as HIV and TB improve their health status while incarcerated is robust. That is, prison-based health care is effective. After release to the community, however, the picture becomes bleaker. Springer et al. (2004), Stephenson et al. (2005), Baillargeon et al. (2010), and Wohl et al. (2011) provided evidence that individuals living with HIV tended to get healthier while incarcerated, but were either lost to follow-up in the community or returned from the community to prison in poor health. With HIV among the few diseases for which we have had relatively strong community continuity-of-care systems, this does not bode well for other diseases with fewer community resources devoted to continuity of care. Whether this situation will change with universal health insurance mandates remains to be seen.

To better understand how the disease conditions prisoners bring back to the community affect public health, it is instructive to examine what former prisoners die from upon their release. This area of inquiry has become relatively active since the early 2000s, perhaps more outside the United States than inside. One of the first studies of causes of death of released state prisoners took place in Washington state (Binswanger et al., 2007). The researchers noted that within two weeks of release, the cohort had an age-adjusted death rate 12.7 times higher than other state residents; within two years it had diminished to 3.5 times higher. Leading causes of death in the cohort were drug overdose, cardiovascular disease, homicide, and suicide.

Spaulding et al. (2011) followed a one-year cohort of released inmates from the GDOC in 1991 for 15 years focusing on "excess mortality" ("defined as the sum of the excess deaths from each cause [observed minus expected] divided by the total number of excess deaths"). They found that the cohort had a higher rate of mortality than the general population of Georgia. Specifically, deaths from HIV, homicide, accidental poisoning, cancer, traffic fatalities, and cirrhosis and other liver diseases contributed the bulk of the deaths. HIV and homicide were the greatest contributors to excess mortality. Cardiovascular diseases, curiously, did not differ greatly as a cause of death among the released persons relative to the general state population.

A challenge for the healthy prison is, then, not only to equip departing prisoners with adequate pharmaceuticals to get them to their first community medical appointment but to instill the motivation and understanding of why this is important to the individual and the community. Developing relationships with community resources to make the connections in as supportive a manner as possible becomes a key element of the healthy prison.

The Healthy Prison

As we have outlined in this chapter, there are significant challenges in dealing with health care delivery in prisons along with the disease burden of incoming and departing inmates. Thus, we imagine that the healthy prison should be nimble and adaptable to changing standards of care that are medically reactive and constitutionally adequate. It would engage in preventive care, health promotion, and education among its staff and inmates and do so in a manner that maximizes benefits to inmates while minimizing the cost to public coffers. However, there are challenges that confront this ideal. One challenge comes from the security of an institution when lockdowns and other limitations on inmate mobility within the facility are implemented for operational and safety concerns and that may override or interfere with medical care. Another challenge is continuity of care when inmates are transferred to other facilities or discharged into the community. How does that inmate access the care he or she needs for his or her illness or condition? Along with the continuity-of-care challenge is inmate compliance with therapy or treatment as inmates have a constitutional right to refuse treatment (unless directed by a court order). How do institutions cope with refusal?

Moreover, prison health does not exist in a social vacuum. Public and legislative sentiment can present hurdles as there are those who feel that inmates do not deserve medical care that exceeds the care available to many in the free world. Some may feel that lack of adequate medical care is one of the pains of imprisonment, while others feel that prison already affords inmates health amenities. Take, for example, Justice Scalia who stated in his dissent in *Brown v. Plata* (2011) that most inmates "will undoubtedly be fine physical specimens who have developed intimidating muscles pumping iron in the prison gym" (p. 5).

Lastly, and consistent with the resource dependency perspective of Pfeffer and Salancik (2003), prisons must depend upon others in their organizational environment to provide funding. We have noted their dependence on an occupational marketplace to produce health care workers willing to serve in these settings. As some states (and localities) continue to turn to contracted health care provision, the issues of public sentiment, legislative funding, disease burden, and constitutional mandates will, no doubt, clash.

Developing the Healthy Prison

There are two basic structural formulae that already exist for developing a healthy prison system in the United States. The first is a model similar to the approach used by the Federal Bureau of Prisons (BOP). The BOP utilizes a mixture of civil service employees (approximately 2,250) and Public Health Service Commissioned Corps (approximately 750) health professionals to deliver care across the 117 institutions and approximately 180,000 prisoners under its custody (U.S. Federal Bureau of

Prisons, 2012). This requires a core group of medically licensed public employees who both provide care and manage additional health services, including prevention, education, and health promotion.

The second is a model similar to that encountered in Australia. All Australians participate in the Medicare program, paying a Medicare levy of 1.5% of their taxable income. For those who make above a certain income threshold and do not have private hospitalization coverage, an additional surcharge may be involved (Australian Taxation Office, 2012). Most germane to our discussion is the idea that there is a functioning public health delivery system in the Australian states. Whether in the free world or in a state prison, one has access to health services delivered by the same agency as would serve those in the community. The major drawback to achieving this change in U.S. prison care is the lack of a functioning public health care system in most states. The caveat here is, of course, that access to care does not guarantee effective utilization of health care, particularly preventive health care.

Perhaps under the Affordable Care Act (passed in 2010), we will see the development of a functional public health care delivery system, similar to that of the public health system in Australia. Should this occur, with a dedicated public health work force prison health care would simply be an extension of health care delivered in the community. This would also encourage a seamless continuity-of-care process that can build on the benefits of enforced sobriety and low exposure to unintended injuries reported in studies outlined earlier.

Even with preventive, emergent, and chronic care provision in prison populations that match their communities, we still have to instill the knowledge about and motivation to utilize health care effectively to produce good health. The healthy prison must develop health education/health promotion programs to make prisoners aware of the appropriate use of health care of all types. This will include the necessity of developing motivations to become and/or remain healthy. Just as we can forcibly keep someone sober only to see them overdose shortly after returning to the community because we did not address their addiction, we can also restrict the drinks and foods that are sold in canteens and commissaries in prisons and provided in chow halls to ensure "good" nutrition only to see people return to their poor nutrition back in the community. The same can be said of physical activity. As in the virtuous prison, reciprocity is essential: If we are to demand lasting change in a virtuous and healthy direction, we must provide inmates with the means to achieve these goals.

If we do not change the ways of thinking about nutrition, exercise, and preventive and/or chronic care among those in our prisons, the healthy prison will be little more than a rest stop in the dimension of health among those who pass through. This is a crux of the epidemiological criminology framework; the same dimensions of risk underlie poor health choices and behaviors as underlie those that lead to patterned criminal behaviors (Akers, Potter, & Hill, 2013). To produce lasting change, we must not only help prisoners recognize their need for change and provide them with the tools to change, but also ensure that the changes they make can be maintained back in the free world. Otherwise, we risk adding nothing more than another experience of social control beyond their personal control to the list of many others they experience while in prison.

The structural- and individual-level changes required must also be accompanied by organizational-level changes. Combined with the discussions of the safe prison, we will have to reconceptualize the purpose of imprisonment. We noted earlier that the healthy prison is part of a rehabilitative prison. We see no way in which an organization geared only to the warehousing and/or incapacitation of individuals can be a healthy prison beyond the imposition of oppressive health regimens on the captives within. Prisons must themselves become facilities that model and motivate those held in them to adopt and maintain healthy attitudes and lifestyles. In the end, the healthy prison is truly a reflection of the larger society in which it is embedded. Personal health can be either a product of self-enlightened liberty or of state-imposed coercion. The same is true of freedom.

Conclusion

The healthy prison is part of a healthy society. We mentioned the Australian Medicare situation earlier, in which all residents participate at the emergent care level and a functioning public health and medical care delivery system exists. Even there, we observe many of the same maladies entering the prison system from the community as we observe here in the United States (see, Indig et al., 2010). This is because of behaviors in the community such as substance abuse, as officials of New South Wales Prison Health once explained to one of the authors.

Healthy prisons reflect healthy societies, just as "sick" prisons reflect the health of the communities from which we draw our prison populations currently. At present our U.S. prisons partially reflect the health of those communities and the ravages of substance abuse, mental illness, and violence. To change the health of our prisons may require that we change the health of our communities.

To end on a hopeful note, the healthy prison is not far from where we are now. Orienting our prison system beyond rehabilitation of behavior toward rehabilitation of behavior *and* body is one of the first steps we must take. Rather than settling for a hospital of hope or sanatorium of death, we must embrace the responsibility of providing care for those we deprive of liberty. To this end, criminal justice professionals, applied and academic, should become advocates for effective public health and public health care programs. We should also be informing our public health colleagues more directly about the ways in which our research and theories can be used to address changes needed to produce desired outcomes. A caveat here is that we must do so within the civil and human rights of the residents of our nation, respecting the right to make bad choices and to pay the price for those poor decisions. Otherwise, as we have stated elsewhere (Potter & Rosky, 2012), the iron fist will simply don the latex glove and add another layer of formal social control to bring even more inmates, both hale and infirm, through the healthy prison's gates.

References

Anderson, R. N., & Smith, B. L. (2005). Deaths: Leading causes for 2002. *National Vital Statistics Reports, 53*, 17.

Akers, T. A., Potter, R. H., & Hill, C. V. (2013). *Epidemiological criminology: A public health approach to crime and violence.* San Francisco, CA: Jossey-Bass.

Anno, B. J. (1997). Health behaviors in prisons and correctional facilities. In D. S. Goehman (Ed.), *Handbook of health behaviors research III* (pp. 289–303). New York, NY: Plenum.

Anno, B. J. (2001). *Correctional health care: Guidelines for the management of an adequate delivery system* (2nd ed.). Chicago, IL: National Commission on Correctional Health Care.

Australian Taxation Office. (2012). *Guide to Medicare levy.* Retrieved June 1, 2012, from http://www.ato.gov.au/individuals/content.aspx?doc=/content/00250854 .htm&page=11

Baillargeon, J., Black, S. A., Leach, C. T., Jenson, H., Pulvino, J., Bradshaw, P., & Murray, O. (2004). The infectious disease profile of Texas prison inmates. *Preventive Medicine, 38*, 607–612.

Baillargeon, J., Penn, J. V., Knight, K., Harzke, A. J., Baillargeon, G., & Becker, E. A. (2010). Risk of reincarceration among prisoners with co-occurring severe mental illness and substance use disorders. *Administration and Policy in Mental Health and Mental Health Services Research, 37*, 367–374.

Binswanger, I. A., Stern, M. F., Deyo, R. A., Heagerty, P. J., Cheadle, A., Elmore, J. G., & Koepsell, T. D. (2007). Release from prison—A high risk of death for former inmates. *New England Journal of Medicine, 356*, 157–165.

Brown v. Plata, 563 U.D. (2011).

California Department of Corrections and Rehabilitation. (2011). *June 2011 population report; plans for complying with three-judge court order.* Retrieved June 1, 2012, from http://www.cdcr.ca.gov/News/docs/6.7.11-Response-to-1.12.10-Order.pdf

Clemmer, D. (1949). A beginning in social education in correctional institutions. *Federal Probation, 13*(1), 32–35.

Colsher, P. L., Wallace, R. B., Loeffelholz, P. L., & Sales, M. (1992). Health status of older male prisoners: A comprehensive survey. *American Journal of Public Health, 82*, 881–884.

Cullen, F. T., Sundt, J. L., & Wozniak, J. F. (2001). The virtuous prison: Toward a restorative rehabilitation. In H. N. Pontell & D. Shichor (Eds.), *Contemporary issues in crime and criminal justice: Essays in honor of Gilbert Geis* (pp. 265–286). Upper Saddle River, NJ: Prentice Hall.

Estelle v. Gamble, 429 U.S. 97 (1976).

Fazel, S., & Baillargeon, J. (2011). The health of prisoners. *The Lancet, 377*, 956–965.

Fazel, S., & Benning, R. (2006). Natural deaths in male prisoners: A 20-year mortality study. *European Journal of Public Health, 16*, 441–444.

Garrity, T. F., Hiller, M. L., Staton, M., Webster, J. M., & Leukefeld, K. J. (2002). Factors predicting illness and health services use among male Kentucky prisoners with a history of drug abuse. *The Prison Journal, 82*, 295–313.

Gottfredson, M. R., &, Gottfredson, D. M. (1988). *Decision making in criminal justice.* New York, NY: Plenum.

Hammett, T. M., Harmon, M. P., & Rhodes, W. (2002). The burden of infectious disease among inmates of and releasees from U.S. correctional facilities, 1997. *American Journal of Public Health, 92*, 1789–1794.

Hart J. T. (1971). The inverse care law. *Lancet, 1*, 405–412.

Indig, D., Topp, L., Ross, B., Mamoon, H., Border, B., Kumar, S., & McNamara, M. (2010). *2009 NSW Inmate Health Survey: Key findings report.* Sydney, NSW, Australia: Justice Health.

Joint Commission. (2012). *Main page.* Retrieved June 1, 2012, from http://www .jointcommission.org/

Marquart, J. W., Merianos, D. E., Hebert, J. L., & Carroll, L. (1997). Health condition and prisoners: A review of research and emerging areas of inquiry. *The Prison Journal, 7*, 184–208.

Maruschak, L. (2008). *Medical problems of prisoners.* Washington, DC: U.S. Department of Justice.

Maruschak, L. M., & Beck, A. J. (2001). *Medical problems of inmates, 1997.* Washington, DC: Bureau of Justice Assistance.

McQuillan G. M., Alter, M. J., Moyer, L. A., Lambert, S. B., & Margolis, H. S. (1997). A population-based serologic survey of hepatitis C virus infection in the U.S. In M. Rizzetto, R. H. Purcell, G. L. Gerin, & G. Verme (Eds.), *Viral hepatitis and liver disease* (pp. 267–270.). Turin, Italy: Edizioni Minerva Medica.

Mumola, C. J. (2007). *Medical causes of death in state prisons, 2001–2004.* Washington, DC: Bureau of Justice Statistics.

National Center for Health Statistics, Centers for Disease Control and Prevention. (2004). *Deaths, percent of total deaths, and death rate for the 15 leading causes of death in 5-year age groups, by race and sex: United States, 2004.* Retrieved June 1, 2012, from http:// www.cdc.gov/nchs/data/dvs/LCWK1_2004.pdf

National Center for Health Statistics, Centers for Disease Control and Prevention. (2009–2010). *Fast stats, A–Z.* Retrieved June 1, 2012, from http://www.cdc.gov/nchs/fastats/ Default.htm

National Commission on Correctional Health Care. (2002). *Health status of soon-to-be-released inmates: Vol. 1.* Chicago: Author.

Office of Management and Budget. (1998). *Memorandum for heads of executive departments and agencies, Circular No. A-119, revised.* Washington, DC: Office of Management and Budget. Retrieved June 1, 2012, from http://standards.gov/a119.cfm#4

Pfeffer, J., & Salancik, G. R. (2003). *The external control of organizations: A resource dependence perspective.* Stanford, CA: Stanford University Press.

Potter, R. H., & Rosky, J. W. (2012). The iron fist in the latex glove: The intersection of criminal justice and public health. *American Journal of Criminal Justice.*

Rosen, D. L., Wohl, D. A., & Schoenbach, V. J. (2011). All-cause and cause-specific mortality among Black and White North Carolina state prisoners, 1995–2005. *Annals of Epidemiology, 21*, 719–726.

Rosenberg, P. S. (1995). Scope of the AIDS epidemic in the United States. *Science, 270*, 1372–1375.

Ruiz, J. D., Molitor, F., & Plagenhoef, J. A. (2002). Trends in hepatitis C and HIV infection among inmates entering prisons in California, 1994 versus 1999. *AIDS, 16*, 2236–2238.

Spaulding, A. C., Seals, R. M., McCallum, V. A., Perez, S. D., Brzozowski, A. K., & Steenland, N. K. (2011). Prisoner survival inside and outside of the institution: Implications for health-care planning. *American Journal of Epidemiology, 173*, 479–487.

Spicer v. Williamson, 132 S.E. 291, 293 (N.C. 1926).

Springer, S. A., Pesanti, E., Hodges, J., Macura, T., Doros, G., & Altice, F. L. (2004). Infected prisoners: Reincarceration and the lack of sustained benefit after release to the community. *Clinical Infectious Diseases, 38*, 1754–1460.

Stephenson, B. L., Wohl, D. A., Golin, C. E., Tien, H.-C., Stewart, P., & Kaplan, A. H. (2005). Effect of release from prison and re-incarceration on the viral loads of HIV-infected individuals. *Public Health Reports, 120*, 84–88

Turbyfill, D. (2011, June 16). Bank robber planned crime and punishment. *The Gaston Gazette*. Retrieved August 1, 2012, from http://www.gastongazette.com/articles/bank-58397-richard-hailed.html

U.S. Centers for Disease Control. (1991). Hepatitis B virus: A comprehensive strategy for eliminating transmission in the United States through universal childhood vaccination: Recommendations of the Immunization Practices Advisory Committee (ACIP). *Morbidity and Mortality Weekly Report, 40*(RR-13), 1–19.

U.S. Centers for Disease Control and Prevention. (1997). *HIV/AIDS Surveillance Report, 9*(2), 1–43.

U.S. Federal Bureau of Prisons. (2012). *About the Bureau of Prisons*. Retrieved from August 2, 2012, from http://www.bop.gov/about/index.jsp

Wallace, S., Klein-Saffran, J., Gaes, G., & Moritsugu, K. (1991). Health status of federal inmates: A comparison of admission and release medical records. *Journal of Jail and Prison Health, 10*, 133–151.

Wohl, D. A., Sheyett, A., Golin, C. E., White, B., Matuszewski, J., Bowling, M., & Earp, J. (2011). Intensive case management before and after prison release is no more effective than comprehensive pre-release discharge planning in linking HIV-infected prisoners to care: A randomized trial. *AIDS and Behavior, 15*, 356–364.

Part V

Reinventing the Prison

9

The Private Prison

Kevin A. Wright

Editors' Introduction

The American prison was founded with inordinate optimism. It was to be a place of national pride, a forward-looking invention that would replace barbaric punishments with life in an environment designed to reform the very spirit of offenders. Much contemporary scholarship on prisons, however, is devoted to illuminating how the correctional enterprise has fallen far short of this grand goal. In fact, books on imprisonment often read much like a social problems text, showing how the society of captives is marked by severe crowding, insufficient programs if not idleness, gangs and racial conflict, inmate-on-inmate victimizations, and a correctional staff whose primary orientation is to ensure custodial order at all costs. Not surprisingly, nearly all prominent criminologists decry the current state of American prisons and favor reducing their use.

In this context of institutional failure, an alternative paradigm for constructing and administering prisons emerged: privatization. If the public sector could not operate high quality prisons, why not rely on the private sector to do so? Most criminologists, however, were appalled by this idea. Perhaps their largest fear was that if companies could make money by owning prisons, they would become a powerful interest group for expanding imprisonment in the United States. But at least two problems beset this opposition to privatization. First, the push toward mass imprisonment was already well under way and was being fueled by other powerful political and social forces. Second, these scholars—many of them noted critics of prisons—inadvertently ended up as defenders of existing correctional institutions. This is similar to educational reformers arguing in favor of failing inner-city schools because they do not want to see the emergence of charter schools. It is not clear why privatization should be dismissed out of hand when public institutions are doing an inadequate job of caring for their charges.

None of this is to say that privatization is a panacea for all that ails prisons—or, for that matter, schools—a key point that Kevin Wright makes in the chapter to follow. As he suggests, privatization is a means to an end, not an end in and of itself. Similar to any other resource or policy tool, it can be used wisely or unwisely. Thus far, the jury is still out on whether private companies run better prisons than those in the public sector. More research is needed, but it seems that prisons, regardless of whether they are public or private, have similar effects on recidivism.

Still, as Wright argues, privatization has the potential to be a means to achieve progressive goals. The key is that private companies must sign contracts that stipulate what they must do to turn a profit. If they are paid money to run prisons more cheaply, then this is what they will do—all to the potential detriment of staff (paid less) and inmates (receive fewer programs and amenities). But if their performance-based contracts also were to tie profits to their providing quality, evidence-based programming to offenders, then a powerful incentive would exist for this to occur. That is, capitalism would be used to create the support for and the delivery of treatment programs that work.

In short, Wright is calling for the creation of a "rehabilitation-for-profit private prison." Quite judiciously, he confronts the possibility that such a reform could be corrupted and not achieve the goal of improving inmate care. But he also proposes that such malfeasance is not inevitable; safeguards can be instituted. Most importantly, his work encourages us to set aside our ideology and not settle for doing more of the same within our prisons. Privatization thus must not be seen, in a knee-jerk way, as a panacea or as an anathema, but rather as providing an opportunity to hold an honest conversation about how best to develop pragmatic ways to improve the correctional enterprise.

I n July of 2010, three inmates escaped from a medium security private prison in Kingman, Arizona. The three men—each serving time for committing a violent crime—were aided and abetted by a female accomplice, and the foursome set off on an interstate crime spree as they attempted to evade authorities. At the initial escape, one of the inmates separated from the group and was captured a few days later in Colorado after a brief exchange of gunfire with police. The remaining three traveled to New Mexico, where they carjacked and killed a couple vacationing from Oklahoma. Overcome by the guilt of the escape and subsequent murders, one inmate split off from the other two fugitives, and he was apprehended by authorities shortly after abandoning his plan to commit "suicide by bear" in Yellowstone National Park. The remaining fugitive and the female accomplice were captured at an Arizona campground nearly three weeks after the initial escape.

The sensational Arizona escape and tragic loss of civilian life associated with it fanned the flames of consistent criticism over private participation in the American correctional system. Indeed, a variety of operational and ethical concerns have been repeated by critics since the increased presence of for-profit prison ownership and management in the 1980s. Are private prisons secure? Do they really save money? Do they really provide better care? Should the state turn over the punishment of its citizens to a private entity? Does the profit motive encourage a continued and increased reliance on imprisonment as a form of social control? Are private prison lobbyists unduly involved with the creation of crime control policy and legislation? Perhaps most importantly, can private prisons ensure the safety of inmates, employees, and most critically, the general public?

One of the primary purposes of prisons is to reduce crime—especially by ensuring that offenders who have been sent to prison do not engage in further criminal behavior. Currently, prisons do little to contribute to recidivism reduction (Cullen, Jonson, & Nagin, 2011), and it makes sense to ask how we can better structure our prisons to help discourage further criminal behavior by ex-offenders. In this context, the purpose of the current chapter is to set forth the idea that private prisons provide an opportunity to imagine a different future for the American prison. It acknowledges the long-standing and likely continued presence of privatization within American corrections (Wright, 2010), and instead of primarily seeking answers to the above questions it proposes a new one: Given private prisons are here to stay, how can we benefit from their presence? It will be argued that private prisons provide an opportunity to harness the power of economic incentives in America to achieve more progressive ends in the handling of offenders. Doing so would replace "punishment for profit" with "rehabilitation for profit," and it is possible that private prisons would be newsworthy for reasons other than escapes, corruption, and compromising the safety of the general public.

The Current Private Prison: No Worse (But No Better) Than Public Prisons

Private involvement in American corrections is not a recent development (Durham, 1989a; Feeley, 2002). It exists in various forms, from state or federal institutions contracting out various services to the private sector (e.g., medical care, food) all the way up to private firms building and managing entire prisons. The latter type receives the lion's share of public and scholarly attention and is the primary focus of the current chapter. Briefly, when a state or the federal government decides to contract out an existing institution or seeks to have a new one built and managed by a private entity, it will create a request for proposals that stipulates the terms and expectations of the potential contractor. It is at this point where privatization offers the most promise for corrections: Innovation coupled with competition is assumed to produce a plan for the best possible care of inmates at the best possible price. The government entity will then select the proposal from contractors that is deemed most appropriate given the stated objectives, and the two sides will decide on final terms to be written up in the contract. It is expected that the government will be actively involved in monitoring the performance of the private firm in accordance with the expectations of the contract. Thus, private prisons are not truly "private"—they answer to the state, which conceivably could terminate or fail to renew a contract based on poor performance (for more detail on the procurement process, see Harding, 2001, pp. 295–309).

The most current data available provided by the Bureau of Justice Statistics' (BJS) Census of State and Federal Correctional Facilities indicated that private facilities made up about 8% of all confinement-based adult institutions in the United States in 2005 (Stephan, 2008).[1] This percentage is similar to the share of privately operated facilities in 2000, which at the time represented a significant increase from just five years earlier. In 1995, 29 of 1,160 (2.5%) of all confinement-based institutions in the United States were privately owned or operated. By 2000, this number jumped to 101 of 1,208 (8.4%) of all confinement-based institutions (Stephan & Karberg, 2003). Data from the BJS Correctional Population in the United States series provide a similar picture. From 2000 to 2010, the percentage of inmates held in a federal or state private prison facility ranged from about 6% to 8%. In 2010, a total of nearly 120,000 inmates were held in a state or federal private prison facility (Glaze, 2011). Thus, private presence within corrections increased sharply in the latter half of the 1990s and has remained relatively stable over the last decade (see also Culp, 2011).

The appeal of private prisons is that they can potentially provide the best quality of care at the best possible price. This promise is alluring to correctional administrators who struggle with how to manage overcrowded populations with shrinking budgets (Wright & Rosky, 2011). Most scholars would agree, therefore, that the increased and continued reliance on the private sector within corrections is due to issues of cost and space (Bowditch & Everett, 1987; Ethridge & Marquart, 1993; Shichor & Sechrest, 1995; see also Price & Riccucci, 2005). Accordingly, one strand of scholarly empirical research has been focused on whether private prisons can provide cost savings as compared to their public counterparts. In general, this research finds that private prisons are no more cost-effective than public prisons. Pratt and Maahs (1999) reviewed the findings of 24 independent studies and found prison ownership to be unrelated to the daily per diem cost of operating a correctional facility (i.e., private prisons did not produce higher or lower operation costs). Instead, facility characteristics such as economy of scale and security level were most important to operation costs, and the authors concluded that "relinquishing the responsibility of managing prisons to the private sphere is unlikely to alleviate much of the financial burden on state correctional budgets" (p. 368; see also Lundahl, Kunz, Brownell, Harris, & Van Vleet, 2009).

A related line of research assesses whether private prisons can provide better quality of care than public prisons. Admittedly, quality of care within prisons can be determined through a variety of measures (Armstrong & MacKenzie, 2003; DiIulio, 1987; Logan, 1992)—with everything from the availability of treatment programs to the number of escapes falling under the umbrella of "quality." Putting aside the issue of appropriate indicators, the equivocal findings of prison ownership and cost savings are repeated in assessments of prison ownership and quality of care. Lundahl and colleagues (2009) reviewed 12 independent studies that compared private prisons with public prisons on a number of different quality performance indicators. The studies revealed that there was little difference in quality of care between privately and publicly managed systems, which led the authors to provide the recommendation that "the data we reviewed do not support a move toward privatization at this time," but also that "the data do not clearly discourage privatization" (p. 393). Further muddying the waters is the fact that most of these quality of care studies are plagued with methodological weaknesses, such as comparisons between only one private prison and one public prison that then produce implications for prison privatization on the whole (Perrone & Pratt, 2003).

One final group of studies examines whether inmates who spend the bulk of their custody within private prisons are less likely to reoffend as compared to inmates who were housed in public prisons. Whereas earlier studies find some support for lowered recidivism among private prison inmates (Farabee & Knight, 2002; Lanza-Kaduce, Parker, & Thomas, 1999), more recent studies find either no difference between public and private recidivism rates (Bales, Bedard, Quinn, Ensley, & Holley, 2005) or an increased likelihood of recidivism by inmates from private prisons (Spivak & Sharp, 2008). The latter two studies are arguably more rigorous than the earlier studies due to larger case sizes, better control variables, and multiple measures of private and public prison exposure. Nevertheless, no clear picture emerges as to whether private prisons are able to reduce recidivism rates as compared to public prisons.

The promise of private prisons has largely gone unfulfilled. In terms of cost-efficiency, quality of care, and recidivism reduction, private prisons tend to fare no worse (but no better) than their public counterparts.[2] What we are left with, then, is a private corporation no better at housing inmates than the state—business has continued as usual. Added to this status quo is a host of ethical concerns and highly publicized cases of corruption and putting the general public at risk. It should come as no surprise, therefore, that the privatization of prisons in the American correctional system has been largely viewed with suspicion and pessimism by correctional scholars, human rights organizations, and the general public.

The Future Private Prison: Doing Well By Doing Good

Most reviews and evaluation studies on prison privatization end by concluding that private prisons do not provide better care and are no more cost-efficient than public prisons, but as Maruna (2011, p. 664) points out, "The negative is easier than the positive, but the positive is more important." Merely calling attention to the deficiencies of the current state of private prisons does little to advance our knowledge on how they can be improved or replaced to better contribute to the U.S. correctional system. This section is focused on taking the next step to suggest how prison privatization can play a role in imagining a different future for the American prison. It begins by discussing the larger social and corporate environment that surrounds prison privatization. This environment encourages the pursuit of profit above all else, and by taking this into account, we may envision a future private prison that is guided by contract incentives designed to aid in the reduction of recidivism.

THE CORRECTIONAL ENVIRONMENT OF PRIVATE PRISONS

"How can we make private prisons better?" To answer this question, we must consider the socioeconomic context within which these institutions operate. Much is made in the criminological literature as to how the United States is structured to encourage the proliferation of criminal behavior. For example, Currie (1997, p. 147) writes of the U.S. "market society" as one in which "the pursuit of private gain becomes the dominant organizing principle of social and economic life." Braithwaite (1989, p. 171) identifies the United States as an "extreme case of an individualist society" whereby individual interests take precedence over mutual help and trust among citizens. Finally, Messner and Rosenfeld (2001, p. 7) reason that the United States is a society organized for crime because of a cultural emphasis on monetary achievement that generates pressures to succeed at any cost. Each of these positions makes the argument that the United States is organized for the individual pursuit of profit, and this organization comes at the expense of crime-inhibiting institutions such as the family, community, and educational system.

Private prisons would appear to be the correctional epitome of a focus on the pursuit of profit to the detriment of the well-being of a significant portion of Americans. Yet Clear (2010, p. 587) argues that "with creative thinking, we might find ways to harness the power of the economic realities to produce a dynamic that has the natural tendency to reduce the investment in a relatively unproductive prison and reentry industry in favor of other priorities." Similarly, as Austin (2011, p. 629) notes, "If one wishes to restructure current public policy, then one must take into account the power of capitalism and traditional economic theory." Thus, a better version of the private prison within the correctional system would be one that is geared toward profit balanced against the "expense" of rehabilitating offenders and potentially reducing recidivism. This line of thinking is not necessarily new (see Avio, 1991; Cullen, 1986; Gentry, 1986), but these earlier positions were criticized for expecting the private sector to do what the public could not in addition to assuming that recidivism reductions could be accurately measured (Durham, 1989b).

Two of the central themes of this book are that we have reached a turning point in the mass imprisonment movement and that we have amassed a significant body of correctional research that can be put toward envisioning a different American prison. Each of these critical points allows us to revisit and bolster earlier arguments that private prisons can be structured toward aiding in recidivism reduction. In particular, the evidence-based movement within corrections has documented both the types of programs (MacKenzie, 2006) and the specific principles of effective intervention (Smith, Gendreau, & Swartz, 2009) that reduce the likelihood of recidivism by ex-offenders. Equally important have been advancements in understanding what does *not* work in reducing recidivism—programs based solely on coercion and punishment are unlikely to result in reductions in reoffending (Lipsey & Cullen, 2007). Thus, instead of a focus on recidivism, private prisons can be rewarded for using programs and techniques that have been shown to contribute to reductions in recidivism. An early article critical of private prisons suggested that "the private sector is more interested in doing *well* than in doing *good*" (Robbins, 1989, p. 542; emphasis in the original). But what if doing well also meant doing good?

At the risk of oversimplifying the problem, what is needed then is to change what is profitable for the private sector in corrections. It is readily apparent that those in pursuit of profit often do not care at what expense that profit comes. Nowhere could this be more true than the current practice of making money off of warehousing a significant proportion of our population—especially the poor, minorities, and immigrants. Examples of changing what is profitable leading to innovation in America are plentiful. Twenty years ago, a focus on "green energy" was likely limited to children of the 1960s who were trying to find ways to power their Volkswagen buses with cow manure. Now, individuals and companies receive tax credits for employing green technology, and even the largely blue-collar field of corrections has joined the green movement (see Chapter 10 in this volume). Currently, it is profitable for the private sector to keep prison cells full, which encourages a continued and increased reliance on imprisonment as a form of social control.[3] Instead, if the private sector were held accountable for employing evidence-based practices found to contribute to recidivism reduction, it is likely that they would find ways to do so in the name of profit.

It is reasonable to ask why we should encourage private sector involvement rather than simply expect the public sector to be held accountable to employ evidence-based practices (see Chapter 12 in this volume). The short answer is that it does not have to be one or the other, and the consistent presence of the private sector in corrections necessitates that it also be structured to aid in the reduction of recidivism. An advantage of the private sector is that it is not necessarily tied to a legacy of control in the handling of offenders (Genders, 2003). Thus, the innovation and risk-taking that private prisons can offer may not be in competition with decades of coercive-based practices as experienced in the public sector (see also Gendreau, Smith, & Theriault, 2009). Perhaps the biggest difference, however, is that the private sector is focused on making a profit, which can be tied to employing evidence-based practices through performance incentives built into contracts.

PERFORMANCE-BASED CONTRACTS

In the 2011 NFL season, quarterback Tim Tebow captured the attention of the sports world with his electric play and outspoken religious beliefs. "Tebowmania" followed the Denver Broncos and their quarterback on an improbable run that culminated in the defeat of the defending league champion Pittsburgh Steelers in the playoffs. After the season was over, Denver signed future Hall of Fame quarterback Peyton Manning, and the now expendable Tebow was shipped off to the New York Jets in a trade. The Jets assumed Tebow's original deal with the Broncos that paid him around 10 million dollars over five years, but he could earn more than that based on performance incentives built into his contract. By playing in 70% of the Broncos offensive plays and 70% of the offensive plays in a playoff win, he received an extra $250,000 for the win over the Steelers. A number of additional incentives (e.g., winning the Super Bowl Most Valuable Player) would pay him even larger sums. All told, Tebow's total contract could be worth 33 million dollars instead of 10 million. Many of the incentives are considered impossible to reach, but with Tebow—anything is possible.

Now, we would hope players like Tim Tebow perform to the best of their abilities regardless of performance incentives, but the main point is clear: Those interested in making the greatest amount of money (or profit) possible must achieve the goals set forth in their contracts. The same could be true of private prison contractors. The contract between the state and the private firm would guarantee some minimal base pay regardless of performance. If the private contractor wanted to make money (and keep shareholders happy), then this contractor would need to meet certain expectations beyond that minimal performance. The beauty in this is that if the private prison did not meet these incentives, the state would not be obligated to pay more and thus would save money (see also Burch, 2011, p. 613). If it did meet the incentives, the state would have to settle for knowing that it is paying for evidence-based service that could potentially reduce its costs in the long run (Drake, Aos, & Miller, 2009).

The current form of private prison contracts often expects little more than performance that is equal to that of the state at a lower cost (McDonald, Fournier, Russell-Einhorn, & Crawford, 1998). Most contracts pay private companies for the number of person days of confinement supplied (Lukemeyer & McCorkle, 2006). If the private sector is to make a profit, then it must find ways to run the prison at a price cheaper than this payment. Thus, there is no incentive for the private sector to focus on treatment and rehabilitation (Armstrong & MacKenzie, 2003), and the most progressive contract stipulation is often a requirement that institutions achieve American Correctional Association (ACA) accreditation within a designated time period (but see Harding, 2001, p. 303). Consequently, there is evidence that private prisons offer less programming to inmates than their public counterparts (Wright, 2010), which is particularly disappointing given the rather dismal program offerings in state institutions in the first place (Chamberlain, 2012; Phelps, 2011).

So what would a contract incentive geared toward recidivism reduction look like? The obvious answer would be to reward private prisons that can document reductions in recidivism as compared to the "going rate" for a particular jurisdiction or state-run equivalent. The problem with this is that recidivism studies in general are a messy lot of performance evaluations (see Gaes, 2005). As the private prison recidivism studies cited above make clear, it is difficult to ensure a matched sample from which to draw definitive conclusions on whether prison ownership is responsible for any differences in recidivism between private and public prisons (e.g., the fact that private prisons often house lower risk inmates may be what is most important). The definition of recidivism itself is complex— it could mean rearrest, reconviction, or re-imprisonment, and the follow-up period could be short (e.g., 6 months) or long (e.g., 3 years). Ultimately, it would be difficult to standardize recidivism evaluations so that objective assessments of private prison performance could be carried out in a timely manner. Thus, although contributing to recidivism reduction would be the end goal of rehabilitation for profit, it would be unwise to try to link specific contract incentives with measures of recidivism.

Instead, performance-based incentives should reflect the evidence-based principles that have been shown to lead to recidivism reduction. The most promising approach would be to link incentives with private prison performance on tools like the Correctional Program Assessment Inventory (CPAI). The CPAI was discussed at length in Chapter 1 of this volume and needs no further detail here. The key is that it provides guidance and accountability in both creating and managing an institutional environment that is conducive to offender change. For example, one item on the CPAI may require that a certain percentage of staff be trained in criminal justice or a related field, whereas another might stipulate that the offender treatment method be of a known effective type. A contract incentive may then pay the private prison contractor a substantial bonus for producing scores at various levels of the CPAI upon objective documentation by outside evaluators (i.e., more money for higher scores, no additional money for poor scores). Currently, most programs assessed tend to score low on the CPAI (Matthews, Hubbard, & Latessa, 2001), but those programs that do score higher on the CPAI have been shown to produce meaningful reductions in recidivism (Lowenkamp, Latessa, & Smith, 2006). Additionally, while the full CPAI instrument currently has 133 items, research exists suggesting that some of these items are more correlated with recidivism than others (Lowenkamp et al., 2006) and focusing on those items in particular might produce a more manageable expectation for private contractors. If the private sector is truly innovative and capable of adapting to stated goals, it is reasonable to expect that it might be able to produce scores on the higher end of the CPAI as compared to the public sector.

There exist many other opportunities for creating financial incentives that encourage a private prison fully equipped to help reduce recidivism. One often overlooked component of the correctional institutional environment is the job satisfaction of staff. At first blush, it may seem as if staff morale would be unrelated to offender recidivism, but an emerging body of research has documented how job stress can lead to burnout and an extensive amount of employee turnover in private prisons (Camp & Gaes, 2002; Griffin, Hogan, & Lambert, 2012). A criticism often levied at private prison contractors is that they cut costs by employing fewer people at lower wages, which may not be surprising given as much as 80% of prison operation costs can be labor costs (Genders, 2003). An institution that is characterized by a high degree of employee turnover is likely to contribute to safety problems and is unlikely to provide the stable environment necessary for meaningful change to occur in offenders. Thus, a promising approach would be for incentives to be built into a contract rewarding private prison contractors who themselves provide incentives to attract and retain staff (Camp & Gaes, 2002). Research exists suggesting that employees are well aware of incentives in performance-based contracting environments (Washington, Yoon, Galambos, & Kelly, 2009), and rewarding employees by giving them a financial bonus for reaching a CPAI score, for example, would align employee performance with overall institutional goals (Lutze, Johnson, Clear, Latessa, & Slate, 2012).

One of the principles of effective intervention with offenders states that positive reinforcers should exceed punishers by a ratio of at least 4 to 1 (Gendreau, 1996). This dictum should hold true for the contract management of private prisons as well. Although some have advocated a fine system for enforcing contracts (Gentry, 1986), the best approach would be to clearly define the expectations associated with financially based performance incentives. If they are not reached, then they are not paid. CPAI performance and staff incentive procedures are just two of the possibilities that could be built into private prison contracts; as noted in Chapter 12, it is not up to the criminologist to demand what should be required of prison management. The broader point is that performance-based incentives must be created out of a foundation of evidence-based practice. Once this is done, the state must allow the private sector to "do what it does best"—excessive oversight and demands for change beyond contract stipulations will instead result in the future private prison looking much like the public prison it was to improve upon (Sellers, 2003). Admittedly, this requires a leap of faith by correctional administrators in the public sector. The final section of this chapter therefore details some of the potential dangers associated with creating a private prison designed to maximize profit through the rehabilitation of offenders.

What to Watch Out For

Prison privatization and offender rehabilitation are certainly strange bedfellows, yet the general public favors responses to crime that are both punitive and rehabilitative in nature (Pratt, 2009). In this respect, a private prison that is focused toward rehabilitation-for-profit may represent the perfect blend of confinement and treatment. HMP Dovegate, a privately built and operated prison in the United Kingdom that contains a therapeutic community within prison walls, provides tangible evidence that such a marriage can be challenging yet amicable (Cullen & Mackenzie, 2011). Nevertheless, such a tenuous relationship requires that we anticipate and confront the possible unintended consequences of associating treatment with profit. Three lingering and interrelated issues may threaten the longevity of a private prison designed to achieve more progressive ends. The following sections discuss these three potential concerns.

1. RECIDIVISM RATES REMAIN HIGH

It is inevitable that recidivism reduction will be one of the key indicators of the success of rehabilitation-for-profit private prisons. But what if no appreciable reduction in recidivism is observed? Consistent with the position offered above, we should not worry so much about recidivism rates. This would seem a curious statement given the overall thrust of the current chapter—especially if private prisons are to solve the correctional problems of overcrowding and under-budgeting. Yet scholars interested in offender reentry often point out that the obsession with recidivism reduction obscures success indicated by other markers of reintegration such as job placement or treatment completion (Lynch, 2006). Moreover, recidivism rates can be influenced by system practices (Wilson, 2005), and the use of technical violations in particular could be more a function of organizational behavior than offender behavior (Wright & Rosky, 2011). Again, the study of recidivism is fraught with conceptual and methodological uncertainties, and due to this recidivism should not be the sole measuring stick for the success of the future private prison.

It is reasonable to ask what role prisons (public or private) can even play in reducing recidivism. After all, it seems unfair to expect that prison management and programming can somehow eliminate the presence of deviant peers, alleviate poverty in disadvantaged communities, and overcome difficult childhoods marked by ineffective parenting (see Thomas, 2005). Indeed, they should not be expected to do so, but to argue that prisons cannot play a role in reducing recidivism is not only inconsistent with the purpose of having prisons in the first place, it also ignores a significant body of literature identifying the components of programs that do successfully reduce recidivism (Gendreau, Smith, & French, 2006). Full adherence to the CPAI, for example, cannot change the offender's community, deviant peers, or opportunities to engage in prosocial activities and obtain meaningful employment (Wright, Pratt, Lowenkamp, & Latessa, 2012). It can, however, change the offender by modifying antisocial attitudes and behaviors and by reducing drug and alcohol dependency, and this is the first step in discouraging future criminal behavior (see also Maruna, Immarigeon, & LeBel, 2004, p. 15). Prisons can do offender rehabilitation, but community, family, and institutional rehabilitation will have to come from elsewhere.

The simple truth is that recidivism reduction alone will not relieve us of the unintended consequences brought on by the mass incarceration movement (Clear & Austin, 2009). Thus, even if the future private prison were to show strong reductions in recidivism, it would do little to change the correctional landscape in terms of who is going to prison and for how long. Perhaps more importantly, the institutional population that public and private prisons serve represents only about 20% of the 7 *million* people under the control of the correctional system (Glaze, 2011). In short, the reduction of recidivism through institutional programming represents a small albeit important piece of the mass incarceration problem, and imagining a new American prison may also mean imagining a new American correctional system (Cullen, 2007). What this all means is that the future private prison should be organized so that it may encourage behavior modification without doing further harm to offenders, their families, and their communities. Reductions in recidivism that are directly tied to private prison programming would be a bonus.

2. CORRUPTION IS RAMPANT

Steps need to be taken to limit the amount of corruption associated with the private prison of the future. Currently, highly publicized cases of corruption have only further cemented the idea that inmate welfare and profit are incompatible. For example, two judges in Pennsylvania were found guilty of accepting more than $2.6 million in kickbacks to send teenagers to privately run detention facilities—some for minor offenses such as creating a Myspace page mocking a high school assistant principal (Urbina & Hamill, 2009)! Organizational deviance is commonplace within the corporate culture (Shichor, 1993), and there exists a fine line between a method that is innovative and a method that is criminal. The political influence of these private organizations creates additional thorny issues and opportunities for corruption. It has been suggested that private prison companies (which can be substantial political campaign contributors) were linked with the development of Arizona's controversial SB 1070 immigration legislation (Sullivan, 2010). If enforced to its full degree, the bill would create a need for additional space for suspected illegal immigrant detention—space conveniently provided by private prison corporations in a twist on the *Field of Dreams* adage, "If you build it, he will come."

The good news is that if private prisons were restructured to focus on treatment, many of the occupancy-related incidents of corruption would disappear. The judges in Pennsylvania were ensuring the private detention facility had a population to serve by sentencing juveniles to custody who otherwise might receive probation. The political lobbying in Arizona was an effort to create a new population to serve by ratcheting up immigration enforcement. If profit is no longer tied to cell occupancy and number of inmates served, then these "innovative" methods of business may no longer be profitable. In short, corruption that results in more offenders being treated with the best possible methods available may be more tolerable than corruption that results in the mere warehousing of offenders.

It is likely, however, that new forms of corruption and methods of corner-cutting will emerge with the rehabilitation-for-profit private prison (e.g., the manipulation of records to achieve incentives). An increased emphasis on contract monitoring and accountability may help to prevent corruption from becoming rampant. Monitoring is often treated as an expendable provision (Harding, 2001, p. 306), but it is arguably the most important component in determining contract compliance and corresponding payment (Shichor, 1999). An important step would be for the state to develop a detailed backup plan in the event that contract termination is required. Currently, there is little threat of termination (or even nonrenewal of contracts) given the alternative: The state would need to quickly find a new operator if it owned the facility or would need to find a new institution to house the inmates if it did not. This reality leaves contract termination an impotent threat, and a looming sufficient alternative may make private prison contractors more accountable and less prone to corruption. Corruption will likely be present in any financial incentive system (Clear, 2011); the key is to take steps to prevent and limit this presence.

3. CONTROL IS EXPANDED

The most damaging possibility is that the rehabilitation-for-profit private prison is added to a disappointing history of progressive reforms that have instead resulted in an increased reliance on coercion and control (Cullen & Gilbert, 1982; Pisciotta, 1994; Rothman, 1980). This might seem an unimaginable outcome given the restructuring of what is profitable, but the "corruption of benevolence" (Levrant, Cullen, Fulton, & Wozniak, 1999) has crept into similar well-intentioned reforms that appealed to the political Left, Right, and the general public (Maruna, 2011). The most relevant of these for the current chapter is a group of policies and programs billed as alternatives to incarceration (e.g., intensive supervision, boot camps). An unintended consequence of these programs is that they have expanded the reach of correctional control into the community (Cullen, Wright, & Applegate, 1996).

Admittedly, private prison contractors engaging in evidence-based treatment may represent the "worst bet" to avoid the corruption of benevolence. Feeley (2002) argues that virtually all cases of privatization within criminal justice have translated to increased control (see also Immarigeon, 1985). He points out that the private sector has been successful in identifying niches (e.g., immigration detention) that expand and create *new* forms of social control. A similar argument against private prisons providing rehabilitation is that they would be "in the business of putting themselves out of business" (Genders, 2002, p. 288). Accordingly, new ways would need to be found to stay in business, which likely means finding new inmates who otherwise would avoid confinement.

As the recidivism reduction discussion above makes clear, the running-out-of-clients "problem" is probably avoidable for the time being. Nevertheless, the future American prison may be increasingly reserved for high-risk, violent offenders. We must be careful to think about how private prisons fit into this reality. Currently, most private prisons serve low-risk offenders (Feeley, 2002), and the principles of effective intervention state that the most intensive treatment should be reserved for high-risk offenders (Gendreau et al., 2006). Thus, the long-term future of the rehabilitation-for-profit private prison requires that one of two things must happen: (1) private prison contractors must demonstrate that they can house and serve higher risk offenders, or (2) some restructuring of private prisons must occur so that they provide services such as evidence-based drug treatment in a form that does not require coerced confinement by the state. Put differently, we cannot allow private prisons to assume a role whereby they receive low-risk offenders who otherwise would have avoided system-involvement—even if this involvement is in the name of treatment.

Conclusion: Money for Somethin' and Justice for Free

We should not turn to private prisons as a quick fix to the current problems plaguing corrections—there is little systematic evidence that they are currently capable of supplying the remedy. Instead, we should capitalize on the purported innovation and adaptation championed by the private sector to envision a new American prison that is rooted in justice and does no further harm to offenders, their families, and their communities (Tonry, 2011). If private prisons are not going to save the state money initially, what incentive do correctional administrators have to contract out service? The answer is that private prisons provide the opportunity to achieve more than a short-term fix for a long-term problem. Implementing evidence-based practice under the watch of the private sector may provide a welcome shift from an approach to corrections that is steeped in "quackery" (Latessa, Cullen, & Gendreau, 2002). This chapter has planted the seeds of an idea—it will require the expertise and support of more than just criminologists to make it a reality.

One does not need to be a proponent of privatization to acknowledge that private prisons will continue to play a small but influential role in American corrections. The purpose of this chapter, therefore, has been to argue that the future private prison can be restructured to achieve more progressive ends in the handling of offenders. Specifically, the future private prison will be rewarded for employing the latest methods of evidence-based corrections and for promoting a healthy and stable work environment for staff. Perhaps more importantly, the future private prison will *not* be rewarded for filling cells or for cutting costs at the expense of treatment programs and adequate staffing. Admittedly, the one unique aspect of the private prison is in who owns and operates it, and the challenge should be put forth for private corporations to produce a prison rooted in science rather than solely in economics. Instead of producing a more cost-effective prison or a better quality-of-care prison (however that is measured), the onus should be placed on private contractors to produce the safe prison, the healthy prison, the therapeutic prison, and so on. The broader point is that the profit motive can be tied to incarceration policies and programs that do no further harm to offenders and instead serve to encourage successful reintegration into the community.

As with many seemingly "innovative" ideas, the pieces are already in place for an accountable private prison designed to aid in recidivism reduction, and thus the future American prison does not have to be limited to imagination. Two characteristics of prison privatization within America make this more than just a possibility. First, prison privatization has played a consistent yet not overpowering presence in the U.S. correctional system. Private prisons are here to stay and they provide the perfect setting to allow for meaningful experimentation without overhauling the entire system. If this experiment is successful, then the public sector may choose to employ some of these methods of success on a larger scale (Harding, 1997). Second, reorganizing private prisons in this manner does not require a monumental shift toward a more socially supportive United States. It also does not concede that prisons should be torn down and replaced with treatment and rehabilitation centers. Instead, it envisions the American prison within the existing structure of a society that rewards individualism and the pursuit of profit. Reinventing the prison as one that capitalizes on what the United States does well already may be the most sensible approach to imagining a different future for the American prison.

Endnotes

1. The focus of the current chapter is on confinement-based adult institutions, but it is important to note that private facilities made up 58% of all community-based facilities (e.g., halfway houses, pre-release centers) in 2005. Private facilities accounted for nearly all of the increase in adult correctional facilities from 2000 to 2005, and all but six of these new facilities were community-based (up from 163 in 2000 to 308 in 2005) (Stephan, 2008). Additionally, private (often nonprofit) involvement in juvenile custody has been quite extensive and consistent over time (McDonald, 1992). Each of these points reiterates the position that privatization plays a role in corrections that is unlikely to dissipate in the near future.

2. It is important to note that assessing private prisons in a relative sense assumes that public prisons in their current form provide an unproblematic baseline for comparison (Austin & Coventry, 1999; Dolovich, 2005; Lippke, 1997).

3. Corrections Corporation of America, the nation's largest private prison company, reportedly offered to buy up the prisons of 48 states—provided that they could guarantee a 90% minimum occupancy rate over the 20-year contract period (Kirkham, 2012).

References

Armstrong, G. S., & MacKenzie, D. L. (2003). Private versus public juvenile correctional facilities: Do differences in environmental quality exist? *Crime & Delinquency, 49,* 542–563.

Austin, J. (2011). Making imprisonment unprofitable. *Criminology and Public Policy, 10,* 629–635.

Austin, J., & Coventry, G. (1999). Are we better off? Comparing private and public prisons in the United States. *Current Issues in Criminal Justice, 11,* 177–201.

Avio, K. L. (1991). On private prisons: An economic analysis of the model contract and model statute for private incarceration. *New England Journal on Criminal and Civil Confinement, 265,* 265–300.

Bales, W. D., Bedard, L. E., Quinn, S. T., Ensley, D. T., & Holley, G. P. (2005). Recidivism of public and private state prison inmates in Florida. *Criminology and Public Policy, 4,* 57–82.

Bowditch, C., & Everett, R. S. (1987). Private prisons: Problem within the solution. *Justice Quarterly, 4,* 441–453.

Braithwaite, J. (1989). *Crime, shame and reintegration*. Cambridge, UK: Cambridge University Press.

Burch, J. H. (2011). Encouraging innovation on the foundation of evidence: On the path to the "adjacent possible"? *Criminology and Public Policy, 10,* 609–616.

Camp, S. D., & Gaes, G. G. (2002). Growth and quality of U.S. private prisons: Evidence from a national survey. *Criminology and Public Policy, 1,* 427–450.

Chamberlain, A. W. (2012). Offender rehabilitation: Examining changes in inmate treatment characteristics, program participation, and institutional behavior. *Justice Quarterly, 29,* 183–228.

Clear, T. R. (2010). The prison industry and the marketplace. *Dialectical Anthropology, 34,* 585–587.

Clear, T. R. (2011). A private sector, incentives-based model for justice reinvestment. *Criminology and Public Policy, 10,* 585–608.

Clear, T. R., & Austin, J. (2009). Reducing mass incarceration: Implications of the iron law of prison populations. *Harvard Review of Law and Policy, 3,* 307–324.

Cullen, E., & Mackenzie, J. (2011). *Dovegate: A therapeutic community in a private prison and developments in therapeutic work with personality disordered offenders*. Hook, UK: Waterside Press.

Cullen, F. T. (1986). The privatization of treatment: Prison reform in the 1980s. *Federal Probation, 50,* 8–16.

Cullen, F. T. (2007). Make rehabilitation corrections' guiding paradigm. *Criminology and Public Policy, 6,* 717–727.

Cullen, F. T., & Gilbert, K. E. (1982). *Reaffirming Rehabilitation*. Cincinnati, OH: Anderson.

Cullen, F. T., Jonson, C. L., & Nagin, D. S. (2011). Prisons do not reduce recidivism: The high cost of ignoring science. *The Prison Journal, 91,* 48S–65S.

Cullen, F. T., Wright, J. P., & Applegate, B. K. (1996). Control in the community: The limits of reform? In A. T. Harland (Ed.), *Choosing correctional options that work: Defining the demand and evaluating the supply* (pp. 69–116). Thousand Oaks, CA: Sage.

Culp, R. (2011). Prison privatization turns 25. In K. Ismaili (Ed.), *U.S. criminal justice policy: A contemporary reader* (pp. 183–210). Sudbury, MA: Jones & Bartlett Learning.

Currie, E. (1997). Market, crime and community: Toward a mid-range theory of post-industrial violence. *Theoretical Criminology, 1,* 147–172.

DiIulio, J. J. (1987). *Governing prisons: A comparative study of correctional management*. New York, NY: Free Press.

Dolovich, S. (2005). State punishment and private prisons. *Duke Law Journal, 55,* 437–546.

Drake, E. K., Aos, S., & Miller, M. G. (2009). Evidence-based public policy options to reduce crime and criminal justice costs: Implications in Washington state. *Victims and Offenders, 4,* 170–196.

Durham, A. M. (1989a). Origins of interest in the privatization of punishment: The nineteenth and twentieth century American experience. *Criminology, 27,* 107–139.

Durham, A. M. (1989b). Rehabilitation and correctional privatization: Observations on the 19th-century experience and implications for modern corrections. *Federal Probation, 53,* 43–52.

Ethridge, P. A., & Marquart, J. W. (1993). Private prisons in Texas: The new penology for profit. *Justice Quarterly, 10,* 29–48.

Farabee, D., & Knight, K. (2002*). A comparison of public and private prisons in Florida: During- and post-prison performance indicators.* Los Angeles: Query Research.

Feeley, M. M. (2002). Entrepreneurs of punishment: The legacy of privatization. *Punishment and Society, 4,* 321–344.

Gaes, G. G. (2005). Prison privatization in Florida: Promise, premise, and performance. *Criminology and Public Policy, 4,* 83–88.

Genders, E. (2002). Legitimacy, accountability and private prisons. *Punishment and Society, 4,* 285–303.

Genders, E. (2003). Privatisation and innovation—Rhetoric and reality: The development of a therapeutic community prison. *The Howard Journal of Criminal Justice, 42,* 137–157.

Gendreau, P. (1996). The principles of effective intervention with offenders. In A. T. Harland (Ed.), *Choosing correctional options that work* (pp. 117–130). Thousand Oaks, CA: Sage.

Gendreau, P., Smith, P., & French, S. A. (2006). The theory of effective correctional intervention: Empirical status and future directions. In F. T. Cullen, J. P. Wright, & K. R. Blevins (Eds.), *Taking stock: The status of criminological theory—Advances in criminological theory* (Vol. 15, pp. 449–446). New Brunswick, NJ: Transaction.

Gendreau, P., Smith, P., & Theriault, Y. L. (2009). Chaos theory and correctional treatment: Common sense, correctional quackery, and the law of fartcatchers. *Journal of Contemporary Criminal Justice, 25,* 384–396.

Gentry, J. T. (1986). The panopticon revisited: The problem of monitoring private prisons. *The Yale Law Journal, 96,* 353–375.

Glaze, L. E. (2011). *Correctional population in the United States, 2010.* Washington, DC: U.S Department of Justice.

Griffin, M. L., Hogan, N. L., & Lambert, E. G. (2012). Doing "people work" in the prison setting: An examination of the job characteristics model and correctional staff burnout. *Criminal Justice and Behavior, 39,* 1131–1147.

Harding, R. (2001). Private prisons. In M. Tonry (Ed.), *Crime and justice: A review of research* (Vol. 28, pp. 265–346). Chicago, IL: University of Chicago Press.

Harding, R. W. (1997). *Private prisons and public accountability.* New Brunswick, NJ: Transaction.

Immarigeon, R. (1985). Private prisons, private programs, and their implications for reducing reliance on incarceration in the United States. *The Prison Journal, 65,* 60–74.

Kirkham, C. (2012). Private prison corporation offers cash in exchange for state prisons. *Huffington Post.* Retrieved July 22, 2012, from http://www.huffingtonpost .com/2012/02/14/private-prisons-buying-state-prisons_n_1272143.html

Lanza-Kaduce, L., Parker, K. F., & Thomas, C. W. (1999). A comparative recidivism analysis of releases from private and public prisons. *Crime and Delinquency, 45,* 28–47.

Latessa, E. J., Cullen, F. T., & Gendreau, P. (2002). Beyond correctional quackery—Professionalism and the possibility of effective treatment. *Federal Probation, 66,* 43–49.

Levrant, S., Cullen, F. T., Fulton, B., & Wozniak, J. F. (1999). Reconsidering restorative justice: The corruption of benevolence revisited? *Crime and Delinquency, 45,* 3–27.

Lippke, R. (1997). Thinking about private prisons. *Criminal Justice Ethics, 16,* 26–38.

Lipsey, M. W., & Cullen, F. T. (2007). The effectiveness of correctional rehabilitation: A review of systematic reviews. *Annual Review of Law and Social Science, 3,* 297–320.

Logan, C. H. (1992). Well kept: Comparing quality of confinement in private and public prisons. *The Journal of Criminal Law and Criminology, 83,* 577–613.

Lowenkamp, C. T., Latessa, E. J., & Smith, P. (2006). Does correctional program quality really matter? The impact of adhering to the principles of effective intervention. *Criminology and Public Policy, 5,* 201–220.

Lukemeyer, A., & McCorkle, R. C. (2006). Privatization of prisons: Impact on prison conditions. *American Review of Public Administration, 36,* 189–206.

Lundahl, B. W., Kunz, C., Brownell, C., Harris, N., & Van Vleet, R. (2009). Prison privatization: A meta-analysis of cost and quality of confinement indicators. *Research on Social Work Practice, 19,* 383–394.

Lutze, F. E., Johnson, W. W., Clear, T. R., Latessa, E. J., & Slate, R. N. (2012). The future of community corrections is now: Stop dreaming and take action. *Journal of Contemporary Criminal Justice, 28,* 42–59.

Lynch, J. P. (2006). Prisoner reentry: Beyond program evaluation. *Criminology and Public Policy, 5,* 401–412.

MacKenzie, D. L. (2006). *What works in corrections: Reducing the criminal activities of offenders and delinquents.* Cambridge, UK: Cambridge University Press.

Maruna, S. (2011). Lessons for justice reinvestment from restorative justice and the justice model experience: Some tips for an 8-year-old prodigy. *Criminology and Public Policy, 10,* 661–669.

Maruna S., Immarigeon R., & LeBel, T. P. (2004). Ex-offender reintegration: Theory and practice. In S. Maruna & R. Immarigeon (Eds.), *After crime and punishment: Pathways to offender reintegration* (pp. 3–26). Cullompton, Devon, UK: Willan.

Matthews, B., Hubbard, D. J., & Latessa, E. J. (2001). Making the next step: Using evaluability assessment to improve correctional programming. *The Prison Journal, 81,* 454–472.

McDonald, D., Fournier, E., Russell-Einhorn, M., & Crawford, S. (1998). *Private prisons in the United States: An assessment of current practices.* Cambridge, MA: Abt Associates.

McDonald, D. C. (1992). Private penal institutions. In M. Tonry (Ed.), *Crime and justice: A review of research* (Vol. 16, pp. 132–158). Chicago, IL: University of Chicago Press.

Messner, S. F., & Rosenfeld, R. (2001). *Crime and the American dream* (3rd ed.). Belmont, CA: Wadsworth.

Perrone, D., & Pratt, T. C. (2003). Comparing the quality of confinement and cost-effectiveness of public versus private prisons: What we know, why we do not know more, and where to go from here. *The Prison Journal, 83,* 301–322.

Phelps, M. S. (2011). Rehabilitation in the punitive era: The gap between rhetoric and reality in U.S. prison programs. *Law and Society Review, 45,* 33–68.

Pisciotta, A. W. (1994). *Benevolent repression: Social control and the American reformatory-prison movement.* New York, NY: New York University Press.

Pratt, T. C. (2009). *Addicted to incarceration: Corrections policy and the politics of misinformation in the United States.* Thousand Oaks, CA: Sage.

Pratt, T. C., & Maahs, J. (1999). Are private prisons more cost-effective than public prisons? A meta-analysis of evaluations research studies. *Crime and Delinquency, 45,* 358–371.

Price, B. E., & Riccucci, N. M. (2005). Exploring the determinants of decisions to privatize state prisons. *The American Review of Public Administration, 35,* 223–235.

Robbins, I. P. (1989). The legal dimensions of private incarceration. *The American University Law Review, 38,* 531–854.

Rothman, D. J. (1980). *Conscience and convenience: The asylum and its alternatives in Progressive America.* Boston, MA: Little, Brown.

Sellers, M. P. (2003). Privatization morphs into "publicization": Businesses look a lot like government. *Public Administration, 81,* 607–620.

Shichor, D. (1993). The corporate context of private prisons. *Crime, Law, and Social Change, 20,* 113–138.

Shichor, D. (1999). Privatizing correctional institutions: An organizational perspective. *The Prison Journal, 79,* 226–249.

Shichor, D., & Sechrest, D. K. (1995). Quick fixes in corrections: Reconsidering private and public for-profit facilities. *The Prison Journal, 75,* 457–478.

Smith, P., Gendreau, P., & Swartz, K. (2009). Validating the principles of effective intervention: A systematic review of the contributions of meta-analysis in the field of corrections. *Victims & Offenders, 4,* 148–169.

Spivak, A. L., & Sharp, S. F. (2008). Inmate recidivism as a measure of private prison performance. *Crime and Delinquency, 54,* 482–508.

Stephan, J. J. (2008). *Census of state and federal correctional facilities, 2005.* Washington, DC: U.S. Department of Justice.

Stephan, J. J., & Karberg, J. C. (2003). *Census of state and federal correctional facilities, 2000.* Washington, DC: U.S. Department of Justice.

Sullivan, L. (2010). Prison economics help drive Ariz. immigration law. *NPR.* Retrieved July 24, 2012, from http://www.npr.org/2010/10/28/130833741/prison-economics-help-drive-ariz-immigration-law

Thomas, C. W. (2005). Recidivism of public and private state prison inmates in Florida: Issues and unanswered questions. *Criminology and Public Policy, 4,* 89–100.

Tonry, M. (2011). Making peace, not a desert: Penal reform should be about values not justice reinvestment. *Criminology and Public Policy, 10,* 637–649.

Urbina, I., & Hamill, S. D. (2009). Judges plead guilty in scheme to jail youths for profit. *New York Times.* Retrieved July 29, 2012, from http://www.nytimes.com/2009/02/13/us/13judge.html?_r=1&src=tp&pagewanted=all

Washington, K. T., Yoon, D. P., Galambos, C., & Kelly, M. (2009). Job satisfaction among child welfare workers in public and performance-based contracting environments. *Journal of Public Child Welfare, 3,* 159–172.

Wilson, J. A. (2005). Bad behavior or bad policy? An examination of Tennessee release cohorts, 1993–2001. *Criminology and Public Policy, 4,* 485–518.

Wright, K. A. (2010). Strange bedfellows? Rehabilitation and prison privatization. *Journal of Offender Rehabilitation, 49,* 74–90.

Wright, K. A., Pratt, T. C., Lowenkamp, C. T., & Latessa, E. J. (2012). The importance of ecological context for correctional rehabilitation programs: Understanding the micro- and macro-level dimensions of successful offender treatment. *Justice Quarterly, 29,* 775–798.

Wright, K. A., & Rosky, J. W. (2011). Too early is too soon: Lessons from the Montana Department of Corrections early release program. *Criminology and Public Policy, 10,* 881–908.

10

The Green Prison

Mary K. Stohr and
John F. Wozniak

Editors' Introduction

At the time of the writing of this book and "The Green Prison" chapter (2012), we have reached the 50th anniversary of the publication of Rachel Carson's monumental book, Silent Spring *(1962). With the publication of this book, Carson arguably assumed the status of the founder of the environmental movement in this country. Her case for being credited as the founder of the movement was not just for preservation or conservation, as had been made by John Muir for the Yosemite Valley and the national parks in general, and had been made by Aldo Leopold for wilderness. Rather, her case called for the proactive halting of destructive—some might say criminal—pollution of our land, water, air, and human bodies and the bodies of other creatures, with DDT and other pesticides (see William Souder's [2012] recent* The Life and Legacy of Rachel Carson). *Trained as a biologist, Carson articulated the view, held by other scientists, and ironically voiced by inmates in prisons, that "what goes around, comes around" in the great circle of life. Should you mess with one part of Mother Nature, Carson might argue, something else is sure to go haywire, thus disrupting this circle. She documented the fact that the widespread spraying of DDT in the 1950s to destroy insects had the collateral and unintended effect of killing birds, including the bald eagle, the iconic symbol of our democracy. You do a wrong, as we did then through the indiscriminate spraying of this toxic chemical, and it will come back to you in some negative form (also known as "karma").*

Of course, the obverse of disrupting the environment or doing a social or criminal wrong is to do good, and that too may come back to one in the form of a regenerated species like the bald eagle recovering 40 years after DDT was banned (thanks in large part to Carson), or the recovering addict who received treatment and is now able to contribute to her community by keeping a job, paying taxes, and raising her kids.

In the chapter that follows, Mary Stohr and John Wozniak make the argument that, as currently operated, most prisons are environmental hogs, consuming enormous resources to fit our outsized appetite for incarceration in this country. In addition to the harm this has done to our communities in social, political, and economic ways, large prisons are harming our environment and, predictably Mother Nature does not like this! Environmental harm caused by large prisons results in dirtier air, water, and soil and sickened humans in them and the communities surrounding them. One answer to this problem of overconsumption, of course, would be to build smaller prisons (see Chapter 11 in this book: "The Small Prison"—which would likely necessitate the reduction in the use of prisons). Although Stohr and Wozniak have no objection to the reduction in the use of prisons generally, another solution, which is the focus of their chapter, is to make the prisons that we do have "greener" in their construction and operation.

In this chapter, Stohr and Wozniak detail how such efforts to make corrections "green" have appeared at the local, state, and federal levels. From creating a butterfly habitat to raising organic produce, some prisons are embracing the green movement as a way to reduce costs and waste, to increase health, to give back to their communities, and just generally to do good by making the world a better place. The greening of prisons is certainly something that Mother Nature, and perhaps Rachel Carson, would conceivably approve of, along with state legislatures and governors concerned about the cost of corrections, and therefore is likely to yield better outcomes for prison officials and inmates engaged in such beneficial activities!

There has been a growing concern about environmental degradation in this country and internationally for some time now. Ever since the Industrial Revolution took hold in the United States and in Europe in the mid to late 1800s, the negative effects of the reckless pollution and overconsumption of resources on air, water, and land, on other species, and on human beings have become increasingly apparent. These untoward impacts have reached the point that a number of scientists have warned of an impending environmental collapse within two generations, one from which our species, and others, may not recover (Diamond, 2005; Lovelock, 2006; Solomon et al., 2007).

As a result of these concerns, "green" or environmentally friendly and sustainable initiatives in the areas of production, consumption, and disposal of goods have become increasingly popular. The green movement, which began in the 1960s, has gained in popularity recently as the evidence of environmental degradation mounts—a degradation that affects everything we do, from the food we consume to how we fuel our cars and heat our homes. The energy, transportation, housing, commercial construction, food and clothing production and processing, and medical care, to name but a few sectors of our economy, to some degree are reconsidering and reconfiguring to appear or actually *be* green (Brown, 2001).

Prisons and other correctional organizations are yet another sector of the economy where environmentally friendly practices might be adopted (Lynch, 2007, pp. 213–214). The idea of green prisons, or those that minimize their negative impact on their environment, is a relatively new one. As prisons consume so many resources, they present a number of opportunities for correctional managers interested in going green. The myriad benefits of such efforts are explored in this chapter. We also note how some prisons are reinventing themselves and making progress in this area. We finish the chapter with recommendations and a proposed model for green prisons.

The Meaning of Green

Lynch and Michalowski (2006, pp. 178–179) define *green* as "actions and practices that are consciously designed to protect and preserve both natural and human environments."

According to Lynch and Stretesky (2003), there are contrasting definitions of the word *green*. That is, "one definition is aligned with corporate interests and emerged through corporate redefinitions of green environmentalism," whereas the other definition "highlights common elements in social movements concerned with environmental justice" and the need to apply concepts of race, class, and gender into the analysis (Lynch & Stretesky, 2003, p. 217).

In the first definition, there is often a reconstruction of the meaning of "green." Thus, as Lynch and Stretesky (2003, p. 220) note, corporations appeared to be green through massive public relations and advertising that stressed "consumption" rather than "production" issues about the environment. An example is that consumers could become green by "buying 'green' products from companies that claimed to be green" (Lynch & Stretesky, 2003, p. 220). According to these authors (2003, p. 220), "by appearing green, corporations were able to diffuse and redirect support for environmental issues and movements." A further contradiction is apparent in the practice of greenwashing—in which consumers are persuaded by advertising to believe that the consumption of green products constitutes going green, even though the production of such products may not be environmentally friendly or green.

Green Prisons: The Problem of Fossil Fuels and Oil Supply

In *Big Prisons, Big Dreams*, Lynch (2007, p. 1) examines "whether a bigger prison system, such as the one we have built in America to control crime, necessarily makes for a better prison system." Essentially, the goal of that book is to "review the rapid growth of the U.S. prison system that has been underway (*sic*) and unimpeded since 1973" (p. 17). Hence, the analysis undertaken here is broad based and reviews data over time and across regions from 50 state prison systems in the United States. Although Lynch's book presents various in-depth chapters illustrating ongoing levels of support for its main arguments, it is instructive for our purposes to note these key conclusions about the relationship between the "imprisonment binge and crime" (Lynch, 2007, pp. 200–201). Lynch (2007, p. 19) maintains that America's big prison system is "not an effective mechanism to control crime" and "is a waste of resources in a world facing an energy crisis and problems of mass energy consumption, such as global warming." To address these issues, a chapter in this book (Lynch, 2007, p. 202) focuses on the problems created by the combination of a huge prison system and limited energy sources. In America, we have an ever-burgeoning dependence on oil and a potential likelihood of a declining availability of oil in our country and across the world.

As Lynch (2007, p. 211) suggests, there is a sensible, scientifically informed approach that can be adapted for the U.S. prison system's potential problems of oil distribution and rising energy costs. According to Lynch (2007, p. 211) four points that are relevant to this discussion are:

- To change the prison system is not extraordinarily difficult. What will be difficult is to change the opinions of the public and lawmakers and to convince them that such changes are needed.

- Lawmakers and the public need to be taught to recognize that our country must institute a correctional system based on offender reform rather than deterrence and incapacitation (Clear, 1994; Cullen & Gilbert, 1982).

- We ought to adopt correctional models found in small, effective prison systems to deal with crime reduction, escalating prison size and costs, looming energy supply problems, and global warming.

- There is a need, in other words, to unite criminal justice policy and philosophy with green theories and practices (e.g., see Beirne & South, 2006; Frank & Lynch, 1992; Lynch & Stretesky, 2003; South, 1998; South & Beirne, 1998; see also Beirne & South, 2007).

Elements of Green Society

In his chapter on "Ecology, Community and Justice," Benton (2007, p. 5) spelled out the elements of a green society, including:

- Humans would live in ways that minimally disrupt the rest of nature.

- Decision making would be decentralized to small, self-sufficient, and self-governing communities.

- Self-government would take the form of active or participatory democracy.

- Either as a separate principle, or as a consequence of the above, these self-governing communities would be radically egalitarian or "nonhierarchical."

- The purposes of individual and collective life would give priority to aesthetic, spiritual, and convivial sources of fulfillment, as against the "materialist" pursuit of material acquisition and competitive advantage.

- Work to meet basic physical needs would be intrinsically fulfilling and employ tools appropriate to small-scale egalitarian communities and to ecologically sustainable production and consumption.

Prisons by their nature are not decentralized in decision making, nor are they egalitarian; in fact, they are specifically designed to be just the opposite. Nor have attempts to make them "democratic" been popular initiatives with politicians or the public (Murton, 1976). However, some of these elements of a green society might be duplicated in the prison (or jail) environment, such as living "in ways that minimally disrupt the rest of nature" and working "to meet basic physical needs" as "intrinsically fulfilling," and employing "tools appropriate to small-scale . . . communities and to ecologically sustainable production and consumption" (Benton, 2007, p. 5).

Prisons and the Resistance to Greening

Correctional institutions, as a rule, and until very recently, have not been as ready to embrace green initiatives or to become anything approaching a "green society." This reluctance to "get on board" with green initiatives is probably a reflection of the politics of going green, with some conservative politicians denying that human activities have had any negative effect on global warming (despite the overwhelming evidence to the contrary—that is, IPCC, 2008; Spray & McGlothlin, 2002; Wachholz, 2007), let alone on other areas of the environment (Walsh, 2011). Yet as recently as 2008, both the Republican and Democratic candidates for president acknowledged the effect that human actions had on warming the earth's atmosphere (Walsh, 2011). Some attribute this shift to denial by conservative candidates and politicians, and the few scientists who support them, to the millions of dollars from "big oil" and the Koch brothers that have flowed to them (Walsh, 2011; Werrell, 2011). Therefore, with this political climate in mind, it would be difficult for correctional institutions in states with conservative legislatures or governors to move in the direction of greening their facilities or practices *unless* the case can be made that money can be saved by doing so, and such a case is being made by the National Institute of Corrections (NIC), the American Correctional Association, and correctional managers in a number of states (Feldbaum, Greene, Kirschenbaum, Mukamal, Welsh, & Pinderhughes, 2011).

Besides politics and the money that all too often fuels it, other barriers to going green, both physical and perceptual, have prevented such a move. Correctional institutions tend to be removed from conventional society in many respects, both in the case of their physical presence for some prisons and in the closed-in nature of prisons and jails. Physically, many prisons are located in smaller communities or on the outskirts of larger ones, making them less subject to the latest trends in thoughts and beliefs. Furthermore, access to the inside of prisons is restricted and tightly controlled or "closed," a fact that also has the effect of making them less aware of, and receptive to, what is popular in the larger culture. Both of these factors also make the greening of prisons (as well as jails) and their operations less likely.

Prisons are not internally structured to be participative or democratic. Instead, they have a bureaucratized structure with paramilitary operations. Neither staff nor inmates have much say in prison operations above the line level, though this is less true in some prisons. In this regard, and as described by Benton (2007), American prisons do not have a natural fit in a green society.

The American Prison as a Toxic Environmental Hog

Yet in every way imaginable, there is an incredible need for American prisons to go green! As currently operated and as a group, they likely consume more energy and natural resources than almost any other social or private institution—more than schools, hospitals, and shopping malls and more than most businesses (Snyder, Tan, & Hoffman, 2004; Stephan, 2004; Vera Institute of Justice, 2012). The amount of money it takes to keep correctional institutions and programming operational at the state level was over $52 billion in 2009 (the latest year for which data were available at this writing) (Sigritz, Cummings, Husch, & Mazer, 2010). Most of them are large institutions, holding hundreds, and often thousands, of inmates who must be watched and held securely 24 hours a day for years at a time. Their inmates also must be fed, clothed, and supervised while they work, go to school, or attend other programming or recreation. Prisons are constructed of several layers of steel, concrete, wood, and glass, all materials requiring transportation to the build site by truck, rail, or ocean container ships. Their actual construction can take years and require the operation of oil-dependent equipment. Lighting, and a great deal of it, must be on all of the time. Security doors, alarms, cameras, and other electrical devices also must be kept on. Inmates must be allowed to shower, which many will choose to do once per day, and their clothing and bedding must be washed regularly. Food must be prepared, and their kitchen equipment is engaged in constant cooking to accommodate the three meals that must be produced and served daily. Power tools and other machinery that make work possible in prisons must have a fuel source. Prison buses, cars, and trucks must be serviced and filled with gasoline and oil. Inmate clothing and bedding must be purchased, or at least the material must be, and made into items of use. The electricity, water, oil and gasoline, coal, and other fuel sources that power these prisons, not to mention the pesticides and fertilizers used in agriculture to produce the food and the toxins in building materials, all contribute to the pollution of prisons and their environs and consume the resources equivalent to a small town every day (Feldbaum et al., 2011).

As prison buildings and their infrastructure degrade, they potentially poison their residents with toxic residue in their old pipes, asbestos in their walls, and waste in their soil and water. Cleaning products, laundry detergents, pest sprays, and lawn fertilizers all can contribute to a mix of toxins that directly, or indirectly, impair the health of inmates and staff in prisons and jails—as can the paints used on the walls and the industrial processing agents used in some work. The cumulative effect of this high energy consumption, older facilities, and the use of products and processes that can poison and sicken inmates and staff, as well as any neighbors sharing a water source or residing downwind, creates institutions in dire need of environmental reform (Environmental Working Group, 2011; Feldbaum et al., 2011).

The Benefits Derived From Going Green

Prisons and jails interested in going green are likely to reap a number of direct and indirect benefits for their state, their community, their staff, and their inmates. The first obvious benefit, after an initial capital investment, will be a reduction in costs for those states and institutions situated to take advantage of solar, wind, wave, and geothermal sources of energy (Atherton & Sheldon, 2011; Feldbaum et al., 2011; Webster, 2010). Recycling and refurbishing materials are also likely to lead to lower costs as are efforts to grow organic foods on their grounds for consumption at the prison or in the prison system.

A second related (indeed, they are all related) benefit will be the improvement in health from reducing the pollution from oil, gas, and other toxins in the environment for the local community and the prison and from eating fewer processed foods (Feldbaum et al., 2011). The exercise required to "work" the garden benefits the inmate workers assigned to it, while also providing something meaningful for them to do. Using greener products to clean dishes and bathrooms and floors, as well as clothing, or electing to use greener methods and practices (e.g., replacing lawns with native grasses or landscaping that requires less water and fewer chemicals) might all reduce the toxicity of the air, water, and soil in the correctional and local environment (Environmental Working Group, 2011).

A third benefit would be the opportunity that going green presents for inmates to have a healthier living environment all around. They could consume less, and what they consume would be more healthful for them. They can give more to others both in their prison and the larger community. Engagement in green jobs also keeps inmates of prisons out of trouble while they do something productive with their time.

A fourth benefit would be the provision of a positive role model for other state, federal, and local public and private social institutions regarding environmental issues. If prisons (and jails), typically vessels for socially conservative values, moved in the direction of greening, it would suddenly make benign environmental practices mainstream and worthy of emulating by the larger culture. Rather than being on the fringe, green policies and practices would suddenly become just normal correctional practice and perhaps typical community practice.

A fifth benefit, of vital importance if the IPCC's dire predictions of a looming environmental disaster by the Intergovernmental Panel on Climate Change (a Nobel Prize–winning consortium of scientists around the world) are true, would be a reduction in the environmental impact of prisons (and jails), both in their local environment and globally. As redundant already mentioned in the redundant foregoing, prisons are energy and resource hogs, and cutting back on their energy and resource consumption and on their direct and indirect output of toxic waste can only be seen as extremely beneficial all around.

A sixth, and last, obvious benefit would be the creation of jobs for construction, maintenance, and recycling staff or workers in the free community who would be engaged in installing green-energy equipment, maintaining it, and processing prison waste materials and for the inmates who would assist them (Webster, 2010). Those same inmates might be able to take the training and experience with green materials, products and maintenance, and gardening work that they would receive in the prison and translate that into work in the free community once released (Feldbaum et al., 2011). According to a recent report by the Brookings Institute (Muro, 2011, p. 4), the "clean economy," or the sector of the economy that usually encompasses low carbon and environmental goods and services that provide environmental benefits (often also termed green), "employs some 2.7 million workers, [and] encompasses a significant number of jobs in establishments spread across a diverse group of industries." It is a sector of the economy whose number of jobs grew despite the recession and whose pay is better for low-skilled workers than is the larger economy.

According to the Pew Center report, *In Brief: Clean Energy Markets: Jobs and Opportunities* (2011a), many countries are investing heavily in the clean economy, with an annual growth rate of 32% between 2004 and 2010 (p. 1). The authors of the Pew report recommend that the United States invest heavily in clean-energy technology and manufacture as a means of creating jobs and positioning this sector of the economy for profits from sale of goods to government and the private sector, both here and abroad. As a first step toward making the production of green goods attractive, the authors recommend that federal, state, and local laws address energy policy such that investment in the clean economy becomes attractive. Should the United States craft policies that sensibly regulate greenhouse gas emissions and other environmental toxins, the thinking goes, there will be greater investment and job creation in the green or clean sector of the economy.

Indicators of a Green Movement in Prisons and Jails

According to the Pew Center (2011b, p. 1), fully 21 states in 2011 alone passed laws or created commissions to study, or action plans to address, such issues as climate change and greenhouse gas reporting and reductions. The National Institute of Corrections issued a 2011 report titled *The Greening of Corrections: Creating a Sustainable System* in which the authors detail how states might create a sustainable model for correctional institutions, for correctional industries, and for reentry programs (Feldbaum et al., 2011).

As a means of controlling costs for all of the activities prisons must engage in, and as a way to reduce the environmental impact that prisons present for their communities, some state and federal prisons and jails in a few localities have begun the effort to go green. As an indication of the momentum for such a movement, in June 2011 the National Institute of Corrections cosponsored the National Symposium on Sustainable Corrections, with the Indiana Department of Corrections, where some of these efforts were showcased and where "green building" vendors offered their products and services. As further evidence of this momentum, also discussed at the symposium was the American Correctional Association's new accreditation standard that requires "facilities seeking accreditation to demonstrate that they have examined, and where appropriate and feasible, implemented strategies that promote recycling, energy and water conservation, pollution reduction and utilization of renewable energy alternatives" (Atherton & Sheldon, 2011, p. 3). Although the desire by private businesses to sell products and services primarily to public correctional institutions appeared to provide some of the impetus for the symposium, if the discussion of those products and services in the symposium report is any indicator, there is enough independent progress in corrections toward greening that one might almost give it the moniker of "movement."

WASHINGTON STATE PRISONS

In Washington state, inmates of the Ahtanum View Work Release plant and the Cedar Creek work camp nurture and harvest foods from their organic gardens and the greenhouse at the latter institution. Located 25 miles from Olympia, the state capital, the Cedar Creek prison recycles all food waste as compost and thousands of pounds of paper and cardboard per year. As well, it recycles "shoe scraps that are made into playground turf" (Judd, 2008).

At the Cedar Creek facility, they grow organic tomatoes and lettuce and have a beehive whose honey is used to supplement the food and whose beeswax is used to create lotion (Webster, 2010). Engaging in these activities has had the effect of saving costs, providing fresh food for the inmates, and diverting waste from landfills (Washington State Department of Corrections, 2011; Webster, 2010). The department's website notes as well that the gardens are part of the Department of Corrections sustainability efforts in Washington state. This correctional center also utilizes "water catchment basins, low water toilets, energy conservation, and field crews with the Department of Natural Resources for tree planting and wildland firefighting" (The Evergreen State College and Washington State Department of Corrections, 2012).

Further, at the Cedar Creek Correctional Center, the Washington State Department of Corrections and Evergreen State College began in 2004 a prison sustainability partnership, which fostered involvement throughout the prison community. A faculty member (whose specialty was forest ecology) at Evergreen coordinated several students at this state college to work with offenders and staff members at the Cedar Creek Center to work together on the Moss-in-Prison Project. This project was designed to explore how to farm mosses for the horticulture trade, determine which species could be cultivated to alleviate pressures of sustainable harvesting in old growth forests, and provide intellectual and emotional stimulation for the inmates, who typically have little or no access to nature (The Evergreen State College and Washington State Department of Corrections, 2012).

Another initiative by inmates in Washington state can be seen at Mission Creek Corrections Center, where they breed and care for the Taylor's Checkerspot butterfly (Chittim, 2011). The women monitor the progress of this butterfly, which is on the brink of being listed on the endangered species list, at a local artillery range for the United State Army. Male inmates from a local prison are engaged in growing the natural grasses for the butterflies' meadow. In addition, at the Washington Corrections Center for Women, activities included "composting, horticulture greenhouse (Tacoma Community College certificate), water and energy conservation, a Prison Pet Partnership Program (dog training and grooming), and field crews for an independent organic farm that supports local food banks" (Sharp, 2010). Likewise, at the Stafford Creek Corrections Center, sustainability efforts consist of "recycling, composting, horticulture greenhouse, beekeeping, water and energy conservation, motorless lawn mowing, the Bicycles from Heaven refurbishing program with the Grays' Harbor Lions Club, and the K–9 Rescue program to rehabilitate troubled dogs for adoption by families" (The Evergreen State College and Washington State Department of Corrections, 2012).

Three other correctional centers in the state of Washington are identified as "green prisons." First is the Monroe Correctional Complex. This was the state's first LEED—Leadership in Energy and Environment Design—facility. It is equipped with low energy lighting and a rainwater collection system for toilet flushing water. Second is the Coyote Ridge Prison, which uses energy-efficient boilers and ventilation system, along with tall and skinny windows for cooling cells in the summer and heating cells in the winter. This facility uses over five million fewer gallons of water than similar sized prisons. And, third is the Cedar Creek Corrections Center. This institution adopts a program that selects inmates to assist in research by raising endangered spotted frogs, compost prison food waste, grow organic vegetables, collect rainwater for gardens, raise bees, and hand-sort recyclables (Schenkel, 2011).

MARYLAND PRISONS

State inmates from the Patuxent Institution in Maryland planted and nurtured almost 500 trees that are destined for county parks (Maryland Department of Public Safety and Correctional Services, 2011). When announcing this initiative, the county manager said that the partnership between the county and the state Department of Corrections in Maryland was undertaken both to "protect the environment" and to show that the "government was working smarter and more efficiently" (Maryland Department of Public Safety and Correctional Services, 2011, p. 1). Across the state of Maryland, inmates from the prison system in the last few years have been involved in picking up trash along the highways and roadways, the refurbishing of several cemeteries, the planting of more trees (over one million), the building of Habitat for Humanity houses, assisting in the restoration of the habitat for oyster beds, the planting and care of institutional gardens, and the demolition of a decrepit house of correction whose materials were recycled (Maryland Department of Natural Resources, 2011, p. 1; Maryland Department of Public Safety and Correctional Services, 2011, pp. 1–2).

INDIANA PRISONS

The Indiana Department of Corrections has instituted recycling programs, LED lighting, horticulture programs, and biomass boilers at three different prisons (Indiana Department of Corrections, 2011). In addition, a wood chipper at one prison, a windmill turbine at another, and solar panels at a third are projected to save those facilities on heat and water to the tune of millions of dollars over the lifetime of this technology.

CALIFORNIA PRISONS

In California, as of 2008, there were 16 facilities being retrofitted to reduce their energy consumption and six additional solar projects were in the works at several institutions (Webster, 2010, p. 192). All of these endeavors were projected to save hundreds of thousands of dollars in the short run and potentially millions in the future. They would also reduce greenhouse gases by significant amounts.

OTHER STATE PRISONS

The Michigan Department of Corrections contracted for energy-efficient building modifications at the Muskegon and Marquette prisons. The contract for these medium-security prisons led to the "installation of simple energy efficient technology, including replacing and adding insulation, converting lighting, replacing old thermostats with energy efficient controls, installing heat recovery systems, and heating and cooling zone controls" (Lynch, 2007, p. 218). At the Utah State Prison in Bluffdale, an extensive renovation was carried out that involved the installation of wind-powered generators and geothermal energy (Lynch, 2007, p. 218). In its prison system, the state of Tennessee implemented energy-efficiency projects, one to improve insulation and the other to furnish geothermal energy (Lynch, 2007, p. 218).

FEDERAL PRISONS

There are also federal prisons involved in green activities. Federal correctional institutions in New Jersey, Colorado, and Arizona have installed solar panels on their roofs to assist with heating costs, thereby reducing carbon emissions by hundreds of thousands of pounds per year while at the same time saving thousands of dollars (Schenkel, 2011). The Butner Federal Correctional Institution in North Carolina (a medium-security facility known for housing Ponzi-schemer Bernie Madoff) has features such as energy-smart landscaping, low-flow plumbing fixtures, an alternative fuel refueling station, a parking lot for alternative fuel vehicles, and encouragement of bicycles as a form of green transportation (Schenkel, 2011). Furthermore, other federal correctional institutions are going green with solar power systems utilized at the Federal Correction Institution in Fairton, New Jersey; the Federal Correction Institute in Englewood, Colorado; the Federal Correctional Institute, Phoenix, Arizona; and the Wallkill State Correctional Facility in Wallkill, New York.

JAILS IN CALIFORNIA AND MINNESOTA

Similarly, the Santa Rita Jail in Dublin, California, installed solar panels on its roof, providing both electricity and savings to the county (Schenkel, 2011). Another jail, this one in Mankato, Minnesota, was built to the U.S. Green Building Council's LEED standards and is likely to save electricity, water, waste, and money by using geothermal heating, lights, and holding ponds to filter water (Linehan, 2009). Also notable is that this jail (the Blue Earth County Justice Center) was designed and constructed with recycled and local building materials (Schenkel, 2011).

Green Planning and Operations for Prisons: A Sustainable Model

As these examples would indicate, what it means to have some green in a prison operation can involve a number of approaches. Some of these prisons (and jails) that have engaged in greening have focused on the physical structure of the facility and how to power it, while others are more about how their inmates might contribute to improving the environment. In this regard, systematic advice on how to "green up" a prison has been presented in the National Institute of

Correction's (NIC) document *The Greening of Corrections*. The report's authors, Feldbaum et al. (2011, p. 48–49), make four general recommendations about how to green up a prison or a jail: First, create a sustainability work group; second, hold a retreat for your executive team; third, implement budget savings strategies and offender employment opportunities; and fourth, provide performance management: Inspect what you expect. These points warrant further discussion.

Regarding the first recommendation, Feldbaum and colleagues advise prison and jail managers to gather together those they employ who are interested in reducing the negative impact of their facility on the environment. They note that such folk should come from all sectors of the facility, including programming and treatment, custody, personnel, budgeting, and maintenance. The sustainability team should develop expectations for the facility and a plan, gain a buy-in from affected staff, and then monitor whether the plan is implemented.

At the recommended retreat for the executive team (number two of the above), the NIC document authors note the need to educate this group about what "green" means for prisons. Ideas and opinions of team members should be solicited. Experts and stakeholders should be used to "develop a smart business strategy that assists in reducing costs, employing offenders, and engaging community partners" (Feldbaum et al., 2011, p. 48).

The third recommendation was more specific, involving eight action items: "mine your waste," or use inmates to recycle and compost and then rethink what they throw away; "support local partnerships," or provide services to the community like repairing old bikes or giving plants or produce that you do not use to food banks; reduce the number of institutional vehicles and switch to vehicles that produce the lowest carbon footprint; develop a dog training/sheltering program with the local humane society shelter as a means of giving offenders something to care for and care about; partner with universities or the military on biodiversity projects; partner with colleges and the local public sector on relevant training and curricula; work with living creatures to enhance their environment (e.g., beehives); use offender emails to reduce waste and improve efficiency in communication (Feldbaum et al., 2011, p. 48).

Under the fourth recommendation, Feldbaum et al. (2011, p. 49) describe the process of selecting a performance management system, then the need to collect baseline data in areas of sustainability such as "energy, solid waste, recycling, water use, gardening and other innovation programs." These data should be published and monitored monthly so that progress in sustainability might be noted and behavior might be adjusted as needed.

Conclusions and Recommendations for a Model Green Prison

For all practical purposes, the discussion so far delineates core ideas, emphases, and practices to be adhered to in taking steps toward developing a "model green prison." In particular, the "meaning of green" and the "elements of green society," which are specified in the beginning of our chapter, need to be incorporated as interconnected guideposts within each basic type of a green prison. Efforts toward establishing a model green prison would also do well to recognize and address the resistance among lawmakers, criminal justice practitioners, and the general public toward notions of greening and global warming. It is certainly not an easy endeavor to change the minds of people who have negative or even hostile attitudes and feelings about such environmental themes. However, to bring about a model green prison, such efforts in changing skeptical minds about greening and global warming are essential.

As illustrated earlier in our chapter, recognizing how the present American prison system, for the most part, consumes more energy and natural resources than virtually all other social private institutions in our country is another compelling reason to develop a model green prison. It is truly not an overstatement, for example, to conceive of any U.S. prison as a "toxic environmental hog"; a model green prison must be designed to avoid as much energy wasting as possible.

Our chapter further pointed out several immediate "benefits from going green in prisons" (i.e., reduction in operating costs, improvement of health through eliminating pollution from environmental toxins, enabling a healthier living environment for inmates, creation of jobs in the community for construction, maintenance, and recycling workers) that each model green prison should incorporate into its proposal justifications and its general mission in society on the whole.

Furthermore, each model prison would do well to follow the energy-sustaining paths undertaken in other green prisons (described in this chapter), such as those in the states of Washington, Maryland, Indiana, and California and in other federal and state facilities.

In this context, our chapter was designed to show that "green principles can be used to reinvent the prison." Drawing insights from green criminology, various writings, and Internet links, images of ways that a green prison can be created (as well as some of the obstacles involved) were discussed in respect to a series of themes and issues associated with green technology and sustainable approaches to living. All in all, the chapter thus takes concerns of criminology and criminal justice in an important direction: It projects in various ways what such a green prison might look like, while also drawing attention to many other efforts to incorporate a movement toward a "greening of American prisons." Why is this important to do? As Lynch (2007, p. 219) puts it, "The longer the need for energy related criminal justice reform is ignored, the more likely it becomes that the criminal justice system will be inadequately prepared to provide for public safety in the future."

In our view, a model green prison does not arise out of thin air but requires a substantive conceptual/theoretical/policy-oriented framework to guide its immediate proposal, support, construction, and provision. Adopting an environmentally friendly plan of action, such as the one recommended by Lynch (2007), also is essential for any movement toward building a model green prison. Parenthetically, other writings within green criminology, critical criminology (see DeKeseredy, 2010; Schwartz & Hatty, 2003), and environmental justice (see Bullard, 2005; Shrader-Frechette, 2005) could be applied to a model green prison's environmentally friendly plan. Based on these myriad sources, we think that it is important for a model green prison to include the following seven components.

COMPONENT 1: SMALLER SIZE

Lynch (2007) maintains prisons do not reduce crime, and the prisons we do have should be smaller. In addition, he observes that our correctional system is composed of large prisons that are unnecessarily costly and resource dependent. Therefore, one step, which can be taken when prisons are being built, is to build smaller, a step that will force us to incarcerate less and use fewer resources in the construction and operation of the prison.

COMPONENT 2: PRISONS MUST SUPPLY
THEIR OWN CLEAN ENERGY NEEDS

Certainly a smaller prison is more likely to be able to attain energy independence, but even medium-and larger-sized prisons can supplement their needs with clean energy. A model green prison, as Lynch (2007, p. 214) observes, is best set up with geothermal heating and cooling systems (to reduce heating and cooling costs) and wind-powered electrical generators (to be used as alternative energy sources). Why is this a better way to proceed? Lynch (2007, p. 214) states that such energy-conscious alternatives "drastically reduce or eliminate the need for fossil-fuel-generated electricity, and perhaps even yield a surplus of energy that could be sold to utilities or channeled to local power grids to provide free energy for street lights—another crime reduction tool."

COMPONENT 3: PRISONS SHOULD BE
SITED CLOSER TO URBAN AREAS

In addition, these prisons should be built in closer proximity to urban and suburban areas as this will reduce the energy costs needed for transporting inmates, moving goods to and from the institution, and staff travel.

COMPONENT 4: PRISONS, THEIR INMATES,
AND STAFF SHOULD BE ENGAGED IN
ENVIRONMENTALLY FRIENDLY ENDEAVORS

In keeping with Lynch's (2007) theoretical rationale and suggested directions for a model green prison (as identified above), it seems beneficial, at this point, to consider the host of previously mentioned examples of greening activities and practices adopted in U.S. prisons at state and federal levels. These greening efforts (when listed all in one place) certainly offer very specific ways that a model green prison can develop in the beginning and broaden out in the future. As such, we showed that these green prisons involved tree planting; nurturing of organic gardens; trash pickup along roads and highways; refurbishing cemeteries; building and fixing houses for Habitat for Humanity; recycling materials such as paper, cardboard, and food waste; beekeeping for food supplement and lotion; using water containment basins; farming for horticulture trade; breeding and care of endangered species; setting up pet-partner projects; composting; water and energy conservation; using energy saving boilers and ventilation; and installing solar panels.

COMPONENT 5: PRISONS MUST FOCUS ON ENVIRONMENTAL WORK AND EDUCATION FOR INMATES

Arguably one of the most promising elements of a model green prison would entail the incorporation of environmental-based work and education in the correctional setting. In recent years, there has been a movement in America toward facilitating both green education and green work opportunities. An example of the former is a 2011 WREX (a local news station) report that Rockford, Illinois, was to receive a quarter of a million dollars to "help launch a multi-year green jobs training program, which will help the city directly by facilitating the creation of much-needed employment opportunities and indirectly by speeding progress toward cheaper substitutes for traditional energy sources, such as wind and solar energy" (Green Jobs Ready, 2011). This link further exhibits green careers are available in hydrology, geoscience, ecology, atmospheric science, geothermal science, and home energy retrofit.

Another example is the Ohio Green Prison Project (OGPP), which is affiliated with the Center on Sentencing and Corrections. In Lancaster, Ohio, OGPP worked on a pilot project devised to: lower operating and energy costs, "demonstrate that training incarcerated people to retrofit prisons with energy-efficient green technology can make facilities more cost effective," and "provide trainees with job skills to prepare them for careers in the burgeoning green economy, making them more likely to succeed when they return to their communities" (Morgan, 2011).

Such green training programs would seem useful to extend into a model green prison, along with enabling its inmates the possibility of enrolling in Oregon for study in Marylhurst University's online MBA program in Sustainable Business— which has four concentrations: natural and organic resources; renewable energy; green development; energy policy and administration (Marylhurst University, 2012). Likewise, Green Mountain College in Vermont has what it calls "the Greenest Green MBA," which consists of an online MBA program in Sustainable Business, providing yet another possible set of studies for inmates who are part of a model green prison.

These types of online MBAs in Sustainable Business do not sound far-fetched in light of reports of "major jobs growth in clean energy between 2003 and

2010—solar thermal and wind grew by 18.4 percent and 14.9 percent, respectively" (Gordon, Kasper, & Lyon, 2011). Inmates in model green prisons who embark upon Sustainable Business master's degrees could join the growing number of "green-collar workers" who find work in renewable energy and energy efficiency industries, which provided in 2010 an estimated 8.5 million jobs in the United States (Moss, 2011). This link further identified several major U.S. cities (San Francisco, Denver, New York City, Los Angeles, Boston, Detroit, Phoenix, Houston) for university graduates seeking green jobs. In this light, a model green prison would do well to augment any of these environmentally oriented endeavors, especially in combination throughout the correctional setting.

COMPONENT 6: PRISONS MUST HIRE AND TRAIN STAFF ON THE VALUE OF, AND THE SKILLS NEEDED FOR, A MODEL GREEN PRISON

Without a staff buy-in regarding a green prison, there is no possibility that it might be fully realized. This is why the NIC efforts in this area are so vital. By showcasing green efforts around the country, and providing a venue from which such information might be shared, the likelihood of more prisons going green increases exponentially. Secondly, if staff members are to be involved in this greening, they must be hired and/or trained in green practices and skills needed to assist inmates.

COMPONENT 7: GREEN PRACTICES AND INITIATIVES SHOULD BE STUDIED

There is value for a model green prison to be spearheaded by a commission or committee that is charged with studying and assembling best practices of green-oriented initiatives for both prison inmates and staff. Data on what works in green prison operation, and just as importantly, what does not, should be collected and reviewed to ensure that efforts to "green" the prison are beneficial for the inmates, staff, and their larger community.

References

Atherton, E., & Sheldon, P. (2011). Plenary address: How to save $1,000 per inmate. *National Symposium on Sustainable Corrections*. Retrieved October 21, 2011, from http://www.GreenPrisons.org

Beirne, P., & South, N. (Eds.). (2006). *Green criminology*. Hampshire, UK: Ashgate.

Beirne, P., & South, N. (Eds.). (2007). *Issues in green criminology: Confronting harms against environments, humanity, and other animals*. Portland, OR: Willan.

Benton, T. (2007). Ecology, community, and justice: The meaning of green. In P. Beirne & N. South (Eds.), *Issues in green criminology: Confronting harms against environments, humanity, and other animals.* (pp. 3–31). Portland, OR: Willan.

Brown, L. R. (2001). *Eco-economy: Building an economy for the Earth.* New York, NY: W. W. Norton.

Bullard, R. D. (Ed.). (2005*). The quest for environmental justice: Human rights and the politics of pollution.* San Francisco, CA: Sierra Club Books.

Carson, R. (1962). *Silent spring.* New York, NY: Houghton Mifflin.

Chittim, G. (2011). *Butterflies behind bars.* Seattle, WA: King 5 News. Retrieved October 21, 2011, from http://www.king5.com/news/local/Butterflies-Behind-Bars

Clear, T. (1994). *Harm in American penology: Offenders, victims, and their communities.* Albany: State University of New York Press.

Cullen, F. T., & Gilbert, K. E. (1982). *Reaffirming rehabilitation.* Cincinnati, OH: Anderson.

DeKeseredy, W. S. (2010). *Contemporary critical criminology.* New York, NY: Routledge.

Diamond, J. (2005). *Collapse: How societies choose to fail or succeed.* New York, NY: Viking Books.

Environmental Working Group. (2011). *Health/toxics.* Retrieved November 18, 2011, from http://www.ewg.org

Feldbaum, M., Greene, F., Kirschenbaum, S., Mukamal, D., Welsh, M., & Pinderhughes, R. (2011). *The greening of corrections: Creating a sustainable system.* Washington, DC: National Institute of Corrections. Retrieved November 26, 2012, from http://nicic.gov/Library/024914

Frank, N., & Lynch, M. J. (1992). *Corporate crime, corporate violence.* Albany, NY: Harrow and Heston.

Gordon, K., Kasper, M., & Lyon, S. (2011). *Green jobs by the numbers: Top clean tech sectors saw explosive growth in 2003–2010 despite the great recession.* Washington, DC: Center for American Progress. Retrieved June 1, 2012, from http://www.americanprogress.org/issues/2011/10/green_jobs_numbers.html

Green Jobs Ready. (2011). *More funding for green jobs training.* Sacramento, CA: Green Jobs Ready. Retrieved June 1, 2012, from http://greenjobsready.com/blog/uncategorized/more-funding-for-green-jobs-training-in-illinois/

Indiana Department of Corrections. (2012). Retrieved June 1, 2012, from http://www.in.gov/idoc/

Intergovernmental Panel on Climate Change. (2008). *IPCC fourth assessment report, 2007: Synthesis for policymakers.* Geneva, Switzerland: IPCC. Retrieved from http://www.ipcc.ch/ipccreports/ar4wg2.htm

Judd, A. (2008). *The green prison movement.* Retrieved June 1, 2012, from http://www.nowpublic.com/environment/green-prison-movement

Linehan, D. (2009). *Justice center's efficiency takes shape.* Mankato, MN: Free Press. Retrieved from October 21, 2011, from http://www.mankatofreepress.com/local

Lovelock, J. (2006). *The revenge of Gaia: Earth's climate crisis and the fate of humanity.* New York, NY: Basic Books.

Lynch, M. J. (2007). *Big prisons, big dreams: Crime and the failure of America's penal system.* New Brunswick, NJ: Rutgers University Press.

Lynch, M. J., & Michalowski, R. (2006). *Primer in radical criminology: Critical perspectives on crime, power, and identity* (4th ed.). Monsey, NY: Criminal Justice Press.

Lynch, M. J., & Stretesky, P. B. (2003). The meaning of green: Contrasting criminological perspectives. *Theoretical Criminology, 7,* 217–238.

Maryland Department of Natural Resources. (2011). *Maryland forest brigade exceeds tree goal—Governor O'Malley plants one millionth tree with inmates.* Retrieved November 26, 2012, from http://dnr.maryland.gov/dnrnews/pressrelease2011/sgg_050411.asp

Maryland Department of Public Safety and Correctional Services. (2011). *Howard County parks to receive 490 transplanted pine trees.* Retrieved October 21, 2011, from http://www.dpscs.state.md.us

Marylhurst University. (2012). *MBA in sustainable business.* Portland, OR: Marylhurst University. Retrieved June 1, 2012, from http://www.marylhurst.edu/academics/schools-colleges-departments/school-business/department-sustainable-business/programs/mba-sustainable-business.html/

Morgan, L. (2011). *Ohio green prison project.* New York, NY: Vera Institute. Retrieved June 1, 2012, from http://www.vera.org/project/ohio-green-prison-project

Moss, L. (2011). Top 10 cities for new grads seeking green jobs. *Mother Nature Network.* Retrieved June 1, 2012, from http://www.mnn.com/money/green-workplace/photos/top-10-cities-for-new-grads-seeking-green-jobs/green-collar-workers

Muro, M. (2011). *Sizing the clean economy: A national and regional green jobs assessment.* Washington, DC: Brookings Institute. Retrieved October 21, 2011, from http://www.brookings.org

Murton, T. O. (1976). *The dilemma of prison reform.* New York, NY: Praeger.

National Institute of Corrections. (2011). *The greening of corrections: Creating a sustainable system.* Washington, DC: Author. Retrieved October 21, 2011, from http://www.GreenPrisons.org

Pew Center. (2011a). *In brief: Clean energy markets: Jobs and opportunities.* Washington, DC: Pew Center on Global Climate Change. Retrieved October 21, 2011, from http://www.pewclimate.org

Pew Center. (2011b). *U.S. states and regions news.* Washington, DC: Pew Center Global on Climate Change. Retrieved October 21, 2011, from http://www.pewclimate.org/states-regions/news

Schenkel, A. (2011). 14 green prisons. *Mother Nature Network.* Retrieved June 1, 2012, from http://www.mnn.com/money/green-workplace/photos/14-green-prisons/eco-life-behind-bars

Schwartz, M. D., & Hatty, S. E. (Eds.). (2003). *Controversies in critical criminology.* Cincinnati, OH: Anderson.

Sharp, R. (2010). *Green prison: Where security meets ecology.* London: The Independent. Retrieved August 1, 2012, from http://www.independent.co.uk/environment/green-living/green-prison-where-security-meets-ecology-2054270.html

Shrader-Frechette, K. (2005). *Environmental justice: Creating equality, reclaiming democracy.* New York, NY: Oxford University Press.

Sigritz, B., Cummings, L., Husch, B., & Mazer, S. (2010). *Fiscal year 2009: State expenditure report.* Washington, DC: National Association of State Budget Officers. Retrieved November 18, 2011, from http://www.nasbo.org

Snyder, T. D., Tan, A. G., & Hoffman, C. M. (2004). *Digest of education statistics 2003.* Washington, DC: U.S. Department of Education, National Center for Education Statistics.

Solomon, S., Qin, D., Manning, M., Chen, Z., Marquis, M., Averyt, K. B., Tignor, M., & Miller, H. L. (Eds.). (2007). *Contribution of Working Group I to the Fourth Assessment Report of the Intergovernmental Panel on Climate Change.* Cambridge, UK: Cambridge University Press. Retrieved November 18, 2011, from http://www.ipcc.ch/publications_and_data/ar4/wg1/en/contents.html

Souder, W. (2012). *On a farther shore: The life and legacy of Rachel Carson.* New York, NY: Crown.

South N. (1998). A green field for criminology? A proposal for a perspective. *Theoretical Criminology, 2,* 211–233.

South, N., & Beirne, P. (1998). [Editors' introduction]. *Theoretical Criminology, 2,* 147–148.

Spray, S., & McGlothlin, K. (2002). *Global climate change.* Lanham, MD: Rowman and Littlefield.

Stephan, J. J. (2004). *State prison expenditures, 2001.* Washington, DC: U.S. Department of Justice, Bureau of Justice Statistics.

Vera Institute of Justice. (2012). *The price of prisons: What incarceration costs taxpayers, fact sheet.* New York, NY: Author.

Wachholz, S. (2007). "At risk": Climate change and its bearing on women's vulnerability to male violence. In P. Beirne & N. South (Eds.), *Issues in green criminology: Confronting harms against environments, humanity, and other animals* (pp. 161–185). Portland, OR: Willan.

Walsh, B. (2011). Going green: Who's bankrolling the climate-change deniers? *Time.* Retrieved November 18, 2011, from http://www.time.com/time/health/article/0,8599,2096055,00.html

Washington State Department of Corrections. (2011). *Organic gardens bloom at work release and Monroe Correctional Complex.* Retrieved October 21, 2011, from http://www.doc.wa.gov/news/stories/2011/092111

Webster, A. (2010). Environmental prison reform: Lower costs and greener world. *New England Journal on Criminal and Civil Confinement, 36,* 175–195.

Werrell, J. (2011). Commentary: Science trumps climate change deniers. *Kansas City Star.* Retrieved November 18, 2011, from http://www.kansascity.com/2011

Part VI

Making Prisons Perform

11

The Small Prison

*Cheryl Lero Jonson, John E. Eck,
and Francis T. Cullen*

Editors' Introduction

Many, if not most, readers have lived their entire lives in the midst of the mass imprisonment movement—an effort to enlarge America's inmate population that extends from the early 1970s. Until very recently, prison populations had risen year in and year out. A decade or so into the mass imprisonment movement, when the number of inmates had doubled, it seemed that this growth could not continue for much longer. But it did, until the financial crisis in 2008 made politicians of all major parties come to their senses. Facing shrinking public treasuries, government officials—especially governors tasked with the job of balancing budgets—initiated steps to reverse the costly practice of caging offenders on the state's dime.

There is, of course, ample reason to incarcerate offenders who commit heinous crimes or who are assessed to be at high risk of recidivating. Virtually everyone would prefer to have a predator safely tucked away in a prison cell as opposed to living next door. The issue is thus not whether prisons will be used as an instrument of crime control but rather how often and in what way. Today there is an emerging national consensus that current levels of imprisonment are no longer sustainable. Imprisonment has simply grown too big and cannot be afforded. The utility of bigness also has been called into question. Criminologists tell us that, past a certain point, locking up an ever-increasing number of offenders yields diminishing returns in preventing crime.

But if levels of imprisonment are to be rolled back, how will such smallness be achieved? And if achieved, what should correctional institutions look like? In this chapter, Cheryl Lero Jonson, John Eck, and Francis Cullen identify a core reason why incarcerating offenders is difficult to resist: Those most responsible for handing out lengthy prison terms—prosecutors and judges—do not have to pay for it. As elected officials, they must be wary that offenders that they release into the community might recidivate or commit a highly publicized heinous crime. Risk averse, they have every reason to send offenders to prison; they are protected politically and the state must pick up the tab for the years of incarcerations they have handed out. But what if local counties had to pay for all those that their locally elected prosecutors and judges placed behind bars? Then, more care might be taken in deciding which offenders truly warranted an expensive stay in prison. Furthermore, it might be possible to establish a strategy for controlling each county's use of imprisonment. Jonson and her colleagues propose a system used to regulate pollution: cap-and-trade.

As the pursuit of bigness is replaced with the pursuit of smallness as the reigning correctional ideology, it would also become possible to rethink the practice of cramming more and more inmates into crowded prison warehouses. Bigness breeds impersonality and the processing of offenders as mere numbers who must be bedded down and fed daily. By contrast, a small prison comes with the expectation that the privilege of low numbers be used for some social purpose, such as equipping inmates with the moral and human capital needed to avoid reoffending. Jonson, Eck, and Cullen thus call for a "criminology of smallness" that would be devoted to uncovering how smallness in corrections could be achieved and foster positive outcomes for inmates and for public safety.

S ize matters. In fact, in the correctional domain, nothing matters more than size, because accomplishing good things is often fundamentally inhibited by the sheer scale of the incarcerated population. Despite a spending and building spree, states have struggled to keep up with the influx of offenders walking through their prison gates. Even as correctional budgets have mushroomed and facilities have been opened regularly, the inmate population has outstripped the designed capacity for many institutions. Depending on the criteria used, anywhere from 19 to 26 states' prison populations exceed capacity (Guerino, Harrison, & Sabol, 2011). Unlike hotel managers, wardens cannot say that their institution is booked up for the evening and to find lodging elsewhere. With little choice, they have double- and triple-celled inmates. And they have transformed gymnasiums into dormitories filled with bunk beds, or crammed inmates into any other plausible nook or cranny that can accommodate a mattress. This structural density has made it impossible in many facilities to provide adequate rehabilitative programming and work assignments. For example, half of all inmates in California serve out their sentences in idleness, receiving no work assignment or rehabilitation programs (Petersilia, 2008). The capacity to provide adequate medical services, including substance abuse treatment, and to properly supervise inmate safety has been compromised. Preparing inmates for successful reentry too often falls into the category of wishful thinking.

There is now a general consensus that maintaining current levels of incarceration is not sustainable. In the face of budget crises and declining state revenues, governors from both political parties have set aside "get tough" ideology and started to address the problem of a bloated prison system. For nearly 40 years, state after state has engaged in a correctional orgy in which offenders have been sent to prison with little thought of how this would be financed. State treasuries always seemed to have enough capital to pay for another few thousand inmates. At times, this has meant cutting services elsewhere, such as support for higher education. But the public did not seem to care too much, reelecting politicians who promised to place more and more "super-predators" behind bars. Now, however, the money has run out. There is no more budgetary fat that can be trimmed. It is either reduce prison populations or cut services that voters care about. Notably, on January 1, 2010, the count of offenders in state prisons declined for the first time in 39 years. The reductions in scale have been marginal, not massive. Still, the intractable rise in incarceration seems to have hit its ceiling. Policy makers are now willing to consider fresh ideas to create a different correctional future.

This context may be a propitious time to entertain radical thoughts on how to make "smallness" a priority in correctional policy. California, of course, is reducing its prison population by upwards of 30,000 due the U.S. Supreme Court decision of *Brown v. Plata* (563 U.S. 2011). Other states also have passed legislation intended to reserve prison space for high-risk offenders and to reinvest savings in locally based alternatives to incarceration (see, e.g., Diroll, 2011; Justice Center, 2011; Pew Center on the States, 2012a). Still, the fundamental dynamic causing the excessive use of imprisonment is left untouched by these reforms. They certainly can achieve marginal, even meaningful, effects. But the core of the apple, so to speak, remains rotten, and thus the problem will certainly persist.

In this chapter, we thus identify and propose solutions for the core problem underlying mass imprisonment: Those who send inmates to prison accrue political capital and do not have to pay for it. The cost-benefit ratio thus leads decision makers to err on the side of incarceration—an option that incurs no political risk and does not cost them anything. Reversing this system of incentives is critical to harnessing prison populations. We also offer comments on how to create smallness within a context of large institutions. These reforms will be best served by overall reductions in the scale of imprisonment. Still, some useful strides can be taken in the short run. We begin with a brief review of the scale of imprisonment in the United States and of why the pursuit of bigness has yielded only limited advances in public safety.

In Pursuit of Bigness

Writing in 1985, Elliott Currie was deeply troubled by the sudden, precipitous rise in America's prison population. He ominously warned that "much greater increases in incarceration would turn the American penal system, already swollen out of all proportion, into a home-grown Gulag of dreadful proportions" (1985, p. 91). Looking back from today's vantage point, Currie's commentary appears both prescient and quaint. It is prescient because the nation's penal system would become just what Currie feared: swollen to the point of being dreadful. It is quaint because the number that so shocked him—an increase of the state and federal prison population to 450,000—would prove to be much like a mile marker on a highway that the prison van is quickly passing at breakneck speed. Currie could not have imagined that in the decades ahead, the "home-grown Gulag" would come to exceed 1.6 million offenders in state and federal institutions and surpass 2.4 million when local jail populations were included in the calculations (Cullen & Jonson, 2012).

If we had lived in 1970, the size of the inmate nation would not have captured too much of our attention. As Blumstein and Cohen (1973) showed at the time, the rate of incarceration had remained remarkably stable during the previous half century, despite fluctuating economic times and horrendous wars. Examining data from 1930 to 1970, they discovered that the imprisonment rate had "an average value of 110.2 prisoners per 100,000 population and a standard deviation during that time . . . of 8.9 prisoners per 100,000 population" (1973, p. 201). Further, they reported that since 1961 the imprisonment rate had "shown a distinct downward trend" (p. 202). Then, everything changed. The United States went from modest imprisonment to mass imprisonment. Much as the nation is marked by big

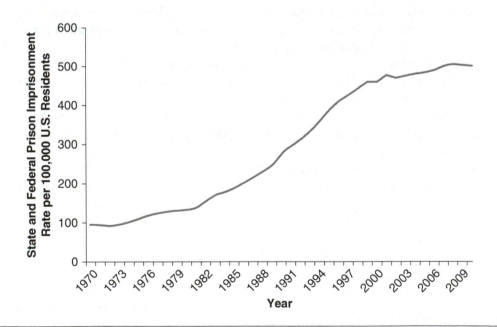

Figure 11.1　State and Federal Prison Imprisonment Rates, 1970–2010

SOURCE: Bureau of Justice Statistics. (2011). *Sourcebook of Criminal Justice Statistics*. Washington, DC: U.S. Department of Justice, Office of Justice Programs.

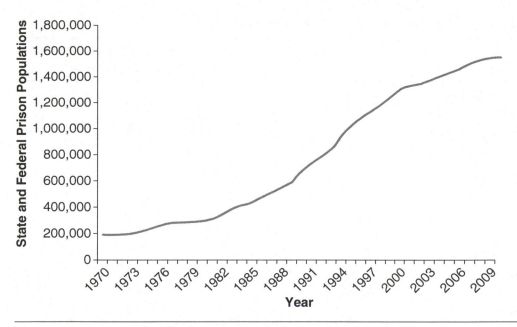

Figure 11.2 State and Federal Prison Populations, 1970–2010

SOURCE: Bureau of Justice Statistics. (2011). *Sourcebook of Criminal Justice Statistics*. Washington, DC: U.S. Department of Justice, Office of Justice Programs.

business, it became marked by big corrections—a behemoth that consumes more than $50 billion a year (The Sentencing Project, 2012).

Thus, in 1970, the state and federal imprisonment rate per 100,000 stood at 96. In 2010, it had multiplied more than five-fold to 497. In raw numbers, the inmate population jumped from 196,429 in 1970 to 1,543,206 in 2010—nearly a nine-fold increase (see Figures 11.1 and 11.2). But let us put this in more human terms. A 2008 study by Pew Charitable Trusts found that on any given day, one in every 100 adults in the United States is behind bars in a jail or prison. For men ages 20 to 34, the ratio narrows to one in every 30. For African American men of this age group, the figure is even more disquieting: One in every nine is locked up (Pew Charitable Trusts, 2008).

It might be argued that much like the spread of the global economy, the spread of mass imprisonment was a worldwide phenomenon—that this was not a case of American exceptionalism but of the nation just following the international crowd. But as Table 11.1 reveals, this was not the case. The United States' embrace of big imprisonment was indeed unusual. In fact, it should be a mark of national embarrassment that the United States stands atop the chart as the world's number one incarcerator. The countries that we most often compare ourselves to—Canada and the Western European nations—have rates of incarceration many-fold lower. Thus, Canada has a rate (114) that is 6.5 times lower. Further, as the United States has been in pursuit of correctional bigness, Canada has enjoyed stable rates of imprisonment since the 1960s and 1970s (Webster & Doob, 2007).

Table 11.1   International Rates of Incarceration, 2011

Country	Prison Population Rates per 100,000 National Population
United States	743
Rwanda	595
Russia	568
Brazil	253
Spain	159
Australia	133
China	122
Canada	114
France	96
Germany	85
Sweden	78
Denmark	74
India	32

SOURCE: Walmsley, R. (2011). *World Population List* (9th ed.). Essex, UK: International Centre for Prison Studies.

The Limits of Bigness

Pointing out the United States is the world leader in imprisoning its citizens does not necessarily make it a bad idea. It could be that as an affluent nation that places a high value on public safety, we have the luxury of locking up as many offenders as we wish. In contrast to the rest of the world, Americans prefer football to soccer. Maybe we just prefer imprisonment to letting predators run free.

This kind of thinking, however, runs up against a stubborn piece of reality: Prisons have their limits as effective instruments of crime control. Kleiman (2009) has captured the consensus of criminologists on this issue with the title of his book: *When Brute Force Fails*. He follows this title with a subtitle that suggests what policy analysis should focus on: *How to Have Less Crime and Less Punishment* (see also Durlauf & Nagin, 2011; Eck & Eck, 2012; Waller, 2006).

Why are prisons limited in their impact on crime? The issue of understanding and estimating such influence is complicated, involving complex conceptual and statistical considerations (Raphael & Stoll, 2009). But three factors serve to constrain how much public safety prisons can produce. First, there is now mounting evidence that prisons do not have a specific deterrence effect (Cullen, Jonson, & Nagin, 2011; Nagin, Cullen, & Jonson, 2009; Villettaz, Killias, & Zoder, 2006). Hard as it may be to believe, people sent to prison reoffend at the same, or higher, rates as people given a community sanction. Even if some inmates decide that crime does not pay, others are unaffected or are made more criminogenic by spending years behind bars associating with other criminals and cut off from conventional social roles. On balance, the effect on crime is a wash—or, if anything, slightly crime producing.

Second, it would be foolish to argue that taking more than two million offenders off the street does not save some crime (Spelman, 2000). When active criminals and predators are caged, there is an incapacitation effect. Still, the bigger imprisonment becomes, the less crime it seems to prevent. As the proportion of the offender population sent to prison expands, the amount of crime saved through sheer incapacitation reaches a point of diminishing returns. This occurs because prison growth depends on sending to the penitentiary not just the worst of the lot but more and more low-risk and moderate-risk offenders—those who are unlikely to recidivate in the time ahead. As Liedka, Piehl, and Useem (2006, p. 272) note, "Policy discussion should be informed by the limitation of the fact that prison expansion, beyond a certain point, will no longer serve any reasonable policy purpose. It seems that that point has been reached."

Third, the opportunity cost of imprisonment is high. Money spent on caging offenders is not spent on rehabilitating them or on other programs that might lower the crime rate, such as early intervention for at-risk children (Donohue, 2009). Importantly, when a big-imprisonment ideology is hegemonic, we simply shove one offender after another through the prison gates. The more there are, the merrier we are! We do not stop to ask more difficult, responsible questions: How much crime reduction will enlarging the prison system achieve? How much will this cost us—both in terms of money spent on incarceration and also money diverted from other correctional and social welfare programs? How should we balance all these factors in devising a rational prison policy?

The problem is that for four decades, nobody has shown much restraint in their willingness to lock up more and more offenders. We have thus used the term *prison orgy* because this is precisely what has occurred. The nation's prison system is bloated, and many of its institutions are in ill health—having descended into custodial warehouses that do little to improve their charges (Kruttschnitt & Gartner, 2005; Petersilia, 2008). We can do better, but only if we find ways to curb our appetite for incarceration.

Why Are Prisons Big?

Although the factors fueling America's mass imprisonment are undoubtedly complex, we can identify three plausible sources. First, a system that has a lot of input (offenders) will have a lot of output (inmates); second, get tough policies achieve what they are intended to achieve (many offenders locked up); and third, prosecutors and judges, and the localities they represent, do not have to pay when offenders are sent to prison. We discuss all three sources, but it is the last one that concerns us.

First, there is an endless flow of offenders that can be imprisoned each year in the United States. In 2010 alone, over 1.2 million violent and 9 million property crimes were reported to law enforcement agencies (Federal Bureau of Investigation, 2011). In response to these offenses, the United States has relied extensively on incarceration as the preferred method of punishment, too often ignoring the various alternatives to incarceration that are currently available. Judges have habitually failed to consider the array of sanctions that were born from the intermediate sanction or "smart sentencing" movement that intended to provide alternatives to incarceration at a cost savings to the public, instead equating prison time with punishment and anything less as doing nothing or not enough to control the crime problem (Byrne, Lurigio, & Petersilia, 1992; Morris & Tonry, 1990; Petersilia, Lurigio, & Bryne, 1992). These alternatives to incarceration are quite varied and include sanctions such as day reporting centers, restorative justice programs, home confinement, electronic monitoring, community service, halfway houses, and monetary penalties such as fines and restitution (Braithwaite, 1989; Bryne et al., 1992; Caputo, 2004).

Not only have judges refused to consider these intermediate sanctions as alternatives to incarceration, but rather they have often used these intermediate punishments as "add-ons" to traditional probation (Caputo, 2004). This practice has resulted in the widening of the net of correctional control and has ultimately contributed to our large prison populations. By increasing the control and surveillance of offenders who would have customarily received traditional probation, the likelihood that offenders will have their probation revoked and could potentially be sent to prison due to technical violations dramatically increases (Caputo, 2004). Consequently, by not applying intermediate sanctions to their intended target populations—those who otherwise would have received a prison sentence—judges have inadvertently contributed to our burgeoning prison population (Corbett & Marx, 1992).

One stark example of a target population where the decision to incarcerate has trumped the use of alternatives to incarceration is drug offenders. In 1980, the United States incarcerated 41,000 drug offenders; by 2010, the number of drug offenders placed behind bars had ballooned to 507,000 (Guerino et al., 2011; Mauer & King, 2007). One may ask, however, whether this dramatic increase in the incarceration of drug offenders simply reflects the increased use of illicit drugs over time. The answer to that question is an unequivocal "no." Estimates of high school senior and adult illicit drug use have shown only marginal increases over the past 20 years, with use among youngsters actually decreasing over this same time period (Johnston, O'Malley, Bachman, & Schulenberg, 2012; Substance Abuse and Mental Health Services Administration, 2009). Consequently, the over 12-fold increase in the use of incarceration between 1980 and 2010 occurred at a time when drug use remained stable or increased only slightly. To be clear, we are not arguing that drug offenders should escape criminal justice intervention, but only that the extraordinary choice to rely on prison as the preferred sanction has not been due to an escalating drug problem. A conscious decision was made to collectively incarcerate drug offenders as opposed to selectively incarcerate those who posed the most danger to society. Thus, in the case of drug offenders, prison has become not a sanction of last resort, but rather the sanction of first resort.

A second plausible explanation for the exorbitant number of people behind bars in the United States can be traced to various forms of get tough legislation that mandated more stringent sentencing in the form of lengthy terms of incarceration. Under the pretense that harsher punishments, particularly imprisonment, would result in the public's safety, states across America began to implement mandatory minimum, three-strikes, and truth-in-sentencing policies that resulted in more offenders being sentenced to prison and for longer periods of time. Consequently, the states and the federal government removed discretion from judges, forcing them to impose mandatory sentences that ensured that certain types of offenders would see the bars of a prison cell.

By 1980, each state as well as the federal government had enacted some form of mandatory minimum sentencing legislation requiring a specific prison sentence for certain offenses, with the number of offenses qualifying for a mandatory prison sentence continuing to rise over the last 30 years (Sorenson & Stemen, 2002; Tonry, 1996). In fact, the federal government has increased the number of offenses carrying a mandatory minimum sentence from 98 in 1991 to 195 in 2010 (United States Sentencing Commission, 2011). Although these policies target a variety of offenses (including identity, sex, and firearm offenses), these mandatory minimum sentences disproportionately target drug offenders (Stemen, Rengifo, & Wilson, 2005; United States Sentencing Commission, 2011). Oftentimes, these mandatory minimum sentences are exceptionally lengthy even for the possession and sale of a small amount of drugs. For example, the average minimum sentence across the United States for a first-offense possession of one ounce of cocaine is roughly two and a half years, while the first-offense selling of one ounce of cocaine is over three years (Stemen et al., 2005). In Delaware, possession of three grams of any controlled substance earns an offender an automatic three years in prison (Clear, 2007). Consequently, these mandatory minimum sentences have not been reserved for our most violent and dangerous criminals; rather they have been and continue to be inflicted upon low-level dealers and users, contributing to the explosion in our prison populations.

Habitual offender laws, which often take the form of three-strikes laws, have also factored into our mushrooming prison populations, with 41 states having implemented a three-strikes law by 2002 (Schiraldi, Colburn, & Lotke, 2004; Stemen et al., 2005). These laws mandate that offenders with prior convictions for any felony offense or prior incarcerations receive increased sentences up to life imprisonment (Stemen et al., 2005). Although these laws are often not used extensively in the 41 states that have them on the books, the three states that have made extensive use of them—California, Florida, and Georgia—have shown increases in their prison populations (Stemen et al., 2005).

Another get tough policy, truth-in-sentencing, has also contributed to the escalation of our prison populations. Truth-in-sentencing legislation mandates that offenders serve a certain percentage of their sentence, often 85% or more, before eligible for release. By 2002, 28 states had adopted this form of legislation (Sabol, Rosich, Kane, Kirk, & Dubin, 2002; Stemen et al., 2005). Truth-in-sentencing policies were enacted to ensure that the time served by inmates closely matched the sentence that they were given by the court (Sorenson & Stemen, 2002). Consequently, many "backdoor" policies allowing for the early release of offenders were abolished. Thus, with states and the federal government increasing the number of offenders sentenced to prison through mandatory minimums and then requiring those offenders to serve longer terms and a greater percentage of their sentence, the prison population began to escalate at an extraordinary rate.

It is not difficult to understand how the failure of judges to consider alternative sanctions to imprisonment and the passing of get tough policies by state and federal legislatures would have resulted in the dramatic increase of people incarcerated. However, a third plausible explanation for our overreliance on incarceration is much more subtle and rarely discussed. We argue that there is a fundamental incentive structure for prosecutors and judges to be tough on crime by seeking offenders and sentencing them to incarcerative sanctions. Because prosecutors and judges are generally elected officials, they are sensitive to any public appearance of being soft on crime that might make them politically vulnerable during the next reelection campaign. Consequently, judges and prosecutors are reluctant to ratchet down punishments, instead favoring harsh and severe sanctions, particularly imprisonment, that portray them as defenders of public safety. Their self-interest thus aligns with assigning more, rather than less, imprisonment.

Furthermore, prosecutors and judges are particularly wary of the "heinous case"—that one case where an offender they have placed on probation subsequently kidnaps, rapes, and/or kills a helpless victim. They would then face an unanswerable question that could ruin their elected careers: How could you have put that predator back on the street? When doubt about an offender's risk exists, their clear incentive is thus to incarcerate and place responsibility for this defendant's future in the hands of the state prison system.

One crucial factor that comes into the play with prosecutors' and judges' love affair with imprisonment is that they can impose this risk-averse, career-protecting sanction *with absolutely no cost to them*. Therefore, when an offender is sentenced to prison, the state is faced with the financial burden of this decision. The state's taxpayers pay an equal share regardless of the number of offenders in their local county sentenced to prison. Thus, counties that incarcerate a greater number of offenders and receive the benefit of removing offenders from their streets are not required to pay more than those counties that rarely incarcerate offenders. In essence, the costs of imprisonment are split evenly across the state while the benefits are felt differentially and locally. Imprisonment is a free endeavor that judges and prosecutors can impose copiously without shouldering any financial responsibility. They are in simplest terms getting "something for nothing" or are on a sort of "judicial or prosecutorial welfare" where they are essentially receiving a political and self-interested benefit on the government's dime. Consequently, because imprisonment comes with no costs but results in multiple political benefits, nothing is stopping these criminal justice officials from relying on imprisonment as their sanction of choice.

How to Make Prisons Smaller

In light of tightening state and federal budgets and the emerging evidence that prisons are not effective in substantially reducing the recidivism of those who are confined behind their walls, the time has come for the United States to enter rehab and cure this "addiction to incarceration" (Cullen & Jonson, 2012). The United States can no longer afford the financial burden that this overreliance on imprisonment has produced, while providing only limited benefits for the public's safety (Pew Center on the States, 2012b). Rather, we need to reduce our prison populations and begin responding to the crime problem in ways that are innovative and proven effective.

RETHINKING "GET TOUGH"

One way to lower prison populations is through state legislation. States across the nation are beginning to rethink the get tough positions that they adamantly touted in more financially prosperous times. In 2009, the United States spent, on average, $29,000 annually for a *single* prisoner (Pew Center on the States, 2009). Using this average rate, state and federal prisoners cost $43.5 billion each year, with one dollar of every 15 state general discretionary dollars spent on corrections (Pew Center on the States, 2009).

In an attempt to save money, multiple states have begun to enact legislation that seeks to lower the number of people that are serving time in correctional facilities. Much of this legislation has sought to reduce the number of low-level offenders, particularly low-level drug offenders, sentenced to incarcerative sanctions (Justice Center, 2011; Pew Center on the States, 2012b). For example, in 2004, New York reduced many of its mandatory minimum sanctions for drug offenders. Specifically, the minimum sentence for a class A-1 drug offense was slashed by almost half, from 15 years to 8 years (New York State Department of Correctional Services, 2004). Kentucky followed suit in 2011, recommending presumptive probation for low-level drug offenders rather than prison. Furthermore, Kentucky lowered the sentence associated with small-time drug dealing, reclassifying this offense from a Class C felony to a Class D felony (American Civil Liberties Union [ACLU], 2011).

Ohio has also decreased sentences for drug and nonviolent offenders (ACLU, 2011). Thus, state officials reduced the mandatory minimum sentence associated with marijuana violations. They also increased the point at which a property crime would qualify for felony status. Before the passage of HB 86, a property crime was classified as a felony when the monetary value reached $500; with the passing of HB 86, this threshold was increased to $1,000. Furthermore, Ohio has required that judges sentence offenders to alternatives to incarceration for low-level felonies and misdemeanors (ACLU, 2011; Diroll, 2011).

JUDICIAL AND PROSECUTORIAL ACCOUNTABILITY

Although state and federal legislatures played a large role in the expansion of the American correctional enterprise, it is not solely upon their shoulders to reduce the prison population. Prosecutors and judges, with their reluctance to sentence people to alternatives to incarceration and their political self-interest, are also to blame for our standing as the world's number one leader in imprisonment. Consequently, part of the solution to lowering prison populations falls to judges and prosecutors. The incentive system that favors imprisonment over noncustodial sanctions must be unmasked and then replaced with a system that focuses on public safety and cost savings to the constituents of a particular locality. With the incentive to incarcerate removed, it becomes possible for prison populations to be reduced substantially.

One potential way to revamp this current incentive structure is to make the costs of imprisonment local. We can no longer allow prosecutors and judges to receive "something for nothing." Instead, counties must "pay to imprison." Currently, the system is arranged so that each taxpayer in the state pays an equal share to the correctional budget regardless of how much their home county utilizes the state's prison space. For example, citizens in a county that sends 1,000 offenders to a state facility pay the exact same amount for prison space as those who live in a county sentencing only 500 offenders to prison. Thus, there is no reason at the county level for judges and prosecutors to reduce their reliance on imprisonment since they and their localities do not have to pay for their greater use of prison space.

By forcing counties to "pay to imprison," judges and prosecutors will have to become more selective in their use of incarceration. No longer would prison be seen as the sanction of first resort. Instead, alternatives to incarceration would have to be seriously considered and imposed on appropriate offenders, reserving prison for those who are at most risk for recidivism. Prosecutors and judges would evolve into criminologists, so to speak, in the sense that they would have to become discerning readers of the research and experts in risk assessments, effective interventions, alternatives to incarceration, and the impact of imprisonment. In essence, we would create a system of sentencing experts who could assign offenders the most appropriate criminal justice sanction.

Furthermore, prosecutors and judges would become more accountable to their constituents. They would have a fiscal responsibility not to bankrupt their counties by frivolously using incarceration as a sanction. They would have to consider the price that the county would pay to send offenders to prison and how that would impact their reelection chances. Thus, both judges and prosecutors would have the mission to protect the public's safety in the most financially responsible way possible. Again, this would require them to become experts on appropriate sanctions for various types of offenders.

CAP-AND-TRADE

One specific way to make counties fiscally responsible is to use a cap-and-trade system concerning imprisonment. The cap-and-trade system was first created in the

United States to control sulfur dioxide emissions and has been found to be effective in reducing environmental pollution (Eck & Eck, 2012). In an innovative article, Eck and Eck were the first to apply this environmental regulatory concept to places where crime runs rampant, shifting the "financial burden for crime fighting to owners of criminogenic locations" (p. 280). When owners have to take fiscal responsibility for their crime problem, they are more likely to engage in effective interventions aimed at lowering their risk for criminal victimization, instead of blindly relying on the criminal justice system. Taking Eck and Eck's lead, we argue that a cap-and-trade system could be similarly applied to the penal system and would be an effective policy at substantially reducing the prison population.

A state imprisonment cap-and-trade system would be designed as follows. First, the state would set a cap or limit on the number of people who could be sentenced to prison. Next, the state would allocate prison space to each county based on population size, with more populated counties receiving more prison beds and less populated counties receiving fewer prison beds. Therefore, each county would be given a set number of slots allocated for incarcerative sanctions. Prosecutors and judges would be free to use these slots as they see fit; however, once they reached their cap, their counties would be forced to pay the state to imprison each additional offender. This fixed number of prison beds would force judges and prosecutors to make calculated and informed decisions on whom to send to prison. Additionally, this would make them accountable to their counties, as their individual county would have to pay for any excess offenders sentenced to prison. One important caveat to this, however, is that a state could decide not to count certain types of offenders toward a county's prison bed allotment. To counter claims that the cap-and-trade policy would endanger public safety, the state might create an exemption for serious, violent crimes and not require counties to "pay to imprison" offenders convicted of these acts. For example, if a county sentenced a convicted murderer to prison, that county would not lose one of its allocated prison spaces.

A second component of this cap-and-trade system involves those counties that do not reach their allotment of prison beds. Those counties that underutilized their prison bed space could do one of three things. First, they could "trade" (e.g., for future cap space) or sell their extra allotments to another county that is in need of prison bed space. Thus, the county could make a profit on their extra prison beds. Second, they could "roll over" those allotments, allowing them to send more people to prison the following year. Finally, counties could receive money from the state for each allotment that they did not use to put toward other endeavors, such as community-based alternatives to incarceration or other crime prevention measures (e.g., early intervention programs, more police officers).

The final component in the cap-and-trade system would require the state to gradually reduce the cap each successive year. By successively lowering the cap, or the number of offenders that the state would permit into the prison system each year, substantial reductions in the prison population could be achieved. For example, if the state lowered its cap by 2,000 offenders overall each year for 10 years, the cap at the end of the decade would be a full 20,000 less than at the beginning of the decade. By the gradual lowering of the cap, counties would be given time to research and learn what are the most effective interventions with offenders. Also, the slow movement away from incarceration would reduce resistance from judges and prosecutors who would most likely oppose sweeping prison reforms occurring in a short period of time.

In Pursuit of Smallness

The ultimate goal would be to have states, and counties within states, start to embrace a policy of smallness as opposed to bigness. As officials began to take more local ownership of how best to intervene with their community's offenders, the possibility for innovation would grow, unleashing a new wave of fresh ideas. In particular, as prison populations were gradually and responsibly reduced, states might begin to reject the view that their prisons must be little more than human warehouses into which an unending flow of inmates must be fit (Irwin, 2005). Instead, they might see the pursuit of smallness as a new correctional paradigm. This might well include a commitment to create "small prisons."

Why might smallness matter—whether in a community, a school classroom, or a prison? One way to answer this question is to look at the obverse—what largeness brings. In most social institutions, the main benefit of size is economies of scale. Thus, it is less expensive to put 100 students in a classroom than 10; or it is less expensive to have one cafeteria that serves 2,000 inmates than four that serve 500 inmates apiece. Size also may allow for more diverse offerings, such as more majors in a college or more types of treatment programming in a prison. But size has its drawbacks as well. Perhaps the most obvious consequence is impersonality—the notion that everyone becomes simply "a number." Thus, when a professor looks up into a sea of 250 students in a lecture hall or a warden looks out upon a sea of 2,000 inmates in prison yard, the individuality of their charges recedes. They become a largely anonymous crowd—a group of impersonal objects—to be managed, hopefully without incident, through their academic or prison term. And when size is allowed to run amok, special problems ensue, such as college students being closed out of required courses needed for graduation or inmates placed in crowded living conditions that expose them to sustained idleness, contagious diseases, or heightened risk of victimization.

In the society of captives, excessive size is particularly dangerous when it is married to a punitive ideology that views the prison as an instrument of pain. When this occurs, little consideration is given to the harshness of prison life. "Penal austerity"—making inmates live in places devoid of any comforts (the so-called no-frills prison)—is seen not as a sign of a debased morality on our part but as a means of making inmates suffer in ways that they richly deserve and that might make them think twice about returning to crime (see, e.g., Applegate, 2001; Finn, 1996). Prisons thus lose what Allen (1981) called their larger "social purpose"—the sense that they ought to be places that seek to improve and ultimately correct offenders. For Irwin (2005), the mixture of size and austerity leads to the "warehouse prison," a place used for the mere "disposal" of inmates seen as intractably dangerous. Echoing these sentiments, Simon (2007, p. 152) has characterized the contemporary prison as a "waste management system" that "no longer works through broad efforts at shaping the personalities and personal relations of inmates." Instead, according to Simon (2007, p. 153):

> the waste management prison needs to make few promises about its ability to penetrate and influence the mentality or will of criminal offenders. Indeed, the state can produce more security on this theory simply by building more prisons and filling them, no matter what happens inside those walls.

Smallness does not eliminate the possibility of penal austerity, but it certainly makes it less likely. With smallness comes an implicit social exchange: You are given fewer people to process, but you are expected to do more with them. In a college setting, professors teaching a seminar of 10 students are expected to give writing assignments and to teach critical thinking skills. In probation, small caseloads are assigned with the expectation of more intensive supervision or more extensive delivery of treatment services. And in a prison, we might imagine that a smaller institution would be designed with the hope that inmates would receive a higher level of service and emerge from this experience more prepared to reenter society. In short, bigness produces lower expectations—multiple-choice tests for lecture halls of 250 students and waste management for prisons crowded to the brim with one inmate after another. Smallness, however, comes with accountability: We expect more from those in charge, whether it is a president of a small liberal arts college or a warden of a small prison.

Smallness does not translate ineluctably into quality. Rather, it presents an opportunity to change course and to achieve goals that bigness precludes. In this regard, the chief benefit of smallness is that it is an ideal conduit for the delivery of individualized human services. Just as a small college or classroom allows professors to know their students, so too does a small prison allow wardens and correctional officers to know the inmates they supervise. They will be positioned to invest time in their charges, using evidence-based approaches to assess and rehabilitate offenders (Andrews & Bonta, 2010). Rather than simply managing "waste" and getting through another day, the occupational culture will be to use correctional expertise to create a safe and therapeutic environment.

The small prison might be fostered in three ways. First, one reason why we focused on a system's overall population is that reducing the number of inmates might well lower the size of existing institutions. States that reduce their populations will be sorely tempted to close institutions, for this is what truly saves money. Still, it might be possible, even on an experimental basis, to keep a facility—or a wing of a facility—in operation to assess the benefits of placing inmates in a small prison environment.

Second, smallness is not just an objective reality but also a mind-set. As the cap on prison populations is lowered and the number of inmates at institutions recedes to designed capacity, it might become feasible to experiment with the division of larger institutions into smaller units, each with its own mission. Obviously, this task would be facilitated if a prison already had podular architecture, where self-contained units are separated physically. But if not, it might still be possible to use housing placements (wings) to create some sense of commonality among inmates. If nothing else, it could be possible to design virtual prisons, with inmates assigned to a particular "house" as in Harry Potter's Hogwarts School of Witchcraft and Wizardry. Of course, it would be better if their houses more closely approximated Gryffindor than Slytherin! But the point is that membership in a particular "small prison" could be identified by clothing, colors, and purpose.

What might such small prisons or "houses" entail? Endless possibilities can be imagined, but one option is to define a prison's membership by the core activity in which inmates are engaged. Thus, smaller units, whether physical or virtual, within a larger prison could be organized around the following: the education prison, the industrial training prison, the computer technology prison, the drug therapy prison, the faith-based prison, and the reentry prison (for those soon to return to society). This approach would give those living and working in such small prisons a clear purpose—a goal of human improvement. Even recalcitrant inmates might be placed in a token economy prison, where they might receive skilled behavioral management and be given the chance to earn their way back into another prison.

Third, as money is freed up by tightening a state's prison population cap, it might be possible to fund public, private, or nonprofit organizations to finance "charter" small prisons. These might be designed to house 100 to 200 inmates and be placed geographically close to inmates' residences (so as to increase family visitation to and community involvement in them). The goal would be to undertake diverse experimentation to find models that "worked" and could be copied elsewhere.

Conclusion

In trumpeting the small prison, we are arguing for a paradigm shift in corrections. For four decades, the United States has been in the grip of a mass imprisonment movement. Bigness and big prisons have become the norm taken for granted— realities that are beyond change. But now there is more than a glimmer of hope. An enduring financial crisis has prompted politicians of all stripes to become pragmatic about the size of imprisonment. In a perfect world in which we could choose to tolerate no risk whatsoever, it might be possible to incarcerate all those who bother us. It also might be nice to have unlimited military resources and ensure that liberty is found in every nation on the globe. But the stubborn fact is that it is not possible to eliminate all risk from crime or to spread freedom everywhere. There are budgetary limits, and hard choices must be made.

Bigness thus is a luxury that we can no longer afford. Still worse, it was a bad idea to begin with. If we were to design a prison system from scratch, nobody would create the swollen behemoth we are currently stuck with—one that costs and damages a great deal, but that only modestly enhances public safety. Any rational correctional system would reserve prisons for those who perpetrate heinous crimes and for those who are at high-risk for recidivating. An effort would be made to avoid excessively long sentences that serve no crime control purpose. The system would have a clear sense of limits—that it was irresponsible to allow prisons to grow like weeds in a garden, out of control.

But it also is the case that we would not erect prison facilities quickly and with the sole aim of housing as many offenders as possible. The pursuit of bigness thus pushes aside other critical considerations. Instead, we would start with a clear idea of what we wished each prison to accomplish. As the waste management philosophy of big corrections was abandoned, we would instead seek to create environments that would allow us to deprive offenders of their freedom but in a way that enabled them to acquire moral and human capital—and to return to society not as criminals but as better citizens. We would realize that small prisons would allow for high-quality intervention and, by achieving better outcomes for reentering inmates, be worth the up-front investment. At the very least, we would experiment extensively with small prisons, determining the optimum size, architecture, and internal management for reforming offenders.

It has taken us four decades to build a big prison system. It may take us four decades to make it small once again. But for this to occur, policy makers must be provided with ideas on how to restrain prison populations and ideas on how to organize prisons to be small in size and in practice. In this context, we need a *criminology of small prisons*, one that is devoted not simply to identifying the ills of bigness but also to illuminating pragmatic ways to move beyond big prisons. This chapter thus is best seen as a first step in this direction—as a way of sharing some small ideas that we hope will inspire some big changes.

References

Allen, F. A. (1981). *The decline of the rehabilitative ideal: Penal policy and social purpose.* New Haven, CT: Yale University Press.

American Civil Liberties Union. (2011). *Smart reform is possible: States reducing incarceration rates while protecting communities.* New York, NY: Author.

Andrews, D. A., & Bonta, J. (2010). *The psychology of criminal conduct* (5th ed.). New Providence, NJ: Anderson/LexisNexis.

Applegate, B. K. (2001). Penal austerity: Perceived utility, desert, and public attitudes toward prison amenities. *American Journal of Criminal Justice, 25,* 253–268.

Blumstein, A., & Cohen, J. (1973). A theory of the stability of punishment. *Journal of Criminal Law and Criminology, 64,* 198–206.

Braithwaite, J. (1989). *Crime, shame and reintegration.* Cambridge, UK: Cambridge University Press.

Brown v. Plata, 563 U.S. (2011).

Byrne, J. M., Lurigio, A. J., & Petersilia, J. (Eds.). (1992). *Smart sentencing: The emergence of intermediate sanctions.* Newbury Park, CA: Sage.

Bureau of Justice Statistics. (2011). *Sourcebook of criminal justice statistics*. Washington, DC: U.S. Department of Justice, Office of Justice Programs.

Caputo, G. A. (2004). *Intermediate sanctions in corrections*. Denton: University of North Texas Press.

Clear, T. R. (2007). *Imprisoning communities: How mass incarceration makes disadvantaged neighborhoods worse*. New York, NY: Oxford University Press.

Corbett, R. P., Jr., & Marx, G. T. (1992). Emerging technofallacies in the electronic monitoring movement. In J. M. Byrne, A. J. Lurigio, & J. Petersilia (Eds.), *Smart sentencing: The mergence intermediate sanctions* (pp. 85–100). Newbury Park, CA: Sage.

Cullen, F. T., & Jonson, C. L. (2012). *Correctional theory: Context and consequences*. Thousand Oaks, CA: Sage.

Cullen, F. T., Jonson, C. L., & Nagin, D. S. (2011). Prisons do not reduce recidivism: The high cost of ignoring science. *The Prison Journal, 91*(3), 48S–65S.

Currie, E. (1985). *Confronting crime: An American challenge*. New York, NY: Pantheon.

Diroll, D. J. (2011). *H.B. 86 summary: The 2011 changes to criminal and juvenile law*. Columbus, OH: Ohio Criminal Sentencing Commission.

Donahue, J. J., III. (2009). Assessing the relative benefits of incarceration: Overall changes and the benefits on the margin. In S. Raphael & M. A. Stoll (Eds.), *Do prisons make us safer? The benefits and costs of the prison boom* (pp. 119–150). New York, NY: Russell Sage.

Durlauf, S. N., & Nagin, D. S. (2011). Imprisonment and crime: Can both be reduced? *Criminology and Public Policy, 10,* 13–54.

Eck, J. E., & Eck, E. B. (2012). Crime place and pollution: Expanding crime reduction options through a regulatory approach. *Criminology and Public Policy, 11,* 279–316.

Federal Bureau of Investigation. (2011). *Uniform crime reports for the United States, 2010*. Washington, DC: Government Printing Office.

Finn, P. (1996). No-frills prisons and jails: A movement in flux. *Federal Probation, 60*(3), 35–44.

Guerino, P., Harrison, P. M., & Sabol, W. J. (2011). *Prisoners in 2010*. Washington, DC: U.S. Department of Justice, Bureau of Justice Statistics.

Irwin, J. (2005). *The warehouse prison: Disposal of the new dangerous class*. Los Angeles, CA: Roxbury.

Johnston, L. D., O'Malley, P. M., Bachman, J. G., & Schulenberg, J. E. (2012). *Monitoring the future national results on adolescent drug use: Overview of the key findings, 2011*. Ann Arbor: The University of Michigan, Institute for Social Research.

Justice Center. (2011). *Justice reinvestment in Ohio: Policy framework to reduce corrections spending and reinvest savings in strategies that can reduce crime*. New York, NY: The Council of State Governments Justice Center.

Kleiman, M. A. R. (2009). *When brute force fails: How to have less crime and less punishment*. Princeton, NJ: Princeton University Press.

Kruttschnitt, C., & Gartner, R. (2005). *Marking time in the Golden State: Women's imprisonment in California*. New York, NY: Cambridge University Press.

Liedka, R. V., Piehl, A. M., & Useem, B. (2006). The crime-control effect of incarceration: Does scale matter? *Criminology and Public Policy, 5,* 245–276.

Mauer, M., & King, R. S. (2007). *A 25-year quagmire: The War on Drugs and its impact on American society*. Washington, DC: The Sentencing Project.

Morris, N., & Tonry, M. (1990). *Between prison and probation: Intermediate punishments in a rational sentencing system*. New York, NY: Oxford University Press.

Nagin, D. S., Cullen, F. T., & Jonson, C. L. (2009). Imprisonment and reoffending. In M. Tonry (Ed.), *Crime and justice: A review of research* (Vol. 38, pp. 115–200). Chicago, IL: University of Chicago Press.

New York State Department of Correctional Services. (2004). Pataki signs Rocky drug reform into law. *Docs Today, 13,* 4–5.

Petersilia, J. (2008). California's correctional paradox of excess and deprivation. In M. Tonry (Ed.), *Crime and justice: A review of research* (Vol. 37, pp. 207–278). Chicago, IL: University of Chicago Press.

Petersilia, J., Lurigio, A. J., & Bryne, J. M. (1992). Introduction: The emergence of intermediate sanctions. In J. Byrne, A. J. Lurigio, & J. Petersilia (Eds.), *Smart sentencing: The emergence of intermediate sanctions* (pp. ix–xv). Newbury Park, CA: Sage.

Pew Center on the States. (2009). *One in 31: The long reach of American corrections.* Washington, DC: Pew Charitable Trusts.

Pew Center on the States. (2012a). *2012 Georgia public safety reform: Legislation to reduce recidivism and cut corrections costs.* Washington, DC: Pew Charitable Trusts.

Pew Center on the States. (2012b). *Time served: The high cost, low return of longer prison sentences.* Washington, DC: Pew Charitable Trusts.

Pew Charitable Trusts. (2008). *One in 100: Behind bars in America 2008.* Washington, DC: Author.

Raphael, S., & Stoll, M. A. (Eds.). (2009). *Do prisons make us safer? The benefits and costs of the prison boom.* New York, NY: Russell Sage.

Sabol, W. J., Rosich, K., Kane, K. M., Kirk, D., & Dubin, G. (2002). *Influences of truth-in-sentencing reform changes in states' sentencing practices and prison populations.* Washington, DC: U.S. Department of Justice.

Schiraldi, V., Colburn, J., & Lotke, E. (2004). *Three strikes and you're out: An examination of the impact of strikes laws 10 years after their enactment.* Washington, DC: Justice Policy Institute.

The Sentencing Project. (2012). *Trends in U.S. corrections.* Washington, DC: Author.

Simon, J. (2007). *Governing through crime: How the War on Crime transformed American democracy and created a culture of fear.* New York, NY: Oxford University Press.

Sorenson, J., & Stemen, D. (2002). The effect of state sentencing policies on incarceration rates. *Crime and Delinquency, 48,* 456–475.

Spelman, W. (2000). What recent studies do (and don't) tell us about imprisonment and crime. In M. Tonry (Ed.), *Crime and justice: A review of research* (Vol. 27, pp. 419–494). Chicago, IL: University of Chicago Press.

Stemen, D., Rengifo, A., & Wilson, J. (2005). *Of fragmentation and ferment: The impact of state sentencing policies on incarceration rates, 1975–2002.* Washington, DC: U.S. Department of Justice.

Substance Abuse and Mental Health Services Administration. (2009). *Results from the 2000–2008 National Survey on Drug Use and Health: National Findings, Office of Applied Studies.* Washington, DC: U.S. Department of Health and Human Services.

Tonry, M. (1996). *Sentencing matters.* New York, NY: Oxford University Press.

United States Sentencing Commission. (2011). *Report to Congress: Mandatory minimum penalties in the federal criminal justice system.* Washington, DC: Author.

Villettaz, P., Killias, M., & Zoder, I. (2006). *The effects of custodial vs. noncustodial sentences on re-offending: A systematic review of the state of knowledge.* Philadelphia, PA: Campbell Collaboration Crime and Justice Group.

Waller, I. (2006). *Less law, more order: The truth about reducing crime*. Westport, CT: Praeger.

Walmsley, R. (2011). *World population list* (9th ed.). Essex, UK: International Centre for Prison Studies.

Webster, C. M., & Doob, A. N. (2007). Punitive trends and stable imprisonment rates in Canada. In M. Tonry (Ed.), *Crime and justice: A review of research* (Vol. 36, pp. 297–370). Chicago, IL: University of Chicago Press.

12

The Accountable Prison

*Francis T. Cullen, Cheryl Lero Jonson,
and John E. Eck*

Editors' Introduction

To borrow a phrase from Jeffrey Reiman, it appears that prisons are "designed to fail." Admittedly, they perform one function well: They keep offenders off the street, allowing few to escape during their prescribed time behind bars. But otherwise, any claim to being a successful American social institution would be difficult to sustain. Nearly all inmates return to society, most within two to three years. Yet upon reentering their communities, there is no evidence that they have been made less criminal; in fact, some likely have had their risk of recidivating increased. Many will be rearrested, reconvicted, and resentenced to prison. Such failure will be especially pronounced in the first few months after release. And what does this persistent record of poor performance cost the taxpayers? In most states the bill for each inmate year in prison is about $30,000—far more than the state allocates to subsidize a student's academic year at one of its public universities.

Many correctional officials will undoubtedly claim that constant failure of prisons to prevent recidivism "is not our fault." Many excuses can be made: The inmates are career criminals and do not want to change their lifestyles; we do not have the resources to provide quality treatment programming; we are not responsible for what happens when offenders are returned to the same criminogenic communities from which they came. Of course, there is a kernel of truth in all of these rejoinders. But they should not be used as rationales for inaction—for viewing the status quo as acceptable. Even if difficult challenges must be surmounted, better performance should be pursued.

As Francis Cullen, Cheryl Lero Jonson, and John Eck observe in the chapter to follow, there is much to be learned about doing a better job from the innovation that has swept across American policing in the last two decades. In the 1970s and 1980s, a growing belief emerged that, due to the secretive and planned nature of most criminal acts, police practices could not have any impact on crime rates. But then a generation of smart analysts—some in academia, some in police departments—rejected this prevailing belief that "nothing works" in law enforcement. They started to map "hot spots" in crime, to see such concentrations as problems to be solved, and to design strategies for knifing off criminal opportunities. Most important, however, they no longer accepted the excuse that lowering illegality was beyond the control of police management. Instead, they started to hold these officials accountable for increasing public safety. Crime, and the problems that nourished it, did not vanish. But requiring managers to meet performance standards created important incentives for these officials to focus their talents and energy on the reduction of lawlessness. And, lo and behold, many communities—especially in major cities—experienced significant decreases in serious street crimes.

In a similar way, Cullen, Jonson, and Eck argue that a fundamental problem for the American prison is that correctional officials are mainly paid to ensure security and custody—to prevent inmate violence (including riots) and to prevent inmate escapes. Directors of departments of corrections and wardens of correctional institutions are not paid, ironically, to correct their charges. Unsurprisingly, they place a high premium on accomplishment of the goals on which their jobs depend.

But should not the public expect more from our correctional leaders? To be sure, security and custody are important. But recall that nearly all inmates eventually return to their—indeed, our—communities. It seems an incredible oversight that nobody is held accountable—other than the offenders themselves—if reentering inmates continue to pose as much of a danger to innocent citizens as when they first entered the prison gates. Consider if hospital administrators and their physicians were not responsible for making patients healthier. What if it were discovered that patients who remained under the care of their family doctor in the community were as likely to regain their health as those who received more invasive and expensive hospital care? Such an admission would not be a time for excuses; it would be a time for malpractice lawsuits.

As Cullen, Jonson, and Eck argue, American prisons will never achieve a higher level of performance—will never be an agency truly committed to reducing inmate recidivism—unless correctional managers are held accountable for what occurs when offenders return to society. Without any performance standards, there is unlikely to be any performance. Thus, the authors call for diverse prison-accountability experiments in which correctional staff are rewarded for lowering inmates' reoffending. Successful innovations could then serve as models for the spread of accountability across American corrections.

Many directors of corrections, wardens, and prison staff might initially resist the offer to help invent an "accountable prison." Change, especially when job security might be in jeopardy, can be unnerving. But in the end, the accountable prison is an expression of faith in those who now administer the nation's correctional institutions.

It is based on the belief that they can do more than serve as custodians. Accountability assumes strongly that similar to their policing counterparts, correctional managers and officers have the talent to ensure that prisons are designed not for failure but for success. By enriching the purpose and practices of their work, they thus can transform their institutions from places of pessimism into places of performance.

A core correctional wisdom is that prison wardens are fired only if inmates riot or escape. Undoubtedly, this "truism" is pregnant with more than a touch of hyperbole. But the central message expresses the reality that a warden's job hinges mainly on maintaining order and on making the prison walls impenetrable from the inside out. There is irony, however, in this primacy granted to the custodial function. Prisons were invented not as holding cells but as "penitentiaries" with the mission of transforming the wayward into the upstanding (Rothman, 1971). Even today, we call prisons "correctional" institutions, and the agencies governing prison systems embrace titles such as the "Department of Rehabilitation and Correction." There are no Departments of Inmate Custody or even Ministries of Justice.

A variety of opinion polls and scholarly surveys show that the public wants prisons to be places that make offenders less likely to recidivate. Virtually no support exists for prisons to function mainly as warehouses devoid of a broader social purpose (Cullen, Fisher, & Applegate, 2000). Further, prisons are at the core of the nation's crime-control efforts. On any given day in the United States, more than 2.2 offenders—about 1 in 100 adults—are behind bars (Glaze & Parks, 2012; Pew Center on the States, 2008). The price of this policy is nearly $52 billion annually (Pew Center on the States, 2011). Research reveals that such mass imprisonment saves some crime—the precise amount is in dispute—simply due to incapacitation (Cullen & Jonson, 2012; Spelman, 2000). Still, given the enormous human and financial costs exacted by incarceration, we should expect more from prisons than a warehousing effect. We do not like hospitals that do not cure, nor schools that do not educate. And we should not like prisons that do not rehabilitate. Consequently, there is no inherent reason why wardens—and departments of corrections generally—should be judged only on their custodial acumen. They should be judged by how much they help reduce crime.

In this essay, we begin by documenting how prisons fail and why this failure is accepted. We then dispute the idea that prisons are beyond redemption and cannot play a more positive role in crime control. We point out that similar views once pervaded policing and, through successful reforms, were shown to be false. From the policing field, we draw the important lesson that a key element to success in any area is that those in charge must be held accountable and that incentives must be structured to achieve a desired end—in our case, low offender recidivism. We show that within corrections, the knowledge now exists to rehabilitate offenders and to reduce recidivism—but that prison managers have little incentive to use this treatment knowledge to reform offenders. Toward this end, we lay out the core elements of designing an "accountable prison" that takes seriously the goal of diminishing inmates' reoffending. Finally, we make the broader point that we—from criminologists to policy makers to practitioners—can no longer accept the status quo. It is time to choose a different correctional future.

The Failure of Prisons

Simply put, prisons do a poor job at reducing recidivism—regardless of whether one considers data on absolute levels of recidivism, or data on the relative levels of recidivism for those that receive a custodial versus those receiving a noncustodial sanction. Langan and Levin (2002; see also Beck & Shipley, 1989) conducted the gold standard study on inmate recidivism. They examined what happened to prisoners released in 1994 over the following three years. Within three months, about 30% of the inmates had been rearrested, a figure that rose to 67.5% by the end of the three-year study period. Following the sample members deeper into the criminal justice system, they discovered that 46.9% were eventually reconvicted of a new crime and that 25.4% were resentenced to prison.

Similarly dismal results were reported recently in a study by the Pew Center on the States (2011), called the *State of Recidivism: The Revolving Door of America's Prison*. These researchers followed for three years two sets of inmates released from state prisons—those released in 1999 and those released in 2004. Overall, the statistics for offenders returned to prison were 45.4% for the 1999 cohort and 43.3% for the 2004 cohort. Recidivism in this study included those re-incarcerated for either a new crime or for a technical violation. For releasees in 1999, the split was 19.9% for a new crime and 25.5% for a technical violations; for releasees in 2004, the split was more titled for the new crime group—22.3% versus 21.0%.

It might be argued that the fact that a lot of inmates end up back behind bars does not mean that prisons are ineffective. The argument could be made that if inmates were not placed in prison, they would be even more likely to recidivate. If this view were put forward, however, it would be wrong. Although the quality of the research is suspect, there is growing evidence that compared to noncustodial sanctions, imprisonment either has no effect, or a slight criminogenic effect, on recidivism (Cullen & Jonson, 2012; Cullen, Jonson, & Nagin, 2011). Four lines of review firmly support this conclusion.

First, led by a group of Canadian psychologists, the systematic reviews of the research conducted by Gendreau, Goggin, Cullen, and Andrews (2000) and later by Smith, Goggin, and Gendreau (2002) have found no specific deterrent effect of imprisonment. In both meta-analyses, imprisonment was associated with a 7% increase in recidivism when compared to community sanctions. If prisons were hospitals, this backfire would be called an "iatrogenic" effect—the treatment is increasing patient harm. Prisons' iatrogenic effects became even more pronounced, increasing to 11%, when Smith et al. included in their analyses only studies coded as strong in methodological quality. Second, these findings were confirmed by Villettaz, Killias, and Zoder (2006). Using a sample of only the highest quality studies (e.g., randomized and natural experiments), Villettaz et al. meta-analyzed five studies and also discovered custodial sanctions to have a criminogenic rather than a preventative effect on recidivism. Third and more recently, Nagin, Cullen, and Jonson's (2009) ballot-box review of 48 studies also concluded that prisons have a null or slight criminogenic effect on recidivism. Fourth, drawing upon the Nagin et al. study, Jonson (2010) conducted the most comprehensive meta-analysis to date on the effect of a custodial versus a noncustodial sanction on reoffending. Analyzing 57 studies, imprisonment was found to result in a 14% increase in recidivism. Even when outliers were deleted from the analysis, imprisonment still resulted in a 5% increase in recidivism. Thus, no systematic review of the research has shown imprisonment to have a specific deterrent effect. In fact, quite the opposite has been found, leading researchers to conclude that "prisons ... should not be used with the expectation of reducing criminal behaviour" (Smith et al., 2002, p. ii).

An equally troubling aspect of the pronounced prison recidivism rate is that it is treated as though it is intractable. Both conservatives and liberals are guilty of this belief in correctional impotence. Admittedly, conservatives are less culpable, because some believe that if prisons are made miserable enough, inmates will learn their lesson and not offend again (Hepburn & Griffin, 1998). Unfortunately, this conservative wisdom turns out to be incorrect. The more painful prisons are, the more likely they are to increase recidivism (see, e.g., Chen & Shapiro, 2007; Gaes & Camp, 2009; Jonson, 2010; Listwan, Sullivan, Agnew, Cullen, & Colvin, 2013; cf. Windzio, 2006). In any event, other conservatives provide a rationale for why prisons do not deter well and mainly serve to incapacitate: They contain wicked people (Wilson, 1975). The only way to stop crime is to put these wicked apples in a separate barrel.

Thus, Bennett, DiIulio, and Walters (1996, p. 49) note that beyond some marginal deterrence, the threat of sentence in a no-frills or spartan prison would lead few street criminals to "forgo the immediate pleasures of crime (sex, drugs, money)." Such "super-predators," who are cold-blooded chronic offenders that victimize without remorse, are beyond redemption. Indeed, "we will have little choice," note Bennett et al., "but to pursue genuine get-tough law enforcement strategies" against them (p. 206). We must stop revolving door justice and use prison bars to restrain these irredeemable youths. Our attention should focus on future super-predators "who are now in diapers" and who "can be saved" (p. 206). The challenge is to fight "moral poverty," the supposed root cause of crime, by bringing strong moral influences into their lives, through loving, responsible adults and through a clear affirmation of religion "as the best and most reliable means we have to reinforce the good." (p. 208).

For liberals, the reason why prisons cannot reduce crime is that the barrel is wicked, not the apples inside. This argument comes in two interrelated versions. First, building on Zimbardo and colleagues' Stanford Prison Experiment, there is an assumption that by their very nature, prisons produce coercion and inhumanity (Zimbardo, 2007). Second, sociological studies have long identified why inmates develop strong oppositional cultures and, in many respects, come to control institutional life. Officials' control was diminished further by a confluence of events in the 1970s and beyond: court rulings that outlawed coercive practices; the infusion of gangs into prisons; and the emergence of racial conflict that make prisons dangerous places (see, e.g., Jacobs, 1977). In this view, there is little that can be done to uproot inmate society and make prisons more governable (see DiIulio, 1987). This is especially the case now that the state has turned prisons into a "warehouse" used as a "disposal" for the "new dangerous class" (Irwin, 2005; see also Wacquant, 2001).

In sum, there is a certain resignation that prisons are what they are: either necessary evils (conservatives) or overused evils (liberals). In either case, there is a consensus that they cannot be changed in any fundamental way and not changed so as to reduce crime by making inmates less likely to reoffend. We disagree with this dystopian view.

From Failure to Success: Lessons from Policing

Our belief that prisons can reduce recidivism is not rooted in utopianism but in the grounded truth of the real-world experience of policing. In the 1970s and 1980s, nothing works thinking—what Matthews (2009, p. 357) calls impossibilism— prevailed in policing (Sherman, 1993). From the mid-1980s through the 1990s to the present, impossibilism was challenged, attacked, and driven back by police practitioners allied with academic researchers. By 2004, the National Academy of Science report on police was able to state that specific policing strategies had the capabilities to reduce crime and disorder (National Research Council, 2004). This successful attack on impossiblism worked on four fronts.

First, scholars such as Herman Goldstein (1990) showed that the police should shift their emphasis from means to ends—from a fixation on bureaucratic processes, equipment, and symbols to the reduction of problems faced by members of the public. The movement he instigated, known as "problem-oriented policing" or by its acronym of "POP," created a vision of how policing should be done. Second, a body of scientific research began to accurately describe crime patterns and ways crime patterns could be suppressed. This scientific movement, called environmental criminology (Wortley & Mazerolle, 2008), created a scientific foundation for understanding how this vision could be achieved. Third, evaluation evidence began to accumulate to show that highly focused policing strategies—targeting offenders, places, or victims—were effective at reducing crime (Braga, 2005; Eck & Guerette, 2012; Farrell, 2005; Tillyer & Kennedy, 2008). The accumulating evidence showed that pursuing this vision was achieving the goals intended. Finally, a new generation of police leaders in the 1990s began using new technologies to hold their organizations accountable for crime and disorder (Weisburd, Mastrofski, McNally, Greenspan, & Willis, 2003). The examples of these leaders demonstrated to other police policy makers—including chiefs, sheriffs, city managers, mayors, members of city councils, and local opinion makers—that pursuing this vision would be worthwhile.

The Compstat process of the New York City Police is the best known of these approaches. The San Diego Police, for example, adopted a problem-oriented approach. The Boston Police used a problem-oriented approach to create a highly targeted and successful homicide reduction strategy. Regardless of what the strategy was called in each police department, what crimes it addressed, or the particulars of the procedures, each had three characteristics. First, it focused on outcomes and developed processes to achieve the outcomes. Second, it made police accountable for achieving the outcome—if the process did not work, it was modified to improve effectiveness. Third, it placed the analysis of data central to the operation: to identify and analyze problems; to craft solutions; and to determine if the solutions were reducing crime. Today, the dogma of impossiblism has been driven from policing. It has been replaced by an outcome-based creed that is data driven and evidence based. We believe something very much like this can improve corrections.

For our purposes, the main lessons to draw from policing is that failed performance is not inevitable in criminal justice, that a fresh paradigm can be realistic rather than utopian, and that embracing accountability is a conduit to effective reform. Of course, the tasks and nature of corrections differ greatly from those of policing, especially since prison officials supervise offenders 24/7 while they are incarcerated and then have no contact with offenders once they are released. On the other hand, policing is a far more complex enterprise than prison administration. Thus, police deal with a bewildering assortment of public demands, many having little or nothing to do with crime; the "client" population is similarly diverse and most are not offenders; and most of policing is highly visible to the public. In contrast, prisons have a far more limited set of responsibilities: contain people being sanctioned by the courts in safe and humane conditions, and then return them to their communities where they can lead crime free lives. We are not asserting that being held accountable for lowering crime among parolees does not pose special challenges—only that these are not beyond the expertise of correctional managers and their staff to meet. As the lessons from policing show, impossibilism—denying that success can be achieved and giving up before one tries—is likely the greatest barrier to success.

Using What We Know About Effective Rehabilitation

The reform of policing began with accepting accountability for crime and then building a science of crime that showed how police could be effective. The reform of the prison reverses this sequence. There is already a solid, scientifically validated, body of evidence supporting the effectiveness of rehabilitation. The only question remaining is whether correctional officials will apply this knowledge in prisons. Just so that there is no ambiguity, we will briefly review this evidence before returning to the question of accountability.

In 1974, Robert Martinson published an article that, in essence, argued that "nothing works" to rehabilitate offenders. Despite limitations to his analysis and the fact that he published a second study in 1979 tempering this claim, this "nothing works" doctrine became enshrined as public policy wisdom. It is amazing that, even today, naysayers will cite Martinson or the "nothing works" doctrine as though it were still true. It is not, as a variety of literature reviews and meta-analyses have convincingly demonstrated (see, e.g., Lipsey & Cullen, 2007). What is accurate is that many treatment programs now used in prison are of questionable effectiveness, mainly because they are not based on solid science or done properly. One reason for this poor quality of treatment service delivery is that *nobody is held accountable for the use of ineffective programs*. Again, we trust that correctional managers and staff would prefer to use interventions that work—that they would prefer to be responsible professionals. But unless they are incentivized to do so, they are unlikely to rock the boat and call for the status quo to be transformed.

There are a number of resources on effective interventions that correctional managers can consult, perhaps the best being Doris MacKenzie's (2006) *What Works in Corrections*. More important, there is now a coherent treatment paradigm that can be used to achieve meaningful reductions in recidivism. Based on three decades of theory and research, this approach was developed and shown to be effective by Canadian psychologists, the most prominent being Don Andrews, James Bonta, and Paul Gendreau (Cullen & Smith, 2011). Other sources describe this paradigm in detail (Andrews & Bonta, 2010), but we will highlight two key considerations. First, these Canadian scholars articulated three clear principles that, if followed, produce treatment success. The paradigm is sometimes known by the acronym of these three principles—"RNR":

- *R—the risk principle*: Focus interventions on high-risk offenders.

- *N—the need principle*: Target for change deficits—or "criminogenic needs"— in offenders that have been shown empirically to cause recidivism and that are "dynamic" or changeable (e.g., antisocial attitudes).

- *R—the responsivity principle*: When targeting criminogenic needs in high-risk offenders, use treatment modalities that are capable of changing these needs and thus of reducing recidivism. That is, use "responsive" treatments. Cognitive-behavioral approaches have been shown to be particularly effective.

Second, these Canadian scholars also designed the technology to implement their principles of effective treatment. Most notably, they developed various versions of the Level of Service Inventory, which is an instrument that can be used to assess the risk level of offenders (Andrews & Bonta, 2010; Smith, Cullen, & Latessa, 2009; Vose, Cullen, & Smith, 2008). Further, they invented an instrument to assess whether correctional agencies are arranged to deliver appropriate treatment services, which they called the Correctional Program Assessment Inventory (CPAI) (Andrews & Bonta, 2010).

In short, we have considerable evidence that offenders can be rehabilitated and blueprints for achieving this goal. The only question is whether those managing prisons will apply it.

The Accountable Prison

In this section, we try to make our proposal for an accountable prison more concrete—to flesh out enough of the general orientation and details that this reform moves, in readers' minds, from the realm of the utopian to the possible. Thus, we discuss how to make accountability matter, why and how carrots should be used to incentivize accountability, some sticky issues that could gum up the works of accountability if not resolved carefully, and some current examples in corrections where the use of incentives has enjoyed a measure of success.

MAKING ACCOUNTABILITY MATTER

The *core goal of the accountable prison is to reduce inmates' recidivism*. This is not to say that custody is deemphasized; rather it is to assert that maintaining order and preventing escapes are no longer the exclusive criteria on which job performance will be judged. In fact, maintaining order and preventing escapes are necessary, though not sufficient, conditions for this core goal. From this point forward, correctional managers and staff will be expected to achieve a broader social purpose—to advance public safety in communities outside the prison.

In this new correctional paradigm, wardens and prison personnel will be *held accountable for making offenders less likely to return to prison*. Every former prisoner who returns is a prison failure. Some resistance to this new responsibility is to be expected. But in another sense, the accountable prison will be increasing the status of and faith placed in correctional managers. They will be elevated from screws and hacks—from mere custodians—to professionals who are expected to use their expertise to reduce crime. In this sense, their jobs will be enriched (see Toch & Klofas, 1982).

What will an accountable prison look like? On one level, we do not care. The key to a successful accountable prison is not micro-management by criminologists. In fact, we would prefer to unleash a giant wave of innovation in which prison leaders and staff take ownership of this reform and proactively work as correctional problem-solvers devoted to figuring out how best to reduce recidivism. However, we are certain that, to enjoy success, correctional managers will need to seek out what is known about how best to reduce recidivism. Particularly in the early days of developing an accountable prison, they will need incentives to become criminologically literate and familiar with evidence-based corrections. They might be inspired to hire staff versed in the "what works" literature and/or to invite in consultants to guide their efforts. If so, then they might well attempt to implement interventions based on the principles of effective treatment (Andrews & Bonta, 2010). They also might well become strong advocates for ending inmate idleness, ending unsuccessful programs, and ending prison conditions that inspire rather than diminish criminal propensities.

They also will now be quite concerned about the transition that offenders make from prison and into the community. It is possible, therefore, that they will become an important advocacy group for the implementation of appropriate reentry programs. If they are going to be held accountable for inmates' behavior in the community, they thus will have a stake in ensuring that their efforts to reform inmates are not undermined. Thus, prison administrators will have to build working relationships with community corrections agencies, local police, prosecutors, and courts. Right now, of course, they have no reason to care what happens to offenders once they step beyond the prison walls, or the effects iatrogenic prisons have on other participants in the criminal justice system.

Of course, some correctional managers might attempt to develop a painful prison in hopes of scaring offenders straight. We are confident that these efforts will fail and place managers at a disadvantage (see Hepburn & Griffin, 1998). That is, based on current scientific knowledge, we are willing to bet that the only way an accountable prison will work to reduce crime is by making it more humane and more oriented to the delivery of human services. As Stephen Colbert is reported to have said, "reality"—that is, the scientific facts—have "a well known liberal bias." If so, we have nothing to worry about; our reform will produce much good. If we are wrong, we will not be happy, but we will take solace in the fact that there is less crime.

CARROTS (MOSTLY) AND STICKS (NOT OFTEN)

Perhaps the key to making the accountable prison feasible is developing a reward system that will motivate correctional wardens and staff to make reducing recidivism a priority. In the movie "Star Wars," Darth Vader had an effective motivational tool. He would look at a failed commander and say, "You have failed me for the last time." The unfortunate officer would then be subjected to the dark side of the force. Our message is not to embrace the Darth Vader School of Motivation. Precisely the opposite; unless a manager is truly oppositional and incompetent, we would not favor the use of negative sanctions—sticks—to coerce compliance with efforts to reduce recidivism. In the long run, such meanness would risk creating collective defiance and a failed reform.

Instead, therefore, we favor a context of encouragement. Most generally, such a context starts with a clear message that we consider wardens and their personnel to be *professionals*. Improving policing followed this route. Initial efforts to make policing more accountable for crime relied on officers and supervisors who shared the basic idea that they could be effective. Only later, as evidence increasingly showed that accountable policing was achievable, and police had a body of knowledge of how to achieve their objective did police administrators begin compelling subordinates to become accountable. But even today, most accountable policing is fostered by carrots rather than sticks.

Regardless, we expect correctional managers have—or are capable of developing—the expertise and the ethical commitment to improve their charges. We should start this enterprise with high, not low, expectations. We should rev them up about the fact that they certainly are smart enough to make inmates less likely to recidivate.

Unlike criminologists and policy makers, they are the ones—much like physicians and nurses in hospitals—who are with their "clients" 24/7. If they cannot change offenders, then who else are we to turn to? Put another way, we need to reiterate that as professionals, part of their job is to return inmates to society improved and less threatening to public safety. This is not an unreasonable request for citizens to make.

Within this context, we must—as noted previously—incentivize the outcomes we value, which in this case is lower recidivism rates. What these incentives might involve will depend, of course, on how large a pool of money states or the federal government will allocate. But within these parameters, our advice is not to impose incentive structures onto prison leaders and their employees. Rather, we would prefer that a number of focus groups be held with correctional personnel to ask them what they would value as incentives for lowering recidivism.

In the end, we suspect that a system of incentives would most likely involve merit pay—just as is being done with teachers and other public employees. In fact, state laws and union contracts might limit the kinds of incentives that can be allocated. Still, we would not wish to close the door to other types of incentives. Borrowing strategies from the world of business—for example, from sales—might be relevant. Here, not only are year-end bonuses allocated but also other rewards that employees value, such as trips to Hawaii and similar exotic locations. Sales units are often recognized as being regional or national leaders in profits. In a similar way, it might be useful to hold award ceremonies, giving trophies to units or prisons that achieve the highest reductions in recidivism—allow staff to chant, "We're #1! We're #1!" In any event, as time progresses and experimental evidence is available, we should be able to know more clearly what combination of incentives is most powerful in motivating efforts to make inmates less criminal.

CORE ISSUES

In any reform of this sort, the devil is in the details. Understanding the nature and calibration of incentives is, as just noted, one challenge to be addressed. But we anticipate that a host of others will emerge—most of which we cannot know or resolve here. Still, there are four core issues that we will consider: experimentation, defining and measuring success, access to the means of success, and the dynamic or evolving approach to how to reward accountability.

Experimentation. We are not so foolish as to suggest that the accountable prison be implemented across an entire prison system. As with any reform, it could turn out to be a bad idea! In fact, the history of corrections is littered with reforms—some progressive and some mean-spirited—that have either proved merely impotent (no effects) or have had disquieting iatrogenic effects. Further, asking that any idea be undertaken on a grand scale usually amounts to it not being undertaken at all. Rather, our recommendation is experimentation. We would prefer that states, or the National Institute of Justice, allocate sufficient funds to test the accountability principle across a limited number of sites. These experiments would allow us to see if accountability works and to see how to fine-tune the idea so that it works better in other locations. In short, the plan is to start modestly with experimentation, build evidence, and then, if warranted, move to a larger scale.

In the initial phase of this reform, coercing a prison to join the experiment is inappropriate: Until there is a strong body of evidence supporting the efficacy of accountable prisons, we should rely on volunteers. There is some selection bias when one starts a reform with only those motivated to engage in participating. But if the accountable prison cannot succeed with motivated participants, it likely will not succeed generally. By contrast, if positive results can be achieved with those wishing to participate, then a firm basis exists for asking other wardens and their staff to join in this reform effort. And though it is not our preference, truly resistant correctional personnel can be removed and replaced by those who are ready "to get with the program." Such an action would be justified, however, on the basis that evidence exists that accountability works and is now a legitimate expectation of a warden's job.

Defining and Measuring Success. For the accountable prison to be effective, the process by which success and failure is measured must be fair. Again, we advise including correctional staff in the process of deciding how this is to be accomplished. An initial challenge is to compute what a prison's "institutional recidivism rate" has been in recent years. A subsequent challenge is to decide what constitutes "success." How much does the recidivism rate have to decline to be attributed to the prison and not some random fluctuation? It is important to select a goal that is achievable. Another issue is how to compute recidivism rates by who the offenders are. It might be necessary to assess recidivism not across all offenders but to standardize it by types of offenders—that is, by low-risk, medium-risk, and high-risk offenders. This will entail using well-validated assessment instruments, such as the Level of Service Inventory (Andrews & Bonta, 2010; Smith et al., 2009; Vose et al., 2008). Most generally, sensitivity must be devoted to developing a recidivism assessment system that prison personnel agree in advance will give them a fair shake.

As the reform proceeds and knowledge grows as to what is achievable, an attempt should be made to develop increasingly precise objectives. Again, this level should vary by offender risk category (and, of course, exclude offenders who will not be released from prison). Regardless, the objectives should be stated in a concrete, unambiguous way: "The XYZ prison will reduce recidivism of released high-risk offenders so that no more than 20% are arrested within one year."

To achieve these objectives, quantitative measures need to be developed that provide easily interpreted measures of performance. Because recidivism tends to be highest in the first months after release, a measurement system might count, for example, the proportion of offenders who have not been arrested for a felony the first year following release from prison. Whether arrest, felony offense, or one year's time constitute the specific criteria is an open question, but the measurement must include the criminal justice action that triggers a failure, the seriousness of the event that triggers the action, and the time period for counting. If prisons are to be made accountable, then the action trigger should be set low (such as an offender's arrest as opposed to re-incarceration). It is important to remember that the decision to send a parolee back to prison does not have to be tightly coupled with this global measure of prison accountability. That is, a prison that has few prisoners return but has most of its former prisoners arrested for felonies cannot be considered successful.

Providing the Means to Be Successful. Again, we do not wish a priori to compel correctional managers to engage in specific evidence-based practices that are "best bets" to reduce recidivism. At the same time, it would be unfair to deprive wardens and their staff of the means to be successful. As noted above—and as is increasingly well known in the field of corrections—there is now a theoretically informed, empirically based rehabilitation paradigm: the principles of effective treatment developed by Andrews, Bonta, Gendreau, and others. To review: This paradigm specifies which offenders should receive intervention (high-risk), what criminogenic needs treatments should target (e.g., antisocial attitudes and cognitions), and what modalities are most capable of reforming offenders (e.g., cognitive-behavioral). It also includes the technology to assess offenders (i.e., Level of Service Inventory) and a blueprint for organizing and administering an agency capable of delivering services that reduce recidivism (i.e., the Correctional Program Assessment Inventory) (see also Chapter 1 in this volume). The ability to intervene effectively with offender thus clearly exists.

Unfortunately, at present, prison managers have no incentive to become well versed in this paradigm, to be trained in its technology, and to implement programs based on its principles. The embrace of quality evidence-based programming is thus episodic at best. As noted above, with the accountable prison, this situation might change. Officials now held responsible for lowering inmate recidivism would have every reason to demand access to this knowledge base and to have the resources required to establish programs that work. Equally important, those holding them accountable would have pressure to provide training and support lest they be accused of and held accountable for a given prison's failure to reduce recidivism. Put more broadly, whereas no incentives now exist to pursue evidence-based treatment, accountability might be a key factor in creating a willingness, rooted in self-interest, to do so.

Incentives and Accountability. To sum up: To move forward as a successful reform, the accountable prison must embrace experimentation. In this process, it must define clear objectives, develop quantitative and understandable measures of success (and thus of failure), and provide the means that correctional managers can use—beyond their own ingenuity—to achieve reductions in recidivism. We then return to the issue of accountability and incentives, which we have said should be tilted strongly in a positive direction. Still, as time passes, the nature of the incentive contingencies should be viewed as dynamic, not static. At the beginning of the reform effort, the means for achieving reductions in recidivism will be quite uncertain—or, at the least, not yet demonstrated. At this stage, the inducements to lower reoffending should be decidedly positive. But as knowledge grows and examples of success in recidivism reduction become more commonplace, then higher levels of accountability are to be expected. Correctional managers who refuse to avail themselves of evidence-based practices or who are incapable of implementing such practices should face consequences; poor performance should be negatively sanctioned. That said, because we would want prison administrators not only to achieve given performance levels but also to exceed them, positive encouragement should always be the dominant approach.

Social Impact Bonds

It is even possible that we could privatize aspects of the accountable prison using an exciting new initiative known as "social impact bonds"—a social experiment to which President Obama's 2012 budget has allocated up to $100 million (Goldmark, 2011). How does this work? If the government wishes to reduce recidivism among inmates, for example, it would allow an investor to enroll inmates in treatment services. The money to pay for these services would be raised by a "social impact bond issuing organization" or SIBIO. The SIBIO would secure financing from investors. The SIBIO would then use this money to contract for treatment services with a provider. Now here is the key: The SIBIO would receive payment only if an agreed-upon reduction in recidivism was achieved. No reduction in recidivism, the government pays nothing. But if lower reoffending is realized, then the government pays the SIBIO an amount that would yield profits for investors (Liebman, 2011).

This initiative is not a pie-in-the-sky idea but is being implemented at Petersborough Prison in England. Social Finance, a SIBIO, is raising $7.9 million to fund the provision of services to male inmates who are serving short sentences and typically have a reoffending rate of 60% within a year. Social Finance and its investors will receive no payment unless recidivism is reduced by 7.5% for the 3,000 inmates. If reoffending can be cut by 12.5%, investors will receive a return of about 13% (BBC News, 2010; Liebman, 2011).

Social impact bonds are appealing because they incentivize accountability and provide a mechanism for funding offender services. They also provide an alternative to relying solely on government agencies to reduce recidivism, thus introducing useful competition. But as is the case with accountable prisons in general, we have no empirical evidence that the social impact bond version of accountable prisons will live up to its promises. We must conduct rigorous experiments to learn when social impact bonds work and to determine if they have negative side effects (see Liebman, 2011). As noted, a first step in this direction is being taken at the Petersborough Prison.

Conclusion: Choosing a Different Future

It is a truism that futures are chosen in the sense that the intersection of decisions by correctional policy makers and practitioners determines who goes to prison, how long they stay there, and how they will be treated while behind bars. But such choices can also be tightly bounded by the constructed and objective realities in which people become enmeshed. Ways of doing corrections can be seen as inevitable— backed up by political ideology, administrative preference, and organizational routinization. We have discovered that in universities, choosing a different future— such as eliminating time-consuming committees that have no discernable reasons for their existence—can take years of effort! We recognize, therefore, that trying to transform corrections so as to choose the accountable prison will not be an easy sell.

Nonetheless, there are two considerations that give us a glimmer of optimism for why our idea for an accountable prison might have some credibility to it. First, it is an idea that potentially will appeal to those on the political Right and on the political Left. For those on the Right, the accountable prison embraces free market principles, believing that incentives will unleash innovation and allow goals to be achieved. How can capitalism be opposed? For those on the Left, the payoff is that the accountable prison might inspire concerted efforts from inside the correctional system to take an interest in offenders and to genuinely try to make their return to the prison world less likely. How can doing good for offenders be opposed?

In fact, accountability is surfacing in various ways within current-day corrections— beyond the social impact bond experiment in the United Kingdom. In Washington state, for example, the legislature has mandated that treatment programs be assessed for their cost effectiveness, based on how expensive they are to deliver and on how much money is saved due to reduced recidivism and related costs (Aos, 2011; Washington State Institute for Public Policy, 2010). More relevant to our spe- cific proposal, recent programs throughout the country have begun to provide incentives to agencies that reduce the number of offenders sent to prison. Thus, in 2007, the Kansas legislature passed Senate Bill 14, which allows the state to award $4 million each year in state grants to community corrections agencies that reduce revocations and re-incarcerations by 20% (Austin, 2010; Kansas SB 14, 2007; Pew Center on the States, 2011). Similarly, Arizona passed SB 1476 in 2008. This bill allows the state to financially reward probation departments for reducing the num- ber of probationers returned to prison for either a new crime or a technical viola- tion. Specifically, departments can be given 40% of funds that the state saved by incarcerating fewer people to develop victims services initiatives, substance abuse programs, and other evidenced-based treatments for offenders (Arizona SB 1476, 2008; Austin, 2010; Pew Center on the States, 2011).

Incentive-based legislation has also been passed in four other states. First, in 2009, California passed legislation that created the Community Corrections Performance Incentives Fund. This fund allows county agencies that used evidenced-based practices with probationers and reduce their revocation and re-incarceration to be rewarded (Austin, 2010; California SB 678, 2009; Pew Center on the States, 2011). Second, also in 2009, Colorado House Bill 1022 made available up to $200,000 in grants for probation and parole agencies that reduced recidivism rates among mentally ill offenders (Austin, 2010; Colorado HB 1022, 2009). Third, Illinois's Crime Reduction Act of 2009 allows state money to be given to probation agencies that adopted evidence-based programs to reduce the number of nonviolent offenders sent to state prisons (Austin, 2010; Illinois SB 1289, 2009; Pew Center on the States, 2011). Fourth, in 2010, South Carolina passed a bill that awards the Department of Probation, Parole, and Pardon Services 35% of the state's savings for not returning probationers and parolees to prison (Austin, 2010; Pew Center on the States 2011; South Carolina SB 1154, 2010). These developments reveal that innovation based on accountability is feasible and is currently being implemented all across the country.

Second and perhaps most importantly, we have reached a moment in correctional history where a turning point is at hand. It is now clear that the punitive paradigm that has controlled prison policy and thinking has exhausted itself. Part of its loss of hegemony lies in the empirical evidence showing that its capacity to protect public safety has been modest. But part of its diminished appeal is in how this paradigm, and its embrace of mass incarceration, is now bankrupting many state treasuries. Many governors, including Republican governors, have faced the stubborn reality that they cannot balance state budgets if they must finance bloated prison systems. Accordingly, they are willing to listen to fresh ideas about how to protect public safety at a lower cost. A time for correctional change is now at hand.

In this context, a proposal for an accountable prison might not be dismissed as a misguided idea cooked up by college professors who know nothing about corrections. Of course, this might well be true! But the serious message here is that we should no longer have a commitment to doing "more of the same" in our prisons. Criminologists have long assumed the position of critics, pointing out all that is wrong with the society of captives (e.g., violence, gangs, disease, crowding). Such critical commentary is valuable, but it has not often led to improving the lives of inmates inside and then outside of prison. By contrast, the accountable prison proposal takes a very different pathway. In advancing it, we assume that prisons are not beyond redemption and that how they are governed matters (see DiIulio, 1987). They can be administered poorly and harshly or they can be administered well and with a human services orientation. Our goal thus has been to find a way of thinking that moves beyond mere criticism of the existing prison order and that identifies a strategy for inspiring a concrete reform that promises to make correctional work more professional and exciting, that creates an interest in helping offenders to stay out of prison, and that improves public safety. That is, as we now sit at a policy fork in the road, we need to illuminate not simply why the old correctional road should not be taken but why we should choose to travel a new road and where this adventure might take us.

In the end, doing more of the same strikes us as inexcusable. The stubborn reality is that prisons have failed at reducing recidivism. We know how to rehabilitate offenders, so there is no excuse for not applying this knowledge in prisons. We have substantial evidence from policing that holding police accountable for crime can reduce crime. In short, there is no excuse for rejecting the idea of the accountable prison outright. That said, until we have built a body of evidence on accountable prisons, we cannot know if this is just a plausible idea, or if it is a plausible idea that actually works. Consequently, we suggest a rolling implementation process. First, prison administrators who are willing to experiment with this idea should conduct proof-of-concept projects. Second, if the evidence from these case studies is plausible, states should engage in systematic research and evaluation to rigorously examine how to implement accountable prisons and evaluate their performance. Third, if these studies continue to show the accountable prison has the weight of evidence behind it, then states should engage in a full-scale rollout of accountability across their prison systems. In short, do not take our word for it. Test it.

References

Andrews, D. A., & Bonta, J. (2010). *The psychology of criminal conduct* (5th ed.). New Providence, NJ: Anderson/LexisNexis.

Aos, S. (2011). Using evidence to maximize return on taxpayer investment. In K. Bogenschneider, O. Little, & S. Eddy (Eds.), *Evidence-based budgeting: Making decisions to move Wisconsin forward* (pp. 1–6). Madison: Wisconsin Family Impact Seminars.

Arizona SB 1476. (2008).

Austin, A. (2010). *Criminal justice trends: Key legislative changes in sentencing policy, 2001–2010.* New York, NY: Vera Institute of Justice.

BBC News. (2010). Private backers fund scheme to cut prisoner reoffending. Retrieved May 24, 2011, from http://www.bbc.co.uk/news/uk-11254308

Beck, A. J., & Shipley, B. E. (1989). *Recidivism of prisoners released in 1983.* Washington, DC: U.S. Department of Justice, Bureau of Justice Statistics.

Bennett, W. J., DiIulio, J. J., Jr., & Walters, J. P. (1996). *Body count: Moral poverty and how to win America's war against crime and drugs.* New York: Simon and Shuster.

Braga, A. A. (2005). Hot spots policing and crime prevention: A systematic review of randomized controlled trials. *Journal of Experimental Criminology, 1,* 317–342.

California Community Corrections Performance Incentive Act of 2009, California SB 678. (2009).

Chen, M. K., & Shapiro, J. M. (2007). Do harsher prison conditions reduce recidivism? A discontinuity-based approach. *American Law and Economic Review, 9,* 1–29.

Colorado HB 1022. (2009).

Crime Reduction Act, Illinois SB 1289. (2009).

Cullen, F. T., Fisher, B. S., & Applegate, B. K. (2000). Public opinion about punishment and corrections. In M. Tonry (Ed.), *Crime and justice: A review of research* (Vol. 14, pp. 1–79). Chicago, IL: University of Chicago Press.

Cullen, F. T., & Jonson, C. L. (2012). *Correctional theory: Context and consequences.* Thousand Oaks, CA: Sage.

Cullen, F. T., Jonson, C. L., & Nagin, D. S. (2011). Prisons do not reduce recidivism: The high cost of ignoring science. *The Prison Journal, 91,* 48S–65S.

Cullen, F. T., & Smith, P. (2011). Treatment and rehabilitation. In M. Tonry (Ed.), *The Oxford handbook of crime and criminology* (pp. 156–178). New York, NY: Oxford University Press.

DiIulio, J. J., Jr. (1987). *Governing prisons: A comparative study of correctional management.* New York, NY: Free Press.

Eck, J. E., & Guerette, R. T. (2012). Place-based crime prevention: Theory, evidence, and policy. In B. C. Welsh & D. P. Farrington (Eds.), *Oxford handbook of crime prevention.* New York, NY: Oxford University Press.

Farrell, G. (2005). Progress and prospects in the prevention of repeat victimization. In N. Tilley (Ed.), *Handbook of crime prevention and community safety* (pp. 143–170). Cullompton, Devon, UK: Willan.

Gaes, G. G., & Camp, S. D. (2009). Unintended consequences: Experimental evidence for the criminogenic effect of prison security level placement on post-release recidivism. *Journal of Experimental Criminology, 5,* 139–162.

Gendreau, P., Goggin, C., Cullen, F. T., & Andrews, D. A. (2000). The effects of community sanctions and incarceration on recidivism. *Forum on Corrections Research, 12*(May), 10–13.

Glaze, L. E. & Parks, E. (2012). *Correctional populations in the United States, 2011.* Washington, DC: U.S. Department of Justice, Bureau of Justice Statistics.

Goldmark, A. (2011). The most exciting 0.003% of Obama's budget: Social impact bonds. *Fast Company.com,* February 16. Retrieved May 25, 2011, from http://www.fast company.com/1728321/the-most-exciting-0003-of-obama-s-budget-social

Goldstein, H. (1990). *Problem-oriented policing.* New York, NY: McGraw-Hill.

Hepburn, J. R., & Griffin, M. L. (1998). *Jail recidivism in Maricopa County: A report submitted to the Maricopa County Sheriff's Office.* Tempe: Arizona State University.

Illinois SB 1289. (2009).

Irwin, J. (2005). *The warehouse prison: Disposal of the new dangerous class.* Los Angeles, CA: Roxbury.

Jacobs, J. B. (1977). *Stateville: The penitentiary in mass society.* Chicago, IL: University of Chicago Press.

Jonson, C. L. (2010). *The impact of imprisonment on reoffending: A meta-analysis.* Unpublished doctoral dissertation, University of Cincinnati. Available from http://etd .ohiolink.edu/view.cgi?acc_num=ucin1285687754

Langan, P. A., & Levin, D. J. (2002). *Recidivism of prisoners released in 1994.* Washington, DC: U.S. Department of Justice, Bureau of Justice Statistics.

Liebman, J. B. (2011). *Social impact bonds: A promising new financing model to accelerate social innovation and improve government performance.* Washington, DC: Center for American Progress.

Lipsey, M. W., & Cullen, F. T. (2007). The effectiveness of correctional rehabilitation: A review of systematic reviews. *Annual Review of Law and Social Sciences, 3,* 297–320.

Listwan, S. J., Sullivan, C. J., Agnew, R., Cullen, F. T., & Colvin, M. (2013). The pains of imprisonment revisited: The impact of strain on inmate recidivism. *Justice Quarterly, 30,* 144–168.

MacKenzie, D. L. (2006). *What works in corrections: Reducing the criminal activities of offenders and delinquents.* New York, NY: Cambridge University Press.

Martinson, R. (1974). What works? Questions and answers about prison reform. *The Public Interest, 35,* 22–54.

Martinson, R. (1979). New findings, new views: A note of caution regarding sentencing reform. *Hofstra Law Review, 7*(Winter), 243–258.

Matthews, Roger. (2009). Beyond "so what" criminology: Rediscovering realism. *Theoretical Criminology, 13,* 341–362.

National Research Council. (2004). *Fairness and effectiveness in policing: The evidence.* Committee to Review Research on Police Policy and Practices, W. Skogan, & K. Frydl (Eds.), *Committee on law and justice, division of behavioral and social sciences and education.* Washington, DC: National Academies Press.

Nagin, D. S., Cullen, F. T., & Jonson, C. L. (2009). Imprisonment and reoffending. In M. Tonry (Ed.), *Crime and justice: A review of research* (Vol. 38, pp. 115–200). Chicago, IL: University of Chicago Press.

Omnibus Crime Reduction and Sentencing Reform Act of 2010, South Carolina SB 1154. (2010).

Pew Center on the States. (2008). *One in 100: Behind bars in America 2008.* Washington, DC: Pew Charitable Trusts.

Pew Center on the States. (2011). *State of recidivism: The revolving door of America's prisons.* Washington, DC: Pew Charitable Trusts.

Risk Reduction Initiative, Kansas SB 14. (2007).

Rothman, D. J. (1971). *The discovery of the asylum: Social order and disorder in the new republic.* Boston, MA: Little, Brown.

Sherman, L. W. (1993). Why crime control is not reactionary. In D. Weisburd & C. Uchida (Eds.), *Police innovation and control of the police* (pp. 71–189). New York, NY: Springer-Verlag.

Smith, P., Cullen, F. T., & Latessa, E. J. (2009). Can 14,737 women be wrong? A meta-analysis of the LSI-R and recidivism for female offenders. *Criminology and Public Policy, 8,* 183–208.

Smith, P., Goggin, C., & Gendreau, P. (2002). *The effects of prison sentences and intermediate sanctions on recidivism: General effects and individual differences.* Ottawa, Canada: Solicitor General of Canada.

Spelman, W. (2000). What recent studies do (and don't) tell us about imprisonment and crime. In M. Tonry (Ed.), *Crime and justice: A review of research* (Vol. 27, pp. 419–494). Chicago, IL: University of Chicago Press.

Tillyer, M. S., & Kennedy, D. M. (2008). Locating focused deterrence approaches within a situational crime prevention framework. *Crime Prevention and Community Safety, 10*(2), 75–84.

Toch, H., & Klofas, J. (1982). Alienation and desire for job enrichment among correction officers. *Federal Probation, 46*(1), 35–44.

Villettaz, P., Killias, M., & Zoder, I. (2006). *The effects of custodial vs. noncustodial sentences on re-offending: A systematic review of the state of knowledge.* Philadelphia, PA: Campbell Collaboration Crime and Justice Group.

Vose, B., Cullen, F. T., & Smith, P. (2008). The empirical status of the Level of Service Inventory. *Federal Probation, 72*(3), 22–29.

Wacquant, L. (2001). Deadly symbiosis: When ghetto and prison meet and mesh. *Punishment and Society, 3,* 95–134.

Washington State Institute for Public Policy. (2010). *Return on (taxpayer) investment: Evidence-based options to improve statewide outcomes.* Olympia: Washington State Institute for Public Policy.

Weisburd, D., Mastrofski, S. D., McNally, A. M., Greenspan, R., & Willis, J. J. (2003). Reforming to preserve: Compstat and strategic problem solving in American policing. *Criminology and Public Policy, 2,* 421–456.

Wilson, J. Q. (1975). *Thinking about crime.* New York, NY: Vintage.

Windzio, M. (2006). Is there a deterrent effect of pains of imprisonment? The impact of "social costs" on the hazard rate of recidivism. *Punishment and Society, 8,* 341–364.

Wortley, R. & Mazerolle, L. (2008). Environmental criminology and crime analysis: Situating the theory, analytic approach and application. In R. Wortley & L. Mazerolle (Eds.), *Environmental criminology and crime analysis* (pp. 1–18). Cullompton, Devon, UK: Willan.

Zimbardo, P. G. (2007). *The Lucifer effect: Understanding how good people turn evil.* New York, NY: Random House.

Part VII

The American Prison

13

Lessons Learned

From Penal Harm to Penal Help

Mary K. Stohr, Cheryl Lero Jonson, and Francis T. Cullen

We live in exciting times for students and scholars studying crime and justice in this country. The drug war is waning. The death penalty and harsh punishments are losing favor with the general public. The stolid belief in the infallibility of the criminal justice process has slackened among the public, just as, or possibly because, the number of exonerations is rising. The amount of crime continues a 30-year slide. Decarceration of prisons is afoot in the states and localities, and it appears a paradigm shift is in process. The belief in the validity of rehabilitation programming has gained converts. Restorative justice programming has spread through all sectors of corrections. Reentry has become a major focus of policy and research. It is difficult to append a label to a period of time, particularly when one is in the midst of it, but all of these developments might signify that we have entered another age of reform.

As students of history know, such "ages" appeared during the Renaissance (14th to 17th centuries) and the "Age of Reason" and the Enlightenment (17th and 18th centuries) in Europe spurred by the weakening of the feudal economic model and a shift in perspective from religious control and influence to science, philosophy, education, literature, and the arts. No doubt the improvement in the dispersal of knowledge, via the printing press, had no small influence on precipitating these shifts as it made possible the spread of ideas. More recently, in this country, we have experienced such ages of reform with the Progressive Era (1890s to 1920s) and the 1960s Age of Aquarius (which includes the 1960s decade but is often extended to the early 1970s). The Progressive Era was fueled by a shift from the farm to the industrial economic model, the perception that corruption was widespread in the private and public sectors, and efforts to recover from a major war (the Civil War). The backdrop to the Age of Aquarius was the fight against a war (the Vietnam War) and widespread movements to improve the rights of racial minorities and women. Such periods were marked by civil and social unrest, major public and private reforms, and, finally, a sense of hope that the world had the potential to be better and the people had the power to make it so (Hofstadter, 1955).

In our age, in our time, we too are experiencing worldwide economic shifts as marked by the Great Recession, the shift of jobs abroad and the rise of China, and a general weariness with war (in Afghanistan and Iraq). We too are experiencing civil and social unrest (the Tea Party and Occupy movements in the states along with the protests against austerity policies in much of Europe, and the Arab Spring [of 2011], which led to the overthrow of several dictators in the Middle East) and some significant changes in social policies. Such changes encompass the reform of state laws that are liberalizing marijuana use, repealing harsh sentences, and reducing incarceration (Hogan et al., 2012).

The widespread decarceration that has taken hold in many states and localities is a harbinger of change. Because of this decarceration, which may be too premature to term a trend, the related dissatisfaction with the penal harm movement, and the increase in the use and acceptance of rehabilitation, restorative justice, and reentry programming, it appears there are some real possibilities for the remaking of prisons (Cullen, Jonson, & Stohr, 2012; Hogan et al., 2012; Pollock, Hogan, Lambert, Ross, & Sundt, 2012). Perhaps it is now time to think about changing from *penal harm* to *penal help* as the dominant focus of prisons.

In fact, in our sector of the criminal justice universe—corrections—we might title the prison segment of this age of reform the *Penal Help Age*. Such an age might be characterized, as our age is, by the three R's. No, not those three R's (Reading, wRiting and aRithmetic!), but Rehabilitation, Restorative justice, and Reentry programming. Why might this age, the early 21st century, be so different? The answer is simple: This is the first time in two generations that it is possible to dream about a different future for corrections and to know there is a real chance that this dream might come true. For almost 40 years, the constant for prisons in this country was one of growth and penal harm (Clear, 1994). The move to reaffirm, on the institutional level, rehabilitation in the 1990s, when it received renewed notice and interest, not to mention funding, from the federal and state policy makers, did not decelerate this growth in the use of incarceration. Nor, somewhat surprisingly, did declining crime rates that persisted, and still persist, for the last 30 years (Pinker, 2011; Zimring, 2007). It took a confluence of these factors—declining crime rates, disillusionment with the power of punishment or penal harm to reduce crime, good scientific evidence regarding the futility of prison as a crime control technique, solid scientific evidence as to the value of rehabilitation, and, particularly important, reduced state revenues—to reach a "tipping point" whereby real change is possible. As Gladwell (2000) defines it, a tipping point in the arena of social phenomena occurs when an idea becomes wildly popular, thus making widespread change possible. Reaching this tipping point of decarceration has the practical effect of opening up a world of possibilities and, in this case, it might clear the way for reform of prisons, for an age of *Penal Help*.

In the preceding chapters, we explored some of the prototypes for prisons that might take shape as penal harm and the related warehousing of inmates in prisons fade. Whether this remaking, as described in these chapters, comes to full fruition so that more help than harm might be achieved in the prisons of the near future is up to our generation of policy makers, scholars, and students and to those who come after us. We certainly know from our penal history that real and beneficial change is relatively easy to visualize in corrections, but not so easy to realize. The history of corrections is replete with well-intentioned reforms whose implementation went awry for either political or administrative reasons (see, e.g., Rothman, 1980). But the corollary to this point, lest we get too pessimistic, is that much positive change has been accomplished in this world and that these positive changes happened due to the committed efforts of people who were interested in promoting a greater humanity in the world (e.g., most personal and state sanctioned violence of every kind has been dramatically reduced over the centuries) (Pinker, 2011).

In this final chapter of our book, we want to get past this tipping point and step into that world of possibilities for corrections, into that age of penal help. To do so, we delineate seven "lessons learned" from this book-length exploration of the potential future prototypes of American prisons. We do not pretend that our list of lessons is exhaustive. The lessons are also more macro in scope than specific to one prison or another. Nevertheless, we think that the recounting of such lessons provides a means by which to find a common thread between the prototypes, to see how they are inextricably connected to one another and to our time, and to visualize how they might be achievable in this new Age of Penal Help.

Lesson 1: Prisons Must Improve, Not Harm Inmates

This is the core message of several chapters, but especially Chapters 1 through 4 (The Therapeutic Prison, The Restorative Prison, The Faith-Based Prison, and The Virtuous Prison). Our prisons must express our values and our time to be more than mere cages or instruments of punishment. They must achieve some *good*, hopefully beyond just incapacitating and exacting retribution by punishing serious and violent offenders (which is admittedly a "good" in and of itself). Moreover, we have knowledge of how to do this—whether through rehabilitation, restorative justice, or even faith-based programs. We must create "decent" prisons that do more than hold convicted offenders safely. Given that the vast majority of inmates (roughly 95%) will eventually return to the free community, prisons must provide to their occupants the resources, skills, and care that will reduce the likelihood that these returning inmates will harm others or themselves with further crimes or other destructive behaviors (Hughes & Wilson, 2011, p. 1; Johnson, 2002, p. 6). Which strategy to pursue to produce this improvement should be based on the evidence of "what works" in corrections.

As indicated in Chapter 1, efforts to rehabilitate have not always "worked" to reduce recidivism. Yet, even when out of favor with politicians, and when the evidence was supposedly slim as to its effectiveness, the rehabilitative ideal was never wholly abandoned by scholars or the public (Cullen & Gendreau, 2001; Cullen & Gilbert, 1982; Moon, Sundt, Cullen, & Wright, 2000; Palmer, 1994). We will not recount the "nothing works" narrative history here, as most readers are likely well aware of it and it was covered by Paula Smith and Myrinda Schweitzer in Chapter 1. But suffice it to say that the evidence is that when the program is targeted toward high-risk offenders (risk [R]), seeks to change the known deficiency (needs [N]), and is delivered in a cognitive-behavioral manner (responsivity [R]), rehabilitation programming can work very well indeed (Andrews & Bonta, 2010; Andrews et al., 1990; Cullen & Gendreau, 2001; Gendreau & Ross, 1987; Lowenkamp, Latessa, & Smith, 2006).

How effective is rehabilitation programming, you might ask? Well, the answer to that question, not to prevaricate, is as follows: It depends! Cullen and Jonson (2012, p. 169) report, after an extensive review of the research in this area, that those programs that adhere to the RNR principles might reduce recidivism by as much as 25%, or even more.

And, of course, there is much we do not know yet about the effectiveness of programming. We have some idea of what works, we know about some things that do not appear to work, but we are not certain about what might *also work* and for *what* (Cullen & Jonson, 2012; Lee & Stohr, 2012). As George Lombardi, director of Corrections in Missouri, remarked on the subject to an Introduction to Corrections class at Missouri State University in Spring 2012, "In Missouri we like to use 'whatever works' in programming." What he meant primarily was *whatever works* in programming to reduce crime (reduce recidivism), but he also meant whatever works to reduce tension and violence in prisons (to manage inmates and improve their lives), and whatever works to provide benefit to the community generally. At the time he made this comment, he was referencing his department's Puppies for Parole program and the inmate gardens at several prisons. Concerning the Puppies for Parole program, he spoke of inmates in Missouri prisons who raise and train dogs for adoption in the free world. As the director saw it, the presence of these dogs calmed the living units they were placed in, had a salutary effect on the inmates they were placed with (e.g., gave them a companion they could lavish affection on), and benefited the community members who were lucky enough to adopt one of these well-trained dogs. The gardening program was part of a restorative justice effort in the prisons where the produce is donated to food pantries around the state as a means of repairing some of the harm inmates had inflicted on communities through the commitment of their crime. Again, these two programs were unlikely to reduce the post-release criminality of the inmate gardeners or dog trainers, but even if they did not, they gave the inmates something useful and worthwhile to do with their time, kept them out of trouble while they were engaged in these programs, and gave them an opportunity to contribute to the larger free community in a meaningful way.

Therefore, rehabilitation programming might be fruitfully used not only to reduce crime—undoubtedly the most desired end for all of us—but also to manage inmates, to benefit the community, and as recompense for crimes already done (restorative justice). It is also likely that rehabilitation programs do serve another purpose that might have the additional effect of restoring the health or well-being of inmates but that has no immediate, direct, or measurable effect on crime reduction. At a minimum, such programs, much like arts and crafts and weight lifting programs, give inmates another niche in which they can escape the noise, drama, and control of prisons, and allow them to reach a place where they can develop their better (e.g., more adult and responsible or mature) selves (Johnson, 2002).

Restorative justice is all about offenders reaching for that "better self" that abhors what they did to the victims and the community and seeks to "make it right." There is some evidence that restorative justice programming can effectuate a modest reduction in crime but may be most effective in this respect when combined with other rehabilitation programming (see, e.g., Chapter 2 in this volume by Lois Presser; Cullen & Jonson, 2012). If, however, restorative justice programming allows inmates in prisons and jails, or correctional clients on probation or parole, the opportunity to "give back" and/or "repair harm" for their community or their victim, there is nothing wrong with that, even above and beyond any effect on recidivism, as the community benefits and hopefully that better self is more developed when the inmate does leave the institution.

As noted by Byron Johnson in Chapter 3, faith-based programs have been shown to reduce the recidivism of some inmates. As religion-based programming is the most likely of all programming to exist in all prisons, given the low-cost nature of their provision by mostly volunteer community preachers, there is no reason why every prison should not have such programs (and the authors have never seen a prison that did not). Should those inmates embrace the common religious belief of the Golden Rule—doing good things unto others that have been done to them in these programs—this can only be beneficial in terms of reducing behavior problems while in prison, reducing later criminality once released, and giving inmates one more niche or venue from which to better themselves.

This issue of good versus evil, and how to maximize the first in human beings while minimizing the latter, was at the core of the development of prisons in this country (see Chapter 4 and the discussion by Francis Cullen, Jody Sundt, & John Wozniak). For the Quakers, who founded prisons in America, virtue and how to achieve it was a central concern in the early Pennsylvania prisons (e.g., the Walnut Street Jail, the Eastern and Western Pennsylvania Prisons); however, this concern was also prevalent in the New York prison system (e.g., the Newgate Prison in New York City, and later the Albany and Sing Sing prisons). In the prisons of today, with the exception of religious programming, there is not enough talk of virtue. "Doing the right thing" (to paraphrase the title of Spike Lee's 1989 movie *Do the Right Thing*) is implied in a number of correctional programs, but rarely explicitly advocated. The absence of crime from one's life (failing to recidivate) is not quite the same as affirmatively being a virtuous person.

The prison subculture, and often the larger community culture, as exemplified by pop culture, too often showcases the antagonist, the serial killer, the gangster, and the hired gunman, rather than the person who plays by the rules and tries to do good in the world. In fact, *do-gooder* has become slang for someone who is obsequious, weak, or naïve, rather than an admirable figure that people want to emulate.

Yet our prisons, and the inmates housed in them, might truly benefit from a return to an emphasis on virtuousness. It almost goes without saying, but cannot, that staff and management in the Virtuous Prison would need to "practice what they preach" so as to minimize harm and to model the do-gooder in such prisons. In this way, they would maximize the help given to those behind prison walls.

Lesson 2: Prisons Must Be Just

From the beginning, prisons were created as an alternative punishment to shaming in the public square (e.g., putting a person in the stocks), beatings and other corporal punishments, and executions of poor men for the commission of "street" crimes. Women and girls committed far fewer of such crimes, but when they did they were held in men's and boy's prisons, and in states with larger populations, in separate prisons of their own. After the Civil War, and as our country became more diverse racially and ethnically, prisons were populated mostly by poor men and boys of every color who had been sentenced as the result of a street crime (see Chapter 5 on the Feminist Prison by Kristi Holsinger, and Chapter 6 on the Racially Just Prison by Craig Hemmens and Mary Stohr). Since the drug war came into full fruition in the 1980s, the numbers of minority men and women in American prisons have exploded. As the main thrust of this war diminishes, we hope to see a corresponding diminishment in the incarceration of minority men and women.

A "just" prison would be one that held people who had committed serious violations of the law. A just prison, in the authors' estimation, would be one that primarily holds serious street-level offenders (e.g., robbers, rapists, and murderers). Additionally, considering the harm they do to community health and well-being and the threat they pose, a just prison would hold those who committed corporate and environmental crimes, something that state prisons rarely do. However, the authors believe that states could be much more engaged in the prosecutions of such crimes within their borders. The dumping of toxic waste into rivers, streams, and forests, or the pilfering of retirement monies, or the exploitation of workers are no less offenses against the common good and arguably result in much more harm to many more people than a robbery on a darkened street. A truly just prison, then, is possible only if we have a truly just society where all serious criminals are treated to prison for the harm they do.

Within the walls of that prison, however, inmates must be accorded a safe and secure incarceration no matter their race, class, gender, or offense committed. Historically, the races were segregated, as were the genders, resulting in lesser conditions for minorities and for women and girls during incarceration. Since the civil rights and women's rights movements of the 1960s and 1970s, some, but not all, of these disparities have been rectified (see Chapters 5 and 6). A just prison would try to accommodate the special needs that different genders, races, ethnicities, religions, and cultures might require.

Furthermore, and related, in a just prison the needs of mentally ill and aged inmates would be met. When it makes legal and humane sense, such inmates would be redirected to communities and their programs, which are better equipped to handle these conditions (Lemieux, Dyeson, & Castiglione, 2002; Slate & Johnson, 2008).

Lesson 3: Prisons Must Be Healthy and Safe

This lesson would seem to be relevant to the chapters on healthy, safe, and green prisons. As the authors of the chapters on safe (Benjamin Steiner & Benjamin Meade, Chapter 7) and healthy (Roberto Hugh Potter & Jeffrey Rosky, Chapter 8), private (Kevin Wright, Chapter 9), and green (Mary Stohr & John Wozniak, Chapter 10) prisons note, inmates are often harmed by their incarceration in prison, even though the potential exists to help them. We must remember that being sent to prison and staying there are the punishments mandated by law, not the unsafe or unhealthy atmosphere of the prison.

Given the unhealthy and crowded living conditions of many correctional facilities (see, e.g., the recent Supreme Court decision regarding the crowded California prisons, *Brown v. Plata*, 2011, where a majority of the justices determined that crowding created an unhealthy environment), you would think that providing a relatively safe incarceration for inmates, much like providing a healthy one, is rocket science! But it is not! The authors of this chapter and book have worked in, and done research in, prisons and jails that are well run and safe for their inmates and staff, and we have been in correctional facilities that are not (e.g., where abuse, assaults, and poor conditions generally prevail). We feel there is a world of difference between such prisons. The difference does not lie in the type of inmate housed (whether violent or nonviolent) or even primarily in the amount of funding provided, though both of these variables can factor into it. Instead, the difference between a well-run and a poorly operated prison lies in the amount and quality of the staff working in such prisons and in the general conditions of confinement. If staff are poorly trained, inadequately paid, unprofessional, and too few in number to competently manage the prison, if the prison itself is overcrowded, if there is not enough work or activities to keep the inmates busy, and if the physical plant of the prison is decrepit and prevents the ready observation of inmate activity, then there is certainly a greater likelihood of the prison being unsafe for both inmates and staff. Therefore, a safe prison is very possible to achieve, even with violently inclined inmates inside of it, but it takes the attention and knowledge of managers and staff and the provision of adequate funds by policy makers (see Chapter 7).

Because many inmates enter prisons in poor health due to poverty, lack of regular access to health care, and substance abuse, prison administrators face many challenges in meeting the health care needs of their charges. Not the least of these challenges are the costs of health care and attracting and keeping competent staff. Private companies who specialize in providing health care professionals to prisons are one solution that seems to meet the basic health care needs of inmates. Of course, given the problems that privatization poses for corrections (see Chapter 9), such services should be monitored carefully by public sector managers to ensure the services promised are the services delivered, and that the staff have the requisite credentials and experience to provide those services (Marquart, Merianos, Cuvelier, & Carroll, 1996).

Green prisons, particularly those that are green not just to save money but also to improve the conditions of confinement, almost certainly provide a healthier incarcerative environment (see Chapter 10). As the authors of that chapter note, prisons that grow organic and fresh produce, that use nontoxic cleaning and maintenance products, and that produce their own energy that does not harm the environment are more likely not simply to maintain inmate health but also to improve the prison conditions in which offenders must reside.

Lesson 4: Prisons Must Be Accountable

As discussed in Chapter 12 (The Accountable Prison), prisons must fulfill their promise and mission. Such promises, for anything but super-maximum prisons, usually involve much more than just a secure incarceration that also serves to punish. As Francis Cullen, Cheryl Jonson, and John Eck indicate in Chapter 12, prisons have an obligation to rehabilitate and to do so in such a way as to reduce recidivism. Prison managers must be tasked with reducing recidivism, they must be provided with the resources to reduce recidivism, and they must be evaluated on their ability to reduce recidivism. This is so because when all is said and done, there can be no greater good achieved by prisons than the reduction in criminality. Reducing recidivism is a goal central to the creation of prisons and has remained at the very core of their continued existence. If a prison cannot do this, it frankly cannot do much.

At this point in the study of human behavior, we know that prison managers, like all public and private sector managers, need to be motivated to achieve these reductions in recidivism. Humans can be motivated by both positive and negative incentives. The research shows, however, that for high performing and creative managers, the types we would like to attract to prison work, positive incentives to achieve reductions in recidivism will work best (Pink, 2009). Therefore, we should find ways to create incentives for prisons to be successful and for people to be rewarded for keeping inmates out of prison who do not need to be there. In other words, prison wardens and employees should be treated like those in the corporate world, as professionals, and be held accountable for reducing the criminality of inmates placed in their care. Just as in other professions, incentives, such as merit pay, financial bonuses, and recognition with regional and/or national awards, should be provided as motivations to work hard and innovatively to achieve the desired out-come of lower recidivism rates. By holding correctional employees accountable for the lower criminality of their inmates and providing positive incentives to achieve these goals, it is hoped that the focus of the correctional enterprise would be on effectively helping inmates lower their criminal behavior, resulting in an increase in the public's safety while reducing the emphasis of inflicting harm on offenders.

Lesson 5: Prisons Must Be Affordable and Reserved for Violent and Repeat Offenders

Related to the idea of accountability is that of value. Do prisons give value for their cost? The discussion of the Accountable Prison (Chapter 12) would indicate they could do much more to do so. One of the reasons about half the states are currently experiencing some decarceration is likely because state legislators and governors have become convinced that the value provided by imprisonment, for lesser offenders especially, is not equal to the cost (Greene & Mauer, 2010; Guerino, Harrison, & Sabol, 2011). Therefore, a takeaway lesson from this discussion of prisons and their costs is that if they are smaller (e.g., see the discussion by Jonson, Eck, & Cullen in Chapter 11) and more focused on serious, violent, or repeat offenders who commit street, corporate, or environmental crime, then they are more likely to be affordable for states and the federal government and are more likely to deliver on their central premise of reducing recidivism and thus *helping rather than harming*. Furthermore, to reduce the number of people sentenced to correctional institutions, prisons should not be seen as a "free" sanction that prosecutors seek and judges grant at will. Rather, the true costs of prison should be made visible. Judges, prosecutors, and the public should be aware of the tens of thousands of dollars it costs to house one individual behind prison walls. One way to achieve this is to charge the local counties for their use of prisons or to give each county a budget or cap for prison expenses on what they can spend on prisons. By doing this, and by limiting the number of people each county can send to prison, the number of people incarcerated could decrease dramatically. Additionally, this cap on the number of offenders sentenced to expensive incarcerative sanctions will force localities to invest in effective alternatives to incarceration. This movement away from a reliance on imprisonment could shift penal policy from one of inflicting harm to one of providing effective treatment and intervention to offenders.

Lesson 6: Prisons Must Be Developmental for Staff

Prison work can wear people out. Studies have indicated that cynicism, stress, and turnover are high among prison staff and that working in them, especially in poorly operated institutions, can be debilitating for the employees (Pollock et al., 2012). Yet the presence of well-trained and professional staff is key to all of the proposed reforms of prisons discussed here. They are central to any real change in prisons. Without them, no rehabilitation, restorative justice, reentry assistance, or help at all is even possible. We simply cannot have a therapeutic, restorative, feminist, racially just, safe, healthy, well-run private (or public), green, small, and ultimately accountable prison without educated, trained, experienced, ethical in practice, and sufficiently compensated staff. Notably, those five descriptors—educated, trained, experienced, ethical in practice, and sufficiently compensated—are the distinctive characteristics of a profession (Stohr & Collins, 2009). As correctional staff in most prisons and jails do not have the pay, education, training, and experience that would match such professionals as teachers, social workers, lawyers, or even police officers, we can correctly surmise that they are not as "professional" in their ranks as they need to be to accomplish all that we ask of them (Stohr & Collins, 2009). Therefore, one important lesson we learn from this book and these chapters is that there is much reform to be accomplished in regard to prisons, and none of it will happen without talented and committed staff. For this reason, an important lesson is that we need a renewed and continuing push for professionalization of correctional staff in this country.

Lesson 7: The Humaneness Found in Prison Provides Hope for a Better Future

Our last lesson, and a heartening one, about prisons is not so much a prescription for what they should be, but an observation on what they have become. Despite all of the well-justified concern voiced by academics and social commentators over the years as to the harm that prisons do to those housed in them and the injustices they can reinforce, American prisons have become more humane over the years. It is *certainly not* true that prisons are more humane in their expansive use for minor offenders, but they are in the sense of the experiences of their inmates or staff members. Unlike the early English and European prison-like Bridewells, gaols, and poor houses, prisons in the Western world generally supply the basics of life (e.g., food, clothing, shelter, and even basic health care). Unlike the early Pennsylvania and New York prisons, and even the reformist-based Elmira, New York (1870), prison, inmates are no longer beaten by staff, completely cut off from loved ones and the larger community, or viewed by the state as slaves. Unlike the industrial, big house, and warehouse prisons of the late 19th and 20th century, their inmates are afforded more recreation, educational, and rehabilitative programming these days than was true in the past. Unlike these early prisons and despite the point made about the need for greater prison staff professionalization even now, most prison staff have some training and more education (at least GED or high school, if not some college) than was true in years past, which is also undoubtedly aligned with the greater humanity shown inmates in prisons.

Our point here, then, is that most prisons these days are not simply bastions of pain and pessimism. Again, there is much about today's society of captives that is disquieting. But failing to see the progress that has been made over time—and failing to see the positive efforts now undertaken in the nation's institutions—risks socially constructing the reality that "nothing good" can occur in prisons. Such thinking can have the untoward consequence of leading people of conscience and good will to abandon reform efforts and to consign hundreds of thousands of inmates to less fulfilling lives. By contrast, the main message of our project is to embrace hope, not despair—a hope nourished by the long-term historical evolution of corrections in a progressive direction.

In short, we must begin to imagine a different future for the American prison. Part of mapping out this course must involve the critical analysis of what is wrong with existing practices. But the other, more important, part is detailing fresh ideas that can lead us to create a truly new penology—one that embodies the positive correctional models articulated in this book. We must not accept existing institutional practices as inevitable or be afraid to think in ways that mix the utopian with the practical. Indeed, the time has come to choose a different future—one that emphasizes the importance of penal help over penal harm. At the core of this vision is the belief, rooted in empirical data, that humaneness improves inmates and protects public safety. Achieving such an ambitious future will take a great deal of urging and vigilance by students of corrections like yourself. But it is within reach—within *your* reach as tomorrow's practitioners and academics. What you think—your ideas—will have consequences. So go forth into the society of captives with a bold imagination and with a commitment to have a transformative effect on the correctional enterprise.

References

Andrews, D. A., & Bonta, J. (2010). *The psychology of criminal conduct* (5th ed.). New Providence, NJ: Anderson/LexisNexis.

Andrews, D. A., Zinger, L., R. D., Bonta, J., Gendreau, P., & Cullen, F. T. (1990). Does correctional treatment work? A clinically relevant and psychologically informed meta-analysis. *Criminology, 28,* 369–404.

Brown v. Plata, 563 U.S. (2011)

Clear, T. R. (1994). *Harm in American penology: Offenders, victims and their communities.* Albany: State University of New York Press.

Cullen, F. T., & Gendreau, P. (2001). From nothing works to what works: Changing professional ideology in the 21st century. *The Prison Journal, 81,* 313–338.

Cullen, F. T., & Gilbert, K. E. (1982). *Reaffirming rehabilitation.* Cincinnati, OH: Anderson.

Cullen, F. T., & Jonson, C. L. (2012). *Correctional theory: Context and consequences.* Thousand Oaks, CA: Sage.

Cullen, F. T., Jonson, C. L., & Stohr, M. K. (2012). Editor's introduction: Imagining a different future. *Journal of Contemporary Criminal Justice, 28,* 4–6.

Gendreau, P., & Ross, R. R. (1987). Revivification of rehabilitation: Evidence from the 1980s. *Justice Quarterly, 4,* 349–407.

Gladwell, M. (2000). *Tipping point: How little things can make a big difference.* New York, NY: Back Bay Books.

Greene, J., & Mauer, M. (2010). *Downscaling prisons: Lessons from four states*. New York, NY: The Sentencing Project.

Guerino, P., Harrison, P., & Sabol, W. (2011). *Prisoners in 2010*. Washington, DC: U.S. Department of Justice, Bureau of Justice Statistics.

Hofstadter, R. (1955). *The age of reform: From Bryan to F.D.R.* New York, NY: Knopf.

Hogan, N., Garland, B., Wodahl, E., Hass, A. Stohr, M. K., & Lambert, E. (2012, March). *Closing the iron bar inn: The issue of decarceration and its possible effects on inmates, staff and communities*. Paper presentation at the annual Academy of Criminal Justice Sciences Meeting, New York, NY.

Hughes, T., & Wilson, D. J. (2011). *Reentry trends in the United States*. Washington, DC: U.S. Department of Justice, Bureau of Justice Statistics, Office of Justice Programs. Retrieved June 2, 2012, from http://bjs.ojp.usdoj.gov/content/pub/pdf/reentry.pdf

Johnson, R. (2002). *Hardtime: Understanding and reforming the prison* (3rd ed.). Belmont, CA: Wadsworth/Thomson.

Lee, L. C., & Stohr, M. K. (2012). A critique and qualified defense of "correctional quackery." *Journal of Contemporary Criminal Justice, 28*, 4–6.

Lemieux, C. M., Dyeson, T. B., & Castiglione, B. (2002). Revisiting the literature on prisoners who are older: Are we wiser? *The Prison Journal, 82*, 440–458.

Lowenkamp, C. T., Latessa, E. J., & Smith, P. (2006). Does correctional program quality really matter? The importance of adhering to the principles of effective intervention. *Criminology and Public Policy, 5*, 201–220.

Marquart, J. W., Merianos, D. E., Cuvelier, S. J., & Carroll, L. (1996). Thinking about the relationship between health dynamics in the free community and the prison. *Crime and Delinquency, 42*, 331–360.

Moon, M. M., Sundt, J. L., Cullen, F. T., & Wright, J. P. (2000). Is child saving dead? Public support for juvenile rehabilitation. *Crime and Delinquency, 46*, 38–60.

Palmer, T. (1994). *A profile of correctional effectiveness and new directions for research*. Albany: State University of New York Press.

Pink, D. H. (2009). *Drive: The surprising truth about what motivates us*. New York, NY: Riverhead Books.

Pinker, S. (2011). *The better angels of our nature: Why violence has declined*. New York, NY: Penguin.

Pollock, J. M., Hogan, N. L., Lambert, E. G., Ross, J. I., & Sundt, J. L. (2012). A utopian prison: Contradiction in terms? *Journal of Contemporary Criminal Justice, 28*, 60–76.

Rothman, D. J. (1980). *Conscience and convenience: The asylum and its alternatives in progressive America*. Hawthorne, NY: Aldine De Gruyter.

Slate, R. N., & Johnson, W. W. (2008). *Criminalization of mental illness*. Durham, NC: Carolina Academic Press.

Stohr, M. K., & Collins, P. A. (2009). *Criminal justice management: Theory and practice in justice-centered organizations*. New York, NY: Oxford University Press.

Zimring, F. E. (2007). *The great American crime decline*. New York, NY: Oxford University Press.

Index

About the Editors

Francis T. Cullen is a Distinguished Research Professor in the School of Criminal Justice at the University of Cincinnati, where he also holds a joint appointment in sociology. He received a Ph.D. (1979) in sociology and education from Columbia University. Professor Cullen has published over 300 works in the areas of corrections, criminological theory, white-collar crime, public opinion, the measurement of sexual victimization, and the organization of criminological knowledge. His recent publications include *Reaffirming Rehabilitation* (30th Anniversary Edition), *Correctional Theory: Context and Consequences*, *Unsafe in the Ivory Tower: The Sexual Victimization of College Women*, the *Encyclopedia of Criminological Theory*, *The Origins of American Criminology*, and *The Oxford Handbook of Criminological Theory*. Professor Cullen is a Past President of the American Society of Criminology and of the Academy of Criminal Justice Sciences. In 2010, he received the ASC Edwin H. Sutherland Award.

Cheryl Lero Jonson is an Assistant Professor in the Department of Criminal Justice at Xavier University. She received a Ph.D. (2010) in criminal justice from the University of Cincinnati. Her publications include *Correctional Theory: Context and Consequences* and *The Origins of American Criminology*. Her work has appeared in *Criminology and Public Policy*, *Crime and Justice: A Review of Research*, and *Victims and Offenders*. Her current research interests focus on the impact of prison on recidivism, sources of inmate violence, the use of meta-analysis to organize criminological knowledge, early intervention and crime prevention, and work-family conflict among law enforcement officials.

Mary K. Stohr is a Professor in the Department of Criminology and Criminal Justice at Missouri State University. She received a Ph.D. (1990) in political science, with specializations in public administration and criminal justice, from Washington State University. Professor Stohr has published over 75 academic works in the areas of correctional organizations and operation, correctional personnel, inmate needs and assessment, gender, victimization, and program evaluation. Her publications include *Corrections: The Essentials*, *Correctional Assessment, Casework and Counseling*, *Corrections: A Text Reader*, *Criminal Justice Management: Theory and Practice in Justice Centered Organizations*, and *The Inmate Prison Experience*. Within the Academy of Criminal Justice Sciences, she is a past two-term treasurer, received the Academy's Founders Award in 2009, is a co-founder of the Corrections Section, and is currently ACJS's Executive Director.

About the Contributors

Francis T. Cullen is a Distinguished Research Professor in the School of Criminal Justice at the University of Cincinnati, where he also holds a joint appointment in sociology. He received a Ph.D. (1979) in sociology and education from Columbia University. Professor Cullen has published over 300 works in the areas of corrections, criminological theory, white-collar crime, public opinion, the measurement of sexual victimization, and the organization of criminological knowledge. His recent publications include *Reaffirming Rehabilitation* (30th Anniversary Edition), *Correctional Theory: Context and Consequences, Unsafe in the Ivory Tower: The Sexual Victimization of College Women*, the *Encyclopedia of Criminological Theory, The Origins of American Criminology*, and *The Oxford Handbook of Criminological Theory*. Professor Cullen is a Past President of the American Society of Criminology and of the Academy of Criminal Justice Sciences. In 2010, he received the ASC Edwin H. Sutherland Award.

John E. Eck is a professor of criminal justice at the University of Cincinnati. For over three decades, he has assisted local police services in developing more effective approaches to reducing crime. His work helped to establish problem-oriented policing as a major worldwide strategy for police in democratic societies. He has written extensively on police matters in academic journals and for practitioners.

Craig Hemmens is Department Head and Professor in the Department of Criminology and Criminal Justice at Missouri State University. He holds a J.D. from North Carolina Central University School of Law and a Ph.D. in Criminal Justice from Sam Houston State University. He has published 19 books and more than 100 articles on a variety of criminal justice–related topics. His primary research interests are criminal law and procedure and corrections. He has served as the editor of the *Journal of Criminal Justice Education* and as a guest editor of *The Prison Journal* and *The Journal of Contemporary Criminal Justice*.

Kristi Holsinger is an Associate Professor of criminal justice and criminology at the University of Missouri–Kansas City. Her research interests are in the areas of theory, correctional interventions and policy related to criminalized females, innovations in teaching, and youth mentoring programs. Her publications include a newly released book, *Teaching Justice: Solving Social Justice Problems Through*

University Education, and articles in *Feminist Criminology, Journal of Child and Adolescent Trauma, Journal of Criminal Justice Education,* and *Journal of Research in Crime and Delinquency.*

Byron R. Johnson is a Distinguished Professor of the Social Sciences at Baylor University. He is the founding director of the Baylor Institute for Studies of Religion (ISR) as well as Director of the Program on Prosocial Behavior. Before joining the faculty at Baylor University, Professor Johnson directed research centers at Vanderbilt University and the University of Pennsylvania. He recently completed a series of studies for the Department of Justice on the role of religion in prosocial youth behavior and is a member of the Coordinating Council for Juvenile Justice and Delinquency Prevention (Presidential Appointment). He is a leading authority on the scientific study of religion, the efficacy of faith-based initiatives, and criminal justice. His recent publications have examined the impact of faith-based programs on recidivism reduction and prisoner reentry.

Cheryl Lero Jonson is an Assistant Professor in the Department of Criminal Justice at Xavier University. She received a Ph.D. (2010) in criminal justice from the University of Cincinnati. Her publications include *Correctional Theory: Context and Consequences* and *The Origins of American Criminology.* Her work has appeared in *Criminology and Public Policy, Crime and Justice: A Review of Research,* and *Victims and Offenders.* Her current research interests focus on the impact of prison on recidivism, sources of inmate violence, the use of meta-analysis to organize criminological knowledge, early intervention and crime prevention, and work-family conflict among law enforcement officials.

Benjamin Meade received his Ph.D. in criminology and criminal justice from the University of South Carolina in 2012. He currently works as an Assistant Professor in the Justice Studies Department at James Madison University. His research interests focus on issues related to corrections, the link between religion and deviance, and the role of religion in corrections. His recent and forthcoming work appears in the *Journal of Criminal Justice,* the *Journal of Research in Crime and Delinquency,* and *Justice Quarterly.*

Roberto Hugh Potter has spent the past two decades researching and working at the intersections among criminal justice, public health, health care, and social control. For 10 years he worked on violence prevention, substance abuse, and correctional health issues at the Centers for Disease Control and Prevention (CDC), before returning to academia in his native Florida. This experience culminated in the text *Epidemiological Criminology: A Public Health Approach to Crime and Violence* (Akers, Potter, & Hill, 2013). Parts of his chapter here can be traced to one of his projects at the CDC, the never-published *Surgeon General's Call to Action on Corrections and Community Health,* that explored the nexus between health care delivery in correctional facilities and the nonexistent public health care delivery system in the United States. Former Surgeon General Richard Carmona used that project as an example of science-based projects that were "interfered with" by political entities in congressional testimony. He continues his interest in the use of noncriminal justice forms of social control to regulate daily behaviors, which he and Jeffrey W. Rosky have described as "the iron fist in the latex glove." He received his Ph.D. in sociology from the University of Florida in 1982 and returned to the Florida University System at the University of Central Florida in 2008, where he serves as the Director of Research Partnerships and Professor in the Department of Criminal Justice.

Lois Presser is an Associate Professor of sociology at the University of Tennessee. She studied at Cornell University (B.S., 1987), Yale University (M.B.A., 1994), and the University of Cincinnati (Ph.D., 2002). Her scholarly work pertains to intersections of culture and harm, power, and justice, and to restorative justice practices. She is the author of *Been a Heavy Life: Stories of Violent Men* (University of Illinois Press). Her work has been published in such journals as *Justice Quarterly, Signs,* and *Social Problems.* Her next book, *Why We Harm* (in press, Rutgers University Press), presents a general cultural theory of harmful action.

Jeffrey W. Rosky is an Assistant Professor in the Department of criminal justice at the University of Central Florida. He received his Ph.D. (2010) in criminal justice from Washington State University. He also holds a B.A. in statistics from Rutgers University and an M.S. in biometrics from the University of Colorado. His work has appeared in *Criminology and Public Policy, Sexual Abuse, Journal of Offender Rehabilitation,* and *American Journal of Criminal Justice.* His research interests include criminological theory, jail systems, prison health care delivery, correctional treatment programs, sex offending, and research methods. Prior to his academic career, he worked as a researcher in the Montana and Colorado state correctional systems and as a biostatistician in environmental science, public health, infectious disease, and cardiac research.

Myrinda Schweitzer is an Associate Director with the Corrections Institute at the University of Cincinnati. She received her B.A. in psychology from the University of Cincinnati and her M.A. in forensic psychology from John Jay College of Criminal Justice. She has published two works on the implementation of evidence-based practices in the community and in a prison setting. She has managed over 30 projects, including a statewide correctional treatment program evaluation, the development and implementation of cognitive-behavioral programs, and recent initiatives to implement effective practices for community supervision. She also has practical experience working in both juvenile and adult rehabilitation programs.

Paula Smith is an Associate Professor in the School of Criminal Justice and Director of the Corrections Institute at the University of Cincinnati. She received her Ph.D. in psychology from the University of New Brunswick, Saint John, in 2006. She has coauthored the book *Corrections in the Community,* and written over 30 publications in the area of corrections. Her research interests include meta-analysis, the assessment of offender treatment and deterrence programs, the development of risk and need assessments for clinicians and managers in prisons and community corrections, the effects of prison life, and the transfer of knowledge to practitioners and policy makers. She has also directed federal- and state-funded research projects, including studies of prisons, community-based correctional programs, juvenile drug courts, probation and parole departments, and mental health services.

Benjamin Steiner is an Assistant Professor in the School of Criminology and Criminal Justice at the University of Nebraska at Omaha. He holds a Ph.D. from the University of Cincinnati. His research interests focus on issues related to juvenile justice and to institutional and community corrections. He has published over 50 journal articles and book chapters related to these topics. Some of his most recent work has appeared in *Journal of Research in Crime and Delinquency*, *Law and Society Review*, *Justice Quarterly*, and *Crime and Delinquency*. He is currently the coprincipal investigator on a study funded by the National Institute of Justice that examines the effects of exposure to different types of violence on inmate maladjustment. His other current projects involve examining the causes and correlates of inmate victimization and rule breaking, along with the official responses to inmate rule violations.

Mary K. Stohr is a Professor in the Department of Criminology and Criminal Justice at Missouri State University. She received a Ph.D. (1990) in political science, with specializations in public administration and criminal justice, from Washington State University. Professor Stohr has published over 75 academic works in the areas of correctional organizations and operation, correctional personnel, inmate needs and assessment, gender, victimization, and program evaluation. Her publications include *Corrections: The Essentials*, *Correctional Assessment, Casework and Counseling, Corrections: A Text Reader, Criminal Justice Management: Theory and Practice in Justice Centered Organizations*, and *The Inmate Prison Experience*. Within the Academy of Criminal Justice Sciences, she is a past two-term treasurer, received the Academy's Founders Award in 2009, is a co-founder of the Corrections Section, and is currently ACJS's executive director.

Jody L. Sundt is an Associate Professor and Graduate Coordinator in the Division of Criminology and Criminal Justice, Hatfield School of Government, Portland State University. Her research focuses on the effectiveness of correctional policy, religion in prison, and public attitudes toward crime and punishment. The American Society of Criminology's Division of Corrections and Sentencing named Dr. Sundt a Distinguished New Scholar in 2006.

John F. Wozniak is Chair and Professor of Sociology in the Department of Sociology and Anthropology at Western Illinois University. He received a Ph.D. (1993) in sociology at McMaster University (Hamilton, Ontario, Canada). Professor Wozniak served two years as president of the Justice Studies Association. He is a coeditor of *Transformative Justice: Critical and Peacemaking Themes Influenced by Richard*

Quinney. His published works on peacemaking criminology and other criminal justice topics have appeared in *Criminology, Crime and Delinquency*, the *Journal of Criminal Justice, Contemporary Justice Review, Crime, Law, and Social Change*, and the *Journal of Criminal Justice Education*. His current research interests include green criminology and critical criminology.

Kevin A. Wright is an Assistant Professor in the School of Criminology and Criminal Justice at Arizona State University. He earned his Ph.D. in criminal justice from Washington State University in 2010. His research interests include criminological theory and correctional policy, with particular emphasis placed on how they intersect. His published work has appeared in *Criminology and Public Policy, Justice Quarterly*, and the *Journal of Offender Rehabilitation*.

⊛SAGE researchmethods

The essential online tool for researchers from the world's leading methods publisher

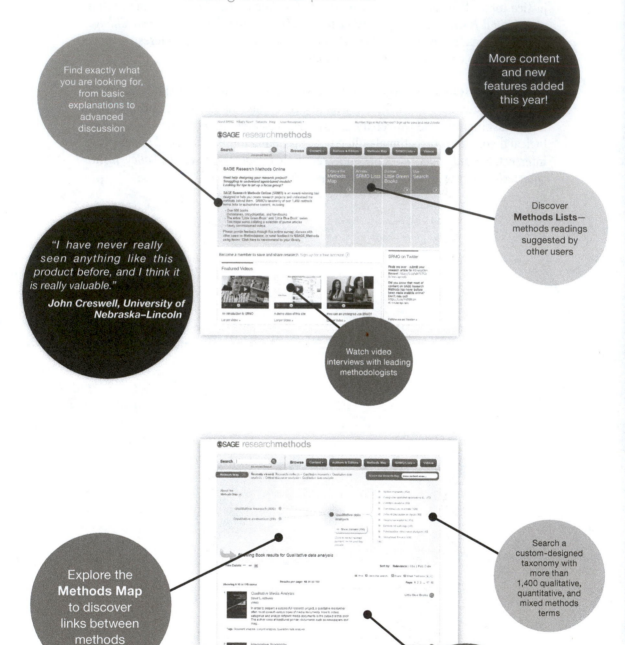

Find exactly what you are looking for, from basic explanations to advanced discussion

More content and new features added this year!

Discover **Methods Lists**— methods readings suggested by other users

"I have never really seen anything like this product before, and I think it is really valuable."

John Creswell, University of Nebraska–Lincoln

Watch video interviews with leading methodologists

Explore the **Methods Map** to discover links between methods

Search a custom-designed taxonomy with more than 1,400 qualitative, quantitative, and mixed methods terms

Uncover more than 120,000 pages of book, journal, and reference content to support your learning

Find out more at
www.sageresearchmethods.com